Objective Knowledge

An Evolutionary Approach

D0082883

KARL R. POPPER

Objective Knowledge

An Evolutionary Approach

OXFORD
AT THE CLARENDON PRESS
1972

Oxford University Press, Ely House, London W. 1

GLASGOW NEW YORK TORONTO MELBOURNE WELLINGTON
CAPE TOWN IBADAN NAIROBI DAR ES SALAAM LUSAKA ADDIS ABABA
DELHI BOMBAY CALCUTTA MADRAS KARACHI LAHORE DACCA
KUALA LUMPUR SINGAPORE HONG KONG TOKYO

PRINTED IN GREAT BRITAIN
AT THE UNIVERSITY PRESS, OXFORD
BY VIVIAN RIDLER
PRINTER TO THE UNIVERSITY

Dedicated to Alfred Tarski

Preface

THE phenomenon of human knowledge is no doubt the greatest miracle in our universe. It constitutes a problem that will not soon be solved, and I am far from thinking that the present volume makes even a small contribution to its solution. But I hope that I have helped to restart a discussion which for three centuries has been bogged down in preliminaries.

Since Descartes, Hobbes, Locke, and their school, which includes not only David Hume but also Thomas Reid, the theory of human knowledge has been largely subjectivist: knowledge has been regarded as a specially secure kind of human belief, and scientific knowledge as a specially secure kind of human knowledge.

The essays in this book break with a tradition that can be traced back to Aristotle—the tradition of this commonsense theory of knowledge. I am a great admirer of common sense which, I assert, is essentially selfcritical. But while I am prepared to uphold to the last the essential truth of *commonsense realism*, I regard the *commonsense theory of knowledge* as a subjectivist blunder. This blunder has dominated Western philosophy. I have made an attempt to eradicate it, and to replace it by an objective theory of essentially conjectural knowledge. This may be a bold claim but I do not apologize for it.

But I feel that I ought to apologize for certain overlaps: I have left the various chapters, whether or not previously published, very nearly in the state in which they were written, even when they are partially overlapping. This is also the reason why I speak here, in Chapters 3 and 4, of the 'first', 'second', and 'third world', although I now prefer to speak of 'world 1', 'world 2', and 'world 3', as in Chapter 2, following a suggestion of Sir John Eccles in his *Facing Reality*.

KARL R. POPPER

Penn, Buckinghamshire
24 July 1971

Acknowledgements

I AM deeply indebted to David Miller, Arne F. Petersen, Jeremy Shearmur, and most of all to my wife, for their patient and indefatigable help.

K. R. P.

Contents

1. Conjectural Knowledge: My Solution of the Problem of Induction

> The growth of unreason throughout the nineteenth century and what has passed of the twentieth is a natural sequel to Hume's destruction of empiricism.
>
> BERTRAND RUSSELL

I THINK that I have solved a major philosophical problem: the problem of induction. (I must have reached the solution in 1927 or thereabouts.[1]) This solution has been extremely fruitful, and it has enabled me to solve a good number of other philosophical problems.

However, few philosophers would support the thesis that I have solved the problem of induction. Few philosophers have taken the trouble to study—or even to criticize—my views on this problem, or have taken notice of the fact that I have done some work on it. Many books have been published quite recently on the subject which do not refer to any of my work, although most of them show signs of having been influenced by some very indirect echoes of my ideas; and those works which take notice of my ideas usually ascribe views to me which I have never held, or criticize me on the basis of straightforward misunderstandings or misreadings, or with invalid arguments. This chapter is an

---

[1] I had earlier (in the winter of 1919–20) formulated and solved the problem of demarcation between science and non-science and I did not think it worth publishing. But after I had solved the problem of induction I discovered an interesting connection between the two problems. This made me think that the problem of demarcation was important. I started to work on the problem of induction in 1923, and I found the solution about 1927. See also the autobiographical remarks in *Conjectures and Refutations* (*C. & R.* for short), chapters 1 and 11.

This chapter was first published in *Revue internationale de Philosophie*, 25ᵉ année, no. 95–6, 1971, fasc. 1–2.

attempt to explain my views afresh, and in a way which contains a full answer to my critics.

My first two publications on the problem of induction were my note in *Erkenntnis* of 1933,[2] in which I briefly presented my formulation of the problem and my solution, and my *Logik der Forschung* (*L.d.F.*) of 1934.[3] The note and also the book were very compressed. I expected, a little optimistically, that my readers would find out, with the help of my few historical hints, why my peculiar *reformulation* of the problem was decisive. It was, I think, the fact that I reformulated the traditional philosophical problem which made its solution possible.

By *the traditional philosophical problem of induction* I mean some formulation like the following (which I will call '*Tr*'):

Tr What is the justification for the belief that the future will be (largely) like the past? Or, perhaps, What is the justification for inductive inferences?

Formulations like these are wrongly put, for several reasons. For example, the first *assumes* that the future will be like the past —an assumption which I, for one, regard as mistaken, unless the word 'like' is taken in a sense so flexible as to make the assumption empty and innocuous. The second formulation assumes that there are inductive inferences, and *rules* for drawing inductive inferences, and this, again, is an assumption which should not be made uncritically, and one which I also regard as mistaken. Therefore I think that both formulations are simply uncritical, and similar remarks would hold for many other formulations. My main task will be, therefore, to formulate once more *the problem which I think lies behind* what I have called the traditional philosophical problem of induction.

The formulations which by now have become traditional are historically of fairly recent date: they arise out of Hume's criticism of induction and its impact upon the commonsense theory of knowledge.

I shall return to a more detailed discussion of the traditional formulations after presenting, first, the commonsense view, next

---

[2] 'Ein Kriterium des empirischen Charakters theoretischer Systeme', *Erkenntnis*, **3**, 1933, pp. 426 f.

[3] *Logik der Forschung*, Julius Springer Verlag, Vienna, 1934 (later referred to as '*L.d.F.*'). Cp. *The Logic of Scientific Discovery*, Hutchinson, London, 1959 (later referred to as '*L. Sc. D.*').

Hume's view, and then my own reformulations and solutions of the problem.

1. The Commonsense Problem of Induction

The commonsense theory of knowledge (which I have also dubbed 'the bucket theory of the mind') is the theory most famous in the form of the assertion that 'there is nothing in our intellect which has not entered it through the senses'. (I have tried to show that this view was first formulated by Parmenides —in a satirical vein: Most mortals have nothing in their erring intellect unless it got there through their erring senses.[4])

However, we do have *expectations*, and we strongly *believe in certain regularities* (laws of nature, theories). This leads to the commonsense problem of induction (which I will call '*Cs*'):

Cs How can these expectations and beliefs have arisen?

The commonsense answer is: Through *repeated* observations made in the past: we believe that the sun will rise tomorrow because it has done so in the past.

In the commonsense view it is simply taken for granted (without any problems being raised) that our belief in regularities is justified by those repeated observations which are responsible for its genesis. (Genesis *cum* justification—both due to repetition—is what philosophers since Aristotle and Cicero have called '*epagōgē*' or '*induction*'.[5])

2. Hume's Two Problems of Induction

Hume was interested in the status of human *knowledge* or, as he might have said, in the question of whether any of our beliefs —and which of them—can be *justified* by sufficient reasons.[6]

He raised two problems: a logical problem (H_L) and a psychological problem (H_{Ps}). One of the important points is that his two answers to these two problems in some way clash with each other.

---

[4] See my *Conjectures and Refutations* (*C. & R.*) Addendum 8 to the third edn., 1969, esp. pp. 408–12.

[5] Cicero, *Topica*, X. 42; cp. *De inventione*, Book I; xxxi. 51 to xxxv. 61.

[6] See David Hume, *Enquiry Concerning Human Understanding*, ed. L. A. Selby-Bigge, Oxford, 1927, Section V, Part I, p. 46. (Cp. *C. & R.*, p. 21.)

Hume's logical problem is:[7]

H_L Are we justified in reasoning from [repeated] instances of which we have experience to other instances [conclusions] of which we have no experience?

Hume's answer to H_L is: No, however great the number of repetitions.

Hume also showed that the logical situation remained *exactly the same* if in H_L the word '*probable*' is inserted before 'conclusions', or if the words 'to instances' are replaced by 'to the *probability* of instances'.

Hume's psychological problem is:[8]

H_{Ps} Why, nevertheless, do all reasonable people expect, and *believe*, that instances of which they have no experience will conform to those of which they have experience? That is, Why do we have expectations in which we have great confidence?

Hume's answer to H_{Ps} is: Because of 'custom or habit'; that is, because we are conditioned, by *repetitions* and by the mechanism of the association of ideas; a mechanism without which, Hume says, we could hardly survive.

3. *Important Consequences of Hume's Results*

By these results Hume himself—one of the most rational minds ever—was turned into a sceptic and, at the same time, into a believer: a believer in an irrationalist epistemology. His result that repetition has no power whatever as an argument, although it dominates our cognitive life or our 'understanding',

---

[7] Hume, *Treatise on Human Nature*, ed. Selby-Bigge, Oxford, 1888, 1960, Book I, Part III, section vi, p. 91; Book I, Part III, section xii, p. 139. See also Kant, *Prolegomena*, pp. 14 f., where he calls the problem of the existence of *a priori* valid statements 'Hume's problem'. To my knowledge I was the first to call the problem of induction 'Hume's problem'; though of course there may have been others. I did so in 'Ein Kriterium des empirischen Charakters theoretischer Systeme', *Erkenntnis*, 3, 1933, pp. 426 f., and in *L.d.F.*, section 4, p. 7, where I wrote: 'If, following Kant, we call the problem of induction "Hume's problem", we might call the problem of demarcation "Kant's problem".' This very brief remark of mine (supported by a few remarks such as on p. 29 of *L. Sc. D.*, that Kant took the principle of induction as '*a priori* valid') contained hints of an important historical interpretation of the relationship between Kant, Hume, and the problem of induction. See also this volume, Chapter 2, pp. 85 ff. and p. 93, where these points are discussed more fully.

[8] See *Treatise*, pp. 91, 139.

led him to the conclusion that argument or reason plays only a minor role in our understanding. Our 'knowledge' is unmasked as being not only of the nature of belief, but of rationally indefensible belief—of *an irrational faith*.[9]

It will become obvious in the next section, and in sections 10 and 11, that no such irrationalist conclusion can be derived from my solution of the problem of induction.

Hume's conclusion was even more forcefully and desperately stated by Russell, in the chapter on Hume of his *A History of Western Philosophy*, published in 1946 (thirty-four years after his *Problems of Philosophy*, which contained a beautifully clear statement of the problem of induction without reference to Hume).[10] Russell says about Hume's treatment of induction: 'Hume's philosophy . . . represents the bankruptcy of eighteenth-century reasonableness' and, 'It is therefore important to discover whether there is any answer to Hume within a philosophy that is wholly or mainly *empirical*. If not, *there is no intellectual difference between sanity and insanity*. The lunatic who believes that he is a poached egg is to be condemned solely on the ground that he is in a minority. . . .'

Russell goes on to assert that if induction (or the principle of induction) is rejected, 'every attempt to arrive at general scientific laws from particular observations is fallacious, and Hume's scepticism is inescapable for an empiricist'.[11]

Thus Russell stresses the clash between Hume's answer to H_L and (a) rationality, (b) empiricism, and (c) scientific procedures.

It will become obvious in sections 4 and 10 to 12 that all these clashes disappear if my solution of the problem of induction is accepted: there is no clash between my theory of non-induction and either rationality, or empiricism, or the procedure of science.

[9] Since Hume, many disappointed inductivists have become irrationalists (just as have many disappointed Marxists).

[10] Hume's name does not occur in chapter VI ('On Induction') of Russell's *The Problems of Philosophy* (1912 and many later reprints), and the nearest to a reference is in chapter VIII ('How *A Priori* Knowledge is Possible'), where Russell says of Hume that 'he inferred the far more doubtful proposition that nothing could be known *a priori* about the connection of cause and effect'. No doubt, causal expectations have an inborn basis: they are psychologically *a priori* in the sense that they are prior to experience. But this does not mean that they are *a priori* valid. See *C. & R.*, pp. 47–8.

[11] The quotations are from Bertrand Russell, *A History of Western Philosophy*, London, 1946, pp. 698 f. (The italics are mine.)

4. *My Way of Approaching the Problem of Induction*

(1) I regard the distinction, implicit in Hume's treatment, between a logical and a psychological problem as of the utmost importance. But I do not think that Hume's view of what I am inclined to call 'logic' is satisfactory. He describes, clearly enough, processes of *valid inference*; but he looks upon these as 'rational' *mental processes*.

By contrast, one of my principal methods of approach, whenever *logical* problems are at stake, is to translate all the subjective or psychological terms, especially 'belief', etc., into *objective* terms. Thus, instead of speaking of a 'belief', I speak, say, of a 'statement' or of an 'explanatory theory'; and instead of an 'impression', I speak of an 'observation statement' or of a 'test statement'; and instead of the 'justification of a belief', I speak of 'justification of the claim that a theory is true', etc.

This procedure of putting things into the objective or logical or 'formal' mode of speaking will be applied to H_L, but not to H_{Ps}; however:

(2) Once the logical problem, H_L, is solved, the solution is transferred to the psychological problem, H_{Ps}, on the basis of the following *principle of transference*: what is true in logic is true in psychology. (An analogous principle holds by and large for what is usually called 'scientific method' and also for the history of science: what is true in logic is true in scientific method and in the history of science.) This is admittedly a somewhat daring conjecture in the psychology of cognition or of thought processes.

(3) It will be clear that my principle of transference guarantees the elimination of Hume's irrationalism: if I can answer his main problem of induction, including H_{Ps}, without violating the principle of transference, then there can be no clash between logic and psychology, and therefore no conclusion that our understanding is irrational.

(4) Such a programme, together with Hume's solution of H_L, implies that more can be said about the logical relations between scientific theories and observations than is said in H_L.

(5) One of my main results is that, since Hume is right that there is no such thing as induction by repetition in *logic*, by the principle of transference there cannot be any such thing in *psychology* (or in scientific method, or in the history of science): the idea of induction by repetition must be due to an error—a

kind of optical illusion. In brief: *there is no such thing as induction by repetition.*

5. *The Logical Problem of Induction: Restatement and Solution*

In accordance with what has just been said (point (2) of the preceding section 4), I have to restate Hume's H_L in an objective or logical mode of speech.

To this end I replace Hume's 'instances of which we have experience' by 'test statements'—that is, singular statements describing observable events ('observation statements', or 'basic statements'); and 'instances of which we have no experience' by 'explanatory universal theories'.

I formulated Hume's logical problem of induction as follows:

L_1 Can the claim that an explanatory universal theory is true be justified by 'empirical reasons'; that is, by assuming the truth of certain test statements or observation statements (which, it may be said, are 'based on experience')?

My answer to the problem is the same as Hume's: No, we cannot; no number of true test statements would justify the claim that an explanatory universal theory is true.[12]

But there is a second logical problem, L_2, which is a generalization of L_1. It is obtained from L_1 merely by replacing the words 'is true' by the words 'is true or that it is false':

L_2 Can the claim that an explanatory universal theory is true or that it is false be justified by 'empirical reasons'; that is, can the assumption of the truth of test statements justify either the claim that a universal theory is true or the claim that it is false?

To this problem, my answer is positive: Yes, *the assumption of the truth of test statements sometimes allows us to justify the claim that an explanatory universal theory is false.*

This reply becomes very important if we reflect on the problem situation in which the problem of induction arises. I have in mind a situation in which we are faced with *several explanatory theories* which compete *qua* solutions of some problem of explanation—for example a scientific problem; and also with the fact that we have to, or at least wish to, choose between them. As we have seen, Russell says that without solving the problem of

---

[12] An explanatory theory goes essentially beyond even an infinity of universal test statements; even a law of low universality does so.

induction, we could not *decide between* a (good) scientific theory and a (bad) obsession of a madman. Hume too had competing theories in mind. 'Suppose [he writes] a person . . . advances propositions, to which I do not assent, . . . that silver is more fusible than lead, or mercury heavier than gold. . . .'[13]

This problem situation—that of choosing between several theories—suggests a third reformulation of the problem of induction:

L_3 Can a *preference*, with respect to truth or falsity, for some competing universal theories over others ever be justified by such 'empirical reasons'?

In the light of my answer to L_2 the answer to L_3 becomes obvious: Yes; sometimes it can, if we are lucky. For it may happen that our test statements may refute some—but not all—of the competing theories; and since we are searching for a true theory, we shall prefer those whose falsity has not been established.

6. *Comments on My Solution of the Logical Problem*

(1) According to my reformulations, the central issue of the logical problem of induction is the validity (truth or falsity) of universal laws *relative to some 'given' test statements*. I do not raise the question, 'How do we decide the truth or falsity of test statements?', that is, of singular descriptions of observable events. The latter question should not, I suggest, be regarded as part of the problem of induction, since Hume's question was whether we are justified in reasoning from experienced to unexperienced 'instances'.[14] Neither Hume nor any other writer on the subject before me has to my knowledge moved on from here to the *further questions*: Can we take the 'experienced instances' for granted? And are they really prior to the theories? Although these further questions are some of those problems to which I was led by my solution of the problem of induction, they go beyond the original problem. (This is clear if we consider the kind of thing for which philosophers have been looking when trying to solve the problem of induction: if a 'principle of induction', permitting us *to derive universal laws from singular statements*,

---

[13] Hume, *Treatise*, p. 95.   [14] Op. cit., p. 91.

could be found, and its claim to truth defended, then the problem of induction would be regarded as solved.)

(2) L_1 is an attempt to translate Hume's problem into an objective mode of speech. The only difference is that Hume speaks of future (singular) *instances* of which we have no experience—that is, of expectations—while L_1 speaks of universal laws or theories. I have at least three reasons for this change. First, from a logical point of view, 'instances' are relative to some universal law (or at least to a statement function which could be universalized). Secondly, our usual method of reasoning from 'instances' to other 'instances' is with the help of universal theories. Thus we are led from Hume's problem to the *problem of the validity of universal theories* (their truth or falsehood). Thirdly, I wish, like Russell, to connect the problem of induction with *the universal laws or theories of science*.

(3) My negative answer to L_1 should be interpreted as meaning that we must regard *all laws or theories as hypothetical or conjectural*; that is, as guesses.

This view is by now fairly popular,[15] but it took quite a time to reach this stage. It is, for example, explicitly combated in an otherwise excellent article of 1937 by Professor Gilbert Ryle.[16] Ryle argues (p. 36) that it is wrong to say 'that all the general propositions of science . . . are mere hypotheses'; and he uses the term 'hypothesis' in exactly the same sense in which I have always used it and in which I am using it now: as a 'proposition . . . which is only conjectured to be true' (loc. cit.). He asserts against a thesis like mine: 'We are often sure, and warranted in being sure, of a law proposition' (p. 38). And he says that some general propositions are 'established': 'These are called "laws", and not "hypotheses".'

This view of Ryle's was indeed almost the 'established' standard at the time I wrote *L.d.F.*, and it is by no means dead. I first turned against it because of Einstein's theory of gravity: there never was a theory as well *'established'* as Newton's, and it is unlikely that there ever will be one; but whatever one may think about the status of Einstein's theory, it certainly taught us to look at Newton's as a 'mere' hypothesis or conjecture.

[15] See Mr. Stove's commencing remark in *Australas. Journ. of Philos.* **38**, 1960, p. 173.
[16] See *Arist. Soc. Supplementary Volume*, **16**, 1937, pp. 36–62.

A second such case was the discovery by Urey in 1931 of deuterium and heavy water. At that time, water, hydrogen, and oxygen, were the substances best known to chemistry, and the atomic weights of hydrogen and oxygen formed the very standards of all chemical measurement. Here was a theory upon the truth of which *every* chemist would have staked his life, at least before Soddy's isotope conjecture in 1910, and in fact long afterwards. But it was here that a refutation was found by Urey (and thus a theory of Bohr's corroborated).

This led me to look more closely into other 'established laws' and especially into the three standard examples of the inductivists:[17]

    (a) that the sun will rise and set once in 24 hours (or approximately 90,000 pulse beats),

    (b) that all men are mortal,

    (c) that bread nourishes.

In all three cases I found that these established laws were actually refuted in the sense in which they were originally meant.

(a) The first was refuted when Pytheas of Marseilles discovered 'the frozen sea and the midnight sun'. The fact that (a) was intended to mean 'Wherever you go, the sun will rise and set once in 24 hours' is shown by the utter disbelief with which his report was met, and by the fact that his report became the paradigm of all travellers' tales.

(b) The second was also refuted, though not as obviously. The predicate 'mortal' is a bad translation from the Greek: *thnētos* means 'bound to die' or 'liable to die', rather than merely 'mortal', and (b) is part of Aristotle's theory that every generated creature is bound to decay and to die after a period which, though its length is part of the creature's essence, will vary a little according to accidental circumstances. But this theory was refuted by the discovery that bacteria are not bound to die, since multiplication by fission is not death, and later by the realization that living matter is not in general bound to decay and to die, although it seems that all forms can be killed by

---

[17] These examples, which I have often used in my lectures, have also been used in Chapter 2 (pp. 97 f., and footnote 58). I apologize for the overlap, but these two chapters were written independently and I feel that they should be kept self-contained.

sufficiently drastic means. (Cancer cells, for example, can go on living.)

(c) The third—a favourite of Hume's—was refuted when people eating their daily bread died of ergotism, as happened in a catastrophic case in a French village not very long ago. Of course (c) originally meant that bread properly baked from flour properly prepared from wheat or corn, sown and harvested according to old-established practice, would nourish people rather than poison them. But they *were* poisoned.

Thus Hume's negative reply to H_L and my negative reply to L_1 are not merely far-fetched philosophical attitudes, as implied by Ryle, and by the commonsense theory of knowledge, but are based on very practical realities. In a vein similarly optimistic to that of Professor Ryle, Professor Strawson writes: 'If . . . there is a problem of induction, and . . . Hume posed it, it must be added that he solved it'—that is, by Hume's positive answer to H_{Ps}, which Strawson seems to accept, describing it as follows: 'our acceptance of the "basic canons" [of induction] . . . is forced upon us by Nature. . . . Reason is, and ought to be, the slave of the passions.'[18] (Hume had said: 'ought only to be'.)

I have not seen anything before which illustrates so well the quotation from Bertrand Russell's *A History of Western Philosophy*, p. 699, which I have chosen as a motto for the present discussion.

Yet it is clear that 'induction'—in the sense of a positive reply to H_L or L_1—is *inductively invalid*, and even paradoxical. For a positive reply to L_1 implies that our scientific account of the world is roughly true. (With this I agree, in spite of my negative reply to L_1.) But from this it follows that we are very clever animals, precariously placed in a surrounding that differs greatly from almost every other place in the universe: animals that strive courageously to discover, by some method or other, the true regularities which rule the universe and thereby our surroundings. It is clear that whatever method we might use, our chances of finding true regularities are slim, and our theories will contain many mistakes which no mysterious 'canon of induction', whether basic or otherwise, will prevent us from committing. But this is just what my negative reply to L_1 says. Thus, since the positive reply entails its own negation, it must be false.

If anybody should wish to moralize about this story, he could

[18] See *Philosophical Studies*, **9**, 1958, no. 1–2, pp. 20 f.; cp. Humes's *Treatise*, p. 415.

say: critical reason is better than passion, especially in matters touching on logic. But I am quite ready to admit that nothing will ever be achieved without a modicum of passion.

(4) L_2 is merely a generalization of L_1, and L_3 is merely an alternative formulation of L_2.

(5) My answer to L_2 and L_3 provides a clear answer to Russell's questions. For I can say: yes, at least some of the ravings of the lunatic can be regarded as refuted by experience; that is, by test statements. (Others may be non-testable and thereby distinguished from the theories of science; this raises the problem of demarcation.[19])

(6) Most important, as I stressed in my first paper on the problem of induction, my answer to L_2 is in agreement with the following somewhat weak form of the *principle of empiricism*: *Only 'experience' can help us to make up our minds about the truth or falsity of factual statements.* For it turns out that, in view of L_1 and the answer to L_1, we can determine at most the falsity of theories; and this indeed can be done, in view of the answer to L_2.

(7) Similarly, there is no clash between my solution and the methods of science; on the contrary, we are led by it to the rudiments of a critical methodology.

(8) Not only does my solution throw much light upon the psychological problem of induction (see section 11, below), but it also elucidates the traditional formulations of the problem of induction and the reason for the weakness of these formulations. (See sections 12 and 13, below.)

(9) My formulations and my solutions of L_1, L_2, and L_3, fall entirely within the scope of *deductive logic*. What I show is that, generalizing Hume's problem, we can add to it L_2 and L_3, which allows us to formulate a somewhat more positive answer than the one to L_1. This is so because from the point of view of deductive logic there is an asymmetry between verification and falsification by experience. This leads to the purely logical distinction

---

[19] The 'problem of demarcation' is what I call the problem of finding a criterion by which we can distinguish the statements of empirical science from non-empirical statements. My solution is the principle that a statement is empirical if there are (finite) conjunctions of singular empirical statements ('basic statements', or 'test statements') which contradict it. It is a consequence of this 'principle of demarcation' that an isolated purely existential statement (such as 'There exists a sea-serpent somewhere in the world at some time') is not an empirical statement, though it may contribute, of course, to our empirical problem situation.

between hypotheses which have been refuted, and others which have not; and to the preference for the latter—if only from a theoretical point of view which makes them *theoretically most interesting objects for further tests.*

7. *Preference for Theories and the Search for Truth*

We have seen that our negative reply to L_1 means that all our theories remain guesses, conjectures, hypotheses. Once we have fully accepted this purely logical result, the question arises whether there can be purely rational arguments, including empirical arguments, for preferring some conjectures or hypotheses to others.

There may be various ways of looking at this question. I shall distinguish the point of view of the theoretician—the seeker for truth, and especially for true explanatory theories—from that of the practical man of action; that is, I will distinguish between *theoretical preference* and *pragmatic preference.* In this section and the next I shall be concerned only with theoretical preference and the quest for truth. Pragmatic preference and the problem of 'reliability' will be discussed in the next section but one.

The theoretician, I will assume, is essentially interested in truth, and especially in finding true theories. But when he has fully digested the fact that we can never justify empirically— that is, by test statements—the claim that a scientific theory is true, and that we are therefore at best always faced with the question of preferring, tentatively, some guesses to others, then he may consider, from the point of view of a seeker for true theories, the questions: *What principles of preference should we adopt? Are some theories 'better' than others?*

These questions give rise to the following considerations.

(1) It is clear that the question of preference will arise mainly, and perhaps even solely, with respect to a set of *competing theories*; that is, theories which are offered as solutions to the same problems. (See also point (8) below.)

(2) The theoretician who is interested in truth must also be interested in falsity, because finding that a statement is false is the same as finding that its negation is true. Thus the refutation of a theory will always be of theoretical interest. But the negation of an explanatory theory is not, in its turn, an explanatory

theory (nor has it as a rule the 'empirical character' of the test statement from which it is derived). Interesting as it is, it does not satisfy the theoretician's interest in finding true explanatory theories.

(3) If the theoretician pursues this interest, then finding where a theory breaks down, apart from giving theoretically interesting information, poses an important new *problem* for any new explanatory theory. Any new theory will not only have to succeed where its refuted predecessor succeeded, but it will also have to succeed where its predecessor failed; that is, where it was refuted. If the new theory succeeds in both, it will at any rate be more successful and therefore 'better' than the old one.

(4) Moreover, assuming that this new theory is not refuted at the time *t* by a new test, it will, at any rate at the time *t*, be 'better' in yet another sense than the refuted theory. For it will not only explain all that the refuted theory explained, and more, but it will also have to be regarded as possibly true, since at the time *t* it has not been shown to be false.

(5) Yet the theoretician will value such a new theory not only because of its success, and its being perhaps a true theory, but also because it may perhaps be false: it is interesting as an object of further tests; that is, of new attempted refutations which, if successful, establish not only a new negation of a theory, but with it a new theoretical problem for the next theory.

We can sum up points (1) to (5) as follows.

The theoretician will for several reasons be interested in non-refuted theories, especially because some of them *may* be true. He will prefer a non-refuted theory to a refuted one, provided it explains the successes and failures of the refuted theory.

(6) But the new theory may, like all non-refuted theories, be false. The theoretician will therefore try his best to detect any false theory among the set of non-refuted competitors; he will try to 'catch' it. That is, he will, with respect to any given non-refuted theory, try to think of cases or situations in which it is likely to fail, if it is false. Thus he will try to construct *severe* tests, and *crucial* test situations. This will amount to the construction of a falsifying law; that is, a law which may perhaps be of such a low level of universality that it may not be able to explain the successes of the theory to be tested, but which will, nevertheless, suggest a *crucial experiment*: an experiment which may refute,

depending on its outcome, either the theory to be tested or the falsifying theory.

(7) By this method of elimination, we may hit upon a true theory. But in no case can the method *establish* its truth, even if it is true; for the number of *possibly* true theories remains infinite, at any time and after any number of crucial tests. (This is another way of stating Hume's negative result.) The actually proposed theories will, of course, be finite in number; and it may well happen that we refute all of them, and cannot think of a new one.

On the other hand, *among the theories actually proposed* there may be more than one which is not refuted at a time *t*, so that we may not know which of these we ought to prefer. But if at a time *t* a plurality of theories continues to compete in this way, the theoretician will try to discover how crucial experiments can be designed between them; that is, experiments which could falsify and thus eliminate some of the competing theories.

(8) The procedure described may lead to a set of theories which are 'competing' in the sense that they offer solutions to at least *some* common problems, although each offers in addition solutions to some problems which it does not share with the others. For although we demand of a new theory that it solves those problems which its predecessor solved *and* those which it failed to solve, it may of course always happen that two or more new competing theories are proposed such that each of them satisfies these demands and in addition solves some problems which the others do not solve.

(9) At any time *t*, the theoretician will be especially interested in finding the best testable of the competing theories in order to submit it to new tests. I have shown that this will at the same time be the one with the greatest information content and the greatest explanatory power. It will be the theory most worthy of being submitted to new tests, in brief '*the best*' of the theories competing at time *t*. If it survives its tests, it will also be *the best tested* of all the theories so far considered, including all its predecessors.

(10) In what has just been said about '*the best*' *theory* it is assumed that a good theory is not *ad hoc*. The ideas of *adhocness* and its opposite, which may perhaps be termed 'boldness', are very important. *Ad hoc* explanations are explanations which are

not independently testable; independently, that is, of the effect to be explained. They can be had for the asking, and are therefore of little theoretical interest. I have discussed the question of the degrees of independence of tests in various places;[20] it is an interesting problem, and it is connected with the problems of simplicity and depth. Since then I have also stressed[21] the need to refer it or relativize it to the *problem of explanation* which we are engaged in solving, and to the problem situations under discussion, because all these ideas bear on the degrees of 'goodness' of the competing theories. Moreover, the degree of boldness of a theory also depends on its relation to its predecessors.

The main point of interest is, I think, that for very high degrees of boldness or non-*adhocness* I have been able to give an objective criterion. It is that the new theory, although it has to explain what the old theory explained, *corrects* the old theory, so that it actually *contradicts* the old theory: it contains the old theory, *but only as an approximation*. Thus I pointed out that Newton's theory contradicts both Kepler's and Galileo's theories —*although it explains them*, owing to the fact that it contains them as approximations; and similarly Einstein's theory contradicts Newton's, which it likewise explains, and contains as an approximation.

(11) The method described may be called the *critical method*. It is a method of trial and the elimination of errors, of proposing theories and submitting them to the severest tests we can design. If, because of some limiting assumptions, only a finite number of competing theories are regarded as possible, this method may lead us to single out *the* true theory by eliminating all its competitors. Normally—that is to say, in all cases in which the number of possible theories is infinite—this method cannot ascertain which of the theories is true; nor can any other method. It remains *applicable*, though inconclusive.

(12) The enrichment of the problems through the refutation of false theories, and the demands formulated under (3), make sure that the predecessor of every new theory will—from the point of view of the new theory—have the character of an

---

[20] See, especially, 'Naturgesetze und theoretische Systeme', in *Gesetz und Wirklichkeit*, ed. S. Moser, Innsbruck, 1949, pp. 43 ff., and 'The Aim of Science', *Ratio*, 1, 1957, now respectively the Appendix and ch. 5 below.
[21] See *C. & R.*, p. 241.

approximation towards this new theory. Nothing, of course, can make sure that for every theory which has been falsified we shall find a 'better' successor, or a better approximation—one that satisfies these demands. *There is no assurance that we shall be able to make progress towards better theories.*

(13) Two further points may be added here. One is that what has been said so far belongs, as it were, to *purely deductive logic*—the logic within which L_1, L_2, and L_3 were posed. Yet in trying to apply this to practical situations arising in science, we come up against problems of a different kind. For example, the relationship between test statements and theories may not be as clearcut as is here assumed; or the test statements themselves may be criticized. This is the kind of problem which always arises if we wish to *apply* pure logic to any lifelike situation. In connection with science it leads to what I have called *methodological rules*, the rules of critical discussion.

The other point is that these rules may be regarded as subject to the general *aim of rational discussion, which is to get nearer to the truth.*

8. *Corroboration: The Merits of Improbability*

(1) My theory of preference has nothing to do with a preference for the 'more probable' hypothesis. On the contrary, I have shown that the testability of a theory increases and decreases with its *informative content* and therefore with its *improbability* (in the sense of the calculus of probability). Thus the 'better' or 'preferable' hypothesis will, more often than not, be the *more improbable* one. (But it is a mistake to say, as does John C. Harsanyi, that I have ever proposed an 'improbability criterion for the choice of scientific hypotheses':[22] not only do I have no general 'criterion', but it happens quite often that I cannot prefer the logically 'better' and more improbable hypothesis, since someone has succeeded in refuting it experimentally.) This result has of course been regarded as perverse by many, but my main arguments are very simple (content = improbability), and they have recently been accepted even by some proponents

---

[22] See John C. Harsanyi, 'Popper's Improbability Criterion for the Choice of Scientific Hypotheses', *Philosophy*, **35**, 1960, pp. 332–40. See also the footnote on p. 218 of *C. & R.*

of inductivism and of a probabilistic theory of induction, such as Carnap.[23]

(2) I originally introduced the idea of *corroboration*, or *'degree of corroboration'*, with the aim of showing clearly that every probabilistic theory of preference (and therefore every probabilistic theory of induction) is absurd.

By the degree of corroboration of a theory I mean a concise report evaluating the state (at a certain time *t*) of the critical discussion of a theory, with respect to the way it solves its problems; its degree of testability; the severity of tests it has undergone; and the way it has stood up to these tests. Corroboration (or degree of corroboration) is thus an evaluating *report of past performance*. Like preference, it is essentially comparative: in general, one can only say that the theory *A* has a higher (or lower) degree of corroboration than a competing theory *B*, in the light of the critical discussion, which includes testing, *up to some time t*. Being a report of past performance only, it has to do with a situation which may lead to preferring some theories to others. *But it says nothing whatever about future performance, or about the 'reliability' of a theory.* (Of course this would in no way be affected should anybody succeed in showing that, in certain very special cases, my or someone else's formulae for the degree of corroboration can be given a numerical interpretation.[24])

The main purpose of the *formulae* which I proposed as definitions for the degree of corroboration was to show that, in many cases, the more *improbable* (improbable in the sense of the calculus of probability) hypothesis is preferable, and to show clearly in which cases this holds and in which it does not hold. In this way, I could show that *preferability cannot be a probability in the sense of the calculus of probability*. Of course, one may *call* the preferable theory the more 'probable' one: *words do not matter*, as long as one is not misled by them.

To sum up: We can sometimes say of two competing theories,

[23] See Rudolf Carnap, 'Probability and Content Measure', in P. K. Feyerabend and Grover Maxwell (eds.), *Mind, Matter and Method*, Essays in Honour of Herbert Feigl, Univ. of Minnesota Press, Minneapolis, 1966, pp. 248–60.

[24] It seems to me that Professor Lakatos suspects that the actual contribution of numbers to my degree of corroboration, if possible, would render my theory inductivist in the sense of a probabilistic theory of induction. I see no reason whatever why this should be so. Cp. pp. 410–12 of *The Problem of Inductive Logic*, I. Lakatos and A. Musgrave (eds.), North Holland, Amsterdam, 1968. (Added in proofs: I am glad to learn that I have misunderstood the passage.)

A and *B*, that in the light of the state of the critical discussion at the time *t*, and the empirical evidence (test statements) available at the discussion, the theory *A* is preferable to, or better corroborated than, the theory *B*.

Obviously, the degree of corroboration at the time *t* (which is a statement about preferability at the time *t*) says nothing about the future—for example, about the degree of corroboration at a time later than *t*. It is just a report about the state of discussion at the time *t*, concerning the logical and empirical preferability of the competing theories.

(3) I must emphasize this, because the following passage of my *Logic of Scientific Discovery* has been interpreted—or rather misinterpreted—as showing that I was using corroboration as an index of the *future* performance of a theory: 'Instead of discussing the "probability" of a hypothesis we should try to assess what tests, what trials, it has withstood; that is, we should try to assess how far it has been able to prove its fitness to survive by standing up to tests. In brief, we should try to assess how far it has been "corroborated".'[25]

Some people thought[26] that the phrase 'prove its fitness to survive' shows that I had here intended to speak of a fitness to survive in the *future*, to stand up to future tests. I am sorry if I have misled anybody, but I can only say that it was not I who mixed the Darwinian metaphor. Nobody expects that a species which has survived in the past will therefore survive in the future: all the species which ever failed to survive some period of time *t* have survived up to that time *t*. It would be absurd to suggest that Darwinian survival involves, somehow, an expectation that every species that has so far survived will continue to survive. (Who would say that the expectation for our own species to survive is very high?)

(4) It may perhaps be useful to add here a point about the degree of corroboration of a statement *s* which belongs to a theory *T*, or follows logically from it, but is logically much weaker than the theory *T*.

Such a statement *s* will have less informative content than the theory *T*. This means that *s*, and the deductive system *S* of all those statements which follow from *s*, will be less testable and less corroborable than *T*. But if *T* has been well tested, then we

[25] *L. Sc. D.*, p. 251.   [26] See *Mind*, New Series, **69**, 1960, p. 100.

can say that its high degree of corroboration applies to all the statements which are entailed by it, and therefore to *s* and *S*, even though *s*, because of its low corroborability, could never on its own attain as high a degree of corroboration.

This rule may be supported by the simple consideration that the degree of corroboration is a means of stating *preference with respect to truth*. But if we prefer *T* with respect to its claim to truth, then we have to prefer with it all its consequences, since if *T* is true, so must be all its consequences, even though they can be less well tested separately.

Thus I assert that with the corroboration of Newton's theory, and the description of the earth as a rotating planet, the degree of corroboration of the statement *s* 'The sun rises in Rome once in every twenty-four hours' has greatly increased. For, on its own, *s* is not very well testable; but Newton's theory, and the theory of the rotation of the earth are well testable. And if these are true, *s* will be true also.

A statement *s* which is derivable from a well-tested theory *T* will, *so far as it is regarded as part of T*, have the degree of corroboration of *T*; and if *s* is derivable not from *T* but from the conjunction of two theories, say T_1 and T_2, it will *qua* part of two theories have the same degree of corroboration as the less well tested of these two theories. Yet *s* taken by itself may have a very low degree of corroboration.

(5) The fundamental difference between my approach and the approach for which I long ago introduced the label 'inductivist' is that I lay stress on *negative arguments*, such as negative instances or counter-examples, refutations, and attempted refutations—in short, criticism—while the inductivist lays stress on '*positive instances*', from which he draws 'non-demonstrative inferences',[27] and which he hopes will guarantee the '*reliability*' of the conclusions of these inferences. In my view, all that can possibly be '*positive*' in our scientific knowledge is positive *only* in so far as certain theories are, at a certain moment of time, preferred to others in the light of our *critical* discussion which consists of attempted refutations, including empirical tests. Thus even what may be called 'positive' is so *only* with respect to *negative methods*.

[27] C. G. Hempel, 'Recent Problems of Induction', in R. G. Colodny (ed.), *Mind and Cosmos*, Pittsburgh Univ. Press, 1966, p. 112.

This negative approach clarifies many points, for example the difficulties encountered in explaining satisfactorily what is a 'positive instance' or a 'supporting instance' of a law.

9. *Pragmatic Preference*

So far I have discussed why the theoretician's preference—if he has any—will be for the 'better', that is, more testable, theory, and for the better tested one. Of course, the theoretician may not have *any* preference: he may be discouraged by Hume's, and my, 'sceptical' solution to the problems H_L and L_1: he may say that, if he cannot *make sure* of finding the true theory among the competing theories, he is not interested in any method like the one described—not even if the method makes it reasonably certain that, *if* a true theory should be among the theories proposed, it will be among the surviving, the preferred, the corroborated ones. Yet a more sanguine or more curious 'pure' theoretician may well be encouraged, by our analysis, to propose again and again new competing theories in the hope that one of them may be true—even if we shall never be able to make sure of any one that it is true.

Thus the pure theoretician has more than one way of action open to him; and he will choose a method such as the method of trial and the elimination of error only if his curiosity exceeds his disappointment at the unavoidable uncertainty and incompleteness of all our endeavours.

It is different with him *qua* man of practical action. For a man of practical action has always to *choose* between some more or less definite alternatives, since even *inaction is a kind of action.*

But every action presupposes a set of expectations; that is, of theories about the world. Which theory shall the man of action choose? Is there such a thing as a *rational choice*?

This leads us to the *pragmatic problems of induction*:

Pr_1 Upon which theory should we rely for practical action, from a rational point of view?

Pr_2 Which theory should we prefer for practical action, from a rational point of view?

My answer to Pr_1 is: From a rational point of view, we should not 'rely' on any theory, for no theory has been shown to be true, or can be shown to be true.

My answer to Pr_2 is: But we should *prefer* as basis for action the best-tested theory.

In other words, there is no 'absolute reliance'; but since we *have* to choose, it will be 'rational' to choose the best-tested theory. This will be 'rational' in the most obvious sense of the word known to me: the best-tested theory is the one which, in the light of our *critical discussion*, appears to be the best so far, and I do not know of anything more 'rational' than a well-conducted critical discussion.

Of course, in choosing the best-tested theory as a basis for action, we 'rely' on it, in some sense of the word. It may therefore even be described as the *most* 'reliable' theory available, in some sense of this term. Yet this does not say that it is 'reliable'. It is not 'reliable' at least in the sense that we shall always do well, even in practical action, to foresee the possibility that something may go wrong with our expectations.

But it is not merely this trivial caution which we must derive from our negative reply to L_1 and Pr_1. Rather, it is of the utmost importance for the understanding of the whole problem, and especially of what I have called the traditional problem, that in spite of the 'rationality' of choosing the best-tested theory as a basis of action, this choice is *not* 'rational' in the sense that it is based upon *good reasons* for expecting that it will in practice be a successful choice: *there can be no good reasons* in this sense, and this is precisely Hume's result. (In this our answers to H_L, L_1, and Pr_1 all agree.) On the contrary, even if our physical theories should be true, it is perfectly possible that the world as we know it, with all its pragmatically relevant regularities, may completely disintegrate in the next second. This should be obvious to anybody today; but I said so[28] before Hiroshima: there are infinitely many possibilities of local, partial, or total disaster.

From a pragmatic point of view, however, most of these possibilities are obviously not worth bothering about because we cannot *do* anything about them: they are beyond the realm of action. (I do not, of course, include atomic war among those disasters which are beyond the realm of human action, although most of us think just in this way, because most of us cannot do more about it than about an act of God.)

All this would hold even if we could be certain that our

[28] See *L.d.F.*, section 79 (*L. Sc. D.*, pp. 253 f.).

physical and biological theories were true. But we do not know it. On the contrary, we have reason to suspect even the best of them; and this adds, of course, further infinities to the infinite possibilities of disaster.

It is this kind of consideration which makes Gume's and my own negative reply so important. For we can now see very clearly why we must beware lest our theory of knowledge proves too much. More precisely, *no theory of knowledge should attempt to explain why we are successful in our attempts to explain things.*

Even if we assume that we have been successful—that our physical theories are true—we can learn from our cosmology how infinitely improbable this success is: our theories tell us that the world is almost completely empty, and that empty space is filled with chaotic radiation. And almost all places which are not empty are occupied either by chaotic dust, or by gases, or by very hot stars—all these in conditions which seem to make the application of any method of acquiring physical knowledge locally impossible.

To sum up, there are many worlds, possible and actual worlds, in which a search for knowledge and for regularities would fail. And even in the world as we actually know it from the sciences, the occurrence of conditions under which life, and a search for knowledge, could arise—and succeed—seems to be almost infinitely improbable. Moreover, it seems that if ever such conditions should appear, they would be bound to disappear again, after a time which, cosmologically speaking, is very short.

10. *Background to My Restatement of Hume's Psychological Problem of Induction*

Historically, I found my new solution to Hume's psychological problem of induction before my solution to the logical problem: it was here that I first noticed that induction—the formation of a belief by repetition—is a myth. It was first in animals and children, but later also in adults, that I observed the immensely powerful *need for regularity*—the need which makes them seek for regularities; which makes them sometimes experience regularities even where there are none; which makes them cling to their expectations dogmatically; and which makes them unhappy and may drive them to despair and to the verge of madness if certain assumed regularities break down. When Kant said that our intellect imposes its laws upon nature, he was right—except that he did not notice how often our intellect fails in the attempt: the regularities we try to impose are *psychologically a priori*, but there is not the slightest reason to assume that they are *a priori valid*, as Kant thought. The need to try to impose such regularities upon our environment is, clearly, inborn, and based on drives, or instincts. There is the general need for a world that conforms to our expectations; and there are many more specific needs, for example the need for regular social response, or the need for learning a language with rules for descriptive (and other) statements. This led me first to the conclusion that expectations may arise without, or before, any repetition; and later to a logical analysis which showed that they could not arise otherwise because repetition presupposes similarity, and similarity presupposes a point of view—a theory, or an expectation.

Thus I decided that Hume's inductive theory of the formation of beliefs could not possibly be true, *for logical reasons*. This led me to see that logical considerations may be transferred to psychological considerations; and it led me further to the heuristic conjecture that, quite generally, what holds in logic also holds—provided it is properly transferred—in psychology. (This heuristic principle is what I now call the 'principle of transference'.) I suppose it was largely this result which made me give up psychology and turn to the logic of discovery.

Quite apart from this, I felt that psychology should be regarded as a biological discipline, and especially that any psychological *theory of the acquisition of knowledge* should be so regarded.

Now if we transfer to human and animal psychology that *method of preference* which is the result of our solution of L_3, we arrive, clearly, at the well-known method of trial and error-elimination: the various trials correspond to the formation of competing hypotheses; and the elimination of error corresponds to the elimination or refutation of theories by way of tests.

This led me to the formulation: the main difference between Einstein and an amoeba (as described by Jennings[29]) is that

[29] H. S. Jennings, *The Behaviour of the Lower Organisms*, Columbia University, 1906.

Einstein *consciously seeks for error elimination.* He tries to kill his theories: he is *consciously critical* of his theories which, for this reason, he tries to *formulate* sharply rather than vaguely. But the amoeba cannot be critical *vis-à-vis* its expectations or hypotheses; it cannot be critical because it cannot *face* its hypotheses: they are part of it. (Only objective knowledge is criticizable: subjective knowledge becomes criticizable only when it becomes objective. And it becomes objective when we *say* what we think; and even more so when we *write* it down, or *print* it.)

It is clear that the method of trial and error-elimination is largely based upon inborn instincts. And it is clear that some of these instincts are linked with that vague phenomenon called by some philosophers 'belief'.

I used to take pride in the fact that I am not a belief philosopher: I am primarily interested in ideas, in theories, and I find it comparatively unimportant whether or not anybody 'believes' in them. And I suspect that the interest of philosophers in belief results from that mistaken philosophy which I call 'inductivism'. They are theorists of knowledge, and starting from subjective experiences they fail to distinguish between objective and subjective knowledge. This leads them to believe in belief as the genus of which knowledge is a species ('justification' or perhaps a 'criterion of truth' such as clarity and distinctness, or vivacity,[30] or 'sufficient reason', providing the specific difference).

This is why, like E. M. Forster, I do not believe in belief.

But there are other reasons, and more important ones, for being wary concerning belief. I am quite ready to admit that there exist some psychological states which may be called 'expectations', and that there are shades of expectations, from the lively expectation of a dog which is about to be taken for a walk, to the almost non-existent expectation of a schoolboy who knows, but does not really believe, that if only he lives long enough, he will one day be an old man. But it is questionable whether the word 'belief' is used by philosophers to describe psychological states in this sense. It seems that they more often use it to denote not momentary states but what may be called 'settled' beliefs, including those countless unconscious expectations which make up our horizon of expectations. It is a far cry

[30] See Hume, *Treatise*, p. 265.

from these to formulated hypotheses, and therefore also to state-ments of the form 'I believe that . . .'.

Now almost all such *formulated* statements can be considered critically; and the psychological states which *result* from a critical consideration seem to me very different indeed from an unconscious expectation. Thus even a 'settled' belief changes when it is formulated, and again after it has been formulated. If the result of its critical consideration is 'acceptance', it can range from that fanatical acceptance which attempts to suppress one's doubts and scruples to that tentative acceptance which is ready for reconsideration and revision at a moment's notice, and which may even be linked with an active search for refutations.

I do not think that such distinctions between different 'beliefs' are of any interest for my own objectivist theory of knowledge; but they ought to be interesting for anybody who takes the psychological problem of induction seriously—which I do not.

11. *Restatement of the Psychological Problem of Induction*

For the reasons just explained, I do not regard the psycho-logical problem of induction as part of my own (objectivist) theory of knowledge. But I think that the principle of transfer-ence suggests the following problems and answers.

Ps_1 If we look at a theory critically, from the point of view of sufficient evidence rather than from any pragmatic point of view, do we always have the feeling of complete assurance or certainty of its truth, even with respect to the best-tested theories, such as that the sun rises every day?

I think the answer here is: No. I suggest that the feeling of certainty—the strong belief—which Hume tried to explain was a *pragmatic* belief; something closely connected with action and the choice between alternatives, or else with our instinctive need for, and expectation of, regularities. But if we assume that we are in a position to reflect on the evidence, and what it permits us to assert, then we shall have to admit that the sun may not rise tomorrow over London after all—for example because the sun may explode within the next half-hour, so that there will be no tomorrow. Of course we shall not consider this possibility 'seriously'—that is, pragmatically—because it does not suggest any possible action: we just can't do anything about it.

Thus we are led to consider our pragmatic beliefs. And these can be very strong indeed. We may ask:

Ps₂ Are those 'strong pragmatic beliefs' which we all hold, such as the belief that there will be a tomorrow, the irrational results of repetition?

My reply is: No. The repetition theory is untenable anyway. These beliefs are partly inborn, partly modifications of inborn beliefs resulting from the method of trial and error-elimination. But this method is perfectly 'rational' since it corresponds precisely to that method of preference whose rationality has been discussed. More especially, a *pragmatic belief in the results of science* is not irrational, because there is nothing more 'rational' than the method of critical discussion, which is the method of science. And although it would be irrational to accept any of its results as certain, there is nothing 'better' when it comes to practical action: there is no alternative method which might be said to be more rational.

12. *The Traditional Problem of Induction and the Invalidity of all Principles or Rules of Induction*

I now return to what I call the traditional philosophical problem of induction.

What I call by this name is, I suggest, the result of seeing the commonsense view of induction by repetition challenged by Hume, without taking the challenge quite as seriously as it should be taken. Even Hume, after all, remained an inductivist; thus not every inductivist challenged by Hume can be expected to see that Hume's challenge is one to inductivism.

The fundamental schema of the traditional problem may be stated in various ways, for example:

Tr₁ How can induction be justified (in spite of Hume)?

Tr₂ How can a principle of induction (that is, a non-logical principle justifying induction) be justified?

Tr₃ How can one justify a principle of induction, such as 'the future will be like the past', or perhaps the so-called 'principle of the uniformity of nature'?

As I briefly indicated in my *Logik der Forschung*, I think that Kant's problem 'How can synthetic statements be valid *a priori*?'

was an attempt to generalize Tr_1 or Tr_2. This is why I regard Russell as a Kantian, at least in some of his phases, for he tried to find a solution for Tr_2 by some *a priori* justification. In the *Problems of Philosophy*, for example, Russell's formulation of Tr_2 was: '. . . what sort of general beliefs would suffice, if true, to justify the judgement that the sun will rise tomorrow . . .?'

From my point of view, all these problems are badly formulated. (And so also are the probabilistic versions such as the one implicit in Thomas Reid's principle of induction, 'What is to be will probably be like to what has been in similar circumstances'.) Their authors do not take Hume's logical criticism sufficiently seriously; and they never seriously consider the possibility that we can, and must, do without induction by repetition, and that we actually do without it.

It seems to me that all the objections to my theory which I know of approach it with the question of whether my theory has solved the traditional problem of induction—that is, whether I have justified inductive inference.

Of course I have not. From this my critics deduce that I have failed to solve Hume's problem of induction.

It is, among other reasons, especially for the reason stated in section 9 that the traditional formulations of the principle of induction have to be rejected. For they all assume not only that our quest for knowledge has been successful, but also that we should be able to explain why it is successful.

However, even on the assumption (which I share) that our quest for knowledge has been very successful so far, and that we now know something of our universe, this success becomes miraculously improbable, and therefore inexplicable; for an appeal to an endless series of improbable accidents is not an explanation. (The best we can do, I suppose, is to investigate the almost incredible evolutionary history of these accidents, from the making of the elements to the making of the organisms.)

Once this has been seen, not only Hume's thesis that an appeal to probability cannot change the reply to H_L (and therefore to L_1 and Pr_1) becomes perfectly obvious, but also the invalidity of any 'principle of induction'.

The idea of a principle of induction is that of a statement—to be regarded as a metaphysical principle, or as valid *a priori*, or as probable, or perhaps as a mere conjecture—which, if true, would give *good reasons for our reliance upon regularities*. If by 'reliance' is meant merely pragmatic reliance, in the sense of Pr_2, upon the rationality of our theoretical *preferences*, then clearly no principle of induction is needed: we do not need to rely on regularities—that is, on the truth of theories—to justify this preference. If, on the other hand, 'reliance' in the sense of Pr_1 is intended, then any such principle of induction would simply be false. Indeed in the following sense it would even be paradoxical. It would entitle us to rely on science; whereas today's science tells us that only under very special and improbable conditions can situations arise in which regularities, or instances of regularities, can be observed. In fact, science tells us, such conditions occur hardly anywhere in the universe, and if they occur somewhere (on earth, say) they are liable to occur for periods which will be short from a cosmological point of view.

Clearly this criticism applies not only to any principle which would justify inductive inference based on repetition, but also to any principle which would justify 'reliance', in the sense of Pr_1, on the method of trial and error-elimination, or on any other conceivable method.

13. *Beyond the Problems of Induction and Demarcation*

My solution of the problem of induction occurred to me a considerable time after I had solved, at least to my own satisfaction, the problem of demarcation (the demarcation between empirical science and pseudoscience, especially metaphysics).

Only after the solution of the problem of induction did I regard the problem of demarcation as objectively important, for I had suspected it of giving merely a definition of science. This seemed to me of doubtful significance (owing perhaps to my negative attitude towards definitions), even though I had found it very helpful for clarifying my attitude towards science and pseudoscience.

I saw that what has to be given up is the *quest for justification*, in the sense of the justification of the claim that a theory is true. *All theories are hypotheses*; all *may* be overthrown.

On the other hand, I was very far from suggesting that we give up the search for truth: our critical discussions of theories are dominated by the idea of finding a true (and powerful) explanatory theory; and *we do justify our preferences by an appeal to the idea of truth*: truth plays the role of a regulative idea. *We test for truth,* by eliminating falsehood. That we cannot give a justification—or sufficient reasons—for our guesses does not mean that we may not have guessed the truth; some of our hypotheses may well be true.[31]

The realization that all knowledge is hypothetical leads to the rejection of the 'principle of sufficient reason' in the form 'that a reason can be given for every truth' (Leibniz) or in the stronger form which we find in Berkeley and Hume who both suggest that it is a sufficient reason for unbelief if we 'see no [sufficient] reason for believing'.[32]

Once I had solved the problem of induction, and realized its close connection with the problem of demarcation, interesting new problems and new solutions arose in rapid succession.

First of all I soon realized that the problem of demarcation and my solution, as stated above, were a bit formal and un-realistic: *empirical refutations could always be avoided.* It was always possible to '*immunize*' any theory against criticism. (This excellent expression which, I think, should replace my terms 'conventionalist stratagem' and 'conventionalist twist' is due to Hans Albert.)

Thus I was led to the idea of *methodological rules* and of the fundamental importance of a *critical approach*; that is, of an approach which avoided the policy of immunizing our theories against refutation.

At the same time, I also realized the opposite: the value of a *dogmatic* attitude: somebody had to defend a theory against criticism, or it would succumb too easily, and before it had been able to make its contributions to the growth of science.

The next step was the application of the critical approach to the test statements, the 'empirical basis': I stressed the conjectural and theoretical character of all observations, and all observation statements.

This led me to the view that all languages are theory-impregnated; which meant, of course, a radical revision of

[31] This hardly needs saying. Yet the *Encyclopedia of Philosophy,* 1967, vol. 3, p. 37 attributes to me the view: 'Truth itself is just an illusion.'

[32] Berkeley, *Three Dialogues Between Hylas and Philonous,* second Dialogue: 'It is to me a sufficient reason not to believe . . . if I see no reason for believing.' For Hume, see *C. & R.,* p. 21 (where the *Enquiry Concerning Human Understanding,* Section V, Part I is quoted).

empiricism. It also made me look upon the critical attitude as characteristic of the rational attitude; and it led me to see the significance of the argumentative (or critical) function of language; to the idea of deductive logic as the organon of criticism, and to stressing the retransmission of falsity from the conclusion to the premises (a corollary of the transmission of truth from the premises to the conclusion). And it further led me to realize that only a *formulated* theory (in contradistinction to a believed theory) can be objective, and to the idea that it is this formulation or objectivity that makes criticism possible; and so to my theory of a 'third world' (or, as Sir John Eccles prefers to call it, 'world 3').[33]

These are just a few of the many problems to which the new approach gave rise. There are other problems which are of a more technical character, such as the many problems connected with probability theory, including its role in quantum theory, and the connection between my theory of preference and Darwin's theory of natural selection.

[33] John C. Eccles, *Facing Reality*, Springer-Verlag, Berlin–Heidelberg–New York, 1970.

2. Two Faces of Common Sense: An Argument for Commonsense Realism and Against the Commonsense Theory of Knowledge

1. *An Apology for Philosophy*

IT is very necessary these days to apologize for being concerned with philosophy in any form whatever. Apart perhaps from some Marxists, most professional philosophers seem to have lost touch with reality. And as for the Marxists—'The Marxists have merely *interpreted* Marxism in various ways; the point, however, is to *change* it.'[1]

In my opinion, the greatest scandal of philosophy is that, while all around us the world of nature perishes—and not the world of nature alone—philosophers continue to talk, sometimes cleverly and sometimes not, about the question of whether this world exists. They get involved in scholasticism,[2] in linguistic puzzles such as, for example, whether or not there are differ-

---

[1] Marx, of course, said (in the eleventh of his *Theses on Feuerbach*): 'The philosophers have merely *interpreted* the world in various ways; the point, however, is to *change* it.' The brilliant and timely variation quoted in the text seems to be due to R. Hochhuth. (But I must not mention Hochhuth's brilliance without dissociating myself most emphatically from his quite mistaken attitude towards Winston Churchill.)

[2] I am using the term 'scholasticism' to indicate an attitude of arguing without a serious problem—an attitude that was by no means universal among the schoolmen of the Middle Ages.

This long essay, so far unpublished, is a revised and expanded version of a talk I gave to my former Seminar early in 1970. It is intended as a fairly full answer to the critics of my views on science. I am indebted to John Watkins who has read through an earlier version of the essay and who pointed out to me a serious error which fortunately proved to be not relevant to my main argument. David Miller has most generously given his time to reading the essay thoroughly and repeatedly and has saved me not only from at least three similar errors but also from countless minor muddles of matter and style. I am deeply indebted to him for this.

ences between 'being' and 'existing'. (As in contemporary art, there are no standards in these worlds of philosophy.)

It goes without saying that the widespread anti-intellectual attitude which was so strong among the National Socialists, and which is again becoming strong among disappointed young people, especially students, is just as bad as this kind of scholasticism, and if possible a little worse even than the pretentious and spurious, though sometimes quite brilliant, verbiage of philosophers and other intellectuals. But it is only a very little worse, for the treason of the intellectuals evokes anti-intellectualism as an almost inevitable reaction. If you feed them stones instead of bread, the young people will revolt, even if in so doing they mistake a baker for a stone-thrower.

Under these circumstances there is a need to apologize for being a philosopher, and more particularly for restating (as I intend to do, if only in passing) what should be a triviality, such as *realism*, the thesis of the reality of the world. What is my excuse?

My excuse is this. We all have our philosophies, whether or not we are aware of this fact, and our philosophies are not worth very much. But the impact of our philosophies upon our actions and our lives is often devastating. This makes it necessary to try to improve our philosophies by criticism. This is the only apology for the continued existence of philosophy which I am able to offer.

2. *The Insecure Starting-Point: Common Sense and Criticism*

Science, philosophy, rational thought, must all start from common sense.

Not, perhaps, because common sense is a secure starting-point: the term 'common sense' which I am using here is a very vague term, simply because it denotes a vague and changing thing—the often adequate or true and often inadequate or false instincts or opinions of many men.

How can such a vague and insecure thing as common sense provide us with a starting-point? My answer is: because we do not aim or try to build (as did, say, Descartes or Spinoza or Locke, Berkeley, or Kant) a secure system on these 'foundations'. Any of our many commonsense assumptions—our commonsense background knowledge, as it may be called—

from which we start can be challenged and criticized at any
time; often such an assumption is successfully criticized and
rejected (for example, the theory that the earth is flat). In such
a case, common sense is either modified by the correction, or it
is transcended and replaced by a theory which may appear to
some people for a shorter or longer period of time as being more
or less 'crazy'. If such a theory needs much training to be understood, it may even fail for ever to be absorbed by common sense.
Yet even then we can demand that we try to get as close as
possible to the ideal: *All science, and all philosophy, are enlightened
common sense.*

Thus we begin with a vague starting-point, and we build on
insecure foundations. But we can make progress: we sometimes
can, after some criticism, see that we have been wrong: we can
learn from our mistakes, from realizing that we have made a
mistake.

(Incidentally, I shall try to show later that common sense has
been particularly misleading in the theory of knowledge. For
there seems to be a commonsense theory of knowledge: it is the
mistaken theory that we acquire knowledge about the world by
opening our eyes and looking at it, or, more generally, by
observation.)

My first thesis is thus that our starting-point is common sense,
and that our great instrument for progress is criticism.

But this thesis raises at once a difficulty. It has been said that
if we wish to criticize a theory, say T_1, whether or not it is of
a commonsense character, then we need some other theory, T_2,
which furnishes us with the necessary basis or starting-point or
background for criticizing T_1. Only in the very special case that
we can show T_1 to be inconsistent (a case called 'immanent
criticism', where we use T_1 in order to show that T_1 is false) can
we proceed differently; that is, by showing that absurd consequences follow from T_1.

I think that this criticism of the method of criticism is invalid.
(What it alleges is that all criticism must be either 'immanent'
or 'transcendent', and that in the case of 'transcendent' criticism
we do not proceed critically since we have to assume dogmatically the truth of T_2.) For what really happens is this. If we feel
that we should produce some criticism of T_1, which we can
assume to be a consistent theory, then we either show that T_1

leads to unintended and undesirable consequences (it does not matter so much whether they are logically inconsistent), or we show that there is a competing theory T_2 which clashes with T_1, and which, we try to show, has certain advantages over T_1. This is all that is needed: as soon as we have competing theories, there is plenty of scope for critical, or rational, discussion: we explore the consequences of the theories, and we try, especially, to discover their weak points—that is, consequences which we think may be mistaken. This kind of critical or rational discussion may sometimes lead to a clear defeat of one of the theories; more often it only helps to bring out the weaknesses of both, and thus challenges us to produce some further theory.

The fundamental problem of the theory of knowledge is the clarification and investigation of this process by which, it is here claimed, our theories may grow or progress.

3. Contrast with Other Approaches

What I have said so far may appear quite trivial. To give it a point, I shall very briefly contrast it with other approaches.

Descartes was perhaps the first to say that everything depends upon the security of our starting-point. In order to render this starting-point really secure, he suggested the method of doubt: accept only what is absolutely indubitable.

He then started from his own existence, which seemed to him indubitable, since even doubting our own existence seems to presuppose the existence of a doubter (a doubting subject).

Now I am no more sceptical about the existence of my own self than Descartes was of his. But I also think (as did Descartes) that I shall die soon and that this will make little difference to the world, except to myself and two or three friends. Obviously the issues of one's own life and death are of some significance, but I conjecture (and I think Descartes would agree) that my own existence will come to an end without the world's coming to an end too.

This is a commonsense view, and it is the central tenet of what may be termed 'realism'. (Realism will soon be discussed more fully.)

I admit that the belief in one's own existence is very strong. But I do not admit that it can bear the weight of anything resembling the Cartesian edifice; as a starting-platform it is much too narrow. Nor do I think, incidentally, that it is as

indubitable as Descartes (excusably) believed. In Hugh Routledge's wonderful book, *Everest 1933*, we read of Kipa, one of the
Sherpas who went higher than was good for him: 'Poor old
Kipa's bewildered mind still held doggedly to the idea that he
was dead.'[3] I do not assert that poor old Kipa's idea was common sense, or even reasonable, but it throws doubt on that
directness and indubitability which Descartes was claiming. In
any case, I do not propose to make any similar claim for certainty, even though I gladly admit that it is good, sane common
sense to believe in the existence of one's thinking self. It is not
the truth of Descartes's starting-point which I wish to challenge,
but its sufficiency for what he tries to do with it and, incidentally,
its alleged indubitability.

Locke, Berkeley, and even the 'sceptic' Hume, and their many
successors, especially Russell and Moore,[4] shared with Descartes
the view that subjective experiences were particularly secure
and therefore suitable as a stable starting-point or foundation;
but they relied mainly on experiences of an observational
character. And Reid, with whom I share adherence to realism
and to common sense, thought that we had some very direct,
immediate, and secure perception of external, objective reality.

In opposition to this, I suggest that there is nothing direct or
immediate in our experience: we have to *learn* that we have a
self, extended in time and continuing to exist even during sleep
and total unconsciousness, and we have to learn about our own
and others' bodies. It is all decoding, or interpretation. We learn
to decode so well that everything becomes very 'direct' or
'immediate' to us; but so it is with the man who has learned the
Morse Code, or, to take a more familiar example, who has
learned to read a book: it speaks to him 'directly', 'immediately'.
Nevertheless, we know that there is a complicated process of
decoding going on; the apparent directness and immediacy are
the result of training, just as in piano-playing or car-driving.

---

[3] Hugh Routledge, *Everest 1933*, Hodder & Stoughton, London, 1934, p. 143.
(I had, though perhaps only for a few seconds, a similar experience to Kipa's
when I was once struck by lightning on the *Sonnblick* in the Austrian Alps.)

[4] G. E. Moore was a great realist because he had a strong love for truth and
felt clearly that idealism was false. Unfortunately, he believed in the commonsense subjectivist theory of knowledge, and thus throughout his whole life he hoped,
in vain, that a proof of realism based on perception could be found—a thing
that cannot exist. Russell relapsed from realism into positivism for the same reason.

We have reason to conjecture that there is a hereditary basis to our decoding skills. At any rate, we sometimes do make mistakes in decoding, especially during the learning period, but also later, especially if unusual situations occur. The immediacy or directness of the well-learned decoding process does not guarantee faultless functioning; there is no absolute certainty, though certainty enough for most practical purposes. The quest for certainty, for a secure basis of knowledge, has to be abandoned.

Thus I see the problem of knowledge in a way different from that of my predecessors. Security and justification of claims to knowledge are not my problem. Instead, my problem is the growth of knowledge. In which sense can we speak of the growth or the progress of knowledge, and how can we achieve it?

4. *Realism*

Realism is essential to common sense. Common sense, or enlightened common sense, distinguishes between appearance and reality. (This may be illustrated by examples such as, 'Today the air is so clear that the mountains appear much nearer than they really are'. Or perhaps, 'He appears to do it without effort, but he has confessed to me that the tension is almost unbearable'.) But common sense also realizes that appearances (say, a reflection in a looking-glass) have a sort of reality; or in other words, that there can be a surface reality— that is, an appearance—and a depth reality. Moreover, there are many sorts of real things. The most obvious sort is that of foodstuffs (I conjecture that they produce the basis of the feeling of reality), or more resistant objects (*objectum* = what lies in the way of our action) like stones, and trees, and humans. But there are many sorts of reality which are quite different, such as our subjective decoding of our experiences of foodstuffs, stones, and trees, and human bodies. The taste and weight of foodstuffs and of stones is again another sort of reality, and so are the properties of trees and human bodies. Examples of other sorts in this many-sorted universe are: a toothache, a word, a language, a highway code, a novel, a governmental decision; a valid or invalid proof; perhaps forces, fields of forces, propensities, structures; and regularities. (My remarks here leave it entirely open whether, and how, these many sorts of objects can be related to each other.)

5. *Arguments for Realism*

My thesis is that realism is neither demonstrable nor refutable. Realism like anything else outside logic and finite arithmetic is not demonstrable; but while empirical scientific theories are refutable,[5] realism is not even refutable. (It shares this irrefutability with many philosophical or 'metaphysical' theories, in particular also with idealism.) But it is arguable, and the weight of the arguments is overwhelmingly in its favour.

Common sense is unquestioningly on the side of realism; there are, of course, even before Descartes—in fact ever since Heraclitus—a few hints of doubt whether or not *our ordinary world is perhaps just our dream*. But even Descartes and Locke were realists. A philosophical theory competing with realism did not seriously start before Berkeley, Hume, and Kant.[6] Kant, incidentally, even provided a proof for realism. But it was not a valid proof; and I think it important that we should be clear why no valid proof of realism can exist.

In its simplest form, idealism says: the world (which includes my present audience) is just my dream. Now it is clear that this theory (though you will know that it is false) is not refutable: whatever you, my audience, may do to convince me of your reality—talking to me, or writing a letter, or perhaps kicking me—it cannot possibly assume the force of a refutation; for I

---

[5] This, of course, is one of my oldest theories. See, for example, chapter 1 of my *Conjectures and Refutations*, esp. pp. 37 f. I disagree with those critics of my views who assert, for example, that Newton's theory is no more refutable than Freud's. A refutation of Newton's theory would be, for example, if all the planets except the earth continue to move as at present, while the earth moves on its present orbit but with constant acceleration even when moving away from its perihelion. (Of course, against this refutation and all others any theory whatever can be 'immunized'—to use a term due to Hans Albert; this was stressed by me as long ago as 1934, and it is emphatically not the point at issue here.) I should say that the refutability of Newton's or Einstein's theory is a fact of elementary physics and of elementary methodology. Einstein, for example, said that if the red shift effect (the slowing down of atomic clocks in strong gravitational fields) was not observed in the case of white dwarfs, his theory of general relativity would be refuted. No description whatsoever of any logically possible human behaviour can be given which would turn out to be incompatible with the psychoanalytic theories of Freud, or of Adler, or of Jung.

[6] Positivism, phenomenalism, and also phenomenology are all of course infected by the subjectivism of the Cartesian starting-point.

would continue to say that I am dreaming that you are talking to me, or that I received a letter, or felt a kick. (One might say that these answers are all, in various ways, immunizing stratagems. This is so, and it is a strong argument against idealism. But again, that it is a self-immunizing theory does not refute it.)

Thus idealism is irrefutable; and this means, of course, that realism is indemonstrable. But I am prepared to concede that realism is not only indemonstrable but, like idealism, irrefutable also; that no describable event, and no conceivable experience, can be taken as an effective refutation of realism.[7] Thus there will be in this issue, as in so many, no conclusive argument. *But there are arguments in favour of realism*; or, rather, *against idealism*.

(1) Perhaps the strongest argument consists of a combination of two: (a) that realism is part of common sense, and (b) that all the alleged *arguments* against it are not only philosophical in the most derogatory sense of this term, but are at the same time based upon an uncritically accepted part of common sense; that is to say, upon that mistaken part of the commonsense theory of knowledge which I have called the 'bucket theory of the mind'; see below, sections 12 and 13.

(2) Although science is a bit out of fashion today with some people, for reasons which are, regrettably, far from negligible,

---

[7] The irrefutability of realism (which I am prepared to concede) may be questioned. The great Austrian authoress Marie Ebner von Eschenbach (1830–1916) tells in some memoirs of her childhood that she suspected realism to be mistaken. Perhaps things do disappear when we look away. So she tried to catch the world in its disappearing trick by suddenly turning round, half expecting that she would see how out of nothingness things try quickly to reassemble themselves; and she was both disappointed and relieved whenever she failed. Several comments may be made on this story. First, it is conceivable that this report of childish experimentation is not untypical, but normal and typical, and plays a part in the development of the commonsense distinction of appearance from reality. Secondly (and I am slightly inclined to favour this view) it is conceivable that the report is untypical; that most children are naïve realists, or become so before an age within their memory; and Marie von Ebner certainly was an untypical child. Thirdly, I have experienced—and not only in childhood but also as an adult—something not too far removed from it: for example, when finding something of which I had completely forgotten, I sometimes felt that if nature had let this thing disappear, nobody would have been the wiser. (There was no need for reality to show that it 'really' existed; nobody would have noticed had it not done so.) The question arises whether, if Marie had succeeded, this would have refuted realism or whether it would not merely have refuted a very special form of it. I do not feel obliged to go into this question, but rather *concede* to my opponents that realism is irrefutable. Should this concession be wrong, then realism is even nearer to being a testable scientific theory than I originally intended to claim.

we should not ignore its relevance to realism, despite the fact that there are scientists who are not realists, such as Ernst Mach or, in our own time, Eugene P. Wigner;[8] their arguments fall very clearly in the class just characterized in (1). But let us for a moment forget about atomic physics (quantum mechanics). We can then assert that almost all, if not all, physical, chemical, or biological theories imply realism, in the sense that if they are true, realism must also be true. This is one of the reasons why some people speak of 'scientific realism'. It is quite a good reason. Because of its (apparent) lack of testability, I myself happen to prefer to call realism 'metaphysical' rather than 'scientific'.[9]

However one may look at this, there are excellent reasons for saying that *what we attempt in science is to describe and (so far as possible) explain reality*. We do so with the help of conjectural theories; that is, theories which we hope are true (or near the truth), but which we cannot establish as certain or even as probable (in the sense of the probability calculus), even though they are the best theories which we are able to produce, and may therefore be called 'probable' as long as this term is kept free from any association with the calculus of probability.

There is a closely related and excellent sense in which we can speak of 'scientific realism': the procedure we adopt involves (as long as it does not break down, for example because of anti-rational attitudes) success in the sense that our conjectural theories tend progressively to come nearer to the truth; that is, to true descriptions of certain facts, or aspects of reality.

(3) But even if we drop all arguments drawn from science, there remain the arguments from language. Any discussion of realism, and especially all arguments against it, have to be

---

[8] For Wigner see especially his contribution to *The Scientist Speculates*, I. J. Good (ed.), Heinemann, London, 1962, pp. 284–302. For a criticism see especially Edward Nelson, *Dynamical Theories of Brownian Motion*, Princeton University Press, 1967, §§ 14–16. See also my contributions in Mario Bunge (ed.), *Quantum Theory and Reality*, Springer, Berlin, 1967, and in W. Yourgrau and A. van der Werde (eds.), *Perspectives in Quantum Theory, Essays in Honor of Alfred Landé*, M.I.T. Press, 1971.

[9] See my *Logik der Forschung*, 1934 (*L.d.F.*) where, in section 79 (p. 252 of the English translation *The Logic of Scientific Discovery*, 1959—*L. Sc. D.*) I describe myself as a metaphysical realist. In those days I identified wrongly the limits of science with those of arguability. I later changed my mind and argued that non-testable (i.e. irrefutable) metaphysical theories may be rationally arguable. (See, for example, my paper 'On the Status of Science and Metaphysics', first published in 1958 and now in my *Conjectures and Refutations*, 1963; fourth edn., 1972.)

formulated in some language. But human language is essentially descriptive (and argumentative),[10] and an unambiguous description is always realistic: it is *of* something—of some state of affairs which may be real or imaginary. Thus if the state of affairs is imaginary, then the description is simply false and its negation is a true description of reality, in Tarski's sense. This does not logically refute idealism or solipsism; but it makes it at least irrelevant. Rationality, language, description, argument, are all about some reality, and they address themselves to an audience. All this presupposes realism. Of course, this argument for realism is logically no more conclusive than any other, because I may merely dream that I am using descriptive language and arguments; but this argument for realism is nevertheless strong and *rational*. It is as strong as reason itself.

(4) To me, idealism appears absurd, for it also implies something like this: that it is my mind which creates this beautiful world. But I know I am not its Creator. After all, the famous remark 'Beauty is in the eye of the beholder', though perhaps not an utterly stupid remark, means no more than that there is a problem of the *appreciation* of beauty. I know that the beauty of Rembrandt's self-portraits is not in my eye, nor that of Bach's Passions in my ear. On the contrary, I can establish to my satisfaction, by opening and closing my eyes and ears, that my eyes and ears are not good enough to take in all the beauty that is there. Also, there are other people who are better judges—better able than I to appreciate the beauty of pictures and of music. Denying realism amounts to megalomania (the most widespread occupational disease of the professional philosopher).

(5) Out of many other weighty though inconclusive arguments I wish to mention only one. It is this. If realism is true—more especially, something approaching scientific realism—then the reason for the impossibility of proving it is obvious. The reason is that our subjective knowledge, even perceptual knowledge, consists of dispositions to act, and is thus a kind of tentative adaptation to reality; and that we are searchers, at best, and at any rate fallible. There is no guarantee against error. At

---

[10] Bühler (partly anticipated by W. von Humboldt) clearly pointed out the descriptive function of language. I have referred to this in various places and argued for the need to introduce the argumentative function of language. See, for example, my paper 'Epistemology Without a Knowing Subject' (read in Amsterdam in 1967, and now reprinted as Chapter 3 in the present volume).

the same time, the whole question of the truth and falsity of our opinions and theories clearly becomes pointless if there is no reality, only dreams or illusions.

To sum up, I propose to accept realism as the only sensible hypothesis—as a conjecture to which no sensible alternative has ever been offered. I do not wish to be dogmatic about this issue any more than about any other. But I think I know all the epistemological arguments—they are mainly subjectivist—which have been offered in favour of alternatives to realism, such as positivism, idealism, phenomenalism, phenomenology, and so on, and although I am not an enemy of the discussion of *isms* in philosophy, I regard all the philosophical *arguments* which (to my knowledge) have ever been offered in favour of my list of *isms* as clearly mistaken. Most of them are the result of the mistaken quest for certainty, or for secure foundations on which to build. And all of them are typical philosophers' mistakes in the worst sense of this term: they are all derivatives of a mistaken though commonsensical theory of knowledge which does not stand up to any serious criticism. (Common sense typically breaks down when applied to itself; see section 12 below.)

I will conclude this section with the opinion of the two men whom I regard as the greatest of our time: Albert Einstein and Winston Churchill.

'I do not see', writes Einstein, 'any "metaphysical danger" in our acceptance of things—that is, of the objects of physics . . . together with the spatio-temporal structures which pertain to them.'[11]

This was Einstein's opinion after a careful and sympathetic analysis of a brilliant attempt at refuting naïve realism due to Bertrand Russell.

Winston Churchill's views are very characteristic and, I think, a very fair comment upon a philosophy which may since have changed its colours, crossing the floor of the house from idealism to realism, but which remains as pointless as ever it was: 'Some of my cousins who had the great advantage of University edu-

---

[11] See Albert Einstein, 'Remarks on Bertrand Russell's Theory of Knowledge', in P. A. Schilpp (ed.), *The Philosophy of Bertrand Russell*, The Library of Living Philosophers, vol. v, 1944, pp. 290 f. Schilpp's translation on p. 291 is very much closer than mine, but I felt that the importance of Einstein's idea justified my attempt at a *very* free translation, which, I hope, is still faithful to what Einstein wanted to say.

cation', Churchill writes, 'used to tease me with arguments to prove that nothing has any existence except what we think of it . . .' He continues:

I always rested upon the following argument which I devised for myself many years ago . . . here is this great sun standing apparently on no better foundation than our physical senses. But happily there is a method, apart altogether from our physical senses, of testing the reality of the sun . . . astronomers . . . predict by [mathematics and] pure reason that a black spot will pass across the sun on a certain day. You . . . look, and your sense of sight immediately tells you that their calculations are vindicated . . . *We have taken what is called in military map-making 'a cross bearing'. We have got independent testimony to the reality of the sun. When my metaphysical friends tell me that the data on which the astronomers made their calculations were necessarily obtained originally through the evidence of their senses, I say 'No'. They might, in theory at any rate, be obtained by automatic calculating-machines set in motion by the light falling upon them without admixture of the human senses at any stage . . .* I . . . reaffirm with emphasis . . . that the sun is real, and also that it is hot—in fact as hot as Hell, and that if the metaphysicians doubt it they should go there and see.[12]

I may perhaps add that I regard Churchill's argument, especially the important passages which I have put in italics, not only as a valid criticism of the idealistic and subjectivistic arguments, but as the philosophically soundest and most ingenious argument against subjectivist epistemology that I know. I am not aware of any philosopher who has not ignored this argument (apart from some of my students whose attention I have drawn to it). The argument is highly original; first published in 1930 it is one of the earliest philosophical arguments making use of the possibility of automatic observatories and calculating machines (programmed by Newtonian theory). And yet, forty years after its publication, Winston Churchill is still quite unknown as an epistemologist: his name does not appear in any of the many anthologies on epistemology, and it is also missing even from the *Encyclopedia of Philosophy*.

Of course Churchill's argument is merely an excellent refutation of the specious arguments of the subjectivists: *he does not*

[12] See Winston S. Churchill, *My Early Life—A Roving Commission,* first published Oct. 1930; quoted by permission of the Hamlyn Publishing Group from the Odhams Press edn., London, 1947, chapter IX, pp. 115 f. (The italics are not in the original.) See also the Macmillan edn., London 1944, pp. 131 f.

prove realism. For the idealist can always argue that he, or we, are dreaming the debate, with calculating machines and all. Yet I regard this argument as silly, because of its universal applicability. At any rate, unless some philosopher should produce some entirely new argument, I suggest that subjectivism may in future be ignored.

6. *Remarks on Truth*

Our main concern in philosophy and in science should be the search for truth. Justification is not an aim; and brilliance and cleverness as such are boring. We should seek to see or discover the most urgent problems, and we should try to solve them by proposing true theories (or true statements, or true propositions; there is no need here to distinguish between these); or at any rate by proposing theories which come a little nearer to the truth than those of our predecessors.

But the search for truth is only possible if we speak clearly and simply and avoid unnecessary technicalities and complications. In my view, aiming at simplicity and lucidity is a moral duty of all intellectuals: lack of clarity is a sin, and pretentiousness is a crime. (Brevity is also important, in view of the publication explosion, but it is of lesser urgency, and it sometimes is incompatible with clarity.) Often we are unable to live up to these demands, and we fail to say things clearly and understandably, but this merely shows that we are all not quite good enough as philosophers.

I accept the commonsense theory (defended and refined by Alfred Tarski[13]) that truth is correspondence with the facts (or with reality); or, more precisely, that a theory is true if and only if it corresponds to the facts.

To go just a little into technicalities which, thanks to Tarski, have by now almost become trivialities: truth and falsity are essentially regarded as properties, or classes, of statements, that is, of (unambiguously formulated) theories or propositions (or 'meaningful sentences')[14] of some language L_1 (for example

[13] See A. Tarski, *Logic, Semantics, Metamathematics,* Clarendon Press, Oxford, 1956, pp. 152–278 (a paper first published in Polish 1933 and in German 1936); the same, in *Philosophy and Phenomenological Research,* 4, 1944, pp. 341–76. See ch. 9, below.

[14] The expression 'meaningful sentence' (i.e. a sentence *plus* its 'meaning', i.e. a statement or proposition) is Tarski's (in Woodger's translation). Tarski has been unjustly criticized for holding the view that truth is a property of (mere) sentences, that is, of (meaningless though) grammatically correct sequences of words of a

German) about which we can speak quite freely in another language L_m, also called the *metalanguage*. Phrases of L_m which wholly or exclusively refer to L_1 are called 'metalinguistic'.

Thus let 'P' abbreviate one of the English (L_m) names of the German (L_1) phrase '*Der Mond ist aus grünem Käse gemacht*'. (Note that by the addition of English quotation marks this German phrase has become an English metalinguistic name— a so-called quotation name—of the German phrase.) Then the identity statement 'P = "*Der Mond ist aus grünem Käse gemacht*"' is evidently an English metalinguistic statement; and we can say: 'The German statement "*Der Mond ist aus grünem Käse gemacht*" corresponds to the facts or to the actual state of affairs if, and only if, the moon is made of green cheese.'

Now introduce the general rule that if P is a statement then 'p' is an abbreviation of the English description of the state of affairs described by the statement P. Then we can say, more generally: 'The phrase P of the object language is a statement corresponding to the facts if and only if p.'

In English we should say that 'P is true in L_1', or 'P is true in German'. Nevertheless, truth is not a notion relative to language; for if P_1 is a statement of any language L_1, and P_2 is a statement of any language L_2, then the following holds (in L_m, say): if P_2 is a translation of P_1 from L_1 into L_2, then P_1 and P_2 must be either both true or else both false: they must have the same truth value. Moreover, if a language is rich enough to possess an operation of negation,[15] then we can say that it contains for every false statement a true statement. (Thus we know that there are, roughly speaking, 'as many' true statements as there are false statements in every language which possesses an operation of negation.)

Tarski's theory more particularly makes clear *just what fact* a statement P will correspond to if it corresponds to *any* fact:

language or a formalism. Yet the truth is that, throughout his work, Tarski discusses only the truth of *interpreted* languages. I shall not distinguish here between statements, propositions, assertions, and theories.

[15] So far as is known all natural languages possess an operation of negation, though artificial languages have been constructed which do not possess this operation. (Animal psychologists even claim that something like this can be found in rats which learn to press levers with characteristic signs and to understand symbols which give these signs the logically opposite value to the original value. See the references to R. W. Brown and K. L. Lashley in Hans Hörmann, *Psychologie der Sprache*, Springer, Berlin, 1967, p. 51.)

namely the fact that *p*. And it solves too the problem of false statements; for a false statement *P* is false *not* because it corresponds to some odd entity like a *non*-fact, but simply because it does *not* correspond to *any* fact: it does not stand in the peculiar relation of *correspondence to a fact* to anything real, though it stands in a relation like 'describes' to the spurious state of affairs that *p*. (There is no virtue in avoiding such phrases as 'a spurious state of affairs', or even 'a spurious fact', as long as we bear in mind that a spurious fact simply is not real.)

Although it needed the genius of Tarski to make it clear, it has by now indeed become perfectly clear that, if we want to speak about the correspondence of a statement to a fact, we need a metalanguage in which we can *state* the fact (or the alleged fact) about which the statement in question speaks, and in addition can also speak about the statement in question (by using some conventional or descriptive *name* of that statement). And vice versa: it is clear that once we possess such a metalanguage in which we can speak about (a) the facts described by the statements of some (object) language, by the simple method of stating these facts, and also (b) the statements of this (object) language (by using *names* of these statements) then we can also speak in this metalanguage about the *correspondence* of statements to facts.

Once we can state in this way the conditions under which each statement of the language L_1 corresponds to the facts, we can define, purely verbally, yet in keeping with common sense:[16] *A statement is true if and only if it corresponds to the facts.*

This, as Tarski points out, is an objectivist or absolutist notion of truth. But it is not absolutist in the sense of allowing us to speak with 'absolute certainty or assurance'. For it does not provide us with a criterion of truth. On the contrary, Tarski could prove that, if L_1 is sufficiently rich (for example, if it contains arithmetic), then *there cannot exist a general criterion of truth.* Only for extremely poor artificial languages can there exist a criterion of truth. (Here Tarski is indebted to Gödel.)

Thus the idea of truth is absolutist, but no claim can be made

---

[16] Tarski shows that in order to avoid the Liar paradox a precaution is needed which goes beyond common sense: we have to be careful not to use the metalinguistic term 'true (in L_1)' in the language L_1. See also ch. 9, below.

for absolute certainty: *we are seekers for truth but we are not its possessors.*[17]

7. *Content, Truth Content, and Falsity Content*

In order to clarify what we are doing when we are seeking for truth, we must at least in some cases be able to give reasons for the intuitive claim that we have come *nearer to the truth*, or that some theory T_1 is superseded by some new theory, say T_2, because T_2 is more like the truth than T_1.

The idea that a theory T_1 may be further from the truth than a theory T_2, so that T_2 is a better approximation to the truth (or simply a better theory) than T_1, has been used, intuitively, by many philosophers, including myself. And just as the notion of truth has been regarded as suspect by many philosophers (not entirely without some grain of truth or reason, as became clear from Tarski's analysis of the semantic paradoxes), so has the notion of a better approach or approximation to the truth, or of a nearness to truth or (as I have called it) of a greater '*verisimilitude*'.

In order to allay these suspicions, I have introduced a logical notion of *verisimilitude* by combining two notions, both originally introduced by Tarski: (a) the notion of *truth*, and (b) the notion of the (logical) *content* of a statement; that is, the class of all statements logically entailed by it (its 'consequence class', as Tarski usually calls it).[18]

---

[17] Professor D. W. Hamlyn has done me the great honour of giving a description of my views on 'The nature of science' (Paul Edwards (ed.), *The Encyclopedia of Philosophy*, vol. 3, p. 37). Most of his outline is quite correct, but he has misunderstood me completely when he sums up my views by saying: 'Truth itself is just an illusion.' Are those who disclaim that they can reach absolute certainty about the authorship of Shakespeare's comedies, or about the structure of the world, for this reason committed to the doctrine that the author himself (or herself) of Shakespeare's comedies, or that the world itself, is 'just an illusion'?

(A clearer picture of the great significance that I attach to the concept of truth will be found in various places in my writings, particularly in Chapter 9 of the present volume.)

[18] The difference between the content or consequence class of a single statement or a finite set of statements (such a finite set can always be replaced by one single statement) on the one hand, and a non-axiomatizable (or not finitely axiomatizable) consequence class or content on the other is important, but will not be discussed here. Consequence classes of both sorts are called by Tarski 'deductive systems'; see Tarski, op. cit., chapter XII. Tarski introduced the notion of a consequence class years before me. I arrived at it later, independently, in my *Logik der Forschung*, where I also introduced the closely related concept of the empirical content of a

Every statement has a content or consequence class, the class of all those statements which follow from it. (We may describe the consequence class of tautological statements, following Tarski, as the zero class, so that tautological statements have zero content.) And every content contains a sub-content consisting of the class of all and only all its *true* consequences.

The class of all the *true* statements which follow from a given statement (or which belong to a given deductive system) and which are not tautological can be called its *truth content*.

The truth content of tautologies (of logically true statements) is zero: it consists only of tautologies. All other statements, *including all false statements*, have non-zero truth content.

The class of false statements entailed by a statement—the subclass of its content which consists of exactly all those statements which are false—might be called (by courtesy, as it were) its 'falsity content'; yet it does not have the characteristic properties of a 'content', or a Tarskian consequence class. It is not a Tarskian deductive system, since from any false statement it is possible logically to deduce true statements. (The disjunction of a false statement and any true statement is one of those statements which are true and follow from the false statement.)

In the remaining part of this section I intend to explain the intuitive ideas of truth content and falsity content in a little more detail, in order to prepare for a closer discussion of the idea of verisimilitude; for the *verisimilitude* of a statement will be explained as *increasing with its truth content* and *decreasing with its falsity content*. In this I shall largely utilize ideas of Alfred Tarski, especially his *theory of truth*, and his *theory of consequence classes and deductive systems* (both referred to here in footnote 18; see also Chapter 9 of this volume for a more detailed treatment).

It is possible to explain the falsity content of a statement *a*

statement *S* as the class of the empirical statements incompatible with *S* (or 'forbidden' by *S*). This concept was later taken up by Carnap; see especially his acknowledgement to my *Logik der Forschung*, on p. 406 of his *Logical Foundations of Probability*, 1950. The notion of *verisimilitude* was introduced by me in 1959 or 1960; see the footnote on p. 215 of *Conjectures and Refutations*, third edn., 1969. I might note here that whereas in *Conjectures and Refutations* I talked of 'truth-content' and 'falsity-content' I now prefer to omit the hyphens when the terms are used as nouns (that is, except in phrases—which I hope are rare—such as 'truth-content measure'). In this I am following the advice of Winston Churchill, as reported on p. 255 of the second edition of Fowler's *Modern English Usage*, 1965.

(as distinct from the class of false statements which follow from *a*) in such a way that (a) it is a content (or a Tarskian consequence class), (b) it contains all false statements which follow from *a*, and (c) it contains no true statement. In order to do this, we need only to relativize the concept of a content, which can be done in a very natural way.

Let us call the content or consequence class of a statement *a* by the name '*A*' (so that, generally, *X* is the content of the statement *x*). Let us call with Tarski the content of a logically true statement by the name '*L*'. *L* is the class of all logically true statements, and the common content of all contents and of all statements. We can say that *L* is the *zero content*.

We now relativize the idea of content so that we speak of the relative content of the statement *a*, *given* the content *Y*, and we denote this by the symbol '*a,Y*'. This is the class of all statements deducible from *a* in the presence of *Y*, or with the help of *Y*.

We see at once that if *A* is the content of the statement *a*, then we have, in the relativized mode of writing, $A = a,L$; that is to say, the absolute content *A* of a statement *a* equals the relative content of *a*, given 'logic' (= zero content).

A more interesting case of the relative content of a conjecture *a* is the case a,B_t where B_t is our *background knowledge* at the time *t*; that is, the knowledge which at time *t* is assumed without discussion. We can say that what is interesting in a new conjecture *a* is, in the first instance, the relative content *a,B*; that is to say, that part of the content of *a* which goes beyond *B*. Just as the content of a logically true statement is zero, so the relative content of a conjecture *a*, given *B*, is zero if *a* contains only background knowledge and nothing beyond it: we can say, generally, that if *a* belongs to *B*, or, what amounts to the same, if $A \subset B$, then $a,B = 0$. Thus the relative content of a statement *x, Y* is the information by which *x* in the presence of *Y* transcends *Y*.

We can now define the falsity content of *a*, which we denote by A_F, as the content of *a*, given the *truth content* of *a* (that is, the intersection A_T of *A* and *T*, where *T* is the Tarskian system of true statements). That is to say, we can *define*:

$$A_F = a,A_T.$$

The so-defined A_F answers our desiderata or adequacy conditions: (a) A_F is a content, even though it is a relative content;

after all, 'absolute' contents too are relative contents, given logical truth (or assuming that L is logically true); (b) A_F contains all the *false* statements which follow from a, since it is the deductive system of statements which follow from a, taking the *true* statements as our (relative) *zero*; (c) A_F '*contains*' no true statement in the sense that its true statements are not taken as content, but as its (relative) zero content.

Contents are sometimes logically comparable and sometimes not: they form partially ordered systems, ordered by the inclusion relation, exactly as statements form systems which are partially ordered by the entailment relation. The *absolute* contents A and B are comparable, provided $A \subset B$ or $B \subset A$. With relative contents, the comparability conditions are more complicated.

If X is a finitely axiomatizable content or deductive system, then there exists a statement x such that X is the content of x.

Thus if Y is finitely axiomatizable, we will be able to write

$$x, Y = x, y.$$

Now in this case one can see that x, Y equals the absolute content of the conjunction $x . y$ *minus* the absolute content of y.

Considerations such as these show that a, B and c, D will be comparable if

$$(A \dotplus B) - B \text{ is comparable with } (C \dotplus D) - D,$$

where '$\dotplus$' is Tarski's addition of *deductive systems*: if both are axiomatizable, $A \dotplus B$ is the content of the conjunction $a . b$.

Thus comparability will be rare in these partially ordered systems. But there is a method which shows that these partially ordered systems can be 'in principle'—that is, without contradiction—linearly ordered. The method is the application of the formal theory of probability. (I assert its applicability here only for axiomatizable systems, but we can extend it to non-axiomatizable systems; see also chapter 9 below.)

We can write '$p(x, Y)$' or else

$$p(X, Y)$$

to read 'the probability of x given Y', and apply the formal axiom system for relative probability which I have given elsewhere (for example, in my *Logic of Scientific Discovery*, new appendices *iv and *v).[19] The result is that $p(x,Y)$ will be a number between 0 and 1—usually we have no idea which number—and that we can assert, quite generally, that

$p(a,B)$ and $p(c,D)$ are *comparable in principle*.

Even though we normally have insufficient information at our disposal for deciding whether

$$p(a,B) \leqslant p(c,D) \text{ or } p(a,B) \geqslant p(c,D),$$

we can assert that at least one of these relations must hold.

The result of all this is that we can say that truth contents and falsity contents may be made comparable in principle with the help of the probability calculus.

As I have shown in various places, the content A of a will be the greater, the smaller the logical probability $p(a)$ or $p(A)$. For the more information a statement carries, the smaller will be the logical probability that it is true (accidentally, as it were). We can therefore introduce a *'measure'* of the content (it can be used mainly topologically, that is, as an indicator of linear order),

$$ct(a),$$

that is, the (absolute) content of a, and also relative measures

$$ct(a,b) \text{ and } ct(a,B)$$

that is, the relative content of a given b or B respectively. (If B is axiomatizable, then we have of course $ct(a,b) = ct(a,B)$.) These 'measures' ct can be defined with the help of the calculus of probability; that is to say, with the help of the definition

$$ct(a,B) = 1 - p(a,B).$$

We have now the means at our disposal to define (measures of) truth content, $ct_T(a)$ and falsity content, $ct_F(a)$:

$$ct_T(a) = ct(A_T),$$

where A_T is again the intersection of A and the Tarskian system of all true statements; and

$$ct_F(a) = ct(a,A_T),$$

---

[19] I used a content *measure* first in 1954 (cp. *L.Sc.D.*, p. 400), and measures of truth and falsity content, etc., in *C. & R.* (p. 385). Here and in Chapter 9 I distinguish *measure functions* by *lower case italics* such as p; ct; vs.

that is, the (measure of) the falsity content is the (measure of) the relative content of *a*, given the truth content of A_T of *a*; or, in still other words, the degree to which *a* goes *beyond* those statements which (a) follow from *a* and (b) which are true.

8. *Remarks on Verisimilitude*

With the help of these ideas we can now explain more clearly what we intuitively mean by truthlikeness or *verisimilitude*. Intuitively speaking, a theory T_1 has less verisimilitude than a theory T_2 if and only if (a) their truth contents and falsity contents (or their measures) are comparable, and either (b) the truth content, but not the falsity content, of T_1 is smaller than that of T_2, or else (c) the truth content of T_1 is not greater than that of T_2, but its falsity content is greater. In brief, we say that T_2 is nearer to the truth, or more similar to the truth, than T_1, if and only if more true statements follow from it, but not more false statements, or at least equally many true statements but fewer false statements.

In general we can say that only *competing* theories—such as the Newtonian and Einsteinian theories of gravitation—are intuitively comparable with respect to their (unmeasured) contents; but there are also competing theories which are not comparable.

The intuitive comparability of the contents of Newton's theory (N) and Einstein's (E) can be established as follows:[20] (a) to every question to which Newton's theory has an answer, Einstein's theory has an answer which is at least as precise; this makes (the measure of) the content, in a slightly wider sense

---

[20] This example was briefly discussed by me in footnote 7 to a note first published in *B.J.P.S.* 5, 1954, pp. 143 ff., and republished in my *Logic of Scientific Discovery*, second edn., 1968, new appendix ix; see p. 401. I have elaborated the point ever since. See, for example, my paper in honour of Herbert Feigl, in P. Feyerabend and G. Maxwell (eds.), *Mind, Matter and Method*, 1966, pp. 343–53. I have shown in this paper that if the (non-measured) contents of two deductive theories, *X* and *Y*, are comparable, then their truth contents are comparable also, and are greater or smaller in accordance with the contents. As David Miller has shown, the proof of this theorem can be considerably simplified. It is important that we never forget the following: although the *measure functions* of content, truth content and falsity content are *in principle* comparable (because probabilities are in principle comparable) we have in general no means to compare them other than by way of comparing the unmeasured contents of competing theories, possibly just intuitively.

than Tarski's,[21] of N less than or equal to that of E; (b) there are questions to which Einstein's theory E can give a (non-tautological) answer while Newton's theory N does not; this makes the content of N definitely smaller than that of E.

Thus we can compare intuitively the contents of these two theories, and Einstein's has the greater content. (It can be shown that this intuition is borne out by the content measures $ct(N)$ and $ct(E)$.) This makes Einstein's theory *potentially* or *virtually* the better theory; for even before any testing we can say: if true, it has the greater explanatory power. Furthermore, it challenges us to undertake a greater variety of tests. Thus it offers us new opportunities to learn more about the facts: without the challenge of Einstein's theory, we should never have measured (with the great degree of precision needed) the apparent distance between the stars surrounding the sun during an eclipse, or the red shift of the light emitted by white dwarfs.

These are some of the advantages, existing *even before it has been tested*, of a (logically) stronger theory; that is, of a theory with greater content. They make it a potentially better theory, a more challenging theory.

But the stronger theory, the theory with the greater content, will also be the one with the greater verisimilitude *unless its falsity content is also greater*.

This assertion forms the logical basis of the method of science —the method of bold conjectures and of attempted refutations. A theory is the bolder the greater its content. It is also the riskier: it is the more probable to start with that it will be false. We try to find its weak points, to refute it. If we fail to refute it, or if the refutations we find are at the same time also refutations of the weaker theory which was its predecessor,[22] then we have reason to suspect, or to conjecture, that the stronger theory has no greater falsity content than its weaker predecessor, and, therefore, that it has the greater degree of verisimilitude.

---

[21] In the first instance, Tarski's notion of an (unmeasured) consequence class or content permits us to compare the contents of theories if one of them entails the other. The generalization here given allows us to compare contents (or the measure of contents) if one of them can answer all questions that can be answered by the other, and with at least equal precision.

[22] This at any rate is the present situation with the eclipse effect: the tests give greater values than predicted by E, while N, even on Einstein's favourable interpretation, predicts at most half the result of E.

9. *Verisimilitude and the Search for Truth*

Take a square as representing the class of all statements, and divide it into two equal sub-areas, the true statements (T) and the false ones (F):

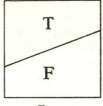

FIG. 1

Now change these arrangements a little, by collecting the class of true statements round the centre of the square.

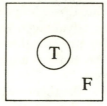

FIG. 2

The task of science is, metaphorically speaking, to cover by hits as much as possible of the target (T) of the true statements, by the method of proposing theories or conjectures which seem to us promising, and as little as possible of the false area (F).

It is very important that we try to conjecture true theories; but truth is not the only important property of our conjectural theories; for we are not particularly interested in proposing trivialities or tautologies. 'All tables are tables' is certainly true —it is more certainly true than Newton's and Einstein's theories of gravitation—but it is intellectually unexciting: it is not what we are after in science. Wilhelm Busch once produced what I have called a rhyme for the epistemological nursery:[23]

[23] From Wilhelm Busch, *Schein und Sein*, 1909. The German text is:

> Zweimal zwei gleich vier ist Wahrheit,
> Schade, dass sie leicht und leer ist.
> Denn ich wollte lieber Klarheit
> Über das, was voll und schwer ist.

See *Conjectures and Refutations*, p. 230, note 16, and E. Nagel, P. Suppes, and

> Twice two equals four: 'tis true
> But too empty and too trite.
> What I look for is a clue
> To some matters not so light.

In other words, we are not simply looking for truth, we are after interesting and enlightening truth, after theories which offer solutions to interesting *problems*. If at all possible, we are after deep theories.

We are not simply trying to hit a point within our target T, but as wide and as interesting an area of our target as possible: twice two equals four, though true, is not in the sense intended here 'a good approximation to the truth', simply because it conveys too little truth to cover the aim of science or even an important part of it. Newton's theory is a much better 'approximation to the truth', even if it is false (as is likely), because of the tremendous number of interesting and informative true consequences which it contains: its *truth content* is very great.

There is an infinity of true statements, and they are of very different value. One way of evaluating them is logical: we estimate the size or measure of their *content* (which in the case of true statements but not of false statements coincides with their truth content). A statement that conveys more information has a greater informative or logical content; it is the better statement. The greater the content of a true statement, the better is it as an approach to our target T; that is, to 'the truth' (more precisely, to the class of all true statements). For we do not wish to learn only that all tables are tables. If we speak about approach or approximation to truth, we mean to 'the whole truth'; that is, the whole class of true statements, the class T.

Now if a statement is false, the situation is similar. Every unambiguous statement is true or false (although we may not know whether it is the one or the other); the logic which I consider here[24] has only these two truth values, and there is no third possibility. However, a false statement may appear to be nearer to the truth than another false statement: 'It is now

A. Tarski (eds.), *Logic, Methodology and Philosophy of Science*, Stanford U.P., 1962, p. 290.

[24] There exist 'many valued systems' of logic with more than two truth values, but they are weaker than two-valued systems, especially from the point of view here adopted (see *Conjectures and Refutations*, p. 64) according to which formal logic is *the organon of criticism*.

9.45 p.m.' seems nearer to the truth than 'It is now 9.40 p.m.' if in fact it is 9.48 p.m. when the remark is uttered.

In this form, however, the intuitive impression is mistaken: the two statements are incompatible and therefore non-comparable (unless we introduce a *measure* like ct). Yet there is some kernel of truth in the mistaken intuition: If we replace the two statements by *interval statements* (see the next paragraph) then the first is indeed nearer to the truth than the second.

We can proceed as follows: the first statement is replaced either by 'It is now *between* 9.45 p.m. and 9.48 p.m.' and the second 'It is now *between* 9.40 p.m. and 9.48 p.m.' In this way, we replace each statement by one that admits a consecutive *range of values*, a *range of error*. Now the two replaced statements become comparable (since the first entails the second), and the first is indeed nearer to the truth than the second; and this must carry over to any consistent measure function of content such as ct and ct_T. But since in a system with a measure function like ct_T our original statements were comparable (in such a system all statements are comparable in principle), we may conclude that the truth content measure ct_T may be so defined that ct_T of the first statement is indeed at least as great as—or greater than—that of the second statement; which justifies up to a point our original intuition.

Note that the word '*between*' in the replaced statements can be interpreted so as to include or exclude either of the bounds. If we interpret it to include the upper bound, then both statements are true, and so $ct = ct_T$ holds for both of them. They are true, yet the first statement has greater verisimilitude because it has a greater truth content than the second. If, on the other hand, we interpret 'between' so as to exclude the upper bound, then both statements become false (though they might be called 'almost true'); but they remain comparable (in the non-measure sense), and we can still assert that the first has a greater truth-likeness than the second. (See also my *Conjectures and Refutations*, pp. 397 f., and my *Logic of Scientific Discovery*, section 37.)

Thus without violating the idea of two valued logic ('every unambiguous statement is true or false, and there is no third possibility'), we can sometimes speak of false statements which are more or less false, or further from the truth or nearer to it. And this idea of higher or lower verisimilitude is applicable both to false statements and to true statements: the essential point is their *truth content* which is a concept lying entirely within the field of two-valued logic.

In other words, it looks as if we could identify the intuitive idea of *approximation to truth* with that of *high truth content*, and low 'falsity content'.

This is important for two reasons: it alleviates the misgivings some logicians have had about operating with the intuitive idea of approximation to truth; and it allows us to say that the aim of science is truth in the sense of better approximation to truth, or greater verisimilitude.

10. *Truth and Verisimilitude as Aims*

To say that the aim of science is verisimilitude has a considerable advantage over the perhaps simpler formulation that the aim of science is truth. The latter may suggest that the aim is completely reached by stating the undoubted truth that all tables are tables or that $1 + 1 = 2$. Obviously, both these statements are true; and just as obviously, neither of them can be said to rank as any sort of scientific achievement.

Moreover, scientists aim at theories like Newton's or Einstein's theory of gravity; and although we are highly interested in the question of the truth of these theories, the theories retain their interest even if we have reason to believe that they are false. Newton never believed that his theory was really the last word, and Einstein never believed that his theory was more than a good approximation to the true theory—the unified field theory which he searched for from 1916 to his death in 1955. All this indicates that the idea of a 'search for truth' is satisfactory only if (a) we mean by 'truth' the set of all the true propositions—that is, our unattainable target set is T (Tarski's class of true propositions)—and if (b) we mean to admit in our search false statements as approximations if they are not 'too false' ('have not too large a falsity content') and contain a great truth content.

Thus the search for verisimilitude is a clearer and a more realistic aim than the search for truth. But I intend to show a little more. I intend to show that while we can never have sufficiently good arguments in the empirical sciences for claiming that we have actually reached the truth, we can have strong and reasonably good arguments for claiming that we may have made progress towards the truth; that is, that the theory T_2 is preferable to its predecessor T_1, at least in the light of all known rational arguments.

Moreover, we can explain the method of science, and much of the history of science, as the rational procedure for getting nearer to the truth. (A further important clarification can be achieved with the help of the idea of verisimilitude in connection with the problem of induction; see especially section 32 below.)

11. *Comments on the Notions of Truth and Verisimilitude*

My defence of the legitimacy of the idea of verisimilitude has sometimes been grossly misunderstood. In order to avoid these misunderstandings it is advisable to keep in mind my view that not only are all theories conjectural, but also all appraisals of theories, including comparisons of theories from the point of view of their verisimilitude.

It is strange that this point, which is all-important for my theory of science, has been misunderstood. As I have often stressed, I believe that all appraisals of theories are *appraisals of the status of their critical discussion*. I therefore believe that clarity is an intellectual value since, without it, critical discussion is impossible. But I do not believe that exactness or precision are intellectual values in themselves; on the contrary, we should never try to be more exact or precise than the problem before us requires (which is always a problem of discriminating between competing theories). For this reason I have stressed that I am not interested in definitions; since all definitions must use undefined terms, it does not, as a rule, matter whether we use a term as a primitive term or as a defined term.

Why, then, have I tried to show that verisimilitude can be defined, or reduced to, other terms (truth content, falsity content and, in the last instance, logical probability)?

Some people have assumed that my aim was something like exactness or precision; or even applicability: that I hoped to find a numerical function which can be applied to theories and which tells us, in numerical terms, what their verisimilitude is (or at least their truth content; or perhaps their degree of corroboration).

In fact, nothing can be further removed from my aims. I do not think that degrees of verisimilitude, or a measure of truth content, or falsity content (or, say, degree of corroboration, or even of logical probability) can ever be numerically determined, except in certain limiting cases (such as 0 and 1). And although the introduction of a measure function makes all contents comparable in principle, or in theory, I believe that in actual application we depend entirely on those rare cases which are comparable on non-metrical and, as it were, qualitative or general logical grounds, such as cases of logically stronger and weaker *competing* theories; that is, theories aimed at solving the same problems. For actual comparison we depend entirely upon these cases (paradoxically, one might say, since measure functions such as probabilities make their arguments in principle *generally* comparable).

What then, one might ask, is the point of my attempts to show that verisimilitude is definable in terms of logical probability? My aim is to achieve (on a lower level of precision) for verisimilitude something similar to what Tarski achieved for truth: the rehabilitation of a commonsense notion which has become suspect, but which is in my opinion much needed for any critical commonsense realism and for any critical theory of science. I wish to be able to say that science aims at truth in the sense of correspondence to the facts or to reality; and I also wish to say (with Einstein and other scientists) that relativity theory is—or so we conjecture—a better approximation to truth than is Newton's theory, just as the latter is a better approximation to truth than is Kepler's theory. And I wish to be able to say these things without fearing that the concept of nearness to truth or verisimilitude is logically misconceived, or 'meaningless'. In other words, my aim is the rehabilitation of a commonsense idea which I need for describing the aims of science, and which, I assert, underlies as a regulative principle (even if merely unconsciously and intuitively) the rationality of all critical scientific discussions.

As I see it, the main achievement of Tarski's invention of a method of defining truth (with respect to formalized languages of finite order) is the rehabilitation of the notion of truth or correspondence to reality, a notion which had become suspect. By defining it in terms of non-suspect (non-semantical) logical notions he established its legitimacy. Having done this, he also showed that it is possible to introduce, by way of axioms, a materially equivalent notion of truth with respect to formalized languages of infinite order, though an explicit definition cannot be given in this case. In my opinion, he thereby rehabilitated the critical use of the undefined notion of truth in non-formalized ordinary or commonsense languages (which are of infinite order), if only we make them slightly artificial by taking care to avoid the antinomies. I should describe such a language as one of critical common sense: I remember how Tarski stressed with great force, in 1935, that in constructing a formalized language, the use of a natural language is unavoidable, even though its uncritical use leads to antinomies. Thus we have, as it were, to reform ordinary language while using it, as described by Neurath in his metaphor of the ship we have to rebuild while trying to keep afloat in it.[25] This indeed is the situation of critical common sense, as I see it.

12. *The Mistaken Commonsense Theory of Knowledge*

Common sense, I said, is always our starting-point, but it must be criticized. And, as might have been expected, it is not too good when it comes to reflect on itself. In fact the commonsense theory of commonsense knowledge is a naïve muddle. Yet it has provided the foundation on which even the most recent philosophical theories of knowledge are erected.

The commonsense theory is simple. If you or I wish to know something not yet known about the world, we have to open our eyes and look round. And we have to raise our ears and listen to noises, and especially to those made by other people. Thus our various senses are our *sources of knowledge*—the sources or the entries into our minds.

I have often called this theory the bucket theory of the mind.

[25] See Otto Neurath, *Erkenntnis* **3**, 1932, p. 206. We have been repeatedly reminded of Neurath's remark by W. V. Quine, for example in his *Word and Object*, M.I.T. Press, 1960, p. 3, or in *Ontological Relativity and other Essays*, Columbia U.P., 1969, pp. 16, 84, and 127.

The bucket theory of the mind is best represented by a diagram:

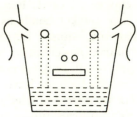

FIG. 3. The Bucket

Our mind is a bucket which is originally empty, or more or less so, and into this bucket material enters through our senses (or possibly through a funnel for filling or reaching it from above), and accumulates and becomes digested.

In the philosophical world this theory is better known under the more dignified name of the *tabula rasa* theory of the mind: our mind is *an empty slate* upon which the senses engrave their messages. But the main point of the *tabula rasa* theory goes beyond the commonsense bucket theory: I mean its emphasis on the perfect emptiness of the mind at birth. For our discussion this is merely a minor point of discrepancy between the two theories, for it does not matter whether we are or are not born with some 'innate ideas' in our bucket—more perhaps in the case of intelligent children, fewer in the case of morons. The important thesis of the bucket theory is that we learn most, if not all, of what we do learn through the entry of experience into our sense openings; so that all *experience consists of information received through our senses.*

In this form, this thoroughly mistaken theory is still very much alive. It still plays a part in theories of teaching, or in 'information theory', for example, though it is admitted now that the bucket is not empty at birth, but endowed with a computer programme.

My thesis is that the bucket theory is utterly naïve and completely mistaken in all its versions, and that unconscious assumptions of it in some form or other still exert a devastating influence especially upon the so-called behaviourists, suggesting the still powerful theory of the conditioned reflex, and other theories which enjoy the highest reputations.

Among the many things which are wrong with the bucket theory of the mind are the following:

(1) Knowledge is conceived of as consisting of things, or thing-like entities in our bucket (such as ideas, impressions, sensa, sense data, elements, atomic experience, or—perhaps slightly better—molecular experiences or '*Gestalten*').

(2) Knowledge is, first of all, *in* us: it consists of information which has reached us, and which we have managed to absorb.

(3) There is *immediate* or *direct* knowledge; that is, the pure, unadulterated elements of information which have got into us and are still undigested. No knowledge could be more elementary and certain than this.

Point (3) can be elaborated as follows:

(3a) All error, all mistaken knowledge, according to the commonsense theory, comes from bad intellectual digestion which adulterates these ultimate or 'given' elements of information by misinterpreting them, or by wrongly linking them with other elements; the sources of error are our subjective admixtures to the pure or given elements of information, which in their turn are not only free from error, but are the standards of all truth, so that it would be completely pointless even to raise the question whether they are perhaps erroneous.

(3b) Thus knowledge, so far as it is free from error, is essentially passively received knowledge; while error is always actively (though not necessarily intentionally) produced by us, either by interfering with 'the given' or perhaps by some other mismanagement: the perfect brain would never err.

(3c) Knowledge which goes beyond the pure reception of the given elements is therefore always less certain than the given or elementary knowledge, which indeed constitutes the standard of certainty. If I doubt anything, I have just to open my eyes again and observe with a candid eye, excluding all prejudices: I have to purify my mind from sources of error.

(4) Nevertheless, we have a practical need of knowledge of a somewhat higher level: of knowledge which goes beyond the mere data or the mere elements. For what we need, especially, is knowledge that establishes expectations by connecting existing data with impending elements. This higher knowledge establishes itself by way of the *association of ideas or elements*.

(5) Ideas or elements are associated if they occur together; and, most important, *association is strengthened by repetition*.

(6) In this way we establish *expectations* (if the idea *a* is strongly associated with the idea *b* then the occurrence of *a* arouses a high expectation of *b*).

(7) In the same way, *beliefs* emerge. True belief is belief in an unfailing association. Erroneous belief is a belief in an association between ideas which, though they occurred together, perhaps sometime in the past, are not unfailingly repeated together.

To sum up: what I call the commonsense theory of knowledge is something very close to the empiricism of Locke, Berkeley, and Hume and not far removed from that of many modern positivists and empiricists.

13. *Criticism of the Commonsense Theory of Knowledge*

Almost everything is wrong in the commonsense theory of knowledge. But perhaps the central mistake is the assumption that we are engaged in what Dewey called *the quest for certainty*.

It is this which leads to the singling out of data or elements, or sense data or sense impressions or immediate experiences, as a secure basis of all knowledge. But far from being this, these data or elements do not exist at all. They are the inventions of hopeful philosophers, who have managed to bequeath them to the psychologists.

What are the facts? As children we learn to decode the chaotic messages which meet us from our environment. We learn to sift them, to ignore the majority of them, and to single out those which are of biological importance for us either at once, or in a future for which we are being prepared by a process of maturation.

Learning to decode the messages which reach us is extremely complicated. It is based upon innate dispositions. We are, I conjecture, innately disposed to refer the messages to a coherent and partly regular or ordered system: to 'reality'. In other words, our subjective knowledge of reality consists of maturing innate dispositions. (This, incidentally, is in my opinion too sophisticated a construction to be used as a strong independent argument in favour of realism.) However this may be, we learn the decoding by *trial and error elimination*, and although we become extremely good and quick at experiencing the decoded message as if it were 'immediate' or 'given', there are always some mistakes, usually corrected by special mechanisms of great complexity and considerable efficiency.

So the whole story of the 'given', of true data, with certainty attached, is a mistaken theory, though part of common sense.

I admit that we experience much as if it were immediately given to us, and as if it were perfectly certain. This is thanks to our elaborate decoding apparatus, with its many built-in checking devices, taking what Winston Churchill would have called 'crossbearings'; systems which manage to eliminate a great many of the mistakes we make in decoding, so that indeed in these cases in which we experience immediacy, we only seldom err. But I deny that these well-adapted experiences should be identified in any sense with 'given' standards of reliability or truth. Nor in fact do these cases establish a standard of 'directness', or of 'certainty', or show that we can never err in our immediate perceptions; it is simply due to our incredible efficiency as biological systems. (A well-trained photographer will rarely make bad exposures. This is due to his training, and not to the fact that his pictures are to be taken as 'data' or 'standards of truth' or perhaps as 'standards of correct exposure'.)

Almost all of us are good observers and good perceivers. But this is a problem to be explained by biological theories, and not to be taken as the basis for any *dogmatism* of direct or immediate or intuitive knowledge. And after all, we do all fail sometimes; we must never forget our fallibility.

14. *Criticism of the Subjectivist Theory of Knowledge*

All this does not of course refute idealism or the subjectivist theory of knowledge. For all I have said about the psychology (or physiology) of perception, it may be merely a dream.

Yet there is a very good argument against the subjectivist and idealist theories which I have not yet used. It runs like this.

Most subjectivists assert with Berkeley that their theories agree in all practical respects with realism, and especially with the sciences; only, they say, the sciences do not reveal to us standards of truth but are nothing but perfect instruments of prediction. There can be no higher standards of certainty (save God-given revelation).[26] But then, physiology comes in and

[26] See my *Conjectures and Refutations*, chapters 3 and 6.

predicts that our 'data' are fallible rather than standards of truth or of certainty. Thus if this form of subjective instrumentalism is true, then it leads to its own refutation. Therefore it cannot be true.

This, of course, does not refute an idealist who would reply that we are only dreaming that we have refuted idealism.

I may perhaps mention in passing that a formally similar argument of Russell's against 'naïve realism', an argument which greatly impressed Einstein, is unacceptable. It was this: 'The observer, when he seems to himself to be observing a stone, *is really, if physics* [physiology] *is to be believed, observing the effects of the stone upon himself.* Thus science seems to be at war with itself. . . . Naïve realism leads to physics, and physics, if true, shows naïve realism to be false. Therefore naïve realism, if true, is false; therefore it is false.'[27]

Russell's argument is unacceptable, because the passage which I have italicized is mistaken. *When the observer observes a stone, he does not observe the effect of the stone upon himself* (though he might do so, say, by contemplating a wounded toe), even though he decodes some of the signals that reach him from the stone. Russell's argument is at the same level as the following: 'When the reader seems to himself to be reading Russell, he is really observing the effects of Russell upon himself and therefore not reading Russell.' The truth is, that reading (i.e. decoding) Russell is partly based upon observations of Russell's text; but there is no problem here worthy of analysis; we all know that reading is a complex process in which we do several sorts of things at once.

I do not think it worth pursuing these exercises in cleverness; and I repeat that, until some new arguments are offered, I shall naïvely accept realism.

15. *The Pre-Darwinian Character of the Commonsense Theory of Knowledge*

The commonsense theory of knowledge is radically mistaken in every point. Its fundamental mistakes can perhaps be cleared up as follows.

[27] Cp. Bertrand Russell, *An Inquiry into Meaning and Truth*, Allen & Unwin, London, 1940 (also New York), pp. 14 f. (Italics not in the original.) See also Einstein's essay in P. A. Schilpp (ed.), *The Philosophy of Bertrand Russell*, 1944, pp. 282 f.

(1) *There is knowledge in the subjective sense, which consists of dispositions and expectations.*

(2) *But there is also knowledge in the objective sense, human knowledge, which consists of linguistically formulated expectations submitted to critical discussion.*

(3) The commonsense theory fails to see that *the difference between* (1) *and* (2) *is of the most far-reaching significance.* Subjective knowledge is not subject to criticism, although it can be changed by various means—for example, by the elimination (killing) of the carrier of the subjective knowledge or disposition in question. Thus knowledge in the subjective sense grows or achieves better adjustments by the Darwinian method of mutation and elimination of the organism. As opposed to this, objective knowledge can change and grow by the elimination (killing) of the linguistically formulated conjecture: the 'carrier' can survive—he can, if he is a self-critical person, even eliminate his own conjecture.

The difference is that linguistically formulated theories can be *critically discussed.*

(4) Apart from this all-important mistake, the commonsense theory is mistaken in different places. It is, essentially, a theory of the genesis of knowledge: the bucket theory is a theory of our acquisition of knowledge—our largely passive acquisition of knowledge—and thus it is also a theory of what I call the *growth of knowledge. But as a theory of the growth of knowledge it is utterly false.*

(5) The *tabula rasa* theory is pre-Darwinian: to every man who has any feeling for biology it must be clear that most of our dispositions are inborn, either in the sense that we are born with them (for example, the dispositions to breathe, to swallow, and so on) or in the sense that in the process of maturation, the development of the disposition is elicited by the environment (for example, the disposition to learn a language).

(6) But even if we forget all about *tabula rasa* theories[28] and assume that the bucket is half-full at birth, or that it changes its structure with the process of maturation, the theory is still most misleading. This is not only because all subjective knowledge is

[28] Some comments about the history of the *tabula rasa* theory will be found in the new addendum on Parmenides in the third edn. of my *Conjectures and Refutations*, 969 and 1972.

dispositional, but mainly because it is not a disposition of the associative type (or the conditioned reflex type). To put my position clearly and radically: *there is no such thing as association or conditioned reflex.* All reflexes are unconditioned; the supposedly 'conditioned' reflexes are the results of modifications which partially or wholly eliminate the false starts, that is to say the errors in the trial-and-error process.

16. *Sketch of an Evolutionary Epistemology*

So far as I know, the term 'evolutionary epistemology' is due to my friend Donald T. Campbell. The idea is post-Darwinian and goes back to the end of the ninteenth century—to such thinkers as J. M. Baldwin, C. Lloyd Morgan, and H. S. Jennings.

My own approach has been somewhat independent of most of these influences, though I read with great interest not only Darwin, of course, but also Lloyd Morgan and Jennings during the years before writing my first book. However, like many other philosophers I laid great stress upon the distinction between two problems of knowledge: its genesis or history on the one hand, and the problems of its truth, validity, and 'justification' on the other. (Thus I stressed, for example, at the Congress in Prague in 1934: 'Scientific theories can never be "justified", or verified. But in spite of this, a hypothesis *A* can under certain circumstances achieve more than a hypothesis *B* . . .'.[29]) I even stressed very early that questions of truth or validity, not excluding *the logical justification of the preference for one theory over another* (the only kind of 'justification' which I believe possible), must be *sharply distinguished from all genetic, historical, and psychological questions.*

However, already when writing my *Logik der Forschung* I came to the conclusion that we epistemologists can claim precedence over the geneticists: logical investigations of questions of validity and approximation to truth can be of the greatest importance for genetic and historical and even for psychological investigations. They are in any case logically prior to the latter type of question, even though investigations in the history of knowledge

---

[29] See *Erkenntnis*, **5**, 1935, pp. 170 ff.; see also my *Logic of Scientific Discovery*, p. 315.

can pose many important problems to the logician of scientific discovery.[30]

Thus I speak here of evolutionary epistemology, even though I contend that the leading ideas of epistemology are logical rather than factual; despite this, all of its examples, and many of its problems, may be suggested by studies of the genesis of knowledge.

This attitude is indeed the precise opposite of that of the commonsense theory and of the classical epistemology of, say, Descartes, Locke, Berkeley, Hume, and Reid: for Descartes and Berkeley, truth is guaranteed by the origin of the ideas, which is ultimately supervised by God. Traces of the view that ignorance is sin are to be found not only in Locke and Berkeley but even in Hume and Reid. For there it is the directness or immediacy of our ideas, or impressions, or perceptions which is their divine seal of truth and which offers the best security for the believer, while in my view we sometimes regard theories as true, or even 'immediately' true, because they are true *and our mental outfit is well adapted* to their level of difficulty. But we are never 'justified' or 'entitled' to claim the truth of a theory, or of a belief, by reason of the alleged immediacy or directness of the belief. This, in my view, is putting the cart before the horse: immediacy or directness may be the result of the biological fact that a theory is true and also (partly for this reason) very useful for us. But to argue that immediacy or directness establishes truth, or is a criterion of truth, is *the fundamental mistake of idealism*.[31]

---

[30] I sometimes speak of the 'principle of transference' when referring to the fact that what holds in logic must hold in genetics or in psychology, so that results may have psychological or, more generally, biological applications. See section 4 of my paper 'Conjectural Knowledge', Chapter 1 in this volume, pp. 37 f.

[31] The epistemological idealist is right, in my view, in insisting that all knowledge, and the growth of knowledge—the genesis of the mutation of our ideas—stem from ourselves, and that without these self-begotten ideas there would be no knowledge. He is wrong in failing to see that without elimination of these mutations through our clashing with the environment there would not only be no incitement to new ideas, but no knowledge of anything. (Cp. *Conjectures and Refutations*, especially p. 117.) Thus Kant was right that it is our intellect which imposes its laws—its ideas, its rules—upon the inarticulate mass of our 'sensations' and thereby brings order into them. Where he was wrong is that he did not see that we rarely succeed with our imposition, that we try and err again and again, and that the result—our knowledge of the world—owes as much to the resisting reality as to our self-produced ideas.

Starting from scientific realism it is fairly clear that if our actions and reactions were badly adjusted to our environment, we should not survive. Since 'belief' is closely connected with expectation and with readiness to act, we can say that many of our more practical beliefs are likely to be true, as long as we survive. They become the more dogmatic part of common sense which, though not by any means reliable, true, or certain, is always a good starting-point.

However, we also know that some of the most successful animals have disappeared, and that past success is far from ensuring future success. This is a fact; and, clearly, although we could do something about it, we cannot do much. I mention this point in order to make it quite clear that past biological success never ensures future biological success. Thus, for the biologist, the fact that theories were successful in the past carries no guarantee whatever of success in the future.

What is the situation? A theory refuted in the past may be retained as useful in spite of its refutation. Thus we can use Kepler's laws for many purposes. But a theory refuted in the past will be *untrue*. And we do not only look for biological or instrumental success. In science we *search for truth*.

A central problem of evolutionary theory is the following: according to this theory, animals which are not well adapted to their changing environment perish; consequently those which survive (up to a certain moment) must be well adapted. This formula is little short of tautological, because 'for the moment well adapted' means much the same as 'has those qualities which made it survive so far'. In other words, a considerable part of Darwinism is not of the nature of an empirical theory, but is a *logical truism*.

Let us make clear what is empirical in Darwinism and what is not. The existence of an environment with a certain structure is empirical. That this environment changes, but not too fast for long periods of time, and not too radically, is empirical; if it is too radical, the sun might explode into a *nova* tomorrow, and all life on earth and all adaptation will come to an end. In brief, there is nothing whatever in logic which explains the existence of conditions in the world under which life and slow (whatever 'slow' may mean here) adaptation to the environment are possible.

But given living organisms, sensitive to environmental changes and changing conditions, and assuming that there is no pre-established harmony between the properties of the organisms and those of the changing environment,[32] we can say something like the following. Only if the organisms produce mutations, some of which are adjustments to impending changes, and thus involve mutability, can they survive; and in this way we shall find, as long as we find living organisms in a changing world, that those which happen to be alive are pretty well adjusted to their environment. If the process of adjustment has gone on long enough, then the speed, finesse, and complexity of the adjustment may strike us as miraculous. And yet, the method of trial and of the elimination of errors, which leads to all this, can be said not to be an empirical method but to belong to the *logic of the situation*. This, I think, explains (perhaps a little too briefly) the logical or *a priori* components in Darwinism.

The tremendous biological advance of the invention of a *descriptive and argumentative language*[33] can now be seen more precisely than before: the linguistic formulation of theories allows us to criticize and to eliminate them without eliminating the race which carries them. This is the first achievement. The second achievement is the development of a conscious and systematic attitude of criticism towards our theories. With this begins the method of science. The difference between the amoeba and Einstein is that, although both make use of the method of trial and error elimination, the amoeba dislikes to err while Einstein is intrigued by it: he consciously searches for his errors in the hope of learning by their discovery and elimination. The method of science is the critical method.

Thus evolutionary epistemology allows us to understand better both evolution and epistemology so far as they coincide with scientific method. It allows us to understand these things better on logical grounds.

---

[32] The following remark is here perhaps of interest. K. Lorenz writes in *Evolution and Modification of Behaviour*, Methuen, London, 1966, pp. 103 f.: 'Any modifiability which regularly proves adaptive, as learning indubitably does, presupposes a programming based on phylogenetically acquired information. To deny this necessitates the assumption of a prestabilized harmony between organism and environment.' See also footnote 34 below.

[33] For the various functions of human language, see, for example, my *Conjectures and Refutations*, pp. 134 f., and chapters 3, 4, and 6, below.

17. *Background Knowledge and Problems*

The aim of science is increase of verisimilitude. As I have argued, the *tabula rasa* theory is absurd: at every stage of the evolution of life and of the development of an organism, we have to assume the existence of some knowledge in the form of dispositions and expectations.

Accordingly, *the growth of all knowledge consists in the modification of previous knowledge*—either its alteration or its large-scale rejection. Knowledge never begins from nothing, but always from some background knowledge—knowledge which at the moment is taken for granted—together with some difficulties, some problems. These as a rule arise from the clash between, on the one side, expectations inherent in our background knowledge and, on the other side, some new findings, such as our observations or some hypotheses suggested by them.

18. *All Knowledge is Theory-Impregnated, Including our Observations*

Knowledge in its various subjective forms is dispositional and expectational. It consists of dispositions of *organisms*, and these dispositions are the most important aspect of the organization of an organism. One type of organism can live only in water today, another only on land; since they have survived so far their very ecology determines part of their 'knowledge'. If it were not absurd to make any estimate, I should say that 999 units out of 1,000 of the knowledge of an organism are inherited or inborn, and that one unit only consists of the modifications of this inborn knowledge; and I suggest, in addition, that *the plasticity needed* for these modifications is also inborn.

From this follows the fundamental theorem:

All acquired knowledge, all learning, consists of the modification (possibly the rejection) of some form of knowledge, or disposition, which was there previously, and in the last instance of inborn dispositions.[34]

From this follows at once a second theorem:

All growth of knowledge consists in the improvement of existing knowledge which is changed in the hope of approaching nearer to the truth.

Because all our dispositions are in some sense adjustments to

[34] For a successful defence of 'innate' or 'inborn' knowledge against behaviourists and other anti-theorists, see Konrad Lorenz, *Evolution and Modification of Behaviour,* quoted in footnote 32 above.

invariant or slowly changing environmental conditions, they can be described as *theory-impregnated*, assuming a sufficiently wide sense of the term 'theory'. What I have in mind is, that there is no observation which is not related to a set of typical situations—regularities—between which it tries to find a decision. And I think we can assert even more: *there is no sense organ in which anticipatory theories are not genetically incorporated.* The eye of a cat reacts in distinct ways to a number of typical situations for which there are mechanisms prepared and built into its structure: these correspond to the biologically most important situations between which it has to distinguish. Thus the disposition to distinguish between these situations is built into the sense organ, and with it the *theory that these, and only these, are the relevant situations for whose distinction the eye is to be used.*[35]

The fact that all our senses are in this way theory-impregnated shows most clearly the radical failure of the bucket theory and with it of all those other theories which attempt to trace our knowledge to our observations, or to the *input* of the organism. On the contrary, *what can be absorbed (and reacted to) as relevant input and what is ignored as irrelevant* depends completely upon the innate structure (the 'programme') of the organism.

19. *Retrospect on the Subjectivist Epistemology*

From the point of view here reached, we must reject as completely baseless any subjectivist epistemology which proposes to choose as a starting-point what appears to it quite unproblematic; that is, our *'direct' or 'immediate' observational experiences.* Admittedly these experiences are, in general, perfectly 'good' and successful (otherwise we should not have survived); but they are neither 'direct' nor 'immediate', and they are not absolutely reliable.

There seems to be no reason why we should not make observational experiences our provisional 'starting-point'—a starting-point, like common sense, not involving commitment to truth or certainty. As long as we are critically inclined it does not matter much where or how we start. But starting from here (which may be perhaps what Russell calls 'naïve realism') we

[35] See, for example, the experiments in T. N. Wiesel and D. H. Hubel, 'Single-cell Responses in Striate Cortex of Kittens Deprived of Vision in One Eye', *Journal of Neurophysiology*, **26**, pp. 1003–17.

come, through physics and biology, to the result that *our obser-*
vations are highly complex and not always reliable though astonishingly
excellent decodings of the signals which reach us from the environment. They must therefore not be elevated to a starting-point
in the sense of a standard of truth.

Thus what appeared as an apparently presupposition-free
subjectivist epistemology or *tabula rasa* theory disintegrates completely. In its place we have to erect a theory of knowledge in
which the knowing subject, the observer, plays an important but
only a very restricted role.

20. *Knowledge in the Objective Sense*

The commonsense theory of knowledge, and with it all
philosophers until at least Bolzano and Frege, mistakenly took
it for granted that there was only one kind of knowledge—
knowledge possessed by some knowing subject.

I will call this kind of knowledge *'subjective knowledge'*, in spite
of the fact that, as we shall see, *genuine or unadulterated or purely*
subjective knowledge simply does not exist.

The theory of subjective knowledge is very old; but it becomes
explicit with Descartes: 'knowing' is an activity and presupposes
the existence of a knowing subject. *It is the subjective self who*
knows.

Now I wish to distinguish between two kinds of 'knowledge':
subjective knowledge (which should better be called organismic
knowledge, since it consists of the dispositions of organisms); and
objective knowledge, or knowledge in the objective sense, which
consists of the logical content of our theories, conjectures,
guesses (and, if we like, of the logical content of our genetic
code).

Examples of objective knowledge are theories published in
journals and books and stored in libraries; discussions of such
theories; difficulties or problems pointed out in connection with
such theories;[36] and so on.

---

[36] I have dealt with this in some detail in my 'Epistemology without a Knowing
Subject' (read in Amsterdam in 1967) and 'On the Theory of the Objective Mind'
(read in Vienna in 1968) now reprinted as Chapters 5 and 6 in the present volume.
See also the important discussion by Sir John Eccles in his brilliant book *Facing*
Reality, Springer, Berlin, 1970, especially chapters x and xi. David Miller has
drawn my attention to the close similarity between my world 3 and the 'third
realm' of F. R. Leavis. See his lecture *Two Cultures?*, 1962, especially p. 28.

We can call the physical world 'world 1', the world of our conscious experiences 'world 2', and the world of the logical *contents* of books, libraries, computer memories, and suchlike 'world 3'.

About this world 3 I have several theses:

(1) We can discover new problems in world 3 which were there before they were discovered and before they ever became conscious; that is, before anything corresponding to them appeared in world 2. *Example*: we discover prime numbers, and Euclid's problem of whether the sequence of prime numbers is infinite arises as a consequence.

(2) Thus there is a sense in which world 3 is *autonomous*: in this world we can make theoretical discoveries in a similar way to that in which we can make geographical discoveries in world 1.

(3) Main thesis: almost all our subjective knowledge (world 2 knowledge) depends upon world 3, that is to say on (at least virtually) *linguistically formulated* theories. *Example*: our 'immediate self-consciousness', or our 'knowledge of self', which is very important, depends very largely upon world 3 theories: on our theories about our body and its continued existence when we fall asleep or become unconscious; on our theories of time (its linearity); on our theory that we can pick up our memory of past experiences in various degrees of clarity; and so on. With these theories are connected our expectations of waking up after falling asleep. I propose the thesis that *full consciousness of self* depends upon all these (world 3) theories, and that animals, although capable of feelings, sensations, memory, and thus of consciousness, do not possess the full consciousness of self which is one of the results of human language and the development of the specifically human world 3.

21. *The Quest for Certainty and the Main Weakness of the Common-sense Theory of Knowledge*

The commonsense theory of knowledge is unaware of world 3, and it thus ignores the existence of knowledge in the objective sense. This is a great weakness of the theory, but it is not its greatest weakness.

In order to explain what I regard as the greatest weakness of the commonsense theory of knowledge, I will first formulate two statements, (a) and (b), which are characteristic of this theory of knowledge.

(a) Knowledge is a special kind of belief or of opinion; it is a special state of the mind.

(b) In order that a kind of belief, or a state of mind, should amount to more than 'mere' belief, and should be capable of sustaining the claim that it amounts to an item of knowledge, we require that the believer should be in possession of *sufficient reasons* for establishing that the item of knowledge is *true with certainty*.

Of these two formulations, (a) can easily be so reformulated that it becomes part—a small part—of an acceptable biological theory of knowledge; for we can say:

(a') Subjective knowledge is a kind of disposition of which the organism sometimes may become conscious in the form of a belief or an opinion or a state of mind.

This is a perfectly acceptable statement, and it may be claimed that it merely says more exactly what (a) was intended to say. Moreover, (a') is perfectly compatible with a theory of knowledge that gives full weight to objective knowledge; that is, to knowledge as part of world 3.

The position of (b) is totally different. As soon as we take objective knowledge into account, we must say that at best only a very small part of it can be given anything like sufficient reasons for certain truth: it is that small part (if any) which can be described as *demonstrable knowledge* and which comprises (if anything) the propositions of formal logic and of (finite) arithmetic.

All else—by far the most important part of objective knowledge, and the part that comprises the natural sciences, such as physics and physiology—is essentially conjectural or hypothetical in character; there simply are no sufficient reasons for holding these hypotheses to be true, let alone certainly true.

Thus (b) indicates that if we were to try so to generalize the commonsense theory of knowledge as to cover objective knowledge, then only demonstrable knowledge (if such there is) could be admitted as objective knowledge. The whole vast and important field of theories which we may describe as 'scientific knowledge' would, owing to its conjectural character, not qualify as knowledge at all. For according to the commonsense theory of knowledge, knowledge is *qualified* belief—belief so qualified that it is certainly true. And it is precisely this kind of qualification which is missing in the vast and important field of conjectural knowledge.

Indeed, the term 'conjectural knowledge' may be claimed to be a contradiction in terms, if the matter is thus approached from the side of the commonsense theory. For the commonsense theory is not very thoroughgoing in its subjectivism; on the contrary, the idea of 'sufficient reason' was originally no doubt an objectivist idea: what were required originally were reasons sufficient for proving or demonstrating the item of knowledge in question, so that (b) indeed turns out to be an extension of the objectivist idea of demonstrable knowledge into the subjectivist world 2, the world of disposition or 'belief'. As a consequence, every adequate generalization or objectivist translation (b′), on lines analogous to (a′), would have to confine objective knowledge to demonstrable knowledge, and thus would have to abandon conjectural knowledge. But with it, it would have to abandon scientific knowledge, the most important kind and the central problem of any theory of knowledge.

This, I think, indicates the greatest weakness of the commonsense theory of knowledge. Not only is it unaware of the distinction between objective and subjective knowledge, but it also accepts, consciously or unconsciously, objective demonstrable knowledge as the paradigm for all knowledge, since it is really only here that we have fully 'sufficient reasons' for distinguishing 'true and certain knowledge' from 'mere opinion' or 'mere belief'.[37]

However, the commonsense theory of knowledge remains essentially subjectivist. Thus it gets into the difficulty of admitting something like subjective sufficient reasons; that is, kinds of personal experience or belief or opinion which, though subjective, are certainly and unfailingly true, and can therefore pass as knowledge.

The difficulty is great, for how can we distinguish within the

[37] Thus we have here an instance of a move characteristic of the commonsense theory of knowledge: an insufficient portion is taken from objective logic and (perhaps unconsciously) transferred into psychology; just as in the case of association theory where the two associated 'ideas' were originally the 'terms' of a categorical proposition, while the association was the copula. (Think of Locke's 'joining or separating of ideas'.)

realm of beliefs? What are the criteria by which we can recognize truth, or a sufficient reason? Either by the strength of the belief (Hume), which is hardly rationally defensible, or by its clearness and distinctness, which is defended (by Descartes) as an indication of its divine origin; or, more straightforwardly, by its origin or its genesis, that is to say by the 'sources' of knowledge. In this way, the commonsense theory is led to the acceptance of some criterion of the 'given' (revealed?) knowledge; to the sense-given or sense datum; or to a feeling of immediacy, or directness, or intuitiveness. It is the purity of the origin that guarantees the freedom from error and thus the purity of the content.[38]

But all these criteria are clearly spurious. The biologist will admit that our sense organs are successful more often than not, and he may even explain their efficiency by Darwinian arguments. But he will deny that they are always or necessarily successful, and that they can be relied on as criteria of truth. Their 'directness' or 'immediacy' is only apparent: it is only another aspect of the miraculous smoothness and efficiency with which they work; yet in fact they work in a highly indirect way, using many intricate mechanisms of control built into the system.

Thus there is nothing like absolute certainty in the whole field of our knowledge. But the doctrine (b) identifies the quest for knowledge with the quest for certainty. This is another reason why it is the weakest part of the commonsense theory of knowledge.

What we have to do is to start from the fact that objective scientific knowledge is conjectural, and then look for its analogue in the field of subjective knowledge. This analogue can be easily identified. It is my thesis that subjective knowledge is part of a highly complex and intricate but (in a healthy organism) astonishingly accurate apparatus of adjustment, and that it works, in the main, like objective conjectural knowledge: by the method of trial and elimination of error, or by conjecture, refutation, and self-correction ('autocorrection').

Common sense is, it appears, part of this apparatus, and its

[38] For a somewhat different account of the doctrine of the sources of our knowledge and of the problem of error see my lecture 'On the Sources of Knowledge and of Ignorance', *Proceedings of the British Academy*, **46,** 1960; also in my *Conjectures and Refutations*, third edn., 1969, pp. 3–30.

status is therefore *not utterly different* from that of other apparently 'direct' or 'immediate' knowledge. (Here Thomas Reid was right, though he greatly overrated the force of the argument from directness or immediacy.)

22. *Analytical Remarks on Certainty*

I am not in the least interested in definitions or in the linguistic analysis of words or concepts. But in connection with the word 'certainty', so much of so little value has been said that something must be said here for the sake of clarity.

There is a commonsense notion of certainty which means, briefly, 'certain enough for practical purposes'. When I look at my watch, which is very reliable, and it shows me that it is eight o'clock, I can hear that it ticks (an indication that the watch has not stopped), then I am 'reasonably certain' or 'certain for all practical purposes' that it is fairly close to eight o'clock. When I buy a book and get 20 pence change from the bookseller, then I am 'quite certain' that the two coins are not counterfeit. (My 'reasons' for this are very complex: they have to do with the inflation which has made it not worth while for coiners to forge tenpenny pieces; even though the coins in question could be old pieces from the good old days when faking florins was profitable.)

If somebody asked me, 'Are you sure that the piece in your hand is a tenpenny piece?' I should *perhaps glance at it again* and say 'Yes'. But should a lot depend on the truth of my judgement, I think I should take the trouble to go into the next bank and ask the teller to look closely at the piece; and if the life of a man depended on it, I should even try to get to the Chief Cashier of the Bank of England and ask him to certify the genuineness of the piece.

What do I wish to say by this? That the 'certainty' of a belief is not so much a matter of its intensity, but of the *situation*: of our expectation of its possible consequences. Everything depends on the importance attached to the truth or falsity of the belief.

'Belief' is connected with our practical everyday life. *We act upon our beliefs.* (A behaviourist might say: a 'belief' is something on which we act.) For this reason, some rather low degree of certainty suffices in most cases. But if much depends upon our belief, then *not only the intensity* of the belief changes, but its whole biological function.

There exists a subjectivist theory of probability which assumes that we can measure the degree of our belief in a proposition by the odds we should be prepared to accept in betting.[39]

This theory is incredibly naïve. If I like to bet, and if the stakes are not high, I might accept any odds. If the stakes are very high, I might not accept a bet at all. If I cannot escape the bet, say because the life of my best friend is at stake, I may feel the need to reassure myself of the most trivial proposition.

With my hands in my pockets, I am quite 'certain' that I have five fingers on each of my hands; but if the life of my best friend should depend on the truth of this proposition, I might (and I think I should) take my hands out of my pockets to make 'doubly' sure that I have not lost one or the other of my fingers miraculously.

What is the upshot of all this? It is that 'absolute certainty' is a limiting idea, and that experienced or subjective 'certainty' depends not merely upon degrees of belief and upon evidence, but also upon the situation—upon the importance of what is at stake. Moreover, the evidence in favour even of a proposition which is, I know, trivially true might be radically revised if what is at stake is sufficiently important. This shows that it is not impossible to improve even on the most certain of certainties. 'Certainty' is not a measure of belief—in a straightforward sense. Rather it is a measure of belief relative to an unstable situation; for the general urgency of the situation in which I am acting has many aspects, and I can switch from one to another. Thus full certainty has not the character of a maximum or a limit. There can always be a certainty which is still more secure.

Apart from *valid and simple* proofs in world 3, objective certainty simply does not exist. And certainty in world 2 is always just a shade of an experience, a shade of the strength of a belief, depending not merely on 'evidence', but on many other things such as the seriousness of the problem situation in which we are acting (or perhaps merely on 'nerves').

It is important to realize in this connection that there are many situations in which refusal to act amounts in itself to an action: in ordinary life we have to act all the time and we have

[39] The theory is often ascribed to F. P. Ramsey but it can be found in Kant.

to do so always on the basis of imperfect certainty (for there is hardly such a thing as perfect certainty). As a rule, the evidence on which we are acting is accepted after the most cursory examination; and *the critical discussion of competing theories which is characteristic of good science goes (as a rule) far beyond the kind of thing with which we are perfectly satisfied in practical life.*

(Science—which is essentially critical—is also more conjectural, and less certain of itself than ordinary life because we have consciously raised to the level of a problem something which normally may have been part of our background knowledge.)

But this does not mean that we ever reach the stage where an ingenious scientific thinker may not detect loopholes in our arguments: possibilities which nobody has thought of so far, and which therefore nobody has attempted to exclude or include.

From the point of view of objective knowledge, all theories therefore remain conjectural. From the point of view of practical life, they may be far better discussed, criticized, and tested than anything we are accustomed to act upon, and to regard as certain.

There is no clash between the thesis that all objective knowledge is objectively conjectural, and the fact that we accept much of it not merely as 'practically certain', but as certain in an extraordinarily highly qualified sense; that is, as much better tested than many theories which we constantly trust our lives to (such as that the floor will not collapse, or that we will not be bitten by a poisonous snake).

Theories are true or false and not *merely* instruments. But they are of course instruments also; for practice or applied science as well as for you and me personally when we wish to make up our minds about a theory in the light of the reported critical discussion of it, including the reported tests. If we receive reports about the results of these tests, and perhaps repeat one or the other of the tests ourselves, then we may use these reports and results in forming our personal subjective convictions and in determining the degree of certainty with which we hold our personal beliefs. (This is one way in which the working of the principle of transference[40] could be explained: we use objective knowledge in the formation of our personal subjective beliefs; and although personal subjective beliefs can always be described as 'irrational' in some sense, this use of objective knowledge

[40] Cp. section 16, footnote 30.

shows that there need not be any Humean conflict here with rationality.)

23. *The Method of Science*

I have so often described what I regard as the self-correcting method by which science proceeds that I can be very brief here: *The method of science is the method of bold conjectures and ingenious and severe attempts to refute them.*

A bold conjecture is a theory with a great content—greater at any rate than the theory which, we are hoping, will be superseded by it.

That our conjectures should be bold follows immediately from what I have said about the aim of science and the approach to truth: boldness, or great content, is linked with great truth content; for this reason, falsity content can at first be ignored.

But an increase in truth content is in itself not sufficient to *guarantee* an increase in verisimilitude; since increase in content is a purely logical affair, and since increase in truth content goes with increase in content, the only field left for scientific debate—and especially to empirical tests—is whether or not the falsity content has also increased. Thus our competitive search for verisimilitude turns, especially from the empirical point of view, into a competitive comparison of falsity contents (a fact which some people regard as a paradox). It seems as if it holds in science also that (as Winston Churchill once put it) wars are never won but always lost.

We can never make absolutely certain that our theory is not lost. All we can do is to search for the falsity content of our best theory. We do so by trying to refute our theory; that is, by trying to test it severely in the light of all our objective knowledge and all our ingenuity. It is, of course, always possible that the theory may be false even if it passes all these tests; this is allowed for by our search for verisimilitude. *But if it passes all these tests then we may have good reason to conjecture that our theory, which as we know has a greater truth content than its predecessor, may have no greater falsity content.* And if we fail to refute the new theory, especially in fields in which its predecessor has been refuted, then we can claim this as one of the objective reasons for *the conjecture that the new theory is a better approximation to truth than the old theory.*

24. *Critical Discussion, Rational Preference, and the Problem of the Analyticity of our Choices and Predictions*

Seen in this way, the testing of scientific theories is part of their critical discussion; or, as we may say, it is part of their rational discussion, for in this context I know no better synonym for 'rational' than 'critical'. The critical discussion can never establish sufficient reason to claim that a theory is true; it can never 'justify' our claim to knowledge. But the critical discussion can, if we are lucky, establish sufficient reasons for the following claim:

'This theory seems at present, in the light of a thorough critical discussion and of severe and ingenious testing, by far the *best* (the strongest, the best tested); and so it seems the one nearest to truth among the competing theories.'

To put it in a nutshell: we can never rationally justify a theory —that is, a claim to know its truth—but we can, if we are lucky, rationally justify a preference for one theory out of a set of competing theories, for the time being; that is, with respect to the present state of the discussion. And our justification, though not a claim that the theory is true, can be the claim that there is every indication at this stage of the discussion that the theory is *a better approximation to the truth* than any competing theory so far proposed.

Let us now consider two competing hypotheses h_1 and h_2. Let us abbreviate by d_t some description of the state of the discussion of these hypotheses at the time t, including of course the discussion of relevant experimental and other observational results. Let us denote by

(1) $$c(h_1, d_t) < c(h_2, d_t)$$

the statement that the *degree of corroboration* of h_1 in the light of the discussion d_t is inferior to that of h_2. And let us ask what kind of assertion (1) is.

In actual fact (1) will be a somewhat uncertain assertion, if for no other reason than that $c(h_1, d_t)$ changes with the time t, and *can* change as fast as thought. In many cases, the truth or falsity of (1) will be just a matter of opinion.

But let us assume 'ideal' circumstances. Let us assume a prolonged discussion which has led to stable results, and especially to agreement on all the evidential components, and let us assume that there is no change of opinion with t for some considerable period.

Under such circumstances we can see that, while the evidential elements of d_t are of course empirical, the statement (1) can be, provided d_t is sufficiently explicit, *logical* or (unless you dislike the term) '*analytic*'.

This is particularly clear if $c(h_1, d_t)$ should be negative, because the agreement of the discussion at time t is that the evidence refutes h_1, while $c(h_2, d_t)$ is positive, because the evidence supports h_2. Example: take h_1 to be Kepler's theory, and h_2 to be Einstein's theory. Kepler's theory may be agreed at time t to be refuted (because of the Newtonian perturbations), and Einstein's theory may be agreed at time t to be supported by the evidence. If d_t is sufficiently explicit to entail all this, then

(1) $$c(h_1, d_t) < c(h_2, d_t)$$

amounts to the statement that some unspecified negative number is smaller than some unspecified positive number, and this is the kind of statement which may be described as 'logical' or 'analytic'.

Of course, there will be other cases; for example, if 'd_t' is merely a name like 'the state of the discussion on 12 May 1910'. But just as one would say that the result of the comparison of two known magnitudes was analytic, so we can say that the result of the comparison of two degrees of corroboration, if sufficiently well known, will be analytic.

But only if the result of the comparison is sufficiently well known can it be said to be the basis of a rational preference; that is, only if (1) holds can we say that h_2 is rationally preferable to h_1.

Let us see further what will happen if h_2 in the sense explained is *rationally preferable* to h_1: we shall base our theoretical predictions as well as the practical decisions which make use of them upon h_2 rather than upon h_1.

All this seems to me straightforward and rather trivial. But it has been criticized for the following reasons.

If (1) is analytic, then the decision to prefer h_2 to h_1 is also analytic, and therefore *no new synthetic predictions* can come out of the preference for h_2 over h_1.

I am not quite certain, but the following seems to me to sum up the criticism which was first advanced by Professor Salmon against my theory of corroboration: either all the steps described are analytic—then there can be no synthetic scientific predictions; or there are synthetic scientific predictions—then some steps cannot be analytic, but must be genuinely synthetic or ampliative, and therefore inductive.

I shall try to show that the argument is invalid as a criticism of my views. h_2 is, as is generally admitted, synthetic, and *all* (non-tautological) *predictions* are derived from h_2 rather than from the inequality (1). This is enough to answer the criticism. The question why we prefer h_2 over h_1 is to be answered by reference to d_t, which, if sufficiently specific, is also non-analytic.

The motives which led to our choice of h_2 cannot alter the synthetic character of h_2. The motives—in contrast to ordinary psychological motives—are *rationally justifiable preferences*. This is why logic and analytic propositions play a role in them. If you like, you can call the motives 'analytic'. But these analytic *motives for choosing h_2* never make h_2 true, to say nothing of 'analytic'; they are at best logically inconclusive reasons for *conjecturing* that it is the most truthlike of the hypotheses competing at the time t.

25. *Science: The Growth of Knowledge through Criticism and Inventiveness*

I see in science one of the greatest creations of the human mind. It is a step comparable to the emergence of a descriptive and argumentative language, or to the invention of writing. It is a step at which our explanatory myths become open to conscious and consistent criticism and at which we are challenged to invent new myths. (It is comparable to the conjectural step in the early days of the genesis of life when types of mutability became an object of evolution through elimination.)

Long before criticism there was growth of knowledge—of knowledge incorporated in the genetic code. Language allows the creation and mutation of explanatory myths, and this is further helped by written language. But it is only science which replaces the elimination of error in the violent struggle for life by non-violent rational criticism, and which allows us to replace killing (world 1) and intimidation (world 2) by the impersonal arguments of world 3.

An Afterthought on Induction

26. *Hume's Problems of Causation and Induction*

So far[41] I have been able to give an outline of epistemology and of the methods used in science to further the growth of knowledge without even mentioning *induction*—neither the word nor the alleged phenomenon. This I think is significant. Induction is a muddle, and because the problem of induction can be solved, in a negative but none the less straightforward manner, induction turns out to play no integral part in epistemology or in the method of science and the growth of knowledge.

In my *Logik der Forschung* (1934) I wrote: 'If, following Kant, we call the problem of induction Hume's problem, we might call the problem of demarcation "Kant's problem".'[42] This passage was, to my knowledge, the first in which the problem of induction was called 'Hume's problem': Kant himself did not call it so, contrary to what I appear to say in the passage just quoted.

What happened was this. Kant originally introduced the name 'Hume's problem' (*'Das Hume'sche Problem'*)[43] for the question of the epistemological status of *causation*; and he then generalized the name to cover the whole question of whether synthetic propositions could be valid *a priori*, since he regarded the principle of causation as the most important of the synthetic principles which were valid *a priori*.

I had proceeded differently. I regarded Hume's own way of looking at the problem of causation as unhelpful. It was largely based upon his untenable empiricist psychology—his version of the bucket theory of the mind, whose subjectivist and psychologistic content offered little that I found important as a contribution to a theory of objective knowledge. But, squeezed into the midst of these few subjectivist contributions, I found

[41] I may perhaps mention that Chapter 2, including this 'Afterthought' was written before the report which now forms Chapter 1 of this volume. There is some overlapping, as may be seen from the fact that my motto to Chapter 1 (from Bertrand Russell's *A History of Western Philosophy*, London, 1946, p. 699) could very well serve here too, especially for section 29. Yet Chapters 1 and 2, especially this 'Afterthought', also complement each other in several respects.

[42] See my 'Ein Kriterium des empirischen Charakters theoretischer Systeme', *Erkenntnis*, **3**, 1933, pp. 426 f., and my *Logic of Scientific Discovery*, section 4 (third paragraph), second English edn., 1968, p. 34; third German edn., 1969, p. 9.

[43] I. Kant, *Prolegomena*, 1st edn., pp. 14 f.

one which I regarded as a gem of priceless value for the theory of objective knowledge: a simple, straightforward, logical refutation of any claim that induction could be a valid argument, or a justifiable way of reasoning.

This Humean argument of the invalidity of induction was, at the same time, the heart of his disproof of the existence of a causal link. But as such I found it neither very relevant nor valid.

Thus for me, what Kant had called 'Hume's problem', the problem of causation, split into two: the *causal problem* (concerning which I disagreed with both Kant and Hume) and the *problem of induction* concerning which I agreed with Hume completely, as far as his logic was concerned. (There was also a psychological aspect of the problem of induction, where of course I disagreed with Hume.)

My next step was to look more closely into Kant's problem situation; and here I found that it was not the principle of causation (as he thought) among his synthetic principles *a priori* which was decisive, but the way he used it; for he used it as a *principle of induction*.

Induction, Hume had shown, was invalid because it led to an infinite regress. Now, in the light of Kant's analysis (and my rejection of *a priori* valid synthetic principles) I was led to the formulation: *induction is invalid because it leads either to an infinite regress or to apriorism.*

This was the formula with which I started the argument of my *L.d.F.* And it led me to christen the logical centre of the whole issue—the problem of induction—'Hume's problem', attributing this name to Kant, who had called the problem of causation (*and* its generalization) 'Hume's problem'.

But I feel that I should, at least briefly, go into more detail.

Hume, I suggest, is a commonsense man. As he points out in his *Treatise*, he is a convinced commonsense realist. It is only his worse half, his commonsense theory of knowledge, his form of the bucket theory of the mind, which makes him 'sceptical' with regard to reality, and drives him into that radical form of idealism—'neutral monism' (as it was called by Mach and Russell). Hume, perhaps even more than Locke and Berkeley, is the paradigm of the philosopher who starts with a strong realistic common sense, but is perverted by his commonsense theory of knowledge into an idealist philosophy, which he finds rationally inescapable, even though it splits his mind in half; it is the schizophrenia between commonsense realism and the common-sense theory of knowledge which drives sensualistic empiricism into an absurd idealism, which only a philosopher could accept; but hardly one as reasonable as Hume.

This schizophrenia is expressed by Hume most clearly in the famous passage:

'As the sceptical doubt arises naturally [= commonsensically] from a profound and intense reflection on those subjects, it always increases, the farther we carry our reflections, whether in opposition or conformity to it. Carelessness and in-attention alone can afford us any remedy. For this reason I rely entirely upon them; and take it for granted, whatever may be the reader's opinion at this present moment, *that an hour hence he will be persuaded there is both an external and an internal world*; . . .'[44]

But Hume was completely convinced of having established that his theory of knowledge was the philosophically deeper and truer one. To show that he thought so, I quote, from an immensity of passages, the following from the *Treatise* in which he argues against the 'error'[45] of our belief in an external world:

From all this it may be infer'd, that no other faculty is requir'd, beside the senses, to convince us of the external existence of body. But to prevent this inference, we need only weigh the three following considerations. *First*, That, properly speaking, 'tis not our body we perceive, when we regard our limbs and members, but certain impressions, which enter by the senses; so that the ascribing a real and corporeal existence to these impressions, or to their objects, is an act of the mind as difficult to explain, as that which we examine at present. *Secondly*, Sounds, and tastes, and smells, tho' commonly regarded by the mind as continu'd independent qualities, appear not to have any existence in extension, and consequently cannot appear to the senses as situated externally to the body. The reason, why we ascribe a place to them, shall be consider'd afterwards. *Thirdly*, Even our sight informs us not of distance or outness (so to speak) immediately and without a certain reasoning and experience, as is acknowledg'd by the most rational philosophers.

This is the bucket theory in purity: our knowledge consists of

---

[44] Hume, *Treatise*, Book I, Part IV, section ii; Selby-Bigge, p. 218. (The italics are mine.)

[45] See *Treatise*, Book I, Part IV, section ii; Selby-Bigge, pp. 190 f., the pen-ultimate paragraph.

our perceptions or 'impressions' which '*enter by the senses*'. And these, once they constitute knowledge, must be in us, and there can be no distance or externality.

(Of course, this philosophical depth is all error. Once we start from the first part of commonsense, from realism, we find that we are animals endowed with sense organs which help us to decode the signals of the external world. We do this astonishingly well, with practically our whole 'external' body co-operating. But this is not our problem here.)

I have briefly sketched Hume's schizophrenia, and the overwhelming role played in his view by the bucket theory of the mind. I now come to explain, against this background, his theory of causality.

This theory is complex and far from consistent, and I will stress only one aspect of it.

Hume regards causation as (a) *a relation between events*, (b) as a 'NECESSARY CONNEXION' (Hume's capitals).[46]

But (he says) when here 'again I turn the object on all sides, in order to discover the nature of this necessary connexion' I find no relations 'but . . . contiguity and succession';[47] there is no sensational basis for the idea of necessity: the idea is baseless.

The nearest to it which is observable is *regular succession*. But if the regular succession of two events were 'necessary', then *it would have to take place with certainty, not only among observed instances but also among unobserved ones*. This is, essentially, the way in which *the logical problem of induction* enters Hume's subjectivist discussion of causation, his bucket-theoretical search for the origin or the basis of the idea of necessity.

I regard this kind of inquiry as completely misconceived; but I regard Hume's formulation and treatment of the *logical problem of induction* (he never uses the term) as a flawless gem. I quote one of the characteristic passages:

'Let men be once fully perswaded of these two principles, *That there is nothing in any object, consider'd in itself, which can afford us a reason for drawing a conclusion beyond it; and, That even after the observation of the frequent or constant conjunction of objects, we have no reason to draw any inference concerning any object beyond those of which*

---

[46] Hume, *Treatise*, Book I, Part III, section ii; Selby-Bigge, p. 77.
[47] Loc. cit.

we have had experience; . . .'[48] These 'two principles' of which Hume tries to persuade us, contain his *negative solution of the problem of induction*. They (and many similar passages) no longer speak of cause or effect, or of necessary connection. They are in my judgement the logical gems buried in the psychological mud of the bucket. And in order to honour Hume for this fundamental discovery, I slightly changed the meaning of Kant's term 'Hume's problem', attaching it to the problem of induction rather than to the problem of causation.

In this sense, Hume's logical problem of induction is the problem whether we are entitled to infer unobserved cases from observed cases, however many; or 'unknown' (unaccepted) statements from 'known' (accepted) statements, however many. Hume's answer to this problem is clearly negative; and, as he points out, it remains negative even if our inference is merely to the *probability* of a connexion that has not been observed rather than to its necessity. This extension to probability is formulated in the *Treatise*: 'According to this account of things, which is, I think, in every point unquestionable, probability is founded on the presumption of a resemblance betwixt those objects, of which we have had experience, and those, of which we have had none; and therefore 'tis impossible this presumption can arise from probability.'[49]

The argument against probabilistic induction is, as will be seen, purely formal; and it is even more clearly so in a passage of Hume's *Abstract* which I have quoted in my *L. Sc. D.*, 1959.[50] That is to say, Hume shows that his reasoning against the validity of inductive inference remains the same whether we try to infer the 'necessity', n of the conclusions or merely their 'probability', p. (The letters 'n' and 'p' would be variables which can be substituted for each other in Hume's argument.)[51]

[48] Hume, *Treatise*, Book I, Part III, section xii; Selby-Bigge, p. 139.

[49] Cp. *Treatise*, Book I, Part III, section vi; Selby-Bigge, p. 90.

[50] Cp. *L. Sc. D.*, 1959, p. 369: this passage is on induction only, while the previously quoted passage, from *Treatise*, p. 91, begins with a discussion of cause and effect.

[51] There is an article by D. Stove, 'Hume, Probability, and Induction', in *The Philosophical Review*, Apr. 1965, reprinted in *Philosophy Today*, 3, pp. 212-32, in which my claim is contested. But since Hume's argument is formal (in the sense that he argues that it makes no difference if we replace n by p), Stove cannot be right.

Besides this logical problem of induction which, I assert, Hume solved completely (though his solution is negative), there is another logical problem of induction which some people call 'Hume's problem of induction'. It is the problem: How can it be shown that inductive inferences (at least probabilistic ones) are valid, or can be valid?

This problem is a typical muddle since it uncritically presupposes the existence of a positive solution to what I have called 'Hume's problem'; but Hume has proved that no positive solution exists.

Ultimately we have Hume's *psychological* problem of induction. It may be put like this: why do most people, and perfectly rational people too, believe in the validity of induction? Hume's answer is the one to which Russell alludes in the motto to our first chapter: the psychological mechanism of association forces them to believe, by custom or habit, that what happened in the past will happen in the future. This is a biologically useful mechanism—perhaps we could not live without it—but it has no rational basis whatever. Thus not only is man an irrational animal, but that part of us which we thought rational—*human knowledge*, including practical knowledge—is utterly irrational.

Thus the clash between Hume's negative solution of the logical problem of induction and his positive solution of the psychological problem destroyed both empiricism and rationalism.

27. *Why Hume's Logical Problem of Induction is Deeper than his Problem of Causation*

There could easily be a little quarrel about the question which is the deeper problem: Hume's problem of causation, or what I have called his problem of induction.

One could argue that if the problem of causation were positively solved—if we could show the existence of a necessary link between cause and effect—the problem of induction would also be solved, and positively. Thus, one might say, the problem of causation is the deeper problem.

I argue the other way round: the problem of induction is negatively solved: we can never justify the truth of a belief in a regularity. But we constantly use regularities, as conjectures,

as hypotheses; and we have good reasons sometimes for preferring certain conjectures to some of their competitors.

At any rate, in the light of a conjecture we can not only
explain cause and effect much better than Hume ever did, but
we can even say what the 'necessary causal link' consists of.

Given some conjectured regularity and some initial conditions
which permit us to deduce predictions from our conjecture, we
can call the conditions the (conjectured) cause and the predicted event the (conjectured) effect. And the conjecture which
links them by logical necessity is the long-searched-for (conjectural) necessary link between cause and effect. (The whole can
be called a 'causal explanation', as I called it in *L.d.F.*, section 12.)

This indicates that we get much further by way of Hume's
negative solution to the problem of induction than by way of his
negative solution to the problem of causation; so that we can
describe the former problem as the 'deeper' one, the one that
lies 'behind' the latter.

28. *Kant's Intervention: Objective Knowledge*

Kant realized that Hume's negative solution of the problem
of induction destroyed the rationality of the foundations of
Newtonian dynamics. Kant, like all his educated contemporaries, did not doubt the truth of Newton's theory. Hume's
analysis reduced it to 'custom' or 'habit'—a quite unacceptable
position.

Hume had shown that induction was threatened by an infinite
regress. Kant pointed out that, with his empiricist dogmatism,
Hume had not considered the possibility that there was a principle of causality (better: a principle of induction) which was
valid *a priori*. This was the position which Kant took up (as I
explained in section 1 of *L.d.F.*) and which Bertrand Russell
took up after him: both tried to save human rationality from
Hume's irrationalism.

Kant divided all sentences according to their logical form into
analytic and synthetic ones, the analytic being those which are
decidable as true or false with the help of logic alone. He further
divided them according to their *a priori* or *a posteriori* validity:
according to whether their claim to truth or falsehood was not

in need of empirical backing (*a priori*) or was so in need (*a posteriori*).

Since, by definition, all analytic statements were *a priori* we thus arrive at the following table.

Division of Statements

		according to logical form:	
		analytic	synthetic
According to basis of claim to truth or falsity:	*a priori*	+	?
	a posteriori	−	+

(The arrows mean 'if . . . then'; for example: if analytic then *a priori*.)

The table indicates that analyticity implies *a priori* character and therefore *a posteriori* character syntheticity. But this leaves the question open: are there or are there not synthetic statements which could be valid *a priori*? Kant said yes, and claimed arithmetic, geometry, the principle of causality (and some major part of Newton's physics) as synthetic and *a priori* valid.

This solved for him Hume's problem. But was it a tenable theory? How could the truth of the principle of causality (for example) be established *a priori*?

Here Kant brought in his 'Copernican Revolution': *it was the human intellect which invented, and imposed, its laws upon the sensual morass, thus creating the order of nature.*

This was a bold theory. But it collapsed once it was realized that Newtonian dynamics was not *a priori* valid but a marvellous hypothesis—a conjecture.

From the point of commonsense realism, quite a bit of Kant's idea could be retained. The laws of nature *are* our invention, they are animal-made and man-made, genetically *a priori* though not *a priori* valid. We *try* to impose them upon nature. Very often we fail, and perish with our mistaken conjectures. But sometimes we come near enough to the truth to survive with our conjectures. And on the human level, when descriptive and argumentative language is at our disposal, we can criticize our conjectures systematically. This is the method of science.

It is important to realize the great contribution made by Kant towards this solution, though Kant did not fully supersede subjectivism in the theory of knowledge. Perhaps the greatest step was his constant discussion of scientific theories, statements, propositions, principles, and the arguments for and against them, where his forerunners had still spoken mainly of sensations or impressions or beliefs.

29. *The Solution of Hume's Paradox: Restoration of Rationality*[52]

Since the days I wrote the passage in which I called the problem of induction 'Hume's problem', this terminology has been universally adopted. I have in vain searched the literature in an attempt to find if somebody before me called the problem of induction 'Hume's problem'. All instances I could find can be traced back to writers who have, more or less carefully, read my book (such as Russell or von Wright). Of course I may have overlooked some earlier writer, and nothing could be less important than to claim priority for introducing a name of a problem. I mention the matter only because it has become fashionable also to call an entirely different problem 'Hume's problem', and some later writers have tried to tell me that 'Hume's problem of induction' is in fact different from the one I have called so.

Obviously there are various different problems which might be called by this name, and I shall refer to two groups:[53]

Group A. How can we justify induction?

Group B. Is induction at all justifiable? And is there any reason why we should think it justifiable?

It will be seen at once that Group B is the more fundamental

[52] This section (like some others) partly overlaps with Chapter 1 of the present volume. I have kept it, however, because it seems to me to complement Chapter 1 in several points. (See also note 41, above.)

[53] John Watkins mentioned to me a 'Group C': Is induction (i.e. something based on repetition) *indispensable*, whether justifiable or not? That it is indispensable (Watkins says) 'is what Hume assumed'. It is exactly what I deny, thereby solving Hume's problem. All we need to assume, in world 3, is realism. In world 2 we are compelled to act and thus as a rule believe in more than can be justified, but we still choose the best of the competing hypotheses: this is a consequence of realism. Watkins thinks that Group C is the most fundamental group of the three, but I cannot see why this should be so. For though *choice* is in a certain sense indispensable, induction is not. (I hope I have not misunderstood Watkins.)

question: if it is solved by giving a clear negative answer, then the Group A question cannot arise.

I claim that I have solved the Group B question in this sense. In other words, I claim to have solved Hume's problem of induction in its deeper form. I say this explicitly because several philosophers have called only Group A 'Hume's problem of induction' and have mistakenly attributed to me[54] the claim that Hume's problem of induction is *insoluble*, while my claim was that I have solved it completely, though negatively.

Hume's problem of induction consists of two elements:

(a) The question of the justification of the validity of the claim to have established with certainty, or at least with probability, the truth of a rule or a generalization, or at least its probable truth, from singular evidence;

(b) The thesis that induction is connected with *repetition* (and that repetition is connected with the strengthening of associations).

One can of course call 'induction' whatever one likes. One can call my theory of criticism and the growth of knowledge my theory of induction. However, I think that that would contribute little to clarity and much to confusion. For of the two elements: the question (a) whether induction is a valid inference —that is, produces valid claims in support of the truth of the induced proposition—seems to me characteristic of Hume's problem and of his negative (logical) answer; and (b) the element of repetition and association appears to me to be characteristic of Hume's problem and makes possible the positive (psychological) part of his answer.

For Hume answered the questions raised by (a) and (b) in two essentially different ways.

(a') He said that induction is completely invalid as an inference. There is not a shadow of a logical argument that would support the inference to a generalization from statements about the past (such as past repetitions of some 'evidence').

(b') He said that in spite of its lack of logical validity, induction plays an indispensable part in practical life. We live by relying on repetition. Association strengthened by repetition is the main mechanism of our intellect, by which we live and act.

Thus here is a paradox. *Even our intellect does not work rationally.*

[54] See G. J. Warnock's review of *L. Sc. D.*, *Mind*, New Series, **69**, 1960, p. 100.

Habit, which is rationally indefensible, is the main force that guides our thoughts and our actions.

This led Hume, one of the most reasonable thinkers of all time, to give up rationalism and look at man not as endowed with reason but as a product of blind habit.

According to Russell this paradox of Hume's is responsible for the schizophrenia of modern man. Whether or not Russell is right in this, I claim that I have solved it.

The solution of the paradox is that not only do we reason rationally, and therefore contrary to the principle of induction, established as invalid by Hume, but that we also act rationally: in accordance with reason rather than with induction. We do not act upon repetition or 'habit', but upon the best tested of our theories which, we have seen, are the ones for which we have good rational reasons; not of course good reasons for believing them to be true, but for believing them to be the *best available* from the point of view of a search for truth or verisimilitude—the best among the competing theories, the best approximations to the truth. The central question for Hume was: do we act according to reason or not? And my answer is: Yes.

With this Hume's paradox is solved. He was right in his logical criticism of the possibility of a valid induction. Where he was wrong was in his association psychology, in his belief that we were acting on the basis of habit, and that habit was the result of sheer repetition.

This solution of Hume's paradox does not, of course, say that we are thoroughly rational creatures. It only says that there is no conflict between rationality and practical action in our human constitution.

It has to be added, of course, that the rational standard of our practical actions often lags far behind the standard applied at the frontiers of knowledge: we often act upon theories which have long been superseded, partly because most of us do not understand what happens at the frontiers of knowledge. I do not think, however, that these remarks are worth pursuing.

30. *Muddles Connected with the Problem of Induction*

Hume himself confused the problem of induction with the problem of the necessary connection between cause and effect;

and Kant saw in the problem of the *a priori* validity of the causal law one of the most fundamental problems of metaphysics. But Hume must be credited with the formulation of the pure logical problem of induction and its solutions (and I am proud that, as far as I know, I was the first to credit him with it). He writes, for example, that we have no *reason* to believe '*that those instances, of which we have had no experience,* [*are likely to*] *resemble those, of which we have had experience*'.[55]

The formulation could not be more clearly separated from the problem of causal necessity which so often bedevils the clarity of Hume's thought. The formulation is also perfectly free from the confusing element of the inference from the past to the future. All that is assumed is that we have empirical evidence of the truth of certain instances, and it is asserted that this does not entitle us to conclude to or extrapolate to analogous experiences at other instances (whether in the past or in the future).

This, then, in all its purity, is what I have christened 'Hume's [logical] problem of induction'.

Hume's answer is as clear as can be: there is no argument of reason which permits an inference from one case to another, however similar the conditions may be; and I completely agree with him in this respect.

I believe, however, that Hume is wrong when he thinks that in practice we make such inferences, on the basis of repetition or habit. I assert that his psychology is primitive.[56] What we do in practice is to jump to a conclusion (often in the form of a Lorenzian 'imprint'); that is to say, to quite inconclusive hypotheses to which we often cling, and with which we may perish, unless we are able to correct them, which is possible especially if, on the human level, they are formulated extrasomatically in written form, and submitted to criticism.

The assertion that we have an irrational inclination to be impressed by habit and repetition is something quite different from the assertion that we have a drive to try out bold hypotheses

[55] David Hume, *Treatise of Human Nature*, 1739–40, Book I, Part III, section vi; Selby-Bigge, p. 89. (The italics are Hume's.) See also my *Logic of Scientific Discovery*, especially p. 369, as referred to above in footnote 50.

[56] There may be other psychologies which are as bad as Hume's but do not clash with logic. Moreover, I assert that there is a psychology which is actually dominated by logic: the rational psychology of trial and error-elimination.

which we may have to correct if we are not to perish. The first describes a typically Lamarckian procedure of instruction; the second a Darwinian procedure of selection. The first one is, as Hume observed, irrational, while the second seems to have nothing irrational in it.

31. *What Remains from the Mistaken Problem of Justifying Induction?*

The mistaken Group A problem—*the problem of justifying induction*—is raised by people who are impressed by the 'Uniformity of Nature': by the fact that the sun rises every day (once in twenty-four hours or once in about 90,000 pulse beats); that all men and all animals are bound to die;[57] and by Hume's famous example that bread nourishes. But all three examples are refuted in the form in which they were originally meant.[58]

'The sun rises every day' was meant to say 'Wherever you go the sun rises every day'. That this was its original meaning is shown by the fact that Pytheas of Marseilles, the first known traveller to cross the polar circle and to describe 'the frozen sea and the midnight sun', was for centuries made the paradigm of a liar, and that the term 'travellers' tales' was derived from him. Aristotle derived the inevitable fate of all men to die from the fact that everything generated and especially every living creature must decay—a thesis which is by no means any longer generally accepted by biologists (who by now have kept a chicken's heart *in vitro* beating for more than half a century). And Hume's example that bread nourishes was tragically refuted when bread baked in the usual way practically wiped out a French village, due to an outbreak of ergotism.

But is this all? It is. It is simply a fact (whatever philosophers may say) that we are commonsensically certain that the sun will rise over London tomorrow. Yet we do not know it for certain. There are millions of possibilities which may prevent it. Anybody who tries to give us positive reasons for believing in it has not grasped the problem. Admittedly we all, Humeans or not,

[57] The Greek word *thnētos*, often translated by 'mortal', actually means 'fated to die'. 'All men are mortal' is therefore better translated 'All men are bound to die'; and in this sense it cannot be said to be valid, because it is derived from 'All generated creatures are (essentially) bound to die', which is refuted by bacteria.

[58] I have used these examples frequently in my lectures, and I used them again in Chapter 1 (pp. 10 f. and footnote 17). But I have decided to let these overlaps stand in order to make the two chapters independently readable.

hope that the sun will continue to rise. Admittedly, this hope is a necessary hope—necessary for action, for life. But even a necessary hope is not objective knowledge, though it may dispose us to belief.

In other words, the reliability of those rules which are still used by philosophers as standard examples of inductive rules, and of their reliability, is false, although quite a good approximation to the truth, it seems.

But this is only to show the unreliability of *so-called* induction. Genuine induction by repetition does not exist. What looks like induction is hypothetical reasoning, well tested and well corroborated and in agreement with reason and common sense. For there is a method of corroboration—the serious attempt to refute a theory where a refutation seems likely. If this attempt fails, the theory can be conjectured, on rational grounds, to be a good approximation to truth—at any rate a better one than its predecessor.

But can we not get something like security? Can we not get security in induction, in countless cases of repetition?

The answer is no. (This is what Hume said.) Commonsense security we can get easily—not so much by repetition as by severe testing. I feel as confident as anyone that the sun will rise tomorrow over London, or that I will die presently, although for the time being bread will continue to nourish me. But I know as a theorist that other things can happen. I even know that the sun does not rise daily everywhere in Europe, that bacteria do not always die but split, and that bread, water, the air, and our most ordinary and reliable surroundings can contain (and it is to be feared will soon contain) deadly poisons.

One can also ask: why do we succeed with our theory-making? Answer: we have succeeded so far, and may fail tomorrow. Every argument showing that we must be successful would prove far too much. All we can do is to conjecture that we live in a part of the cosmos where conditions for life, and for succeeding with our knowledge enterprise, seem to be favourable at the moment. But if we know anything then we also know that almost anywhere else in this cosmos conditions for life and for knowledge are highly unfavourable, because our cosmology tells us that the world is almost everywhere completely empty, and where it is not empty it is almost everywhere too hot.

And the fact that horse-drawn vehicles could be seen every day in London for many centuries has not prevented their disappearance and replacement by the motor car. The apparent 'uniformity of nature' is quite unreliable; and although we can say that the laws of nature do not change, this is dangerously close to saying that there are in our world some abstract connections which do not change (which is quite trivial if we admit that we do not know, but at best conjecture, what these connections are) and that we call them 'laws of nature'.

32. *Dynamic Scepticism: Confrontation with Hume*

The position here defended is radically different from what has in modern times been called 'scepticism', at least since the Reformation. For in modern times scepticism is described as the theory which is pessimistic with respect to the possibility of knowledge. But the view proposed here hopefully adheres to the possibility *of the growth of knowledge, and therefore of knowledge.* It merely removes the quality of certainty which common sense assumed as essential to knowledge, and shows that both certainty and knowledge are different from what the commonsense theory assumed. One will hardly describe as a sceptic a man who believes in the possibility of the unlimited growth of knowledge.

On the other hand, some classic sceptics such as Cicero and Sextus Empiricus were not far removed from the position here defended. *'Scepsis'* could well be translated (though it rarely is) as 'critical inquiry', and 'dynamic scepticism' could be identified with 'forceful critical inquiry', or for that matter even 'hopeful critical inquiry', little as hope itself has an entirely rational basis. It certainly has very little to do with the wish to know where nothing can be known.

In this connection it seems to me of some importance to go back to our starting-point—common sense *plus* critical argument—and to remind ourselves of the result that common sense involves *realism*—perhaps something not too far removed from 'scientific realism'—and that all the known arguments against realism[59] turn out to be critically untenable—or, more precisely,

---

[59] I do not include among these arguments that one valid argument for a kind of idealism which in no way clashes with realism: that human knowledge is the product of men, and that all our theories are of our own invention. See footnote 31 above, and *Conjectures and Refutations*, p. 117.

untenable blunders of the weakest part of common sense: of the commonsense theory of knowledge. Thus we have no reason whatever to abandon realism.

But this means a radical change in the situation of my 'hopeful scepticism', especially when compared with that of David Hume.

Hume argues:

(1) Induction (that is, induction by repetition) is rationally totally invalid.

(2) As a matter of fact, we do rely in our actions (and thus in our belief) on the existence of some reality which is not completely chaotic.

(3) This reliance of ours is, in view of (1), irreparably irrational.

(4) Thus human nature is essentially irrational.

I fully accept Hume's theses (1) and (2). But I reject his thesis (3), the irrationality thesis. I can do so because I do not try to base (2) upon (1), but I assert realism as a so far critically untouched part of common sense which we have no reason to surrender. Hume believed—because of his mistaken commonsense theory of knowledge—that it can be reasonable to accept (2) only when we 'know' it—that is, have sufficient reason to believe in it; and he thought that such belief is based, *de facto*, on induction (which he rightly rejected as irrational). But there exists not only the Humean knowledge of sufficient reason, there exists also objective conjectural knowledge (and its subjective analogue, discussed above in section 20). The status of our commonsense view of reality is not essentially different[60] from that of the immediate perceptions or impressions which Hume accepted as secure: it is conjectural knowledge; and it becomes part of our organic apparatus by the method of trial and error-elimination. Thus there is no reason whatever to base (2) upon (1), or to see it as in need of a positive support other than the absence of tenable critical arguments against it.

To sum up, we need not argue, as Hume did, from induction to realism; there is nothing irrational in the conjecture of realism; and the general arguments against it, in whose validity Hume believed, are part of his mistaken commonsense epistemology.

[60] Here Thomas Reid was right. See above, end of section 21.

Thus we are perfectly free to reject Hume's theses (3) and (4).

A further point may be made about (3) and (4). We *hopefully* believe in realism, and this hopefulness is not a rational one for there are at least some arguments in 'scientific realism' which make us predict the ultimate destruction of all life.

But even this does not support Hume's theses (3) and (4). For it is not irrational to hope as long as we live—and action and decisions are constantly forced upon us.

33. *Analysis of an Argument from the Improbability of Accidents*

As I have briefly indicated (in section 22), subjective probability as a measure of '*rational belief*' seems to me a mistake that has nothing good to offer to the theory of knowledge.

But since nothing depends on words, I do not of course object to calling what I have called here a 'good' (or 'the best') conjecture a 'probable' conjecture (or the most probable of the known conjectures), as long as the word 'probability' is not interpreted in the sense of the calculus of probability. For probability in the sense of the calculus of probability has in my opinion nothing whatever to do with the goodness of a hypothesis. (Only its *im*probability, as already explained, may be used as a measure of its content, and thus of an aspect of its goodness.)

However, there is an old argument with a faintly plausible kernel which can be connected with the calculus of probability as follows.

Let us assume we have a hypothesis H and that this hypothesis is logically very improbable; that is to say, it has a very great content and makes assertions in a number of fields so far completely disconnected. (Example: Einstein's gravitational theory predicted not only Newton's planetary motions, but also a small deviation in the orbit of Mercury, an effect on the path of light rays grazing a heavy body, and a red-shift of spectral lines emitted in heavy gravitational fields.) If all these predictions are successfully tested, then the following argument seems to be intuitively sound and reasonable.

(1) *It can hardly be an accident* that the theory predicts these utterly improbable predictions unless it is true. From this it is argued that there is as great a probability for its truth as there is an improbability for these successes to be due to an accumulation of accidents.

I do not think that this argument (1) can be taken as perfectly valid in this form, but I do believe that there is nevertheless something in it. Let us look more closely into it.

Let us assume that the argument (1) is valid. Then we could calculate *the probability for the theory to be true* as 1 minus the probability that it is only accidentally verified; and if the predicted effects are logically very improbable—for example, because their numerical amount is very precisely and correctly predicted—then the products of these very small numbers would be the number to be deducted from unity. In other words, we should obtain, by this method of calculation, for a good conjecture a probability very close to unity.[61]

The argument at first sounds convincing, but it is obviously invalid. Take Newton's theory (N). It makes so many precise predictions that according to the argument in question it should get a probability very close to unity. Einstein's theory (E) should get an even greater probability. But by the probability calculus we have (writing 'v' for 'or'):

$$p(N \vee E) = p(N) + p(E) - p(NE);$$

and since the theories are incompatible, so that $p(NE) = 0$, we obtain

$$p(N \vee E) = p(N) + p(E) \approx 2$$

(that is, very nearly 2), which is absurd.

The solution of the problem is that argument (1) is specious reasoning. For the following is possible.

(2) The good agreement with the improbable observed result is neither an accident nor due to the truth of the theory, but simply due to its *truthlikeness*.

This argument (2) would explain why many incompatible theories can agree in many fine points in which it would be intuitively highly improbable that they agree by sheer accident.[62]

Thus the argument (1) can be put a little more correctly as follows.

[61] The argument is, in a slightly different form, an old one. Traces of it can be found in Aristotle's *Nicomachean Ethics*, and in Theon of Smyrna, *Liber de Astronomica*, ed. Th. H. Martin, Paris, 1949, p. 293.

[62] I am not sure whether I have ever published this argument before, but I remember that it was an argument I first considered about 1930.

(1′) There is something like verisimilitude, and an accidentally very improbable agreement between a theory and a fact can be interpreted as an indicator that the theory has a (comparatively) high verisimilitude. Generally speaking, a better agreement in improbable points may be interpreted as an indication of greater verisimilitude.

I do not think that much can be said against this argument, even though I should dislike its being developed into yet another theory of induction. But I want to make quite clear that the degree of corroboration of a theory (which is something like a measure of the severity of the tests it has passed) cannot be interpreted simply as a measure of its verisimilitude. At best, it is only an *indicator* (as I explained in 1960 and 1963 when I first introduced the idea of verisimilitude; see for example *Conjectures and Refutations*, pp. 234 f.) of verisimilitude, as it appears at the time *t*. For the degree to which a theory has been severely tested I have introduced the term 'corroboration'. It is to be used mainly for purposes of comparison: for example *E* is more severely tested than *N*. The degree of corroboration of a theory has always a temporal index: it is the degree to which the theory appears well tested at the time *t*. This cannot be a measure of its verisimilitude, but it can be taken as an indication of how its verisimilitude *appears* at the time *t*, compared with another theory. Thus the degree of corroboration is a guide to the preference between two theories at a certain stage of the discussion with respect to their then apparent approximation to truth. But it only tells us that one of the theories offered *seems—in the light of the discussion*—the one nearer to truth.

34. *Summary: A Critical Philosophy of Common Sense*

Once we have seen the need for a critical philosophy the problem of a starting-point arises. Where shall we start? The question seems important, for it seems that there is a danger that an initial mistake may have the most severe consequences.

Concerning this starting-point the views held by most classical and contemporary philosophers and the views which I have proposed here as a half-hearted philosophy of common sense differ radically from each other. I shall here try to sum up the main differences in tabular form.

Earlier Philosophers	*My Critical View*
(1) The choice of our starting-point is decisively important: we must beware not to fall into error at the very start.	(1′) The choice of our starting-point is not decisively important because it can be criticized and corrected like everything else.
(2) Our starting-point should, if possible, be true and certain.	(2′) There is no way to find a starting-point such as this.
(3) It can be found in the personal experience of the self (subjectivism) or in the pure description of behaviour (objectivism).[63]	(3′) Since it can be found neither in subjectivism nor in objectivism, it may be best to start with both, and to criticize both.
(4) In accepting either this kind of subjectivism or this kind of objectivism, philosophers accepted uncritically *a form of the commonsense theory of knowledge*—a theory which may be said to form the weakest point of common sense.	(4′) It is advisable to start from common sense, however vague the views comprised by it may be, but to be critical of all that may be claimed in the name of common sense.
(5) The theory which subjectivists accepted is that the most certain knowledge we can have is about ourselves and our observational or perceptual experiences. (In the emphasis on the certainty of perceptual experiences subjectivists and objectivists coincide.)	(5′) A little critical reflection convinces us that all our knowledge is theory impregnated, and (almost) all also conjectural in character.
(6) There are some hard facts on which knowledge can be built, such as our clear and distinct sensations or sense data: direct or immediate experiences cannot be false.	(6′) Since all knowledge is theory-impregnated, it is all built on sand; but it can be improved by critically digging deeper, and by not taking any alleged 'data' for granted.

[63] This form of objectivism is what is usually called 'behaviourism' or 'operationalism'. It is not closely discussed in the present paper.

(7) This is a clear result of the commonsense theory of knowledge.

(7') It is here that the commonsense theory of knowledge fails: it overlooks the indirect and conjectural character of knowledge. Even our sense organs (to say nothing of the interpretation of their deliverances) are theory-impregnated and open to error, although only occasionally in healthy organisms.

(8) But the commonsense theory of knowledge, which always starts as a form of realism, always ends in the morass of either epistemological idealism or operationalism.

(8') We recognize that even realism and its (biological) theory of knowledge are two conjectures; and we argue that the first is a much better conjecture than idealism.

(9) Common sense, having started from realism and ended in subjectivism, disproves itself. (This may be said to be part of Kant's view.)

(9') The commonsense theory of knowledge is disproved as self-contradictory; but this does not affect the commonsense theory of the world; that is, realism.

An attempt to keep the commonsense theory as an integral whole—realism plus commonsense epistemology—is bound to collapse. Thus, by the method of being sceptical about one's starting-point, the commonsense theory is broken into at least two parts—realism and epistemology—and the latter can be rejected and replaced by an objective theory which utilizes the former.

3. Epistemology Without a Knowing Subject

ALLOW me to start with a confession. Although I am a very happy philosopher I have, after a lifetime of lecturing, no illusions about what I can convey in a lecture. For this reason I shall make no attempt in this lecture to convince you. Instead I shall make an attempt to challenge you, and, if possible, to provoke you.

1. *Three Theses on Epistemology and the Third World*

I might have challenged those who have heard of my adverse attitude towards Plato and Hegel by calling my lecture '*A theory of the Platonic world*', or '*A theory of the objective spirit*'.

The main topic of this lecture will be what I often call, for want of a better name, '*the third world*'. To explain this expression I will point out that, without taking the words 'world' or 'universe' too seriously, we may distinguish the following three worlds or universes: first, the world of physical objects or of physical states; secondly, the world of states of consciousness, or of mental states, or perhaps of behavioural dispositions to act; and thirdly, the world of *objective contents of thought*, especially of scientific and poetic thoughts and of works of art.

Thus what I call 'the third world' has admittedly much in common with Plato's theory of Forms or Ideas, and therefore also with Hegel's objective spirit, though my theory differs radically, in some decisive respects, from Plato's and Hegel's. It has more in common still with Bolzano's theory of a universe of propositions in themselves and of truths in themselves, though it differs from Bolzano's also. My third world resembles most closely the universe of Frege's objective contents of thought.

It is not part of my view or of my argument that we might not

An address given on 25 Aug. 1967, at the Third International Congress for Logic, Methodology and Philosophy of Science, 25 Aug. to 2 Sept. 1967; first published in the proceedings of this Congress, eds. B. van Rootselaar and J. F. Staal, Amsterdam 1968, pp. 333–73.

enumerate our worlds in different ways, or not enumerate them at all. We might, especially, distinguish more than three worlds. My term 'the third world' is merely a matter of convenience.

In upholding an objective third world I hope to provoke those whom I call '*belief philosophers*': those who, like Descartes, Locke, Berkeley, Hume, Kant, or Russell, are interested in our subjective beliefs, and their basis or origin. Against these belief philosophers I urge that our problem is to find better and bolder theories; and that *critical preference* counts, but *not belief*.

I wish to confess, however, at the very beginning, that I am a realist: I suggest, somewhat like a naïve realist, that there are physical worlds and a world of states of consciousness, and that these two interact. And I believe that there is a third world, in a sense which I shall explain more fully.

Among the inmates of my 'third world' are, more especially, *theoretical systems*; but inmates just as important are *problems* and *problem situations*. And I will argue that the most important inmates of this world are *critical arguments*, and what may be called—in analogy to a physical state or to a state of consciousness—*the state of a discussion* or the *state of a critical argument*; and, of course, the contents of journals, books, and libraries.

Most opponents of the thesis of an objective third world will of course admit that there are problems, conjectures, theories, arguments, journals, and books. But they usually say that all these entities are, essentially, symbolic or linguistic *expressions* of subjective mental states, or perhaps of behavioural dispositions to act; further, that these entities are means of *communication*—that is to say, symbolic or linguistic means to evoke in others similar mental states or behavioural dispositions to act.

Against this, I have often argued that one cannot relegate all these entities and their content to the second world.

Let me repeat one of my standard arguments[1] for the (more or less) *independent existence of the third world*.

I consider two thought experiments:

Experiment (1). All our machines and tools are destroyed, and all our subjective learning, including our subjective knowledge of machines and tools, and how to use them. But *libraries*

---

[1] The argument is adapted from Popper, 1962, vol. ii; cp. p. 108. (Bibliographical details of references in this chapter are given in the Select Bibliography on p. 150–2.)

and our capacity to learn from them survive. Clearly, after much suffering, our world may get going again.

Experiment (2). As before, machines and tools are destroyed, and our subjective learning, including our subjective knowledge of machines and tools, and how to use them. But this time, *all libraries are destroyed also*, so that our capacity to learn from books becomes useless.

If you think about these two experiments, the reality, significance, and degree of autonomy of the third world (as well as its effects on the second and first worlds) may perhaps become a little clearer to you. For in the second case there will be no re-emergence of our civilization for many millennia.

I wish to defend in this lecture three main theses, all of which concern epistemology. Epistemology I take to be the theory of *scientific knowledge*.

My first thesis is this. Traditional epistemology has studied knowledge or thought in a subjective sense—in the sense of the ordinary usage of the words 'I know' or 'I am thinking'. This, I assert, has led students of epistemology into irrelevances: while intending to study scientific knowledge, they studied in fact something which is of no relevance to scientific knowledge. For *scientific knowledge* simply is not knowledge in the sense of the ordinary usage of the words 'I know'. While knowledge in the sense of 'I know' belongs to what I call the 'second world', the world of *subjects*, scientific knowledge belongs to the third world, to the world of objective theories, objective problems, and objective arguments.

Thus my first thesis is that the traditional epistemology, of Locke, Berkeley, Hume, and even of Russell, is irrelevant, in a pretty strict sense of the word. It is a corollary of this thesis that a large part of contemporary epistemology is irrelevant also. This includes modern epistemic logic, *if* we assume that it aims at a theory of *scientific knowledge*. However, any epistemic logician can easily make himself completely immune from my criticism, simply by making clear that he does not aim at contributing to the *theory of scientific knowledge*.

My first thesis involves the existence of two different senses of knowledge or of thought: (1) *knowledge or thought in the subjective sense*, consisting of a state of mind or of consciousness or a disposition to behave or to react, and (2) *knowledge or thought in an objective sense*, consisting of problems, theories, and arguments as such. Knowledge in this objective sense is totally independent of anybody's claim to know; it is also independent of anybody's belief, or disposition to assent; or to assert, or to act. Knowledge in the objective sense is *knowledge without a knower*: it is *knowledge without a knowing subject*.

Of thought in the objective sense Frege wrote: 'I understand by a *thought* not the subjective act of thinking but its *objective content* . . .'[2]

The two senses of thought and their interesting interrelations can be illustrated by the following highly convincing quotation from Heyting (1962, p. 195), who says about Brouwer's act of inventing his theory of the continuum:

'If recursive functions had been invented before, he [Brouwer] would perhaps not have formed the notion of a choice sequence which, I think, would have been unlucky.'

This quotation refers on the one hand to some *subjective thought processes* of Brouwer's and says that they might not have occurred (which would have been unfortunate) had the *objective problem situation* been different. Thus Heyting mentions certain possible *influences* upon Brouwer's subjective thought processes, and he also expresses his opinion regarding the value of these subjective thought processes. Now it is interesting that influences, *qua* influences, must be subjective: only Brouwer's subjective acquaintance with recursive functions could have had that unfortunate effect of preventing him from inventing free choice sequences.

On the other hand, the quotation from Heyting points to a certain objective relationship between the *objective contents* of two thoughts or theories: Heyting does not refer to the subjective conditions or the electrochemistry of Brouwer's brain processes, but to an *objective problem situation in mathematics* and its possible influences on Brouwer's subjective acts of thought which were bent on solving these objective problems. I would describe this by saying that Heyting's remark is about the objective or third-world *situational logic* of Brouwer's invention, and that Heyting's remark implies that the third-world situation may affect the second world. Similarly, Heyting's suggestion that it would have been unfortunate if Brouwer had not invented choice sequences

[2] Cp. Frege, 1892, p. 32; italics mine.

is a way of saying that the *objective content* of Brouwer's thought was valuable and interesting; valuable and interesting, that is, in the way it changed the objective problem situation in the third world.

To put the matter simply, if I say 'Brouwer's thought was influenced by Kant' or even 'Brouwer rejected Kant's theory of space' then I speak at least partly about acts of thought in the subjective sense: the word 'influence' indicates a context of thought processes or acts of thinking. If I say, however, 'Brouwer's thought differs vastly from Kant's', then it is pretty clear that I speak mainly about contents. And, ultimately, if I say 'Brouwer's thoughts are incompatible with Russell's', then, by using a *logical term* such as '*incompatible*', I make it unambiguously clear that I am using the word 'thought' only in Frege's objective sense, and that I am speaking only about the objective content, or the logical content, of theories.

Just as ordinary language unfortunately has no separate terms for 'thought' in the sense of the second world and in the sense of the third world, so it has no separate terms for the corresponding two senses of 'I know' and of 'knowledge'.

In order to show that both senses exist, I will first mention three subjective or second-world examples:

(1) 'I *know* you are trying to provoke me, but I will not be provoked.'

(2) 'I *know* that Fermat's last theorem has not been proved, but I believe it will be proved one day.'

(3) From the entry 'Knowledge' in *The Oxford English Dictionary*: *knowledge* is a 'state of being aware or informed'.

Next I will mention three objective or third-world examples:

(1) From the entry 'Knowledge' in *The Oxford English Dictionary*: *knowledge* is a 'branch of learning; a science; an art'.

(2) 'Taking account of the present state of *metamathematical knowledge*, it seems possible that Fermat's last theorem may be undecidable.'

(3) 'I certify that this thesis is an original and significant *contribution to knowledge*.'

These very trite examples have only the function of helping to clarify what I mean when I speak of 'knowledge in the objective sense'. My quoting *The Oxford English Dictionary* should not be interpreted as either a concession to language analysis or as an attempt to appease its adherents. It is not quoted in an attempt to prove that 'ordinary usage' covers 'knowledge' in the objective sense of my third world. In fact, I was surprised to find in *The Oxford English Dictionary* examples of objective usages of 'knowledge'. (I was even more surprised to find some at least *partly* objective usages of 'know': 'to distinguish . . . to be acquainted with (a thing, a place, a person) ; . . . to understand'. That these usages may be partly objective will emerge from the sequel.)[3] At any rate, my examples are not intended as arguments. They are intended solely as illustrations.

My *first thesis*, so far not argued but only illustrated, was that traditional epistemology with its concentration on the second world, or on knowledge in the subjective sense, is irrelevant to the study of scientific knowledge.

My *second thesis* is that what is relevant for epistemology is the study of scientific problems and problem situations, of scientific conjectures (which I take as merely another word for scientific hypotheses or theories), of scientific discussions, of critical arguments, and of the role played by evidence in arguments; and therefore of scientific journals and books, and of experiments and their evaluation in scientific arguments; or, in brief, that the study of a *largely autonomous* third world of objective knowledge is of decisive importance for epistemology.

An epistemological study as described in my second thesis shows that scientists very often do not claim that their conjectures are true, or that they 'know' them in the subjective sense of 'know', or that they believe in them. Although in general they do not claim to know, in developing their research programmes they act on the basis of guesses about what is and what is not fruitful, and what line of research promises further results in the third world of objective knowledge. In other words, scientists act on the basis of a guess or, if you like, of a *subjective belief* (for we may so call the subjective basis of an action) concerning what is promising of impending *growth in the third world of objective knowledge*.

This, I suggest, furnishes an argument in favour of both my *first thesis* (of the irrelevance of a subjectivist epistemology) and

[3] See section 7.1 below.

of my *second thesis* (of the relevance of an objectivist epistemology).

But I have a *third thesis*. It is this. An objectivist epistemology which studies the third world can help to throw an immense amount of light upon the second world of subjective consciousness, especially upon the subjective thought processes of scientists; but *the converse is not true*.

These are my three main theses.

In addition to my three main theses, I offer three supporting theses.

The first of these is that the third world is a natural product of the human animal, comparable to a spider's web.

The second supporting thesis (and an almost crucial thesis, I think) is that the third world is largely *autonomous*, even though we constantly act upon it and are acted upon by it: it is autonomous in spite of the fact that it is our product and that it has a strong feed-back effect upon us; that is to say, upon us *qua* inmates of the second and even of the first world.

The third supporting thesis is that it is through this interaction between ourselves and the third world that objective knowledge grows, and that there is a close analogy between the growth of knowledge and biological growth; that is, the evolution of plants and animals.

2. *A Biological Approach to the Third World*

In the present section of my talk I shall try to defend the existence of an autonomous world by a kind of biological or evolutionary argument.

A biologist may be interested in the behaviour of animals; but he may also be interested in some of the *non-living structures* which animals produce, such as spiders' webs, or nests built by wasps or ants, the burrows of badgers, dams constructed by beavers, or paths made by animals in forests.

I will distinguish between two main categories of problems arising from the study of these structures. The first category consists of problems concerned with *the methods used* by the animals, or *the ways the animals behave* when constructing these structures. This first category thus consists *of problems concerned with the acts of production*; with the behavioural dispositions of the animal; and with the relationships between the animal and the product. The second category of problems is concerned with the *structures themselves*. It is concerned with the chemistry of the materials used in the structure; with their geometrical and physical properties; with their evolutionary changes, depending upon special environmental conditions; and with their dependence upon or their adjustments to these environmental conditions. *Very* important also is the *feedback relation* from the properties of the structure to the behaviour of the animals. In dealing with this second category of problems—that is, with the structures themselves—we shall also have to look upon the structures from the point of view of their biological *functions*. Thus some problems of the first category will admittedly arise when we discuss problems of the second category; for example 'How was this nest built?' and 'What aspects of its structure are typical (and thus presumably traditional or inherited) and what aspects are variants adjusted to special conditions?'.

As my last example of a problem shows, problems of the first category—that is, problems concerned with the production of the structure—will sometimes be suggested by problems of the second category. This must be so, since both categories of problems are dependent upon *the fact that such objective structures exist*, a fact which itself belongs to the second category. Thus the existence of the *structures themselves* may be said to create both categories of problems. We may say that the second category of problems—problems connected with the structures themselves —is more fundamental: all that it presupposes from the first category is the bare fact that the structures are somehow *produced by* some animals.

Now these simple considerations may of course also be applied to products of *human* activity, such as houses, or tools, and also to works of art. Especially important for us, they apply to what we call 'language', and to what we call 'science'.[4]

The connection between these biological considerations and the topic of my present lecture can be made clear by reformulating my three main theses. My first thesis can be put by saying that in the present problem situation in philosophy, few things are as important as the awareness of the distinction between the two categories of problems—production problems on the one

---

4 On these 'artifacts' cp. Hayek, 1967, p. 111.

hand and problems connected with the produced structures themselves on the other. My second thesis is that we should realize that the second category of problems, those concerned with the products in themselves, is in almost every respect more important than the first category, the problems of production. My third thesis is that the problems of the second category are basic for understanding the production problems: contrary to first impressions, we can learn more about production behaviour by studying the products themselves than we can learn about the products by studying production behaviour. This third thesis may be described as an anti-behaviouristic and anti-psychologistic thesis.

In their application to what may be called 'knowledge' my three theses may be formulated as follows.

(1) We should constantly be aware of the distinction between problems connected with our personal contributions to the production of scientific knowledge on the one hand, and problems connected with the structure of the various products, such as scientific theories or scientific arguments, on the other.

(2) We should realize that the study of the products is vastly more important than the study of the production, even for an understanding of the production and its methods.

(3) We can learn more about the heuristics and the methodology and even about the psychology of research by studying theories, and the arguments offered for or against them, than by any direct behaviouristic or psychological or sociological approach. In general, we may learn a great deal about behaviour and psychology from the study of the products.

In what follows I will call the approach from the side of the products—the theories and the arguments—the 'objective' approach or the 'third-world' approach. And I will call the behaviourist, the psychological, and the sociological approach to scientific knowledge the 'subjective' approach or the 'second-world' approach.

The appeal of the subjective approach is largely due to the fact that it is *causal*. For I admit that the objective structures for which I claim priority are caused by human behaviour. Being causal, the subjective approach may seem to be more scientific than the objective approach which, as it were, starts from effects rather than causes.

Though I admit that the objective structures are products of behaviour, I hold that the argument is mistaken. In all sciences, the ordinary approach is from the effects to the causes. The effect raises the problem—the problem to be explained, the explicandum—and the scientist tries to solve it by constructing an explanatory hypothesis.

My three main theses with their emphasis on the objective product are therefore neither teleological nor unscientific.

3. *The Objectivity and the Autonomy of the Third World*

One of the main reasons for the mistaken subjective approach to knowledge is the feeling that a book is nothing without a reader: only if it is understood does it really become a book; otherwise it is just paper with black spots on it.

This view is mistaken in many ways. A wasp's nest is a wasp's nest even after it has been deserted; even though it is never again used by wasps as a nest. A bird's nest is a bird's nest even if it was never lived in. Similarly a book remains a book—a certain type of product—even if it is never read (as may easily happen nowadays).

Moreover, a book, or even a library, need not even have been written by anybody: a series of books of logarithms, for example, may be produced and printed by a computer. It may be the best series of books of logarithms—it may contain logarithms up to, say, fifty decimal places. It may be sent out to libraries, but it may be found too cumbersome for use; at any rate, years may elapse before anybody uses it; and many figures in it (which represent mathematical theorems) may never be looked at as long as men live on earth. Yet each of these figures contains what I call 'objective knowledge'; and the question of whether or not I am entitled to call it by this name is of no interest.

The example of these books of logarithms may seem far-fetched. But it is not. I should say that almost every book is like this: it contains objective knowledge, true or false, useful or useless; and whether anybody ever reads it and really grasps its contents is almost accidental. A man who reads a book with understanding is a rare creature. But even if he were more common, there would always be plenty of misunderstandings and misinterpretations; and it is not the actual and somewhat accidental avoidance of such misunderstandings which turns black spots on white paper into a book, or an instance of knowledge in the objective sense. Rather, it is something more abstract. It is its possibility or potentiality of being understood, its dispositional character of being understood or interpreted, or misunderstood or misinterpreted, which makes a thing a book. And this potentiality or disposition may exist without ever being actualized or realized.

To see this more clearly, we may imagine that after the human race has perished, some books or libraries may be found by some civilized successors of ours (no matter whether these are terrestrial animals which have become civilized, or some visitors from outer space). These books may be deciphered. They may be those logarithm tables never read before, for argument's sake. This makes it quite clear that neither its composition by thinking animals nor the fact that it has not actually been read or understood is essential for making a thing a book, and that it is sufficient that it might be deciphered.

Thus I do admit that in order to belong to the third world of objective knowledge, a book should—in principle, or virtually —be capable of being grasped (or deciphered, or understood, or 'known') by somebody. But I do not admit more.

We can thus say that there is a kind of Platonic (or Bolzano-esque) third world of books in themselves, theories in themselves, problems in themselves, problem situations in themselves, arguments in themselves, and so on. And I assert that even though this third world is a human product, there are many theories in themselves and arguments in themselves and problem situations in themselves which have never been produced or understood and may never be produced or understood by men.

The thesis of the existence of such a third world of problem situations will strike many as extremely metaphysical and dubious. But it can be defended by pointing out its biological analogue. For example, it has its full analogue in the realm of birds' nests. Some years ago I got a present for my garden—a nesting-box for birds. It was a human product, of course, not a bird's product—just as our logarithm table was a computer's product rather than a human product. But in the context of the bird's world, it was part of an objective problem situation, and an objective opportunity. For some years the birds did not even seem to notice the nesting-box. But after some years, it was carefully inspected by some blue tits who even started building in it, but gave up very soon. Obviously, here was a graspable opportunity, though not, it appears, a particularly valuable one. At any rate, here was a problem situation. And the problem may be solved in another year by other birds. If it is not, another box may prove more adequate. On the other hand, a most adequate box may be removed before it is ever used. The question of the adequacy of the box is clearly an objective one; and whether the box is ever used is partly accidental. So it is with all ecological niches. They are potentialities and may be studied as such in an objective way, up to a point independently of the question of whether these potentialities will ever be actualized by any living organism. A bacteriologist knows how to prepare such an ecological niche for the culture of certain bacteria or moulds. It may be perfectly adequate for its purpose. Whether it will ever be used and inhabited is another question.

A large part of the objective third world of actual and potential theories and books and arguments arises as an unintended by-product of the actually produced books and arguments. We may also say that it is a by-product of human language. Language itself, like a bird's nest, is an unintended by-product of actions which were directed at other aims.

How does an animal path in the jungle arise? Some animal may break through the undergrowth in order to get to a drinking-place. Other animals find it easiest to use the same track. Thus it may be widened and improved by use. It is not planned—it is an unintended consequence of the need for easy or swift movement. This is how a path is originally made—perhaps even by men—and how language and any other institutions which are useful may arise, and how they may owe their existence and development to their usefulness. They are not planned or intended, and there was perhaps no need for them before they came into existence. But they may create a new need, or a new set of aims: the aim-structure of animals or men is not 'given', but it develops, with the help of some kind of feedback mechanism, out of earlier aims, and out of results which were or were not aimed at.[5]

---

[5] See Hayek, 1967, chapter 6, especially pp. 96, 100, n. 12; Descartes, 1637, cp. 1931, p. 89; Popper, 1960, p. 65; 1966, section XXIV (i.e. pp. 253–5 below).

In this way, a whole new universe of possibilities or potentialities may arise: a world which is to a large extent *autonomous*.

A very obvious example is a garden. Even though it may have been planned with great care, it will as a rule turn out partly in unexpected ways. But even if it turns out as planned, some unexpected interrelationships between the planned objects may give rise to a whole universe of possibilities, of possible new aims, and of new *problems*.

The world of language, of conjectures, theories, and arguments—in brief, the universe of objective knowledge—is one of the most important of these man-created, yet at the same time largely autonomous, universes.

The idea of *autonomy* is central to my theory of the third world: although the third world is a human product, a human creation, it creates in its turn, as do other animal products, its own *domain of autonomy*.

There are countless examples. Perhaps the most striking ones, and at any rate those which should be kept in mind as our standard examples, may be found in the theory of natural numbers.

Pace Kronecker, I agree with Brouwer that the sequence of natural numbers is a human construction. But although we create this sequence, it creates its own autonomous problems in its turn. The distinction between odd and even numbers is not created by us: it is an unintended and unavoidable consequence of our creation. Prime numbers, of course, are similarly unintended autonomous and objective facts; and in their case it is obvious that there are many facts here for us to *discover*: there are conjectures like Goldbach's. And these conjectures, though they refer indirectly to objects of our creation, refer directly to problems and facts which have somehow emerged from our creation and which we cannot control or influence: they are hard facts, and the truth about them is often hard to discover.

This exemplifies what I mean when I say that the third world is largely autonomous, though created by us.

But the autonomy is only partial: the new problems lead to new creations or constructions—such as recursive functions, or Brouwer's free choice sequences—and may thus add new objects to the third world. And every such step will create *new unintended facts*; *new unexpected problems*; and often also *new refutations*.[6]

There is also a most important feed-back effect from our creations upon ourselves; from the third world upon the second world. For the new emergent problems stimulate us to new creations.

The process can be described by the following somewhat over-simplified schema (see my 1966, especially p. 243, below):

$$P_1 \to TT \to EE \to P_2.$$

That is, we start from some problem P_1, proceed to a tentative solution or tentative theory TT, which may be (partly or wholly) mistaken; in any case it will be subject to error-elimination, EE, which may consist of critical discussion or experimental tests; at any rate, new problems P_2 arise from our own creative activity; and these new problems are not in general intentionally created by us, they emerge autonomously from the field of new relationships which we cannot help bringing into existence with every action, however little we intend to do so.

The autonomy of the third world, and the feed-back of the third world upon the second and even the first, are among the most important facts of the growth of knowledge.

Following up our biological considerations, it is easy to see that they are of general importance for the theory of Darwinian evolution: they explain how we can lift ourselves by our own bootstraps. Or in more highbrow terminology, they help to explain 'emergence'.

4. *Language, Criticism, and the Third World*

The most important of human creations, with the most important feed-back effects upon ourselves and especially upon our brains, are the higher functions of human language; more especially, the *descriptive function* and the *argumentative function*.

Human languages share with animal languages the two lower functions of language: (1) self-expression and (2) signalling. The self-expressive function or symptomatic function of language is obvious: all animal language is symptomatic of the state of some organism. The signalling or release function is likewise obvious:

---

[6] An example of the latter is Lakatos's 'concept-stretching refutation'; see Lakatos, 1963–4.

we do not call any symptom linguistic unless we assume that it can release a response in another organism.

All animal languages and all linguistic phenomena share these two lower functions. But human language has many other functions.[7] Strangely enough, the most important of the higher functions have been overlooked by almost all philosophers. The explanation of this strange fact is that the two lower functions are always present when the higher ones are present, so that it is always possible to 'explain' every linguistic phenomenon, in terms of the lower functions, as an *'expression'* or a *'communication'*.

The two most important higher functions of human languages are (3) the *descriptive* function and (4) the *argumentative* function.[8]

With the descriptive function of human language, the regulative idea of *truth* emerges, that is, of a description which fits the facts.[9]

Further regulative or evaluative ideas are content, truth content, and verisimilitude.[10]

The argumentative function of human language presupposes the descriptive function: arguments are, fundamentally, about descriptions: they criticize descriptions from the point of view of the regulative ideas of truth; content; and verisimilitude.

Now two points are all-important here:

(1) Without the development of an exosomatic descriptive language—a language which, like a tool, develops outside the body—there can be *no object* for our critical discussion. But with the development of a descriptive language (and further, of a written language), a linguistic third world can emerge; and it is only in this way, and only in this third world, that the problems and standards of rational criticism can develop.

(2) It is to this development of the higher functions of lan-

---

[7] For example, advisory, hortative, fictional, etc.

[8] See Popper, 1963, especially chapters 4 and 12, and the references on pp. 134, 293, and 295 to Bühler, 1934. Bühler was the first to discuss the decisive difference between the lower functions and the descriptive function. I found later, as a consequence of my theory of criticism, the decisive distinction between the descriptive and the argumentative functions. See also Popper, 1966, section XIV and note 47; see also p. 235, below.

[9] One of the great discoveries of modern logic was Alfred Tarski's re-establishment of the (objective) correspondence theory of truth (truth = correspondence to the facts). The present essay owes everything to this theory; but I do not of course wish to implicate Tarski in any of the crimes here committed.

[10] See the previous note and Popper, 1962a, especially p. 292; and Popper, 1963, chapter 10 and Addenda; also pp. 44–60 above and ch. 9, below.

guage that we owe our humanity, our reason. For our powers of reasoning are nothing but powers of critical argument.

This second point shows the futility of all theories of human language that focus on *expression and communication*. As we shall see, the human organism which, it is often said, is intended to express itself, depends in its structure very largely upon the emergence of the two higher functions of language.

With the evolution of the argumentative function of language, criticism becomes the main instrument of further growth. (Logic may be regarded as *the organon of criticism*; see my 1963, p. 64.) The autonomous world of the higher functions of language becomes the world of science. And the schema, originally valid for the animal world as well as for primitive man,

$$P_1 \to TT \to EE \to P_2$$

becomes the schema of the growth of knowledge through error-elimination by way of systematic *rational criticism*. It becomes the schema of the search for truth and content by means of rational discussion. It describes the way in which we lift ourselves by our bootstraps. It gives a rational description of evolutionary emergence, and of our *self-transcendence by means of selection and rational criticism*.

To sum up, although the meaning of 'knowledge', like that of all words, is unimportant, it is important to distinguish between different senses of the word.

(1) Subjective knowledge which consists of certain inborn dispositions to act, and of their acquired modifications.

(2) Objective knowledge, for example, scientific knowledge which consists of conjectural theories, open problems, problem situations, and arguments.

All work in science is work directed towards the growth of objective knowledge. We are workers who are adding to the growth of objective knowledge as masons work on a cathedral.

Our work is fallible, like all human work. We constantly make mistakes, and there are objective standards of which we may fall short—standards of truth, content, validity, and others.

Language, the formulation of problems, the emergence of new problem situations, competing theories, mutual criticism by way of argument, all these are the indispensable means of scientific growth. The most important functions or dimensions of the human language (which animal languages do not possess) are the descriptive and the argumentative functions. The growth of these functions is, of course, of our making, though they are unintended consequences of our actions. It is only within a language thus enriched that critical argument and knowledge in the objective sense become possible.

The repercussions, or the feed-back effects, of the evolution of the third world upon ourselves—our brains, our traditions (if anybody were to start where Adam started, he would not get further than Adam did), our dispositions to act (that is, our beliefs),[11] and our actions, can hardly be overrated.

As opposed to all this, *traditional epistemology* is interested in the second world: in knowledge as a certain kind of belief—justifiable belief, such as belief based upon perception. As a consequence, this kind of belief philosophy cannot explain (and does not even try to explain) the decisive phenomenon that scientists criticize their theories and so kill them. *Scientists try to eliminate their false theories, they try to let them die in their stead. The believer—whether animal or man—perishes with his false beliefs.*

5. Historical Remarks

5.1. Plato and Neo-Platonism

For all we know, Plato was the discoverer of the third world. As Whitehead remarked, all Western philosophy consists of footnotes to Plato.

I will make only three brief remarks on Plato, two of them critical.

(1) Plato discovered not only the third world, but part of the influence or feed-back of the third world upon ourselves: he realized that we try to grasp the ideas of his third world; also that we use them as explanations.

(2) Plato's third world was divine; it was unchanging and, of course, true. Thus there is a big gap between his and my third world: my third world is man-made and changing. It contains not only true theories but also false ones, and especially open problems, conjectures, and refutations.

---

[11] The theory that beliefs may be gauged by readiness to bet was regarded as well known in 1771; see Kant, 1778, p. 852.

And while Plato, the great master of dialectical argument, saw in it merely a way leading to the third world, I regard arguments as among the most important inmates of the third world; not to speak of open problems.

(3) Plato believed that the third world of Forms or Ideas would provide us with ultimate explanations (that is, explanation by essences; see my 1963, chapter 3). Thus he writes for example: 'I think that if anything else apart from the idea of absolute beauty is beautiful, then it is beautiful *for the sole reason* that it has some share in the idea of absolute beauty. *And this kind of explanation applies to everything.*' (Plato, *Phaedo*, 100 c.)

This is a theory of *ultimate explanation*; that is to say, of an explanation whose explicans is neither capable nor in need of further explanation. And it is a theory of *explanation by essences*; that is, by hypostasized words.

As a result, Plato envisaged the objects of the third world as something like non-material things or, perhaps, like stars or constellations—to be gazed at, and intuited, though not liable to be touched by our minds. This is why the inmates of the third world—the forms or ideas—became concepts of things, or essences or natures of things, rather than theories or arguments or problems.

This had the most far-reaching consequences for the history of philosophy. From Plato until today, most philosophers have either been nominalists[12] or else what I have called essentialists. They are more interested in the (essential) meaning of words than in the truth and falsity of theories.

I often present the problem in the form of a table (see the next page).

My thesis is that *the left side of this table is unimportant*, as compared to the right side: what should interest us are theories; truth; argument. If so many philosophers and scientists still think that concepts and conceptual systems (and problems of their meaning, or the meaning of words) are comparable in importance to theories and theoretical systems (and problems of their truth, or the truth of statements), then they are still suffering from Plato's main error.[13] For concepts are partly means of

---

[12] Cp. Watkins, 1965, chapter VIII, especially pp. 145 f., and Popper, 1959 pp. 420–2; 1963, pp. 18 ff., 262, 297 f.

[13] The error, which is traditional, is known as 'the problem of universals'. This

formulating theories, partly means of summing up theories. In any case their significance is mainly instrumental; and they may always be replaced by other concepts.

IDEAS
that is

| DESIGNATIONS *or* TERMS *or* CONCEPTS | STATEMENTS *or* PROPOSITIONS *or* THEORIES |

may be formulated in

| WORDS | ASSERTIONS |

which may be

| MEANINGFUL | TRUE |

and their

| MEANING | TRUTH |

may be reduced, by way of

| DEFINITIONS | DERIVATIONS |

to that of

| UNDEFINED CONCEPTS | PRIMITIVE PROPOSITIONS |

The attempt to establish (rather than reduce) by these means their

| MEANING | TRUTH |

leads to an infinite regress

Contents and objects of thought seem to have played an important part in Stoicism and in Neo-Platonism: Plotinus preserved Plato's separation between the empirical world and Plato's world of Forms or Ideas. Yet, like Aristotle,[14] Plotinus destroyed the transcendence of Plato's world by placing it into the consciousness of God.

should be replaced by 'the problem of theories', or 'the problem of the theoretical content of all human language'. See Popper, 1959, sections 4 (with the new footnote *1) and 25.

Incidentally, it is clear that of the famous three positions—*universale ante rem, in re,* and *post rem*—the last, in its usual meaning, is anti-third-world and tries to explain language as expression, while the first (Platonic) is pro-third-world. Interestingly enough, the (Aristotelian) middle position (*in re*) may be said either to be anti-third-world or to ignore the problem of the third world. It thus testifies to the confusing influence of conceptualism.

[14] Cp. Aristotle, *Metaphysics*, XII (*Λ*), 7: 1072b21 f.; and 9: 1074b15 to 1075a4. This passage (which Ross sums up: 'the divine thought must be concerned with the most divine object, which is itself') contains an implicit criticism of Plato. Its affinity with Platonic ideas is especially clear in lines 25 f.: 'it thinks of that which is most divine and precious, and it does not change; for change would be change for the worse . . .'. (See also Aristotle, *De Anima*, 429b27 ff., especially 430a4.)

Plotinus criticized Aristotle for failing to distinguish between the First Hypostasis (Oneness) and the Second Hypostasis (the divine intellect). Yet he followed Aristotle in identifying God's acts of thought with their own contents or objects; and he elaborated this view by taking the Forms or Ideas of Plato's intelligible world to be the immanent states of consciousness of the divine intellect.[15]

5.2. *Hegel*

Hegel was a Platonist (or rather a Neo-Platonist) of sorts and, like Plato, a Heraclitean of sorts. He was a Platonist whose world of Ideas was changing, evolving. Plato's 'Forms' or 'Ideas' were objective, and had nothing to do with conscious ideas in a subjective mind; they inhabited a divine, an unchanging, heavenly world (super-lunar in Aristotle's sense). By contrast Hegel's Ideas, like those of Plotinus, were conscious phenomena: thoughts thinking themselves and inhabiting some kind of consciousness, some kind of mind or 'Spirit'; and together with this 'Spirit' they were changing or evolving. The fact that Hegel's 'Objective Spirit' and 'Absolute Spirit' are subject to change is the only point in which his Spirits are more similar to my 'third world' than is Plato's world of Ideas (or Bolzano's world of 'statements in themselves').

The most important differences between Hegel's 'Objective Spirit' and 'Absolute Spirit' and my 'third world' are these:

(1) According to Hegel, though the Objective Spirit (comprising artistic creation) and Absolute Spirit (comprising philosophy) both consist of human productions, man is not creative. It is the hypostasized Objective Spirit, it is the divine self-consciousness of the Universe, that moves man: 'individuals . . . are instruments', instruments of the Spirit of the Epoch, and their work, their 'substantial business', is 'prepared and appointed independently of them'. (Cp. Hegel, 1830, paragraph 551.) Thus what I have called the autonomy of the third world, and its feed-back effect, becomes with Hegel omnipotent: it is only one of the aspects of his system in which his theological background manifests itself. As against this I assert that the individual creative element, the relation of give-and-take between

[15] Cp. Plotinus, *Enneades*, II. 4. 4 (1883, p. 153, 3); III. 8. 11 (1883, p. 346, 6); V. 3. 2–5; V. 9. 5–8; VI. 5. 2; VI. 6. 6–7.

a man and his work, is of the greatest importance. In Hegel this degenerates into the doctrine that the great man is something like a medium in which the Spirit of the Epoch expresses itself.

(2) In spite of a certain superficial similarity between Hegel's dialectic and my evolutionary schema

$$P_1 \to TT \to EE \to P_2$$

there is a fundamental difference. My schema works through error-elimination, and on the scientific level through conscious criticism under the regulative idea of the search for truth.

Criticism, of course, consists in the search for contradictions and in their elimination: the difficulty created by the demand for their elimination constitutes the new problem (P_2). Thus the elimination of error leads to the objective growth of our knowledge—of knowledge in the objective sense. It leads to the growth of objective verisimilitude: it makes possible the approximation to (absolute) truth.

Hegel, on the other hand, is a relativist.[16] He does not see our task as the search for contradictions, with the aim of eliminating them, for he thinks that contradictions are as good as (or better than) non-contradictory theoretical systems: they provide the mechanism by which the Spirit propels itself. Thus rational criticism plays no part in the Hegelian automatism, no more than does human creativity.[17]

(3) While Plato lets his hypostasized Ideas inhabit some divine heaven, Hegel personalizes his Spirit into some divine consciousness: the Ideas inhabit it as human ideas inhabit some human consciousness. His doctrine is, throughout, that the Spirit is not only conscious, but a self. As against this, my third world has no similarity whatever to human consciousness; and though its first inmates are products of human consciousness, they are totally different from conscious ideas or from thoughts in the subjective sense.

5.3. *Bolzano and Frege*

Bolzano's statements in themselves and truths in themselves are, clearly, inhabitants of my third world. But he was far from clear about their relationship to the rest of the world.[18]

---

[16] See Popper, 1963, chapter 15; Popper, 1962, Addendum to vol. ii: 'Facts, Standards and Truth: A Further Criticism of Relativism'.

[17] See Lakatos, 1963–4, p. 234, note 1 (Offprint, p. 59).

[18] Bolzano, 1837, vol. i, § 19, p. 78, says that statements (and truths) in

It is, in a way, Bolzano's central difficulty which I have tried to solve by comparing the status and autonomy of the third world to those of animal products, and by pointing out how it originates in the higher functions of the human language.

As for Frege, there can be no doubt about his clear distinction between the subjective acts of thinking, or thought in the subjective sense, and objective thought or thought content.[19]

Admittedly, his interest in subordinate clauses of a sentence, and in indirect speech, made him the father of modern epistemic logic.[20] But I think that he is in no way affected by the criticism of epistemic logic which I am going to offer (see section 7 below): as far as I can see, he was not thinking in these contexts of epistemology in the sense of a theory of scientific knowledge.

5.4. *Empiricism*

Empiricism—say, of Locke, Berkeley, and Hume—has to be understood in its historical setting: its main problem was, simply, religion *versus* irreligion; or, more precisely, the rational justification, or justifiability, of Christianity, as compared to scientific knowledge.

This explains why knowledge is throughout regarded as a kind of belief—belief justified by evidence, especially by perceptual evidence, by the evidence of our senses.

Though their positions with respect to the relation of science and religion differ widely, Locke, Berkeley,[21] and Hume agree essentially in the demand (which Hume sometimes feels is an unattainable ideal) that we should reject all propositions—and especially propositions with existential import—for which the evidence is insufficient, and accept only those propositions for which we have sufficient evidence: which can be proved, or verified, by the evidence of our senses.

This position can be analysed in various ways. A somewhat sweeping analysis would be the following chain of equations or

themselves have no being ('*Dasein*'), existence, or reality. Yet he also says that a statement in itself is *not merely* 'something stated, thus presupposing a person who stated it'.

[19] See the quotation in section 1 above from Frege, 1892, p. 32, and Frege, 1894.
[20] The way leads from Frege to Russell, 1922, p. 19 and Wittgenstein, 1922, 5. 542.
[21] For Berkeley's position compare Popper, 1963, section 1 of chapter 3 and chapter 6.

equivalences most of which can be supported by passages from the British empiricists and even from Bertrand Russell.[22]

p is verified or demonstrated by sense experience = there is sufficient reason or justification for us to believe p = we believe or judge or assert or assent or know that p is true = p is true = p.

One remarkable thing about this position which *conflates the evidence, or proof, and the assertion to be proved,* is that anybody who holds it ought to *reject the law of the excluded middle.* For it is obvious that the situation may arise (in fact, it would be practically the normal situation) that neither p nor not-p can be fully supported, or demonstrated, by the evidence available. Yet it seems that this was not noticed by anybody before Brouwer.

This failure to reject the law of the excluded middle is particularly striking in Berkeley; for if

$$esse = percipi$$

then the truth of any statement about reality can be established only by perception statements. Yet Berkeley, very much like Descartes, suggests in his Dialogues[23] that we should reject p if there is 'no reason to believe in it'. The absence of such reasons may be compatible, however, with the absence of reasons to believe in not-p.

6. *Appreciation and Criticism of Brouwer's Epistemology*

In the present section I wish to pay homage to L. E. J. Brouwer.[24]

[22] Cp. Russell, 1906–7, p. 45: 'Truth is a quality of beliefs'; Russell, 1910: 'I shall use the words "belief" and "judgment" as synonyms.' (p. 172, footnote); or: '. . . judgment is . . . a multiple relation of the mind to the various other terms with which the judgment is concerned.' (p. 180). He also holds that 'perception is always true (even in dreams and hallucinations)' (p. 181). Or cp. Russell, 1959, p. 183: '. . . but from the point of view of the theory of knowledge and of the definition of truth it is sentences expressing belief that are important'. See also Russell, 1922, pp. 19 f., and Ducasse's *'epistemic attitudes'* in Ducasse, 1940, pp. 701–11. It is clear that both Russell and Ducasse belong to those traditional epistemologists who study knowledge in its subjective or second-world sense. The tradition far transcends empiricism.

[23] See the second dialogue between Hylas and Philonous (Berkeley, 1949, p. 218, lines 15 f.): 'It is to me a sufficient reason not to believe the existence of any thing, if I see no reason for believing it.' Cp. Descartes, 1637, Part IV (first paragraph): 'Any opinion should be rejected as manifestly false ['*aperte falsa*' in the Latin version] if the slightest reason for doubt can be found in it.'

[24] This section on Brouwer was introduced in order to pay homage to this great mathematician and philosopher who died shortly before the Congress took place

It would be presumptuous of me to try to praise and even more presumptuous to try to criticize Brouwer as a mathematician. But it may be permissible for me to try to criticize his epistemology and his philosophy of intuitionist mathematics. If I dare to do so, it is in the hope of making a contribution, however slight, to the clarification and further development of Brouwer's ideas.

In his Inaugural Lecture (1912) Brouwer starts from Kant. He says that Kant's intuitionist philosophy of geometry—his doctrine of the pure intuition of space—has to be abandoned in the light of non-Euclidean geometry. But, Brouwer says, we do not need it, since we can arithmetize geometry: we can take our stand squarely on Kant's theory of arithmetic, and on his doctrine that arithmetic is based upon the pure intuition of time.

I feel that this position of Brouwer's can no longer be sustained; for if we say that Kant's theory of space is destroyed by non-Euclidean geometry, then we are bound to say that his theory of time is destroyed by special relativity. For Kant says explicitly that there is only *one* time, and that the intuitive idea of (absolute) simultaneity is decisive for it.[25]

It might be argued—on lines somewhat parallel to a remark of Heyting's[26]—that Brouwer might not have developed his epistemological and philosophical ideas about intuitionist mathematics had he known at the time of the analogy between Einstein's relativization of time and non-Euclidean geometry. To paraphrase Heyting, this would have been unfortunate.

However, it is unlikely that Brouwer would have been overmuch impressed by special relativity. He might have given up citing Kant as a precursor of his intuitionism. But he could have retained his own theory of a *personal* time—of a time of our own intimate and immediate experience. (See Brouwer, 1949.) And

at which this paper was read. For those who are not acquainted with Brouwer's (and Kant's) intuitionist philosophy of mathematics it may be easier to omit this section and to continue with section 7, below.

[25] In the Transcendental Aesthetic (Kant, 1778, pp. 46 f.; Kemp-Smith's translation, pp. 74 f.), Kant stresses under point 1 the *a priori* character of simultaneity; under points 3 and 4 that there can be only *one* time; and under point 4 that time is *not a discursive concept*, but 'a pure form of . . . intuition' (or, more precisely, *the* pure form of sensual intuition). In the last paragraph before the Conclusion on p. 72 (Kemp-Smith, p. 90) he says explicitly that the intuition of space and time is not an intellectual intuition.

[26] See the quotation from Heyting in section 1 above.

this was in no way affected by relativity, even though Kant's theory was affected.

Thus we need not treat Brouwer as a Kantian. Yet we cannot sever him from Kant too easily. For Brouwer's idea of intuition, and his use of the term 'intuition', cannot be fully understood without analysing its Kantian background.

For Kant, *intuition is a source of knowledge*; and 'pure' intuition ('the pure intuition of space and time') is an unfailing source of knowledge: from it springs *absolute certainty*. This is most important for the understanding of Brouwer who clearly adopts this epistemological doctrine from Kant.

It is a doctrine with a history. Kant took it from Plotinus, St. Thomas, Descartes, and others. Originally, intuition meant, of course, perception: it is what we see, or perceive, if we look at, or if we direct our gaze onto, some object. But at least from Plotinus on, there developed a contrast between *intuition* on the one hand, and *discursive* thinking on the other. Intuition is God's way of knowing everything at a glance, in a flash, timelessly. Discursive thought is the human way: as in a discourse, we argue step by step, which takes time.

Now Kant upheld the doctrine (against Descartes) that we do not possess a faculty of intellectual intuition, and that, for this reason, our intellect—our concepts—remain empty or analytic, unless indeed they are applied to material which is either given to us by our senses (sense intuition), or unless they are *'concepts constructed in our pure intuition of space and time'*.[27] Only in this way can we obtain synthetic knowledge *a priori*: our intellect is essentially discursive; it is bound to proceed by logic, which is empty —'analytic'.

According to Kant, sense intuition presupposes pure intuition: our senses cannot do their work without ordering their perceptions into the framework of space and time. Thus space and time are prior to all sense-intuition; and the theories of space

---

[27] See Kant, 1778, p. 741: 'To construct a concept means to exhibit this *a priori* intuition [the 'pure intuition'] which corresponds to the concept.' See also p. 747: 'We have endeavoured to make it clear how great the difference is between the discursive use of reason through concepts and the intuitive use through the construction of concepts.' On p. 751, the *'construction of concepts'* is further explained: 'we can determine our concepts in our *a priori* intuition of space and time in as much as we create the *objects themselves* by way of a uniform synthesis'. (The italics are partly mine.)

and time—geometry and arithmetic—are *a priori* valid. The source of their *a priori* validity is the human faculty of *pure intuition*, which is strictly limited to this field, and which is strictly distinct from the intellectual or discursive way of thinking.

Kant maintained the doctrine that the *axioms of mathematics* were based on pure intuition (Kant, 1778, pp. 760 f.): they could be 'seen' or 'perceived' to be true, in a non-sensual manner of 'seeing' or 'perceiving'. In addition, pure intuition was involved in *every step of every proof in geometry* (and in mathematics generally):[28] to follow a proof we need to look at a (drawn) figure. This 'looking' is not sense-intuition but pure intuition, as shown by the fact that the figure might often be convincing even though drawn in a very rough manner, and by the fact that the drawing of a triangle might represent for us, in *one* drawing, an infinity of possible variants—triangles of all shapes and sizes.

Analogous considerations hold for arithmetic which, according to Kant, is based on counting; a process which in its turn is essentially based on the pure intuition of time.

Now this theory of the sources of mathematical knowledge suffers in its Kantian form from a severe difficulty. Even if we admit everything that Kant says, we are left puzzled. For Euclid's geometry, whether or not it uses pure intuition, certainly makes use of intellectual argument, of logical deduction. *It is impossible to deny that mathematics uses discursive thought.* Euclid's discourse moves through propositions and whole books step by step: it was not conceived in one single intuitive flash. Even if we admit, for the sake of the argument, the need for pure intuition *in every single step without exception* (and this admission is difficult for us moderns to make), the stepwise, discursive, and logical procedure of Euclid's derivations is so unmistakable, and it was so generally known and imitated (Spinoza, Newton) that it is difficult to believe that Kant can have ignored it. In fact Kant knew all this probably as well as anybody. But his position was forced upon him, by (1) the structure of the *Critique* in which the

[28] Cp. Kant, 1778, pp. 741–64. See, for example, the end of p. 762 where he says about proofs in mathematics ('even in algebra'): 'all inferences are made safe . . . by placing them plainly before our eyes.' Cp., for example, also the top of p. 745 where Kant speaks of a 'chain of inferences', and 'always guided by intuition'. (In the same passage (p. 748) 'to construct' is explained as 'to represent in intuition'.)

'Transcendental Aesthetic' precedes the 'Transcendental Logic', and by (2) his sharp distinction (I should suggest untenably sharp distinction) between intuitive and discursive thought. As it stands, one is almost inclined to say that there is not merely a lacuna here in Kant's exclusion of discursive arguments from geometry and arithmetic, but a contradiction.

That this is not so was shown by Brouwer who filled the lacuna. I am alluding to Brouwer's theory of *the relation between mathematics on the one hand and language and logic on the other*.

Brouwer solved the problem by making a sharp distinction between *mathematics as such* and *its linguistic expression and communication*. Mathematics itself he saw as an extra-linguistic activity, essentially an activity of mental construction on the basis of our pure intuition of time. By way of this construction we create in our intuition, in our mind, the objects of mathematics which afterwards—after their creation—we can try to describe, and to convey to others. Thus the linguistic description, and the discursive argument with its logic, come after the essentially mathematical activity: they always come after an object of mathematics—such as a proof—has been constructed.

This solves the problem which we uncovered in Kant's *Critique*. What at first sight appears to be a contradiction in Kant is removed, in a most ingenious way, by the doctrine that we must sharply distinguish between two levels, one level intuitive and mental and essential for mathematical thought, the other discursive and linguistic and essential for communication only.

Like every great theory, this theory of Brouwer's shows its worth by its fertility. It solved three great sets of problems in the philosophy of mathematics with one stroke:

(1) *Epistemological problems* concerning the source of mathematical certainty; the nature of mathematical evidence; and the nature of mathematical proof. These problems were solved, respectively, by the doctrine of intuition as a source of knowledge; by the doctrine that we can intuitively see the mathematical objects we have constructed; and by the doctrine that a mathematical proof is a sequential construction, or a construction of constructions.

(2) *Ontological problems* concerning the nature of mathematical

objects and the nature of their mode of existence. These problems were solved by a doctrine which had two sides: on the one side there was *constructivism*, and on the other there was a *mentalism* which located all mathematical objects in what I call the 'second world'. Mathematical objects were constructions of the human mind, and they existed solely as constructions in the human mind. Their objectivity—their character as objects, and the objectivity of their existence—rested entirely in the possibility of repeating their construction at will.

Thus Brouwer in his inaugural lecture could imply that, for the intuitionist, mathematical objects existed in the human mind; while for the formalist, they existed 'on paper'.[29]

(3) *Methodological problems* concerning mathematical proofs.

We may quite naïvely distinguish two main ways of being interested in mathematics. One mathematician may be interested mainly in theorems—in the truth or falsity of mathematical propositions. Another mathematician may be interested mainly in proofs: in questions of the existence of proofs of some theorem or other, and in the character of the proofs. If the first interest is preponderant (which seems to be the case for example with Polya), then it is usually linked with an interest in the discovery of mathematical 'facts' and thus with a Platonizing mathematical heuristic. If the second kind of interest is preponderant, then proofs are not merely means of making sure of theorems about mathematical objects, but they are mathematical objects themselves. This, it seems to me, was the case with Brouwer: those constructions which were proofs were not only creating and establishing mathematical objects, they were at the same time themselves mathematical objects—perhaps even the most important ones. Thus to assert a theorem was to assert the existence of a proof for it, and to deny it was to assert the existence of a refutation; that is, a proof of its absurdity. This leads immediately to Brouwer's rejection of the law of the excluded middle, to his rejection of indirect proofs, and to the demand that existence

---

[29] Cp. the end of the third paragraph of Brouwer, 1912. Brouwer speaks there about the existence not of mathematics but of 'mathematical exactness', and *as it stands*, the passage therefore applies to the problems (1) and (3) even more closely than to the ontological problem (2). But there can be no doubt that it was meant to apply to (2) also. The passage reads in Dresden's translation: 'The question where mathematical exactness does exist is answered differently ... The intuitionist says: in the human intellect. The formalist says: on paper.'

can be proved only by the actual construction—the making visible as it were—of the mathematical object in question.

It also leads to Brouwer's rejection of 'Platonism', by which we may understand the doctrine that mathematical objects have what I call an 'autonomous' mode of existence: that they may exist without having been constructed by us, and thus without having been proved to exist.

So far I have tried to understand Brouwer's epistemology, mainly by conjecturing that it springs from an attempt to solve a difficulty in Kant's philosophy of mathematics. I now proceed to what I announced in the title of this section—to an appreciation and criticism of Brouwer's epistemology.

From the point of view of the present paper, it is one of Brouwer's great achievements that he saw that mathematics—and perhaps, I may add, the third world—is created by man.

This idea is so radically anti-Platonic that it is understandable that Brouwer did not see that it can be combined with a kind of Platonism. I mean the doctrine of the (partial) *autonomy* of mathematics, and of the third world, as sketched in section 3 above.

Brouwer's other great achievement, from a philosophical point of view, was his anti-formalism: his recognition that mathematical objects must exist before we can talk about them.

But let me turn to a criticism of Brouwer's solution of the three main sets of problems of the philosophy of mathematics discussed earlier in the present section.

(1') *Epistemological problems:* Intuition in general, and the theory of time in particular.

I do not propose to change the name 'Intuitionism'. Since the name will no doubt be retained, it is the more important to give up the mistaken philosophy of intuition as an infallible source of knowledge.

There are no authoritative sources of knowledge, and no 'source' is particularly reliable.[30] Everything is welcome as a source of inspiration, including 'intuition'; especially if it suggests new problems to us. But nothing is secure, and we are all fallible.

---

[30] I have dealt with this problem at length in my lecture 'On the Sources of Knowledge and of Ignorance' which now forms the Introduction to Popper, 1963.

Besides, Kant's sharp distinction between intuition and discursive thought cannot be upheld. 'Intuition', whatever it may be, is largely the product of our cultural development, and of our efforts in discursive thinking. Kant's idea of one standard type of pure intuition shared by us all (perhaps not by animals in spite of a similar perceptual outfit) can hardly be accepted. For after having trained ourselves in discursive thought, our intuitive grasp becomes utterly different from what it was before.

All this applies to our intuition of time. I personally find Benjamin Lee Whorf's report on the Hopi Indians[31] and their utterly different intuition of time convincing. But even if this report should be incorrect (which I think unlikely), it shows possibilities which neither Kant nor Brouwer ever considered. Should Whorf be right, then our intuitive grasp of time—the way in which we 'see' temporal relations—would partly depend on our language and the theories and myths incorporated in it: *our own European intuition of time would owe much to the Greek origins of our civilization, with its emphasis on discursive thought.*

At any rate, our intuition of time may change with our changing theories. The intuitions of Newton, Kant, and Laplace differ from Einstein's; and the role of time in particle physics differs from that in the physics of continua, especially optics. While particle physics suggests a razor-like unextended instant, a '*punctum temporis*' which divides the past from the future, and thus a time co-ordinate consisting of (a continuum of) unextended instants, and a world whose 'state' may be given for any such unextended instant, the situation in optics is very different. Just as there are spatially extended grids in optics whose parts co-operate over a considerable distance of space, so there are temporally extended events (waves possessing frequencies) whose parts co-operate over a considerable distance of time. Thus, owing to optics, *there cannot be in physics a state of the world at an instant of time.* This argument should, and does, make a great difference to our intuition: what has been called the specious present of psychology is neither specious nor confined to psychology, but is genuine and occurs already in physics.[32]

[31] Cp. 'An American Indian Model of the Universe' in Whorf, 1956.

[32] Cp. Gombrich, 1964, especially p. 297: 'If we want to pursue this thought to its logical conclusion the *punctum temporis* could not even show as a meaningless dot, for light has a frequency.' (The argument can be supported by considering boundary conditions.)

Thus not only is the general doctrine of intuition as an infallible source of knowledge a myth, but our intuition of time, more especially, is just as subject to criticism and correction as is, according to Brouwer's own admission, our intuition of space.

The main point here I owe to Lakatos's philosophy of mathematics. It is that mathematics (and not only the natural sciences) grows through the criticism of guesses, and bold informal proofs. This presupposes the linguistic formulation of these guesses and proofs, and thus their status in the third world. Language, at first merely a means of communicating descriptions of prelinguistic objects, becomes thereby an *essential part* of the scientific enterprise, even in mathematics, which in its turn becomes part of the third world. And there are layers, or levels, in language (whether or not they are formalized in a hierarchy of metalanguages).

Were the intuitionist epistemology correct, mathematical competence would be no problem. (Were Kant's theory correct, it would not be understandable why we—or more precisely Plato and his school—had to wait so long for Euclid.[33]) Yet it is a problem, since even highly competent intuitionist mathematicians can disagree on some difficult points.[34] It is not necessary for us to inquire which side in the disagreement is in the right. It is sufficient to point out that, once an intuitionist construction can be criticized, the problem raised can only be solved *by using argumentative language in an essential way.* Of course, the essential critical use of language does not commit us to the use of arguments banned by intuitionist mathematics (though there is a problem here, as will be shown). My point at the moment is merely this: once the admissibility of a proposed intuitionist mathematical construction can be questioned—and of course it can be questioned—language becomes more than a mere means of communication which could in principle be dispensed with: it becomes, rather, the indispensable medium of critical discussion. Accordingly it is no longer only the intuitionist construction 'which is objective in the sense that it is irrelevant which subject makes the construction';[35] rather, the objectivity, even

---

[33] Cp. the corresponding remark on Kant's aprioristic view of Newton's physics in Popper, 1963, chapter 2, the paragraph to which the footnote 63 is attached.

[34] Cp. S. C. Kleene's comments in Kleene and Vesley, 1965, pp. 176–83, on Brouwer, 1951, pp. 357–8, which Kleene criticizes in the light of Brouwer's note on page 1248 of Brouwer, 1949.   [35] Heyting in Lakatos, 1967, p. 173.

of intuitionist mathematics, rests, as does that of all science, upon the criticizability of its arguments. But this means that language becomes indispensable as the medium of argument, of critical discussion.[36]

It is for this reason that I regard Brouwer's subjectivist epistemology, and the philosophical justification of his intuitionist mathematics, as mistaken. There is a give-and-take between construction, criticism, 'intuition', and even tradition, which he fails to consider.

I am, however, prepared to admit that even in his erroneous view of the status of language Brouwer was partly right. Although the objectivity of all science, including mathematics, is inseparably linked with its criticizability, and therefore with its linguistic formulation, Brouwer was right in reacting strongly against the thesis that mathematics is *nothing but* a formal language game or, in other words, that there are no such things as extra-linguistic mathematical objects; that is to say, thoughts (or in my view, more precisely, thought contents). As he insisted, mathematical talk is *about* these objects; and in this sense, mathematical language is secondary to these objects. But this does not mean that we could construct mathematics without language: there can be no construction without constant critical control, and no criticism without putting our constructs into a linguistic form and treating them as objects of the third world. Although the third world is not identical with the world of linguistic forms, it arises together with argumentative language: it is a by-product of language. This explains why, once our constructions become problematic, systematized, and axiomatized, language may become problematic too, and why formalization may become a branch of mathematical construction. This, I think, is what Professor Myhill means when he says that '*our formalizations correct our intuitions while our intuitions shape our formalizations*'.[37] What makes this remark particularly worth quoting is that, having been made in connection with Brouwerian intuitionist proof, it seems indeed to provide a correction of Brouwerian epistemology.

(2') *Ontological problems:* That the objects of mathematics owe their existence partly to language was sometimes seen by

---

[36] Cp. Lakatos, 1963–4, especially pp. 229–35.
[37] J. Myhill, 1967, p. 175 (my italics); cp. also Lakatos, (1963–4).

Brouwer himself. Thus he wrote in 1924: 'Mathematics is based upon ["*Der Mathematik liegt zugrunde*"] an unlimited sequence of signs or symbols ["*Zeichen*"] or of finite sequences of symbols . . .'[38] This need not be read as an admission of the priority of language: no doubt the crucial term is 'sequence', and the idea of a sequence is based upon the intuition of time, and upon construction based upon this intuition. Yet it shows that Brouwer was aware that signs or symbols were needed to carry out the construction. My own view is that discursive thought (that is, sequences of linguistic arguments) has the strongest influence upon our awareness of time, and upon the development of our intuition of sequential order. This in no way clashes with Brouwer's constructivism; but it does clash with his subjectivism and mentalism. For the objects of mathematics can now become citizens of an objective third world: though originally constructed by us—the third world originates as our product—the thought contents carry with them their own unintended consequences. The series of natural numbers which we construct creates prime numbers—which we *discover*—and these in turn create problems of which we never dreamt. *This is how mathematical discovery becomes possible.* Moreover, the most important mathematical objects we discover—the most fertile citizens of the third world—are *problems*, and new kinds of *critical arguments*. Thus a new kind of mathematical existence emerges: the existence of problems; and a new kind of intuition: the intuition which makes us see problems, and which makes us understand problems prior to solving them. (Think of Brouwer's own central problem of the continuum.)

The way in which language and discursive thought interact with more immediate intuitive constructions (an interaction which, incidentally, destroys that ideal of absolute evidential certainty which intuitive construction was supposed to realize) has been described in a most enlightening way by Heyting. I may perhaps quote the beginning of a passage of his from which I have derived not only stimulation but also encouragement: 'It has proved not to be intuitively clear what is intuitively clear in mathematics. It is even possible to construct a descending scale of grades of evidence. The highest grade is that of such assertions as $2+2 = 4$. $1002+2 = 1004$ belongs to a lower

---

[38] Brouwer, 1924, p. 244.

grade; we show this not by actual counting, but by reasoning which shows that in general $(n+2)+2 = n+4$. . . . [Statements like this] have already the character of an implication: "If a natural number n is constructed, then we can effect the construction, expressed by $(n+2)+2 = n+4$."'[39] In our present context, Heyting's 'grades of evidence' are of secondary interest. What is primarily important is his beautifully simple and clear analysis of the unavoidable interplay between intuitive construction and linguistic formulation which necessarily involves us in discursive—and therefore logical—reasoning. The point is stressed by Heyting when he continues: 'This level is formalized in the free-variable calculus.'

A last word may be said on Brouwer and mathematical Platonism. The autonomy of the third world is undeniable, and with it, Brouwer's equation '*esse* = *construi*' must be given up; *at least* for problems. This may lead us to look anew at the problem of the logic of intuitionism: *without giving up the intuitionist standards of proof*, it may be important for critical rational discussion to distinguish sharply between a thesis and the evidence for it. But this distinction is destroyed by intuitionist logic which results from the *conflation of evidence, or proof, and the assertion to be proved*.[40]

(3′) *Methodological problems:* The original motive of Brouwer's intuitionist mathematics was security: the search for safer methods of proof; in fact, for infallible methods. Now if you want more secure proofs, you must be more severe concerning the admissibility of demonstrative argument: you must use weaker means, weaker assumptions. Brouwer confined himself to the use of logical means which were weaker than those of classical logic.[41] To prove a theorem by weaker means is (and has always been) an intensely interesting task, and one of the great sources of mathematical problems. Hence the interest of intuitionist methodology.

But I suggest that this holds for proofs only. For criticism, for refutation, we do not want a poor logic. While an organon of demonstration should be kept weak, an organon of criticism

[39] Cp. Heyting, 1962, p. 195.   [40] Cp. section 5.4 above.
[41] These remarks hold only for the *logic* of intuitionism which is part of classical logic, while intuitionist mathematics is not part of classical mathematics. See especially Kleene's remarks on 'Brouwer's principle' in Kleene and Vesley, 1965, p. 70.

should be strong. In criticism we do not wish to be confined to demonstrating impossibilities: we do not claim infallibility for our criticism, and we are often content if we can show that some theory has counter-intuitive consequences. In an organon of criticism, weakness and parsimony are no virtue, since it is a virtue in a theory that it can stand up to strong criticism. (It seems therefore plausible that in the critical debate—the meta-debate—of the validity of an intuitionist construction, the use of full classical logic may be admissible.)

7. *Subjectivism in Logic, Probability Theory, and Physical Science*

In view of what has been said in section 5, especially on empiricism, it is not surprising that neglect of the third world—and consequently a subjectivist epistemology—should be still widespread in contemporary thought. Even where there is no connection with Brouwerian mathematics there are often sub-jectivist tendencies to be found within the various specialisms. I will here refer to some such tendencies in logic, probability theory, and physical science.

7.1. *Epistemic logic*

Epistemic logic deals with such formulae as '*a* knows *p*' or '*a* knows that *p*' and '*a* believes *p*', or '*a* believes that *p*'. It usually symbolizes these by

$$\text{'}Kap\text{'} \text{ or } \text{'}Bap\text{'}$$

where '*K*' and '*B*' respectively stand for the relationships of knowing and of believing, and *a* is the knowing or believing subject and *p* the known or believed proposition or state of affairs.

My first thesis in section 1 implies that this has nothing to do with scientific knowledge: that the scientist, I will call him '*S*', does neither know nor believe. What does he do? I will give a very brief list:

'*S* tries to understand *p*.'
'*S* tries to think of alternatives to *p*.'
'*S* tries to think of criticisms of *p*.'
'*S* proposes an experimental test for *p*.'
'*S* tries to axiomatize *p*.'
'*S* tries to derive *p* from *q*.'

'*S* tries to show that *p* is not derivable from *q*.'
'*S* proposes a new problem *x* arising out of *p*.'
'*S* proposes a new solution of the problem *x* arising out of *p*.'
'*S* criticizes his latest solution of the problem *x*.'

The list could be extended at some length. It is far removed in character from '*S* knows *p*' or '*S* believes *p*' or even from '*S* mistakenly believes *p*' or '*S* doubts *p*'. In fact, it is quite an important point that we may doubt without criticizing, and criticize without doubting. (That we may do so was seen by Poincaré in *Science and Hypothesis*, which in this point may be contrasted with Russell's *Our Knowledge of the External World*.)

7.2. *Probability theory*

Nowhere has the subjectivist epistemology a stronger hold than in the field of the calculus of probability. This calculus is a generalization of Boolean algebra (and thus of the logic of propositions). It is still widely interpreted in a subjective sense, as a *calculus of ignorance, or of uncertain subjective knowledge*; but this amounts to interpreting Boolean algebra, including the calculus of propositions, as a *calculus of certain knowledge*—of certain knowledge *in the subjective sense*. This is a consequence which few Bayesians (as the adherents of the subjective interpretation of the probability calculus now call themselves) will cherish.

This subjective interpretation of the probability calculus I have combated for thirty-three years. Fundamentally, it springs from the same epistemic philosophy which attributes to the statement 'I know that snow is white' a greater epistemic dignity than to the statement 'snow is white'.

I do not see any reason why we should not attribute still greater epistemic dignity to the statement 'In the light of all the evidence available to me I believe that it is rational to believe that snow is white.' The same could be done, of course, with probability statements.

7.3. *Physical science*

The subjective approach has made much headway in science since about 1926. First it took over quantum mechanics. Here it became so powerful that its opponents were regarded as nitwits who should rightfully be silenced. Then it took over statistical mechanics. Here Szilard proposed in 1929 the by now almost universally accepted view that we have to pay for subjective information by physical entropy increase; which was interpreted as a proof that physical entropy is lack of knowledge and thus a subjective concept, and that knowledge or information is equivalent to physical negentropy. This development was neatly matched by a parallel development in information theory which started as a perfectly objective theory of channels of communication, but was later linked with Szilard's subjectivist information concept.

Thus the subjective theory of knowledge has entered science on a broad front. The original point of entry was the subjective theory of probability. But the evil has spread into statistical mechanics, the theory of entropy, into quantum mechanics, and into information theory.

It is of course not possible to refute in this lecture all these subjectivist theories. I cannot do more than mention that I have combated them for years (most recently in my 1967). But I do not harbour any illusions. It may be many more years before the turn of the tide (expected by Bunge, 1967)—if it ever does turn.

There are only two final points I wish to make.

First, I shall try to indicate what epistemology or the logic of discovery looks like from an objectivist point of view, and how it may be able to throw some light on the biology of discovery.

Secondly, I shall try to indicate, in the last section of this lecture, what the psychology of discovery looks like, from the same objectivist point of view.

8. *The Logic and the Biology of Discovery*

Epistemology becomes, from an objectivist point of view, the theory of the growth of knowledge. It becomes the theory of problem-solving, or, in other words, of the construction, critical discussion, evaluation, and critical testing, of competing conjectural theories.

I now think that with respect to competing theories it is perhaps better to speak of their 'evaluation' or 'appraisal', or of the 'preference' for one of them, rather than of its 'acceptance'. Not that words matter. The use of 'acceptance' causes no harm as long as it is kept in mind that all acceptance is tentative and, like belief, of passing and personal rather than objective and impersonal significance.[42]

The evaluation or appraisal of competing theories is partly prior to testing (*a priori*, if you like, though not in the Kantian sense of the term which means '*a priori* valid') and partly posterior to testing (*a posteriori*, again in a sense which does not imply validity). Also prior to testing is the (empirical) content of a theory, which is closely related to its (virtual) explanatory power; that is to say, its power to solve pre-existing problems—those problems which give rise to the theory, and with respect to which the theories are *competing theories*.

Only with respect to some pre-existing set of problems can theories be (*a priori*) evaluated, and their values compared. Their so-called simplicity too can be compared only with respect to the problems in whose solution they compete.

Content and virtual explanatory power are the most important regulative ideas for the *a priori* appraisal of theories. They are closely related to their degree of testability.

The most important idea for their *a posteriori* appraisal is truth or, since we need a more accessible comparative concept, what I have termed 'nearness to truth', or 'verisimilitude'.[43] It is important that while a theory without content can be true (such as a tautology), verisimilitude is based upon the regulative idea of truth content; that is to say, on the idea of the amount of interesting and important true consequences of a theory. Thus a tautology, though true, has zero *truth content* and zero verisimilitude. It has of course the probability *one*. Generally speaking, content and testability and verisimilitude[44] can be measured by *im*probability.

The *a posteriori* evaluation of a theory depends entirely upon the way it has stood up to severe and ingenious tests. But severe tests, in their turn, presuppose a high degree of *a priori* testability or content. Thus the *a posteriori* evaluation of a theory depends largely upon its *a priori* value: theories which are *a priori*

---

[42] For instance, I have no objection whatever to Lakatos's use of the terms 'acceptance$_1$' and 'acceptance$_2$' in his 'Changes in the Problem of Inductive Logic', § 3 (Lakatos, 1968).

[43] Cp. Popper, 1963, especially chapter 10, section 3, and addendum 6; also Popper, 1962a, especially p. 292; see also pp. 17–26, above.

[44] Cp. Popper, 'A theorem on truth content', in Feyerabend and Maxwell, 1966.

uninteresting—of little content—need not be tested because their low degree of testability excludes *a priori* the possibility that they may be subjected to really significant and interesting tests.

On the other hand, highly testable theories are interesting and important even if they fail to pass their test; we can learn immensely from their failure. Their failure may be fruitful, for it may actually suggest how to construct a better theory.

Yet all this stress upon the fundamental importance of *a priori* evaluation could perhaps be interpreted as ultimately due to our interest in high *a posteriori* values—in obtaining theories which have a high truth content and verisimilitude, though they remain of course always conjectural or hypothetical or tentative. What we are aiming at are theories which are not only intellectually interesting and highly testable, but which have actually passed severe tests better than their competitors; which thus solve their problems better; and which, should their conjectural character become manifest by their refutation, give rise to new, unexpected, and fruitful, problems.

Thus we can say that science begins with problems, and proceeds from there to competing theories which it evaluates *critically*. Especially significant is the evaluation of their verisimilitude. This demands severe critical tests, and therefore presupposes high degrees of testability, which are dependent upon the content of the theory, and therefore can be evaluated *a priori*.

In most cases, and in the most interesting cases, the theory will ultimately break down and thus raise new problems. And the advance achieved can be assessed by the intellectual gap between the original problem and the new problem which results from the breakdown of the theory.

This cycle can again be described by our repeatedly used diagram:

$$P_1 \to TT \to EE \to P_2;$$

that is: problem P_1—tentative theory—evaluative error elimination—problem P_2.

The evaluation is always *critical*, and its aim is the discovery and *elimination of error*. The growth of knowledge—or the learning process—is not a repetitive or a cumulative process but one of error-elimination. It is Darwinian selection, rather than Lamarckian instruction.

This is a brief description of epistemology from an objective point of view: the method, or logic, of aiming at the growth of objective knowledge. But although it describes the growth of the third world, it can be interpreted as a description of biological evolution. Animals, and even plants, are problem-solvers. And they solve their problems by the method of competitive tentative solutions and the elimination of error.

The tentative solutions which animals and plants incorporate into their anatomy and their behaviour are biological analogues of theories; and vice versa: theories correspond (as do many exosomatic products such as honeycombs, and especially exosomatic tools, such as spiders' webs) to endosomatic organs and their ways of functioning. Just like theories, organs and their functions are tentative adaptations to the world we live in. And just like theories, or like tools, new organs and their functions, and also new kinds of behaviour, exert their influence on the first world which they may help to change. (A new tentative solution—a theory, an organ, a new kind of behaviour—may discover a new virtual ecological niche and thus may turn a virtual niche into an actual one.) New behaviour or organs may also lead to the emergence of new problems. And in this way they may influence the further course of evolution, including the emergence of new biological values.

All this holds also for sense organs. They incorporate, more especially, theory-like expectations. Sense organs, such as the eye, are prepared to react to certain selected environmental events—to those events which they 'expect', and *only* to those events. Like theories (and prejudices) they will in general be blind to others: to those which they do not understand, which they cannot interpret (because they do not correspond to any specific problem which the organism is trying to solve).[45]

Classical epistemology which takes our sense perceptions as 'given', as the 'data' from which our theories have to be constructed by some process of induction, can only be described as pre-Darwinian. It fails to take account of the fact that the alleged data are in fact adaptive reactions, and therefore interpretations which incorporate theories and prejudices and which, like theories, are impregnated with conjectural expectations; that there can be no pure perception, no pure datum; exactly as

[45] Cp. my remarks in Lakatos and Musgrave, 1968, p. 163.

there can be no pure observational language, since all languages are impregnated with theories and myths. Just as our eyes are blind to the unforeseen or unexpected, so our languages are unable to describe it (though our languages can grow—as can our sense organs, endosomatically as well as exosomatically).

This consideration of the fact that theories or expectations are built into our very sense organs shows that the epistemology of induction breaks down even before taking its first step. It cannot start from sense data or perceptions and build our theories upon them, since there are no such things as sense data or perceptions which are not built upon theories (or expectations—that is, the biological predecessors of linguistically formulated theories). Thus the 'data' are no basis of, no guarantee for, the theories: they are not more secure than any of our theories or 'prejudices' but, if anything, less so (assuming for argument's sake that sense data exist and are not philosophers' inventions). Sense organs incorporate the equivalent of primitive and uncritically accepted theories, which are less widely tested than scientific theories. Moreover, there is no theory-free language to describe the data, because myths (that is, primitive theories) arise together with language. There are no living things, neither animals nor plants, without problems and their tentative solutions which are equivalent to theories; though there may well be, or so it seems, life without sense-data (at least in plants).

Thus life proceeds, like scientific discovery, from old problems to the discovery of new and undreamt-of problems. And this process—that of invention and selection—contains in itself a rational theory of emergence. The steps of emergence which lead to a new level are in the first instance the new problems (P_2) which are created by the error-elimination (EE) of a tentative theoretical solution (TT) of an old problem (P_1).

9. *Discovery, Humanism, and Self-Transcendence*

For a humanist our approach may be important because it suggests a new way of looking at the relation between ourselves —the subjects—and the object of our endeavours: the growing objective knowledge, the growing third world.

The old subjective approach of interpreting knowledge as a relation between the subjective mind and the known object— a relation called by Russell 'belief' or 'judgment'—took those things which I regard as objective knowledge merely as *utterances or expressions* of mental states (or as the corresponding behaviour). This approach may be described as an *epistemological expressionism* because it is closely parallel to the expressionist theory of art. A man's work is regarded as the expression of his inner state: the emphasis is entirely upon the causal relation, and on the admitted but overrated fact that the world of objective knowledge, like the world of painting or music, is created by men.

This view is to be replaced by a very different one. It is to be admitted that the third world, the world of objective knowledge (or more generally of the objective spirit) is man-made. But it is to be stressed that this world exists to a large extent autonomously; that it generates its own problems, especially those connected with methods of growth; and that its impact on any one of us, even on the most original of creative thinkers, vastly exceeds the impact which any of us can make upon it.

But it would be a mistake to leave things at that. What I regard as the most important point is not the sheer autonomy and anonymity of the third world, or the admittedly very important point that we always owe almost everything to our predecessors and to the tradition which they created: that we thus owe to the third world especially our rationality—that is, our subjective mind, the practice of critical and self-critical ways of thinking, and the corresponding dispositions. More important than all this, I suggest, is the relation between ourselves and our work, and what can be gained for us from this relation.

The expressionist believes that all he can do is to let his talent, his gifts, express themselves in his work. The result is good or bad, according to the mental or physiological state of the worker.

As against this I suggest that everything depends upon the give-and-take between ourselves and our work; upon the product which we contribute to the third world, and upon that constant feed-back that can be amplified by conscious self-criticism. The incredible thing about life, evolution, and mental growth, is just this method of give-and-take, this interaction between our actions and their results by which we constantly transcend ourselves, our talents, our gifts.

This self-transcendence is the most striking and important fact of all life and all evolution, and especially of human evolution.

In its pre-human stages it is of course less obvious, and so it may indeed be mistaken for something like self-expression. But on the human level, self-transcendence can be overlooked only by a real effort. As it happens with our children, so it does with our theories: they tend to become largely independent of their parents. And as it may happen with our children, so with our theories: we may gain from them a greater amount of knowledge than we originally imparted to them.

The process of learning, of the growth of subjective knowledge, is always fundamentally the same. It is *imaginative criticism*. This is how we transcend our local and temporal environment by trying to think of circumstances *beyond* our experience: by criticizing the universality, or the structural necessity, of what may, to us, appear (or what philosophers may describe) as the 'given' or as 'habit'; by trying to find, construct, invent, new situations—that is, *test* situations, *critical* situations; and by trying to locate, detect, and challenge our prejudices and habitual assumptions.

This is how we lift ourselves by our bootstraps out of the morass of our ignorance; how we throw a rope into the air and then swarm up it—if it gets any purchase, however precarious, on any little twig.

What makes our efforts differ from those of an animal or of an amoeba is only that our rope may get a hold in a third world of critical discussion: a world of language, of objective knowledge. This makes it possible for us to discard some of our competing theories. So if we are lucky, we may succeed in surviving some of our mistaken theories (and most of them are mistaken), while the amoeba will perish with its theory, its belief, and its habits.

Seen in this light, life is problem-solving and discovery—the discovery of new facts, of new possibilities, by way of trying out possibilities conceived in our imagination. On the human level, this trying out is done almost entirely in the third world, by attempts to represent, in the theories of this third world, our first world, and perhaps our second world, more and more successfully; by trying to get nearer to the truth—to a fuller, a more complete, a more interesting, logically stronger and more relevant truth—relevant to our problems.

What may be called the second world—the world of the mind —becomes, on the human level, more and more the link between the first and the third world: all our actions in the first world are influenced by our second-world grasp of the third world. This is why it is impossible to understand the human mind and the human self without understanding the third world (the 'objective mind' or 'spirit'); and why it is impossible to interpret either the third world as a mere expression of the second, or the second as the mere reflection of the third.

There are three senses of the verb 'to learn' which have been insufficiently distinguished by learning theorists: 'to discover'; 'to imitate'; 'to make habitual'. All three may be regarded as forms of discovery, and all three operate with trial-and-error methods which contain a (not too important and usually much overrated) element of chance. 'To make habitual' contains a minimum of discovery—but it clears the decks for further discovery; and its apparently repetitive character is misleading.

In all these different ways of learning or of acquiring or producing knowledge the method is Darwinian rather than Lamarckian: it is selection rather than instruction by repetition. (But we should not overlook the fact that Lamarckism is a kind of approximation to Darwinism, and that the products of selection therefore often look as if they were products of Lamarckian adaptation, of instruction through repetition: Darwinism, we can say, simulates Lamarckism.) But selection is a two-edged sword: it is not only the environment that selects and changes us—it is also we who select and change the environment, mainly by discovering a new ecological niche. On the human level, we do this by co-operation with a whole new objective world—the third world, the world of objective tentative knowledge which includes objective new tentative aims and values. We do not mould or 'instruct' this world by expressing in it the state of our mind; nor does it instruct us. Both we ourselves and the third world grow through mutual struggle and selection. This, it seems, holds at the level of the enzyme and the gene: the genetic code may be conjectured to operate by selection or rejection rather than by instruction or command. And it seems to hold good at all levels, up to the articulate and critical language of our theories.

To explain this more fully, organic systems may be looked at as the objective products or results of tentative behaviour which was 'free'—that is, not determined—within a certain realm or range circumscribed or bound by its internal situation (especially its genetic make-up) and its external situation (the environment). Ill-success rather than success leads then by natural selection to the comparative fixation of the successful way of reacting. It may be conjectured that the genetic code guides the synthesis of proteins by the same method: by the prevention or elimination of certain potential chemical syntheses rather than by direct stimulation or guidance. This would make the invention of the genetic code through selection understandable. It would turn its apparent instructions into prohibitions, the result of error-elimination; and like a theory, the genetic code would be not only the result of selection, but it would also operate by selection or prohibition or prevention. This is of course a conjecture but, I suggest, an attractive one.

SELECT BIBLIOGRAPHY

ARISTOTLE, *Metaphysics*.
—— *De Anima*.
BERKELEY, *Three Dialogues Between Hylas and Philonous*, in: *Works*, eds. Luce and Jessop, vol. ii, 1949.
BOLZANO, B., *Wissenschaftslehre*, 1837.
BROUWER, L. E. J., Inaugural lecture, 14 October 1912; transl. A. Dresden, *Bull. Am. Math. Soc.* **20**, 1914, 81–96.
—— *Math. Ann.* **93**, 1924.
—— Mathematik, Wissenschaft und Sprache [Vortrag gehalten in Wien am 10. III, 1928], in *Monatsh. Math. Phys.* **36**, 1929, 353–64.
—— Consciousness, Philosophy, and Mathematics, in: *Proc. 10th Intern. Congress of Philosophy*, 1949, vol. i, fascicule ii.
—— On Order in the Continuum, and the Relation of Truth to Non-Contradictority, *Kon. Ned. Acad. Recht. Wet. Proc.* Sect. Sci. **54**, 1951.
BÜHLER, K., *Sprachtheorie*, 1934.
BUNGE, M., *Quantum Theory and Reality*, 1967.
DESCARTES, R., *Discourse de la methode*, 1637; transl. E. S. Haldane and G. R. T. Ross, vol. i, 1931.
DUCASSE, C. J., *J. Phil.* **37**, 1940.
FEYERABEND and MAXWELL, eds., *Mind, Matter and Method, Essays in Philosophy and Science in Honor of Herbert Feigl*, 1966.
FREGE, G., Ueber Sinn und Bedeutung, *Z. Phil. und phil. Kritik*, **100**, 1892, 25–50.
—— Review of Husserl, 1891, *Z. Phil. und phil. Kritik*, **103**, 1894, 313–32.
—— Der Gedanke. *Beiträge zur Philosophie d. deutschen Idealismus*, **1**, 1918.
GOMBRICH, E. H., Moment and Movement in Art, *J. Warburg and Court. Inst.* **27**, 1964.

GOMPERZ, H., *Weltanschauungslehre*, vol. ii/1, 1908.
—— *Über Sinn und Sinngebilde, Verstehen und Erkennen*, 1929.
HAYEK, F. A., *The Constitution of Liberty*, 1960.
—— *Studies in Philosophy, Politics, and Economics*, 1967.
HEGEL, G. W. F., *Enzyklopädie der philosophischen Wissenschaften*, third edn., 1830.
HEINEMANN, F., *Plotin*, 1921.
HENRY, P., Plotinus' Place in the History of Thought, in: *Plotinus, the Enneads*, transl. S. MacKenna, second edn., 1956.
HEYTING, A., After thirty years, in: *Logic, Methodology and Philosophy of Science*, eds. E. Nagel, P. Suppes and A. Tarski, 1962, pp. 194 ff.
—— *Intuitionism*, 1966.
—— Informal rigour and intuitionism, in: LAKATOS, 1967.
HUSSERL, E., *Philosophie der Arithmetik*, 1891.
—— *Logische Untersuchungen*, vol. i, second edn., 1913.
KANT, I., *Kritik der reinen Vernunft*, first edn. 1770, second edn. 1778.
KLEENE, S. C., and R. VESLEY, *The Foundations of Intuitionistic Mathematics*, Amsterdam, North-Holland Publ. Co., 1965.
LAKATOS, I., Proofs and Refutations, *Brit. J. Phil. of Sci.* **14**, 1963–4.
—— editor, *Problems in the Philosophy of Mathematics*, Amsterdam, North-Holland Publ. Co., 1967.
—— editor, *The Problem of Inductive Logic*, Amsterdam, North-Holland Publ. Co., 1968.
—— and A. MUSGRAVE, eds., *Problems in the Philosophy of Science*, Amsterdam, North-Holland Publ. Co., 1968.
MYHILL, J., Remarks on Continuity and the Thinking Subject, in: LAKATOS, 1967.
PLATO, *Phaedo*.
PLOTINUS, *Enneades*, ed. R. Volkmann, 1883, 1884.
POPPER, K. R., *Logik der Forschung*, 1934, *The Logic of Scientific Discovery*, 1959 and later edns.
—— *The Poverty of Historicism*, second edn., 1960.
—— *The Open Society and its Enemies*, fourth edn. 1962 and later edns.
—— Some Comments on Truth and the Growth of Knowledge, in: *Logic, Methodology and Philosophy of Science*, eds. E. Nagel, P. Suppes and A. Tarski, 1962*a*.
—— *Conjectures and Refutations*, 1963 and later edns.
—— *Of Clouds and Clocks*, 1966. (Now in this volume, ch. 6, below.)
—— Quantum Mechanics Without 'The Observer', in: *Quantum Theory and Reality*, ed. Mario Bunge, 1967.
—— On the Theory of the Objective Mind, in: *Akten des XIV. Internationalen Kongresses für Philosophie in Wien*, vol. i, 1968. (Now ch. 4 in this volume.)
—— A Pluralist Approach to the Philosophy of History, in: *Roads to Freedom, Essays in Honour of Friedrich A. von Hayek*, 1969, pp. 181 ff.
—— Eine objektive Theorie des historischen Verstehens, *Schweizer Monatshefte*, **50**, 1970, pp. 207 ff.
RUSSELL, B., On the Nature of Truth, in: *Aristotelian Soc. Proc.* **7**, 1906–7, pp. 28–49.

RUSSELL, B., *Philosophical Essays*, 1910.
—— Introduction to WITTGENSTEIN's *Tractatus*, 1922.
—— *My Philosophical Development*, 1959.
WATKINS, J. W. N., *Hobbes's System of Ideas*, 1965.
WHORF, B. L., *Language, Thought and Reality*, 1956.
WITTGENSTEIN, L., *Tractatus Logico-Philosophicus*, 1922.

4. On the Theory of the Objective Mind

OUR main task as philosophers is, I think, to enrich our picture of the world by helping to produce imaginative and at the same time argumentative and critical theories, preferably of methodological interest. Western philosophy consists very largely of world pictures which are variations of the theme of body-mind dualism, and of problems of method connected with them. The main departures from this Western dualistic theme were attempts to replace it by some kind of monism. It seems to me that these attempts were unsuccessful, and that behind the veil of monistic protestations there still lurks the dualism of body and mind.

1. Pluralism and the Thesis of the Three Worlds

There were, however, not only monistic deviations, but also some *pluralistic* ones. This is almost obvious if we think of polytheism, and even of its monotheistic variants. Yet to the philosopher it may seem doubtful whether the various religious interpretations of the world offer any genuine alternative to the dualism of body and mind. The gods, whether many or few, are either minds endowed with immortal bodies, or else pure minds, in contrast to ourselves.

However, some philosophers have made a serious beginning towards a philosophical pluralism, by pointing out the existence of a *third world*. I am thinking of Plato, the Stoics, and some moderns such as Leibniz, Bolzano, and Frege (but not of Hegel who embodied strong monistic tendencies).

Plato's world of Forms or Ideas was, in many respects, a religious world, a world of higher realities. Yet it was neither

A lecture delivered (in an abbreviated German version) on 3 Sept. 1968 in Vienna. Reproduced from the *Akten des XIV. Internationalen Kongresses für Philosophie*, vol. i, Vienna 1968, pp. 25–53. Some additional material which is now being included was first published (in German) in *Schweizer Monatshefte*, 50. Jahr, Heft 3, 1970, pp. 207–15.

a world of personal gods nor a world of consciousness, nor did it consist of the contents of some consciousness. It was an objective, autonomous third world which existed in addition to the physical world and the world of the mind.

I follow those interpreters of Plato who hold that Plato's Forms or Ideas are different not only from bodies and from minds, but also from 'Ideas in the mind', that is to say, from conscious or unconscious experiences: Plato's Forms or Ideas constitute a third world *sui generis*. Admittedly, they are virtual or possible *objects* of thought—*intelligibilia*. Yet for Plato, these *intelligibilia* are as objective as the *visibilia* which are physical bodies: virtual or possible objects of sight.[1]

Thus Platonism goes beyond the duality of body and mind. It introduces a tripartite world, or, as I prefer to say, a third world.

I will not argue here about Plato, however; rather I will argue about pluralism. And even if I and others should be mistaken in attributing this pluralism to Plato, even then could I appeal to a well-known *interpretation* of Plato's theory of Forms or Ideas as an example of a philosophy which genuinely transcends the dualistic schema.

I wish to make this pluralistic philosophy the starting-point of my discussion, even though I am neither a Platonist nor a Hegelian.[2]

In this pluralistic philosophy the world consists of at least three ontologically distinct sub-worlds; or, as I shall say, there are three worlds: the first is the physical world or the world of physical states; the second is the mental world or the world of mental states; and the third is the world of intelligibles, or of *ideas in the objective sense*; it is the world of possible objects of thought: the world of theories in themselves, and their logical relations; of arguments in themselves; and of problem situations in themselves.

---

[1] For Plato's distinction between the visible (*horaton*) and the intelligible (*noēton*) see, for example, Plato's *Republic*, 509 E. (Cp. *Theaetetus*, 185 D ff.) The physiology of the eye has shown that the processes of visually perceiving *visibilia* closely resemble an elaborate interpretation of *intelligibilia*. (One could claim that Kant anticipated much of this.)

[2] Hegel, following Aristotle, rejected the Platonic third world: he conflated thought processes and objects of thought. Thus he disastrously attributed consciousness to the objective mind, and deified it. (See especially the end of Hegel's *Encyclopedia* with the very apt quotation from Aristotle's *Metaphysics*, 1072b18–30.)

One of the fundamental problems of this pluralistic philosophy concerns the relationship between these three 'worlds'. The three worlds are so related that the first two can interact, and that the last two can interact.[3] Thus the second world, the world of subjective or personal experiences, interacts with each of the other two worlds. The first world and the third world cannot interact, save through the intervention of the second world, the world of subjective or personal experiences.

2. *The Causal Relations Between the Three Worlds*

It seems to me most important to describe and explain the relationship of the three worlds in this way—that is, with the second world as the mediator between the first and the third. Although rarely stated, this view seems to me clearly involved in the three-world theory. According to this theory, the human mind can see a physical body in the literal sense of 'see' in which the eyes participate in the process. It can also 'see' or 'grasp' an arithmetical or a geometrical object; a number, or a geometrical figure. But although in this sense 'see' or 'grasp' is used in a metaphorical way, it nevertheless denotes a real relationship between the mind and its intelligible object, the arithmetical or geometrical object; and the relationship is closely analogous to 'seeing' in the literal sense. Thus the mind may be linked with objects of both the first world and the third world.

By these links the mind establishes an *indirect* link between the first and the third world. This is of the utmost importance. It cannot seriously be denied that the third world of mathematical and scientific theories exerts an immense influence upon the first world. It does so, for instance, through the intervention of technologists who effect changes in the first world by applying certain consequences of these theories; incidentally, of theories developed originally by other men who may have been unaware of any technological possibilities inherent in their theories. Thus these possibilities were hidden in the theories

---

[3] I am using here the word 'interact' in a wide sense, so as not to exclude a psychophysical parallelism: it is not my intention to discuss this problem here. (In other places I have argued for interactionism; see, for example, chapters 12 and 13 of my *Conjectures and Refutations*, 1963, 1965, 1969.)

themselves, in the objective ideas themselves; and they were discovered in them by men who tried to *understand* these ideas.

This argument, if developed with care, seems to me to support the objective reality of all three worlds. Moreover, it seems to me to support not only the thesis that a subjective mental world of personal experiences exists (a thesis denied by the behaviourists), but also the thesis that it is one of the main functions of the second world to grasp the objects of the third world. This is something we all do: it is an essential part of being human to learn a language and this means, essentially, to learn to grasp *objective thought contents* (as Frege called them).[4]

I suggest that one day we will have to revolutionize psychology by looking at the human mind as an organ for interacting with the objects of the third world; for understanding them, contributing to them, participating in them; and for bringing them to bear on the first world.

3. *The Objectivity of the Third World*

The third world or rather the objects belonging to it, the objective Forms or Ideas which Plato discovered, have been more often than not mistaken for subjective ideas or thought processes; that is, for mental states, for objects belonging to the second world rather than the third.

This mistake has a long history. It begins with Plato himself. For although Plato clearly recognized the third-world character of his Ideas, it seems that he did not yet realize that the third world contained not only universal concepts or notions, such as the number 7 or the number 77, but also mathematical truths or propositions,[5] such as the proposition '7 times 11 equals 77', and even false propositions, such as '7 times 11 equals 66', and, in addition, all kinds of non-mathematical propositions or theories.

---

[4] Cp. Gottlob Frege, '*Über Sinn und Bedeutung*', *Zeitschrift für Philosophie und philosophische Kritik*, **100**, 1892, p. 32: 'I understand by thought not the subjective act of thinking but its objective content . . .'.

[5] That for Plato truth and propositions are (usually) not third-world ideas but mental acts (like the mental acts of grasping the notions of likeness, etc., described in *Theaetetus*, 186 A) seems suggested in *Theaetetus*, 189 EF., where Plato says that 'thought is the talk which the soul has with itself about any object whatever'. Cp. *Sophist*, 263 E–264 B where the emphasis is on silent speech (true and false), affirmation, negation, and opinion. But in *Phaedrus*, 247 D to 249 B truth is one of the inmates of the third world grasped by the soul.

This, it seems, was first seen by the Stoics who developed a marvellously subtle philosophy of language. Human language, as they realized, belongs to all three worlds.[6] In so far as it consists of physical actions or physical symbols, it belongs to the first world. In so far as it expresses a subjective or psychological state or in so far as grasping or understanding language involves a change in our subjective state,[7] it belongs to the second world. And in so far as language contains information, in so far as it says or states or describes anything or conveys any meaning or any significant message which may entail another, or agree or clash with another, it belongs to the third world. *Theories, or propositions, or statements are the most important third-world linguistic entities.*

If we say 'I saw something written on papyrus', or 'I saw something engraved in bronze', we speak of linguistic entities as belonging to the first world: we do not imply that we can read the message. If we say 'I was greatly impressed by the earnestness and conviction with which the address was delivered', or 'This was not so much a statement as an angry outburst', we speak of linguistic entities as belonging to the second world. If we say 'But James said today precisely the opposite of what John said yesterday' or 'From what James says it follows clearly that John is mistaken', or if we speak of Platonism, or of quantum theory, then we speak of some objective import, of some *objective logical content*; that is, we speak of the third-world significance of the information or the message conveyed in what has been said, or written.

It was the Stoics who first made the important distinction between the (third-world) objective logical *content* of what we are saying, and the *objects* about which we are speaking. These objects, in their turn, can belong to any of the three worlds: we can speak first about the physical world (either about

---

[6] The Stoics were materialists: they regarded the soul as part of the body, identifying it with 'the breath of life' (Diogenes Laertius, vi. 156 f.). The reasoning power they described as 'the leading part' of the body (Sextus, *Adv. Math.* vii, 39 ff.). This theory may, however, be interpreted as a special form of body-mind dualism, since it presents a special solution of the body-mind problem. If we add to these two worlds (or two parts of the first world) the *content of* '*what has been said*' (*lecton*) we arrive at the Stoic version of the *third world*.

[7] The idea of a *state* of the mind (such as goodness, or truthfulness) seems to be Stoic; it is of course interpreted as a state of the breath, and thus of the body. Cp. Sextus, loc. cit.

physical things or physical states) or secondly about our sub-jective mental states (including our grasp of a theory) or thirdly about the contents of some theories, such as some arithmetical propositions and, say, their truth or falsity.

It seems highly advisable to me that we should try to avoid such terms as 'expression' and 'communication' whenever we speak of speech in the third-world sense. For 'expression' and 'communication' are, essentially, psychological terms, and their subjectivist or personal connotations are dangerous in a field where there is so strong a temptation to interpret the third-world contents of thought as second-world thought processes.

It is interesting that the Stoics extended the theory of the third world not merely from Platonic Ideas to theories or propositions. They also included, in addition to such third-world linguistic entities as declarative statements or assertions, such things as problems, arguments, and argumentative inquiries, and besides even commands, admonitions, prayers, treaties, and, of course, poetry and narration. They also distinguished between a personal state of truthfulness, and the truth of a theory or proposition; that is to say, a theory or proposition to which the third-world predicate 'objectively true' applies.

4. *The Third World as a Man-Made Product*

We can, in the main, distinguish between two groups of philosophers. The first consists of those who, like Plato, accept an autonomous third world and look upon it as superhuman and as divine and eternal. The second consists of those who, like Locke or Mill or Dilthey or Collingwood, point out that *language*, and what it 'expresses' and 'communicates' is *man-made*, and who, for this reason, see everything linguistic as a part of the first and second worlds, rejecting any suggestion that there exists a third world. It is interesting that most students of the humanities belong to this second group which rejects the third world.

The first group, the Platonists, are supported by the fact that we can speak of eternal verities: a proposition is, timelessly, either true or false. This seems to be decisive: eternal verities must have been true before man existed. Thus they cannot be of our making.

The members of the second group agree that eternal verities cannot be of our own making; yet they conclude from this that eternal verities *cannot be 'real'*: 'real' is merely *our usage* of the predicate 'true' and the fact that, at least in certain contexts, we use 'true' as a time-independent predicate. This kind of usage is, they may argue, not so very surprising: while Peter's father Paul may at one time be heavier than Peter, and a year later less heavy, nothing like this can happen to two pieces of metal as long as the one remains a proper one-pound weight and the other a proper two-pound weight. Here the predicate 'proper' plays the same role as the predicate 'true' in connection with statements; in fact, we can replace 'proper' by 'true'. Yet nobody will deny that weights can be man-made, these philosophers may point out.

I think that it is possible to uphold a position which differs from that of both these groups of philosophers: I suggest *that it is possible to accept the reality or (as it may be called) the autonomy of the third world, and at the same time to admit that the third world originates as a product of human activity.* One can even admit that the third world is man-made and, in a very clear sense, superhuman at the same time.[8] It transcends its makers.

That the third world is not a fiction but exists 'in reality' will become clear when we consider its tremendous effect on the first world, mediated through the second world. One need only think of the impact of electrical power transmission or atomic theory on our inorganic and organic environment, or of the impact of economic theories on the decision whether to build a boat or an aeroplane.

According to the position which I am adopting here, the third world (part of which is human language) is the product of men, just as honey is the product of bees, or spiders' webs of spiders. *Like language* (and like honey) human language, and thus larger parts of the third world are *the unplanned product of*

---

[8] Although man-made, the third world (as I understand this term) is superhuman in that its contents are virtual rather than actual objects of thought, and in the sense that only a finite number of the infinity of virtual objects can ever become actual objects of thought. We must beware, however, of interpreting these objects as the thoughts of a superhuman consciousness as did, for example, Aristotle, Plotinus, and Hegel. (See my first note above.) For the super-human character of truth, see pp. 29 f. of my *Conjectures and Refutations*, 1963.

human actions,[9] though they may be solutions to biological or other problems.

Let us look at the theory of numbers. I believe (unlike Kronecker) that even the natural numbers are the work of men, the product of human language and of human thought. Yet there is an infinity of such numbers, more than will ever be pronounced by men, or used by computers. And there is an infinite number of true equations between such numbers, and of false equations; more than we can ever pronounce as true, or false.

But what is even more interesting, unexpected new problems arise as an unintended by-product of the sequence of natural numbers; for instance the unsolved problems of the theory of prime numbers (Goldbach's conjecture, say). These problems are clearly *autonomous*. They are in no sense made by us; rather, they are *discovered* by us; and in this sense they exist,

---

[9] See Karl Bühler's theory of the lower and higher functions of human language, and my development of the theory reported in my *Conjectures and Refutations*, 1963, pp. 134 f., and 295, and also in my *Of Clouds and Clocks*, 1966, see pp. 235–8 below. See also F. A. Hayek, *Studies in Philosophy, Politics and Economics*, 1967, especially chapters 3, 4, and 6. Briefly, Bühler points out that animal and human languages are alike in so far as they are always *expressions* (symptoms of a state of the organism) and *communications* (signals). Yet human language is also different since it has, in *addition*, a higher function: it can be *descriptive*. I have pointed out that there are other higher functions, and especially one which is of decisive importance: the *argumentative or critical* function.

It is important that this theory emphasizes that the lower functions are always present. (It is therefore not touched by the criticism which R. G. Collingwood directs, in his *Principles of Art*, 1938, pp. 262 ff., against the theory of language of I. A. Richards, *The Principles of Literary Criticism*, second edn., 1926.)

Regarding the significance of unintended consequences of intentional human actions, see Hayek, op. cit., p. 100, especially note 12. Concerning the origin of language, it was Hayek (I think) who first drew my attention to a passage in Descartes's *Discourse on Method*, second section (Haldane and Ross, vol. i, p. 89) in which Descartes describes the development and improvement of 'the King's highways' as an unintended consequence of their use, a theory which may be transferred to the development of language. I have dealt with the problem of unintended consequences of intentional actions at some length in my *Poverty of Historicism*, 1944, 1957, p. 65 (published after Hayek's *The Counter Revolution of Science*, 1942, 1952, but written before 1942), where I refer, in a footnote, to Hume, and to 'a Darwinian explanation of the . . . instrumental character of undesigned institutions'; and in my *The Open Society and Its Enemies*, 1945, especially vol. ii, chapter 14, pp. 93–8, and note 11 on pp. 323 f. (for whose criticism I am indebted to Hayek, *Studies in Philosophy*, p. 100, note 12). See also my lecture, 'Epistemology without a Knowing Subject' (read in Amsterdam in 1967), now reprinted as Chapter 3 in the present volume.

undiscovered, before their discovery. Moreover, at least some of these unsolved problems may be insoluble.

In our attempts to solve these or other problems we may invent new theories. These theories, again, are produced by us: they are the product of our critical and creative thinking, in which we are greatly helped by other existing third-world theories. Yet the moment we have produced these theories, they create new, unintended and unexpected problems, autonomous problems, problems to be discovered.

This explains why the third world which, in its origin, is our product, is *autonomous* in what may be called its ontological status. It explains why we can act upon it, and add to it or help its growth, even though there is no man who can master even a small corner of this world. All of us contribute to its growth, but almost all our individual contributions are vanishingly small. All of us try to grasp it, and none of us could live without being in contact with it, for all of us make use of speech, without which we would hardly be human.[10] Yet the third world has grown far beyond the grasp not only of any man, but even of all men (as shown by the existence of insoluble problems). Its action upon us has become more important for our growth, and even for its own growth, than our creative action upon it. For almost all its growth is due to a feed-back effect: to the challenge of the discovery of autonomous problems, many of which may never be mastered.[11] And there will always be the challenging task of discovering new problems, for an infinity of problems will always remain undiscovered. In spite and also because of the autonomy of the third world, there will always be scope for original and creative work.

---

[10] The humanizing power of her dramatic discovery of speech has been most movingly and convincingly described by Helen Keller. Of the specifically humanizing functions of language the argumentative (or critical) function seems to me the most important one: it is the basis of what is called human rationality.

[11] For it can be shown (A. Tarski, A. Mostowski, R. M. Robinson, *Undecidable Theories*, Amsterdam, 1953; see especially note 13 on pp. 60 f.), that the (complete) system of all true propositions in the arithmetic of integers is not axiomatizable and essentially undecidable. It follows that there will always be infinitely many unsolved problems in arithmetic. It is interesting that we are able to make such unexpected discoveries about the third world, which are largely independent of our state of mind. (This result goes largely back to the pioneer work of Kurt Gödel.)

5. *The Problem of Understanding*

I have given here some reasons for the autonomous existence of an objective third world because I hope to make a contribution to *the theory of understanding* ('*hermeneutics*'), which has been much discussed by students of the humanities ('*Geisteswissenschaften*', 'moral and mental sciences'). Here I will start from the assumption that it is *the understanding of objects belonging to the third world* which constitutes the central problem of the humanities. This, it appears, is a radical departure from the fundamental dogma accepted by almost all students of the humanities (as the term indicates), and especially by those who are interested in the problem of understanding. I mean of course the dogma that the objects of our understanding belong mainly to the second world, or that they are at any rate to be explained in psychological terms.[12]

Admittedly, the activities or processes covered by the umbrella term 'understanding' are subjective or personal or psychological activities. They must be distinguished from the

---

[12] In spite of the vogue of anti-psychologism which started with Husserl's *Logische Untersuchungen*, 1900–1 (second edn., 1913, 1921), psychologism—that is, neglect or even denial of the third world—is still powerful, especially among those interested in the theory of understanding ('hermeneutics'). Husserl's anti-psychologism was without doubt the result of Frege's criticism of Husserl's psychologistic *Philosophie der Arithmetik. Psychologische und Logische Untersuchungen*, 1891. In his *Logische Untersuchungen* (in which he refers to Bolzano), Husserl states with marvellous clarity (vol. i, p. 178): 'In all . . . sciences we have to insist upon the fundamental distinction between three kinds of interrelations: (a) The interrelations of our *cognitive experiences* . . .;' (this is, what I here call the *second world*) '(b) The interrelations of the *objects under investigation*. . . .;' (especially my *first world* —but it can be any of the others) 'and (c) The *logical interrelations* . . .'. (These belong to my third world.) It may well be, however, that it is just this most important passage which is to be blamed for the still so prevalent confusion. For in the place after (a) indicated by the dots, Husserl refers to the psychological interrelations of 'judgements, insights, conjectures, questions', and especially also acts of intuitive *understanding* 'in which a long discovered theory is thought out with insight'. The reference to 'judgements', 'conjectures' and 'questions' (on a level with 'insights') might have led to confusion, especially as Husserl speaks under (c) *only* of *truths*, apparently to the exclusion of false propositions, conjectures, questions, or problems: he mentions 'the *truths* of a scientific discipline, more especially of a scientific theory, of a proof or a conclusion'. (It should be remembered that Husserl and many even more recent thinkers looked upon a scientific theory as a scientific hypothesis which has been *proved true*: the thesis of the conjectural character of scientific theories was still widely decried as absurd when I tried to propagate it in the nineteen thirties.) The way in which Husserl refers in this passage to *understanding* (cp. also vol. ii, pp. 62 ff.) may also be responsible for some of the still prevailing psychologistic tendencies.

(more or less successful) *outcome* of these activities, from their result: the 'final state' (for the time being) of understanding, the *interpretation*. Although this *may* be a subjective state of understanding, it may also be a third-world object, especially a theory; and the latter case is, in my opinion, the more important one. Regarded as a third-world object, the interpretation will always be a theory; for example a historical explanation, supported by a chain of arguments and, perhaps, by documentary evidence.

So every interpretation is a kind of *theory* and, like every theory, it is anchored in other theories, and in other third-world objects. And in this way the third-world problem of the *merits* of the interpretation can be raised and discussed, and especially its value for our historical *understanding*.

But even the subjective act or the dispositional state of 'understanding' can be understood, in its turn, only through its connections with third-world objects. For I assert the following three theses concerning the subjective act of understanding.

(1) That every subjective act of understanding is largely anchored in the third world;

(2) that almost all important remarks which can be made about such an act consist in pointing out its relations to third-world objects; and

(3) that such an act consists in the main of operations with third-world objects: we operate with these objects almost as if they were physical objects.

This, I suggest, can be generalized, and holds for every subjective act of 'knowledge': all the important things we can say about an act of knowledge consist of pointing out the third-world objects of the act—a theory or proposition—and its relation to other third-world objects, such as the arguments bearing on the problem as well as the objects known.

6. *Psychological Processes of Thought and Third World Objects*

Even some of those who admit the need to analyse the *final state of (subjective) understanding* in terms of third-world objects will, I fear, reject the corresponding thesis regarding the *subjective or personal activity of grasping or of understanding*: it is generally believed that we cannot do without such subjective procedures *as sympathetic understanding* or empathy, or there-enactment of other people's actions (Collingwood), or the attempt to put ourselves into another person's situation by making his aims and his problems our own.

As against this view my thesis is this. Exactly as a subjective state of understanding finally reached, so a psychological process which leads up to it must be analysed in terms of the third-world objects in which it is anchored. In fact it can be analysed *only* in these terms. The process or activity of understanding consists, essentially, of a sequence of states of understanding. (Whether or not one of these is a 'final' state may often depend, subjectively, on nothing more interesting than a feeling of exhaustion.) Only if an important argument or some new evidence has been reached—that is, some third-world object—can more be said about it. Until then, it is the sequence of the preceding states that constitutes the 'process', and it is the work of criticizing the state reached (that is, of producing third-world critical arguments) that constitutes the 'activity'. Or to put it in another way: *the activity of understanding consists, essentially, in operating with third-world objects.*

The activity can be represented by a *general schema of problem-solving by the method of imaginative conjectures and criticism*, or, as I have often called it, by *the method of conjecture and refutation*. The schema (in its simplest form) is this:[13]

$$P_1 \to TT \to EE \to P_2.$$

Here P_1 is the *problem* from which we start, TT (the 'tentative theory') is the imaginative conjectural solution which we first reach, for example our first *tentative interpretation*. EE ('*error-elimination*') consists of a severe critical examination of our conjecture, our tentative interpretation: it consists, for example, of the critical use of documentary evidence and, if we have at this early stage more than one conjecture at our disposal, it will also consist of a critical discussion and comparative evaluation of the competing conjectures. P_2 is the problem situation as it emerges from our first critical attempt to solve our problems. It leads up to our second attempt (*and so on*). A satisfactory

[13] This tetradic schema, and a more elaborate version of it, may be found in my *Of Clouds and Clocks*, 1966, now reprinted as Chapter 6 in the present volume, section XVIII. It may be regarded as resulting from the critical interpretation of the (non-Hegelian) dialectic schema discussed in my paper 'What is Dialectic', 1940, which now forms chapter 15 of my *Conjectures and Refutations*, 1963.

understanding will be reached if the interpretation, the conjectural theory, finds support in the fact that it can throw new light on new problems—on more problems than we expected; or if it finds support in the fact that it explains many subproblems, some of which were not seen to start with. Thus we may say that we can gauge the progress we have made by comparing P_1 with some of our later problems (P_n, say).

This schematic analysis is very widely applicable; and it operates entirely with third-world objects such as problems, conjectures, and critical arguments. And yet, it is an analysis of what we are doing in our subjective second world when we try to understand.

A more detailed analysis would show that we always pick out our problem against a third-world *background*.[14] This background consists of at least a *language*, which always incorporates many theories in the very structure of its usages (as emphasized for example by Benjamin Lee Whorf), and of many other theoretical assumptions, unchallenged at least for the time being. It is only against a background like this that a problem can arise.

A problem together with its background (and perhaps together with other third-world objects) constitutes what I call a *problem situation*. Further third-world objects with which we operate may be: competition and conflict (between theories and problems, aspects of conjectures, interpretations, and philosophical positions); and comparisons or contrasts or analogies. It is important to note that the relationship between a solution and a problem is a logical relationship and thus an objective third-world relationship; and that, if our tentative solution does not solve our problem, it may solve a substitute problem. This leads to the third-world relation called '*problem shift*' by I. Lakatos, who distinguishes between progressive and degenerating problem shifts.[15]

[14] I am using here the term 'background' rather than '*background knowledge*' because I wish to avoid discussing the admissibility of an objective third-world sense of the term '*knowledge*'. (See, however, *Conjectures and Refutations*, pp. 227 f. For 'background knowledge' see op. cit., especially pp. 112, 238 ff.) The objective sense of 'knowledge' is discussed at length in my paper 'Epistemology without a Knowing Subject' (read in Amsterdam in 1967) now reprinted as Chapter 3 in the present volume.

[15] Cp. I. Lakatos, 'Changes in the Problem of Inductive Logic', in I. Lakatos (ed.), *The Problem of Inductive Logic*, 1968. See now also I. Lakatos, 'Criticism and

7. *Understanding and Problem-Solving*

I wish to suggest here that the activity of understanding is, essentially, the same as that of all problem solving. Admittedly, like all intellectual activities, it consists of subjective second-world processes. Yet the subjective work involved can be analysed, and has to be analysed, as an operation with objective third-world objects. It is an operation that establishes in some cases a kind of familiarity with these objects, and with the handling of these objects. To use an analogy, it can be compared with the activities of a builder of bridges or of houses: in trying to solve some practical problem he operates with, or handles, simple structural units, or more complex structural units, with the help of simple or else sophisticated tools.

Replacing these first-world structural units and tools by third-world structural units and tools, such as problems or theories or critical arguments, we obtain a picture of what we are doing when we try to understand or grasp some third-world structure, or try to make some other problem-solving contribution to the third world. But we obtain more than a mere picture. My central thesis is that any intellectually significant analysis of the activity of understanding has mainly, if not entirely, to proceed by analysing our handling of third-world structural units and tools.

In order to make this thesis a little more palatable, I may perhaps recall that these third-world structural units are *intelligibles*; that is, possible (or virtual) objects of our understanding. No wonder that if we are interested in the *process* of our understanding, or in some of its results, we have to describe what we are doing, or achieving, almost entirely in terms of these objects of understanding, the intelligibles, and their relationships. All else, such as a description of our subjective feelings, of excitement or disappointment or satisfaction, may be very interesting, but has little bearing on our problem; that is, on the understanding of intelligibles, of third-world objects or structures.

I am ready to admit, however, that there are certain subjective experiences or attitudes which do play a part in the process of understanding. I have in mind such things as

the Methodology of Scientific Research Programmes' in I. Lakatos and A. Musgrave (eds.), *Criticism and the Growth of Knowledge*, 1970.

emphasis: the picking out of a problem or a theory as important, even though it may not be precisely the problem or theory under investigation; or the opposite: the *dismissal* of some theory as irrelevant rather than as false; or, say, as irrelevant to the discussion at a certain stage, even though it may be important at another stage; or perhaps even the dismissal of a theory as false *and* as too irrelevant for being discussed explicitly. Logically considered, this amounts to the proposal that its falsity and irrelevance should be relegated to the 'background' of the discussion.

A proposal thus to relegate a theory or a problem (or a narrative or a 'project') is conveyed, more often than not, by expressive and emotional means.[16] It is easily seen that, from the point of view of handling third-world objects, these means operate as a kind of shorthand: in principle, they could be replaced by a more detailed *analysis of the objective problem situation*. The trouble is that this analysis may be complex, may take a long time, and may be felt not to be worth while, because its problem is just to establish the fact that there are irrelevances.

This sketchy analysis of some emotional overtones attempts to illustrate the claim that even such overtones may sometimes be best understood in terms of third-world objects such as problem situations.

This claim should not be confounded with an even more important one—that the task of explaining psychological states such as emotions creates its own theoretical problems, to be solved by its own tentative theories: theories (that is, third-world objects) about the second world. Yet this should not be taken to mean that we can understand persons solely, or mainly, by studying psychological theories about them; nor is it intended to recant or even restrict my thesis that in all understanding, including the understanding of persons and their actions, and thus *in the understanding of history*, the analysis of third-world situations is our paramount task.

On the contrary, one of my main points is that actions, and

---

[16] A good analysis of such a situation may be found in Collingwood's criticism of Richards mentioned above; see *The Principles of Art*, 1938, especially pp. 164 f. In fact, Collingwood's criticism is a beautiful example of an analysis of an emotional content of a third-world object in terms of a problem situation, its background, and its solution.

M

therefore history, can be explained as problem solving, and that my analysis in terms of the *schema of conjectures and refutations* $(P_1 \rightarrow TT \rightarrow EE \rightarrow P_2$, as explained in section 6 above) can be applied to it.

Before proceeding to this important point I will, however, first discuss in some detail an example of the process of understanding a third-world object: a simple arithmetical equation.

8. *A Very Trivial Example*

That 777 times 111 equals 86,247 is a very trivial arithmetical fact. It can be written as an equation. It may also be regarded as a very trivial theorem of the theory of natural numbers.

Do I *understand* this trivial proposition?

Yes and no. I certainly understand the assertion—especially when I see it in writing, as otherwise I may not be able to handle or retain a number as big as 86,247. (I have made the experiment, and I confused it with 86,427.) But in *some* sense I understand it of course at once when I hear it: 777 and 111 are easy to handle, and I understand that the proposition in question is offered as a *solution of the problem*: what numeral in the decadic system is equal to 777 times 111?

As to *solving* this problem, I know of course that there are many people who can find its solution quite easily in their heads; I myself may manage by trying very hard. But if I want to make sure of my result, or even to make sure that I shall not confuse it with a different result in the next minute, I have to make use of what Bridgman calls a 'paper and pencil operation'; I have to put the whole thing into an algorithm in which there are structural units that can be easily handled. (Of course, third-world structural units.) One of the points here is *error-elimination*: the established paper and pencil operations make it easy to detect and eliminate errors.

So far we have used three of the four objects which occur in my schema of problem solving (the schema $P_1 \rightarrow TT \rightarrow EE \rightarrow P_2$, introduced in section 6). In order to understand a proposition, a tentative theory, we asked first: What was the problem? And in order to eliminate error, we made a calculation with pencil and paper. Though we started from a proposition or tentative theory (TT), we proceeded from there to the underlying problem (to P_1); and later to a method of calculation designed to eliminate errors (*EE*). Does a second problem (*P₂*) come in also? It does: the method of error-elimination indeed leads to a problem shift: in our case a very trivial and degenerating problem shift—the replacement of one multiplication problem by three simpler ones and by an addition. The problem shift (from P_1 to P_2) is, of course, degenerating; obviously so, because we have no real theoretical interest here—we are only applying a routine whose point is to make the solution easier to work with and easier to check (that is, to eliminate errors).

Even in this extremely trivial example we can distinguish various degrees of understanding.

(1) The bare understading of what has been said, understanding in the sense in which we may also 'understand' the proposition '777 times 111 equals 68,427' without realizing that it is false.

(2) The understanding that it is a solution of a problem.

(3) The understanding of the problem.

(4) The understanding that the solution is true, which in our case is trivially easy.

(5) The checking of the truth by some method of error elimination, again trivial in our case.

There are, clearly, further degrees of understanding. Especially (3), the understanding of the problem, can be carried further. For some may, and others may not, understand that the problem is verbal in so far as '777 times 111', though not written in the decadic way of writing, is just as good a way, or better, of forming a synonym of the number '8 times 10,000, plus 6 times 1,000, plus 2 times 100, plus 4 times 10, plus 7'; and that '86,247' is only a shorthand method of writing the latter name. This kind of understanding exemplifies an attempt to understand the *background* that is normally taken for granted. Thus it *discovers a problem within that background.*

These degrees of understanding[17] cannot, of course, as a rule

---

[17] Dilthey stresses often, and rightly, that there are degrees of understanding. I am not quite sure, however, whether he always distinguishes between degrees of understanding (that is, of the depth or completeness of understanding) and the certainty ('*Sicherheit*') of understanding, which seems to me quite a different and an altogether mistaken idea. For Dilthey remarks: 'The highest degree of certainty is reached in the field of interpretation of [the objects of] the scientific mind.' (W. Dilthey, *Gesammelte Schriften*, vol. 7, p. 261.) This seems to me to contain

be put into a linear order; new possibilities of further and better understanding may branch off at almost every point, especially in less trivial cases.

Thus we can learn quite a lot from our very simple example. Perhaps the most important thing we can learn is the following. Whenever we try to interpret or to understand a theory or a proposition, even a trivial one like the equation here discussed, we are in fact raising *a problem of understanding*, and this always turns out to be *a problem about a problem*; that is to say, a *higher level problem*.

9. *A Case of Objective Historical Understanding*[18]

All this holds for all problems of understanding, and especially the problem of *historical understanding*. My thesis is that the main aim of all historical understanding is the hypothetical reconstruction of a historical *problem-situation*.

I will try to explain this thesis in some detail with the help of another example: with the help of a few historical considerations of Galileo's *theory of the tides*. This theory has turned out to be 'unsuccessful' (because it denies that the moon has any effect on the tides), and even in our own time Galileo has been severely and personally attacked for his dogmatism in sticking obstinately to such an obviously false theory.

In brief, Galileo's theory says that the tides are a result of accelerations which, in their turn, are a result of the complex movements of the Earth. When, more precisely, the regular rotating Earth is, in addition, moving round the sun, then the

a confusion. Or do I misunderstand this proposition? That *high certainty of understanding* can go with an extremely *low degree of understanding* may be seen when we reflect on the following formulation in R. Carnap, *Introduction to Semantics*, 1942, p. 22: '. . . to understand a sentence, to know what is asserted by it, is the same as to know under what conditions it would be true.' Indeed I know that the equation '777 times 111 = 86,427' would be true precisely under the condition that 777 times 111 does in fact equal 86,427. (In fact it does not.) I know this from Tarski's definition of truth; and I know of *every statement* that this kind of truth-condition holds for it. Thus I *must understand with certainty every statement*, if I understand the language; and this is, indeed, true for an extremely *low degree of understanding*, which is hardly the intended sense of either Dilthey's or Carnap's theory.

[18] *In the remaining notes to this paper I try to illustrate, in connection with problems of historical understanding, the superiority of the third-world method of critically reconstructing problem situations over the second-world method of intuitively re-living some personal experience (a method whose value, limited and subjective yet at the same time indispensably suggestive, I do not wish to reject entirely).*

velocity of any surface point located at the moment on the side opposite the sun will be greater than the velocity of the same point when, after 12 hours, it faces the sun. (For if a is the orbital velocity of the earth and b is the rotational velocity of a point on the equator, then $a+b$ is the velocity of

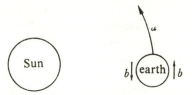

this point at midnight and $a-b$ its velocity at midday.) Thus the velocity changes, which means that there must arise periodical accelerations and retardations. But any periodical retardations and accelerations of a basin of water result, says Galileo, in appearances resembling those of the tides. (Galileo's theory is plausible but incorrect in this form: apart from the constant acceleration due to the rotation of the earth—that is, the centripetal acceleration—which also arises if a is zero, there does not arise any further acceleration and therefore especially no periodical acceleration.[19])

What can we do to improve our historical understanding of this theory which has so often been misinterpreted? My answer to this *problem of understanding* (which I will denote by 'P^u') proceeds along lines similar to those of my answer to the question of understanding discussed before in connection with our trivial arithmetical equation.

I claim that the first and all-important step is to ask ourselves: *what was the (third-world) problem* to which Galileo's theory was a tentative solution? And what was the situation—the logical *problem situation*—in which this problem arose?

---

[19] One might say that Galileo's kinematic theory of the tides contradicts the so-called Galilean relativity principle. But this criticism would be false, historically as well as theoretically, since this principle does *not* refer to *rotational* movements. Galileo's physical intuition—that the rotation of the earth has non-relativistic mechanical consequences—was right; and although these consequences (the movement of a spinning top, Foucault's pendulum, etc.) do not explain the tides, the Coriolis-force at least is not quite without influence upon them. Moreover we get (small) periodical kinematical accelerations as soon as we take into account the curvature of the earth's movement round the sun.

Galileo's problem was, quite simply, to explain the tides. Yet his problem situation was far less simple.

It is clear that Galileo was not even immediately interested in what I have just called his *problem*. It was another problem which led him to the problem of the tides: the problem of the truth or falsity of the Copernican theory—the problem whether the earth was moving or at rest. It was Galileo's hope that he would be able to use a successful theory of the tides as a decisive argument in favour of the Copernican theory.

What I call Galileo's *problem situation* turns out to be a complex affair. Admittedly, the problem situation entails the problem of the tides, but it does so in a specific role: the explanation of the tides is to serve as a touchstone of the Copernican theory. Yet even this remark does not suffice for an understanding of Galileo's problem situation. For Galileo's tentative theory was not merely trying to explain the changing tides: it tried to explain them against a certain *background* and, in addition, *within a certain given theoretical framework*. While the background was unproblematic for Galileo, what I propose to call 'Galileo's framework' was highly problematic, and Galileo was fully aware of this fact.

Thus it turns out that in order to solve our *problem of understanding* (P^u) we have to investigate a fairly complex third-world object. The object consists of the problem of the tides (of which Galileo's theory was a tentative solution) together with its setting—its background, and its framework: it is this complex object which I call the *problem situation*.

Galileo's *problem situation* may be characterized like this.

As a true cosmologist and theoretician Galileo had long been attracted by the incredible daring and simplicity of Copernicus's main idea, the idea that the earth and the other planets are moons of the sun. The explanatory power of this bold idea was very great; and when Galileo discovered the moons of Jupiter, recognizing in them a small model of the solar system, he saw in this an empirical corroboration of this bold conception, in spite of its highly speculative and almost *a priori* character. In addition to all this, he had been successful in testing a prediction derivable from Copernicus's theory: it predicted that the inner planets would show phases, like those of the moon; and Galileo had been able to observe the phases of Venus.

Copernicus's theory was, like Ptolemy's theory, essentially a geometrical cosmological model, constructed by geometrical (and kinematical) means. But Galileo was a physicist. He knew that the real problem was to find a mechanical (or perhaps trans-mechanical) physical explanation; and he actually discovered some of the elements of such an explanation, especially the laws of inertia and the corresponding conservation law for rotary motions.

Galileo boldly tried to base his physics on these two conservation laws only, although he was well aware of the fact that there must be great third-world gaps in his physical knowledge. From the point of view of method Galileo was perfectly right in attempting to explain everything on this very narrow basis; for only if we try to exploit and test our fallible theories to the limit can we hope to learn from their failure.

This explains why Galileo, in spite of his acquaintance with the work of Kepler, stuck to the hypothesis of the circular motion of the planets; and he was quite right in doing so in view of the fact that this circular motion could be explained by his basic conservation laws. It is often said that he tried to cover up the difficulties of the Copernican cycles, and that he oversimplified the Copernican theory in an unjustifiable manner; also that he ought to have accepted Kepler's laws. But all this shows a failure of historical understanding—an error in the analysis of the third-world problem situation. Galileo was quite right to work with bold over-simplifications; and Kepler's ellipses were just as bold over-simplifications as Galileo's circles. But Kepler was lucky in soon having his over-simplifications used, and thereby explained, by Newton, as a test of his solution of the two-body problem.

But why did Galileo reject the already well-known idea of an influence of the moon upon the tides? This question opens up a highly important aspect of the problem situation. First, Galileo rejected the lunar influence because he was an opponent of astrology which essentially identified the planets with the gods; in this sense he was a forerunner of the enlightenment, and also an opponent of Kepler's astrology, although he admired Kepler.[20] Secondly, he worked with a mechanical

[20] See *Conjectures and Refutations*, p. 188.

conservation principle for rotary motions, and this appeared to exclude interplanetary influences. Without Galileo's attempt to explain the tides on this very narrow basis, we might never have found that the basis was too narrow, and that a further idea was needed—Newton's idea of attraction (and with it, that of a force); ideas which almost had the character of astrological ideas, and which were felt to be occult by most enlightened men, such as Berkeley.[21] They were even felt to be occult by Newton himself.

Thus we are led by the analysis of Galileo's problem situation to justify the rationality of Galileo's method in several points in which he has been criticized by various historians; and thus we are led to a better *historical understanding* of Galileo. Psychological explanations which have been attempted, such as ambition, jealousy, or aggressiveness, or the wish to create a stir, become superfluous. They are here replaced by a third-world situational analysis. Similarly it becomes superfluous to criticize Galileo for 'dogmatism' because he stuck to the circular movement, or to introduce the idea of a mysterious psychological attraction in the 'mysterious circular movement'. (Dilthey calls it an archetypical idea or one that is psychologically attractive.[22]) For Galileo's method was correct when he tried to proceed as far as possible with the help of the rational conservation law for rotary motions. (There was not yet any dynamic theory.)

This result should illustrate how together with our understanding of his objective problem situation, our historical understanding of Galileo's role has grown. We may now denote this problem situation by 'P_1', since it plays a role analogous to that P_1 which we had before. And we can denote Galileo's

---

[21] See *Conjectures and Refutations*, p. 188 and chapter 6.

[22] Dilthey speaks of the 'mysterious circular movement' ('*die geheimnisvolle Kreisbewegung*': *Schriften*, vol. 1, pp. 95–6) of the ancient astronomy. This seems to me a misinterpretation, and a point against Dilthey's *degrees of certainty*, discussed in an earlier note. (Dilthey might have perhaps replied that, in this field science only starts with Newton; and that he was speaking of pre-scientific ideas. I do not think that it would be possible to accept this reply, and to deny that Galileo was a scientist: science begins with Anaximander, or even earlier.)

For a brief but thorough treatment of Ptolemy *vs.* Copernicus; see O. Neugebauer, *The Exact Sciences in Antiquity*, 1957, pp. 191 ff. (Owing to his failure to distinguish sharply between geometrical and physical problems, even Neugebauer condemns on p. 204 as dogmatic Copernicus's or Galileo's insistence on using circles.)

tentative theory by '*TT*', and his own and other people's attempts to discuss it critically, and to eliminate errors, we can denote by '*EE*'. Galileo, though hopeful, was far from satisfied with the result of his discussion. We may say that his P_2 was very close to his P_1; that is, the problem was still open.

Much later the matter led to a revolutionary change (due to Newton) in the *problem situation* (P_2): Newton extended Galileo's framework—the framework of the conservation laws within which Galileo's problem had been conceived. Part of Newton's revolutionary change was that he readmitted into the theory the moon, whose banishment from the theory of the tides had been a necessary consequence of Galileo's framework (*and* background).

To sum up the story briefly, Galileo's physical framework was a somewhat simplified form of Copernicus's model of the solar system. It was a system of cycles (and perhaps epicycles) with constant rotational velocity. Even Einstein commented on Galileo's 'attachment to the idea of circular motion' which he held 'responsible for the fact that he did not *fully* recognize the law of inertia and its fundamental significance'.[23] But he forgot that, just as Newton's theory was based upon the law of inertia, or the law of conservation of momentum, so the cycle-epicycle theory, in its simpler forms which adhered to constant velocities—it was the form preferred by Galileo—was based originally upon the law of the conservation of angular momentum. Both conservation laws are no doubt held

---

[23] The quoted words are from p. xi. of Einstein's admirable Foreword to Galileo's *Dialogue Concerning the Two Chief World Systems*, translated by Stillman Drake, revised edn., 1962. Einstein recognizes that Galileo did have the law of inertia; and there can be no doubt that Galileo did not *fully* (the italics are Einstein's) recognize its fundamental significance. I may mention here that Galileo has been much criticized for presenting Copernicus's system in an over-simplified form; and, indeed, he says in a spirit of criticism that 'Ptolemy introduces vast epicycles' (op. cit., pp. 341 f.) but does not say that Copernicus also used epicycles. Here is a problem of historical interpretation. I suggest that Galileo consciously left open the problem raised by the fact that the oversimplified Copernican system, based exclusively on constant velocity circular motion without epicycles, did not fit the observations precisely. He was greatly impressed by the fact that it fitted the observations comparatively very well; and he thought that the *purely geometrical problems* which were left open might be solved *only together with the physical problems*. (He hints that *not so 'vast'* epicycles, or vortices or magnetic forces might furnish possible solutions; cp. op. cit., pp. 398 ff.). This thought turned out to be correct; and we should not forget that even Kepler's geometrical solution was still only an approximation, that is, an over-simplification.

'instinctively', perhaps owing to something like the selection of conjectures under the pressure of practical experience: for the angular momentum law the experience with well-greased cart wheels may have been decisive. We should also remember that the ancient theory of the circular rotation of the heavens (which derives from this experience) was ultimately replaced by the earth's conservation of its angular momentum; an indication that the cycles were neither as naïve nor as mysterious as they are still often thought to be. Within this framework— as opposed to that of the astrologists—there could be no inter- action between the heavenly bodies. Thus the lunar theory of the tides, asserted by the astrologists, had to be rejected by Galileo.[24]

Can we learn anything new from this example? I think we can.

First, the example shows the immense importance of the reconstruction of Galileo's problem situation (P_1) for the understanding of Galileo's theory (TT). The importance of this reconstruction is even greater for the understanding of unsuccessful theories like Galileo's than for successful ones, for its fault (the fault of TT) may be explicable by a fault in the framework or in the background of P_1.

Secondly, in the present case it becomes obvious that the re- construction of Galileo's problem situation (P_1) has in its turn the character of a *conjecture* (and also of an over-simplification or idealization): this is obvious, considering that my analysis of this problem situation (P_1), brief as it is, deviates consider- ably from that of others who have tried to understand this unsuccessful theory of Galileo's. But if my reconstruction of P_1 is a conjecture, *what is the problem which this conjecture tries to solve?* Obviously it is P^u, the *problem of understanding* Galileo's theory.

My *third* point is this: *our problem of understanding, P^u, is on a higher level* than P_1. That is to say, the problem of under-

---

[24] The connection between Galileo's theory of the tides and his rejection of astrology is discussed and interpreted in my *Conjectures and Refutations*, note 4 to chapter 1 (p. 38), and note 4 to chapter 8 (p. 188). This is a typical conjectural interpretation (in the sense of my *Open Society and Its Enemies*, 1945, vol. i, chapter 10, p. 171), and as such can 'throw light upon the historical material': it has helped me *better to understand* the last passage in Galileo's *Dialogue* (op. cit., p. 462; for Galileo's attitude towards astrology see also pp. 109 f.) in which Galileo men- tions Kepler, reproving him for his astrological 'puerilities'.

standing is a *metaproblem*: it is about TT and thus also about P_1. Accordingly, the theory designed to solve the problem of understanding is a *metatheory*, since it is a theory part of whose task it is to discover, in every particular case, what P_1, TT, EE, and P_2 actually consisted of.

This, incidentally, should not be taken to imply that in every particular case *only* the structures of P_1, TT, etc., have to be discovered by the metatheory, while the schema itself $(P_1 \rightarrow TT \rightarrow EE \rightarrow P_2)$ has to be uncritically accepted. On the contrary, the schema, it should be stressed again, is an over-simplification, and should be elaborated or even radically changed whenever the need arises.

My *fourth* point is that every attempt (except the most trivial) to understand a theory is bound to open up a historical investigation about this theory and its problem, which thus become part of the *object* of the investigation. If the theory was a scientific one, the investigation will be one into the history of science. If the theory was, say, a historical one, the investigation will be one into the history of historiography. The problems which these historical investigations try to solve will be meta-problems, to be sharply distinguished from the problems which are the objects under investigation.

My *fifth* point is that the history of science should be treated *not* as a history of theories, but as a history of problem situations and their modifications (sometimes imperceptible, sometimes revolutionary) through the intervention of attempts to solve the problems. Historically, unsuccessful attempts may thus turn out to have been just as important for the further development as successful ones.

My *sixth* point (which merely elaborates the third) is that we have to distinguish clearly between the metaproblems and metatheories of the historian of science (which are on the P^u level) and the problems and theories of the scientists (which are on the P_I level). It is only too easy to mix these two up, for if we formulate the historian's problem by asking: 'What was Galileo's problem?', the answer seems to be 'P_1'; but P_1 (as opposed to 'Galileo's problem was P_1') seems to belong to the object level rather than the meta level;[25] and so the two levels get confused.

[25] Actually, the answer is a historical conjecture *about* Galileo's problem

But there are, in general, no problems common to the different levels.
This is easily seen: two tentative metatheories of the same object
are often very different. Two historians of science who agree
on 'the facts' may understand or interpret them in very different ways (sometimes in complementary ways, sometimes
even in conflicting ways). They may even disagree on what
constitutes their problems. Thus in general they will not share
problems with each other, and even less with the theory which
is the object of their investigation and interpretation.

Also, in order to interpret a theory, the metatheorist is free
to use anything that may be helpful; for example, he may contrast the theory with some radically different competing theories.
*Thus some of the third-world structural units that constitute the meta-
theory may be utterly dissimilar from those that constitute the theory to
be interpreted or understood.*

The point is important. It establishes *a fortiori* that even if
we could speak at all sensibly (which I am inclined to deny)
of such a thing as a *similarity* between third-world *thought-
contents* on the one hand and, on the other, those second-world
thought-processes through which we grasp these contents, even
then I should still deny that there actually is, in general, any
similarity, on any level of problems, between the contents and
the corresponding thought-processes. For the third-world
method of historical understanding which I am trying to
describe is a method which, wherever possible, replaces
psychological explanations by the analysis of *third-world relations*:
in place of psychological explanatory principles we make use of
third-world considerations mainly of a logical character; and
my thesis is that from such analyses our historical understanding
can grow.

My *seventh* and perhaps most important point concerns what
I have sometimes described as *situational logic* or *situational
analysis.*[26] (The latter name may be preferable because the
former may be felt to suggest a deterministic theory of human
action; it is of course far from my intention to suggest anything
like this.)

(P_1). The historian's metaproblems and his conjectural answers will be discussed
more fully later.

[26] I have described the method of *situational logic* or *situational analysis* in my
Open Society, vol. ii, chapter 14, especially p. 97, and in my *Poverty of Historicism*,
1957, sections 31 ('Situational Logic in History': see especially p. 149) and 32.

By a situational analysis I mean a certain kind of tentative or conjectural explanation of some human action which appeals to the situation in which the agent finds himself. It may be a historical explanation: we may perhaps wish to explain how and why a certain structure of ideas was created. Admittedly, no creative action can ever be fully explained. Nevertheless, we can try, conjecturally, to give an idealized reconstruction of the *problem situation* in which the agent found himself, and to that extent make the action 'understandable' (or 'rationally understandable'), that is to say, *adequate to his situation as he saw it*. This method of situational analysis may be described as an application of the *rationality principle*.

It would be a task for situational analysis to distinguish between the situation as the agent saw it, and the situation as it was (both, of course, conjectured).[27] Thus the historian of science not only tries to explain by situational analysis the theory proposed by a scientist as adequate, but he may even try to explain the scientist's failure.

In other words, our schema of problem-solving by conjecture and refutation or a similar schema may be used as an explanatory theory of human actions, since we can interpret an action as an attempt to solve a problem. Thus the explanatory theory of action will, in the main, consist of a conjectural reconstruction of the problem and its background. A theory of this kind may well be testable.

I have tried to answer the question: '*How can we understand a scientific theory, or improve our understanding of it?*' And I have

[27] There are many cases in which we can reconstruct, *objectively* (even though conjecturally), (a) the *situation as it was* and (b) a very different *situation as it appeared to the agent*, or as it was *understood, or interpreted*, by the agent. It is interesting that this can be done *even in the history of science*. An example is Schrödinger's wave mechanics. Schrödinger did not interpret his problem as a statistical one (that it was statistical became clear only after Born's famous '*statistical interpretation*'; see my 'Quantum Mechanics Without "The Observer"', in Mario Bunge (ed.), *Quantum Theory and Reality*, 1967; now chapter three in my *Philosophy and Physics*). But there are many other examples, old and new. Kepler understood his problem as the discovery of a Pythagorean *harmony of the world*. Einstein formulated the problem of general relativity with the help of a demand for *covariance*; and although he accepted the criticism due to E. Kretschmann (*Ann. Physik*, 35, p. 575, 1917) who said that this demand was empty, Einstein clearly believed that it could be restated so as to serve its intended purpose, though he never gave a satisfactory restatement. An example from philosophy (connected with Kant's problem 'How is pure natural science possible?') is analysed in *Conjectures and Refutations*, chapter 2, section x, especially pp. 94–6.

suggested that my answer, in terms of problems and problem situations, can be applied far beyond scientific theory. We may, at least in some cases, apply it even to works of art: we may conjecture what the artist's problem was, and we may be able to support this conjecture by independent evidence; and this analysis may help us to understand the work.[28]

(A somewhat intermediate position between the task of interpreting a scientific theory and interpreting a work of art may perhaps be taken up by the task of reconstructing a damaged work of art—say, reconstructing a poem found in the form of a damaged papyrus.)

10. *The Value of Problems*

It may be objected to my suggested solution of the problem 'How can we understand a scientific *theory*, or improve our understanding of it?' that it merely shifts the question; for it merely replaces it by the related question: 'How can we understand a scientific *problem*, or improve our understanding of it?'

The objection is valid. But as a rule, the problem shift will be a progressive one (to use Professor Lakatos's terminology).

---

[28] Several such analyses can be found in the works of E. H. Gombrich. His *Art and Illusion*, 1959, is partly (though not wholly) a study of the impact on Western Art of the problems raised by the aim, accepted in the past by many artists, of creating an illusion of reality (for example, by using perspective). In his *Norm and Form*, 1966, p. 7, he quotes Ghiberti's own description of his aims: 'I strove . . . to imitate nature as far as I could with all the lines that result in it . . . They [the panels] are all frames so that the eye measures them and so true that standing at a distance they appear in the round.' Gombrich comments that the 'artist works like a scientist. His works exist not only for their own sake but also to demonstrate certain problem-solutions.' Of course, this is part of the analysis of the work of one artist; and even though similar comments may be made on some other artists, it is not suggested that their problems are similar. On the contrary, the problems change: solutions of the old problems—for example, of the problem of creating an illusion of reality or 'nature'—may create the rejection of the old problem, and the search for new ones.

An example of these new problems is how to interest the beholder, and to engage his active co-operation; for example, by posing for him problems of interpretation, or reconstruction. Cp. E. H. Gombrich, *Meditations on a Hobby Horse*, 1963.

I may mention here that Gombrich's analyses shed light on the problem of what may be called *the autonomy of the work of art*: the fact that, though man-made, it creates its own interrelations. (See also my *Of Clouds and Clocks*, section 24 and note 65.) There is a beautiful story about Haydn who, when listening to the first chorus of his *Creation*, broke into tears and said 'I have not written this'.

As a rule, the second question—the metaproblem of understanding a problem—will be more difficult and more interesting than the first. At any rate, I think that it is the more fundamental of the two questions, because I think that science starts from problems (rather than from observations, or even from theories, though admittedly the 'background' of the problem will contain theories and myths).

However that may be, I suggest that this second metaproblem is different from the first. Of course, we can and should always deal with it as we dealt with the first—by way of an idealizing historical reconstruction. But I suggest that this is insufficient.

My thesis is that, in order to gain a *real understanding* of any given problem (say, Galileo's problem situation) more is needed than an analysis of this problem or of any problem for which some good solution is known to us: in order to understand any such 'dead' problem we must at least once in our life, have seriously wrestled with some live problem.

Thus my answer to the metaproblem 'How can we learn to understand a scientific problem?' is: by learning to understand some *live* problem. And this, I assert, can be done only *by trying to solve it, and by failing to solve it.*

Assume a young scientist meets a problem which he does not understand. What can he do? I suggest that even though he does not understand it, he can try to solve it and *criticize his solution himself* (or get it criticized by others). Since he does not understand the problem, his solution will be a failure; a fact which will be brought out by criticism. In this way a first step will be made towards pinpointing *where the difficulty lies*. And this means, precisely, that a first step will be made towards understanding the problem. For a problem is a difficulty, and understanding a problem consists in finding out that there is a difficulty, and where the difficulty lies. And this can only be done by finding out why certain *prima facie solutions do not work.*

So we learn to understand a problem by trying to solve it, and by failing. And when we have failed a hundred times, we may even become experts with respect to this particular problem. That is, if anybody proposes a solution, we may see at once whether there is any prospect of success for this proposal, or whether the proposal will fail because of those difficulties which we know only too well from our own past failures.

Thus, learning to understand a problem is a matter of handling third-world structural units; and to get an intuitive grasp of the problem is to get familiar with these units and their logical interrelations. (All this, of course, is similar to getting an intuitive grasp of a theory.)

I suggest that only someone who has thus wrestled with a live problem can reach a good understanding of a problem like that of Galileo; for only he can gauge his own understanding. And only he will fully understand (on the third level, as it were) the significance of my contention that the vital first step towards understanding a theory is to understand the problem situation in which it arises.

I also suggest that the much discussed problem of the transference of learning from one discipline to another is closely connected with gaining experience in wrestling with live problems. Those who have learned only how to apply some given theoretical framework to the solving of problems which arise within this framework, and which are soluble within it,[29] cannot expect that their training will help them much in another specialism. It is different with those who have themselves wrestled with problems, especially if their understanding, clarification, and formulation, proved difficult.[30]

Thus I think that those who have wrestled with a problem may be compensated by gaining an understanding of fields far removed from their own.

It may be interesting and fruitful to investigate how far we can apply situational analysis (the idea of problem solving) to art, music, and poetry, and whether it can help our understanding in these fields. That it can help in some cases I do not doubt. Beethoven's notebooks for the last movement of the Ninth Symphony show that the introduction to this movement tells the story of his attempts to solve a problem—the problem of breaking into words. To see this helps our understanding of

----

[29] The scientists I am here describing are the practitioners of what is called 'normal science' by Thomas Kuhn, *The Structure of Scientific Revolutions*, 1962. (Second edition 1971.)

[30] In the first two or three pages of chapter 2 of my *Conjectures and Refutations* I have tried to argue that *there are no subject matters but only problems* which, admittedly, may lead to the rise of theories but *which almost always need for their solution the help of widely different theories*. (This shows the self-defeating character of specialization.)

the music and the musician. Whether this understanding helps our enjoyment of the music is a different question.

11. *Understanding* ('*Hermeneutics*') *in the Humanities*

This brings me to the problem of understanding in the humanities (*Geisteswissenschaften*).

Almost all the great students of this problem—I will mention only Dilthey and Collingwood—hold that the humanities differ radically from the natural sciences, and that the most outstanding difference lies in this: that the central task of the humanities is to *understand*, in a sense in which we can understand men, but not nature.

Understanding is said to be based upon our common humanity. It is in its fundamental form a kind of intuitive identification with other men, in which we are helped by expressive motions, such as gestures and speech. It is, further, an understanding of human actions. And it is, ultimately, an understanding of the products of the human mind.

It must be admitted that, in the sense here indicated, we can understand men and their actions and products while we cannot understand 'nature'—solar systems, molecules, or elementary particles. Yet there is no sharp division here. We can learn to understand the expressive movements of higher animals in a sense very similar to that in which we understand men. But what is a 'higher' animal? And is our understanding limited to them? (H. S. Jennings learned to understand unicellular organisms well enough to attribute aims and intentions to them.[31]) On the other end of the scale our intuitive understanding even of our friends is far from perfect.

I am quite prepared to accept the thesis that understanding is the aim of the humanities. But I doubt whether we should deny that it is the aim of the natural sciences also. Of course, it will be 'understanding' in a slightly different sense. But there are already many differences in the understanding of men and their actions. And we must not forget a statement like the following made by Einstein in a letter to Born:

'You believe in the dice-playing God, and I in the perfect

---

[31] Cp. H. S. Jennings, *The Behaviour of the Lower Organisms*, 1906.

rule of law within a world of some objective reality which I
try to catch in a wildly speculative way.'[32]

I am sure that Einstein's wildly speculative attempts to
'catch' reality are attempts to *understand* it, in a sense of the
word 'understand' in which it has at least *four* similarities with
understanding in the humanities. (1) As we understand other
people owing to our shared humanity, we may understand
nature because we are part of it. (2) As we understand men
in virtue of some rationality of their thoughts and actions, so
we may understand the laws of nature because of some kind
of rationality or understandable necessity[33] inherent in them.
This has been a conscious hope of almost all great scientists
at least since Anaximander, not to mention Hesiod and Herodotus;[34] and this hope has reached at least some temporary
fulfilment first in Newton's and then in Einstein's theory of
gravity. (3) The reference to God in Einstein's letter indicates
another sense shared with the humanities—the attempt to
understand the world of nature in the way we understand a
work of art: as a creation. And (4) there is in the natural
sciences that consciousness of an ultimate failure of all our
attempts to understand which has been much discussed by
students of the humanities and which has been attributed to
the 'otherness' of other people, the impossibility of any real
self-understanding, and the inevitability of over-simplification
which is inherent in any attempt to understand anything
unique and real. (We can now add that it seems to matter little
whether this reality is cosmic or microcosmic.)

[32] Einstein's letter is quoted (in the original German and in an English translation) in Max Born, *Natural Philosophy of Cause and Chance*, 1949, p. 122.

[33] I may mention such demands of rationality as principles of symmetry (which
have been stressed especially by Hermann Weyl and E. P. Wigner), and ideas like
what I should call 'Einstein's principle of action and reaction' (it might also be
called his 'reality principle'): that Newton's space and time are unsatisfactory
because they can exert a physical effect on bodies but are not in their turn subject
to any kind of countereffect (while a field is).

[34] The idea of cosmic symmetry may be found in Hesiod's *Theogony*, 720–5;
in Anaximander's theory of the shape and position of the earth; and in Herodotus's
attempt to introduce some symmetry into a geography which he knew was grossly
unsymmetric (the rivers Nile and Danube, of all things, were as far as possible
made symmetrical to each other). Cp. the previous note. In addition, all attempts
to introduce a measure of justice, or reward and punishment, into the universe
(Anaximander, Herodotus) are attempts to find some rationality in it and so to
understand it.

Thus I oppose the attempt to proclaim the method of understanding as the characteristic of the humanities, the mark by which we may distinguish them from the natural sciences. And when its supporters denounce a view like mine as 'positivistic' or 'scientistic',[35] then I may perhaps answer that they themselves seem to accept, *implicitly and uncritically*, that positivism or scientism is *the only philosophy appropriate to the natural sciences*.

This is understandable, considering that so many natural scientists have accepted this scientistic philosophy. Yet students of the humanities might have known better. Science, after all, is a branch of literature; and working on science is a human activity like building a cathedral. No doubt there is too much specialization and too much professionalism in contemporary science, which makes it inhuman; but this unfortunately is true of contemporary history or psychology also, almost as much as of the natural sciences.

Moreover, there is an important field of history—perhaps the most important one—the history of human opinion, of human knowledge, which comprises the history of religion, of philosophy, and of science. Now there are two things about the history of science. One is that only a man who understands science (that is, scientific problems) can understand its history; and the other is that only a man who has some real understanding of its history (the history of its problem situations) can understand science.

Labouring the difference between science and the humanities has long been a fashion, and has become a bore. The method of problem solving, the method of conjecture and refutation, is practised by both. It is practised in reconstructing a damaged text as well as in constructing a theory of radioactivity.[36]

---

[35] The term 'scientism' meant originally 'the slavish imitation of the method and language of [natural] science', especially by social scientists; it was introduced in this sense by Hayek in his 'Scientism and the Study of Society', now in his *The Counter-Revolution of Science*, 1962. In *The Poverty of Historicism*, p. 105, I suggested its use as a name for the aping of what is widely *mistaken* for the method of science; and Hayek now agrees (in his Preface to his *Studies in Philosophy, Politics, and Economics*, which contains a very generous acknowledgement) that the methods actually practised by natural scientists are different from 'what most of them told us . . . and urged the representatives of other disciplines to imitate'.

[36] Of course there are differences everywhere. But there are few things as similar to certain procedures in theoretical physics as the conjectural reconstruction

But I should go even further and accuse at least some professional historians of 'scientism': of trying to copy the method of natural science, *not as it actually is*, but as it is wrongly alleged to be. This alleged but non-existent method is that of collecting observations and then 'drawing conclusions' from them. It is slavishly aped by some historians who believe that they can collect documentary evidence which, corresponding to the observations of natural science, forms the 'empirical basis' for their conclusions.

This alleged method is one that can never be put into effect: you can neither collect observations nor documentary evidence if you do not first have a problem. (A ticket collector collects documents, but he rarely collects historical evidence.)

Worse even than the attempt to apply an inapplicable method is the worship of the idol of certain or infallible or authoritative knowledge which these historians mistake for the ideal of science.[37] Admittedly, we all try hard to avoid error; and we ought to be sad if we have made a mistake. Yet to avoid error is a poor ideal: if we do not dare to tackle problems which are so difficult that error is almost unavoidable, then there will be no growth of knowledge. In fact, it is from our boldest theories, *including those which are erroneous*, that we learn most. Nobody is exempt from making mistakes; the great thing is to learn from them.[38]

12. *Comparison with Collingwood's Method of Subjective Re-Enactment*

In order to illustrate the application of situational analysis to history, and in order to contrast it with the second-world

of a damaged text. A conjecture of this kind is even testable, and some have been refuted. (See for example *Berlin Papyri*, No. 9777, later combined by J. U. Powell with the older *Oxyrhynchus Papyri*, xvii, 2075, fr. i, which made it possible to refute certain conjectural reconstructions.) These, however, are somewhat rare cases; as a rule, 'the tests of . . . [most] historical interpretations' (such as can be found in J. W. N. Watkins, *Hobbes System of Ideas*, 1965; or on pp. 248 to 253 and 319 of vol. i and in other places of my *Open Society*) 'can never be as rigorous as those of a . . . [physical] hypothesis', as I said, op. cit., p. 171; I should have excepted the most interesting kind of all hypotheses—the cosmological ones. Some of these can of course be tested, and some have been even sufficiently precise for refutation. But others, and very interesting ones, seem to be untestable, and may remain so. (On testability see my *Logic of Scientific Discovery*, 1959; first edn., published as *Logik der Forschung*, 1934.)

37 Cp. my *Logic of Scientific Discovery*, section 85.
38 This is the main topic of my *Conjectures and Refutations*; see its Preface.

method of subjective understanding, I will first quote a passage from R. G. Collingwood, the philosopher, historian, and student of historiography.

I shall quote this passage from Collingwood because I can go with him quite a long way, though not all the way. We part company over the issue of the second and third worlds: the issue of choosing a subjective or an objective method. (We agree on the significance of problem situations.) Collingwood's psychological way of putting things is by no means merely a matter of formulation. Rather, it is an essential part of his theory of understanding (as it is of Dilthey's, although Dilthey tried to get rid of subjectivity since he was afraid of arbitrariness).[39]

As the passage from Collingwood illustrates, his thesis is that the historian's understanding of history consists in his re-enactment of past experiences:

Suppose . . . he [the historian] is reading the Theodosian Code, and has before him a certain edict of an emperor. Merely reading the words and being able to translate them does not amount to knowing their historical significance. In order to do that he must envisage the *situation* with which the emperor was trying to deal, and he must envisage it as that emperor envisaged it. Then he must see for himself, just as if the emperor's *situation* were his own, how such a *situation* might be dealt with; he must see the possible alternatives, and the reasons for choosing one rather than another; and thus he must go through the process which the emperor went through in deciding on this particular course. Thus he is re-enacting in his own mind the experience of the emperor; and only in so far as he does this has he any historical knowledge, as distinct from merely philological knowledge, of the meaning of the edict.[40]

[39] This was one of Dilthey's main problems; he spoke, especially of the need to transcend subjectivistic and sceptical tendencies in historiography. In this context, the famous problem may be mentioned which Dilthey and others called 'the hermeneutic circle': the problem that the whole (of a text, of a book, of a philosopher's work, of a period) can be understood only if we understand the constituent parts, while these parts in their turn can be understood only if we understand the whole. It does not seem generally known that this was very well formulated by Bacon, *De Augmentis*, VI. x. vi: 'Out of all the words we have to extract the sense in whose light each single word is to be interpreted.' ('Interpreted' means here simply 'read'; see my final note.) The idea is also to be found in an ironically laboured form in Galileo's *Dialogue* (op. cit., p. 108) where Simplicio is made to say that in order to understand Aristotle one must have 'every saying of his always before the mind'.

[40] Cp. R. G. Collingwood, *The Idea of History*, 1946, p. 283. (The italics are mine.)

You will see that Collingwood lays great stress upon the *situation* closely corresponding to what I call the *problem situation*. But there is a difference. Collingwood makes it clear that the essential thing in understanding history is not the analysis of the situation itself, but the historian's mental process of re-enactment, the sympathetic repetition of the original experience. For Collingwood, the analysis of the situation serves merely as a help—an indispensable help—for this re-enactment. My view is diametrically opposed. I regard the psychological process of re-enactment as inessential, though I admit that it may sometimes serve as a help for the historian, a kind of intuitive check of the success of his situational analysis. *What I regard as essential is not the re-enactment but the situational analysis.* The historian's analysis of the situation is his historical conjecture which in this case is a metatheory about the emperor's reasoning. Being on a level different from the emperor's reasoning, it does not re-enact it, but tries to produce an idealized and reasoned reconstruction of it, omitting inessential elements and perhaps augmenting it. Thus the historian's central metaproblem is: what were the decisive elements in the emperor's problem situation? To the extent to which the historian succeeds in solving this metaproblem, he *understands* the historical situation.

Thus what he has to do *qua* historian is not to re-enact past experiences, but to marshal objective arguments for and against his conjectural situational analysis.

This method may be very successful even in those cases in which any attempt at re-enactment necessarily fails. For there may be acts which are in many ways beyond the historian's capacity for action and therefore for re-enactment. The act which is to be re-enacted may be one of unbearable cruelty. Or it may be an act of supreme heroism, or of despicable cowardice. Or it may be an artistic or literary or scientific or philosophical achievement of an excellence which far exceeds the historian's abilities. Admittedly, if his abilities in the field he tries to analyse are insufficient, his analysis will be uninteresting. But we cannot (as Collingwood does) expect the historian to combine the gifts of Caesar, Cicero, Catullus, and Theodosius. No historian of art can be a Rembrandt, and few will even be able to copy a great masterpiece.

While in the most interesting cases a re-enactment will be impracticable for the historian, in other cases it may be perfectly possible yet completely superfluous. I am thinking of those countless trivial cases in which, once the situation has been analysed, it becomes obvious that the action of the agent was adequate to the situation, in a trivial and ordinary way.

The historian's task is, therefore, so to reconstruct the problem situation as it appeared to the agent, that the actions of the agent become *adequate* to the situation. This is very similar to Collingwood's method, but it eliminates from the theory of understanding and from the historical method precisely the subjective or second-world element which for Collingwood and most other theorists of understanding (hermeneuticists) is its salient point.

Our conjectural reconstruction of the situation may be a real historical discovery. It may explain an aspect of history so far unexplained; and it may be corroborated by new evidence, for example by the fact that it may improve our understanding of some document, perhaps by drawing our attention to some previously overlooked or unexplained allusions.[41]

[41] Besides Galileo's theory of the tides and his relations to Kepler, discussed above, there is another example of an interpretation which may perhaps be mentioned here. On pp. 13 to 15 of *Conjectures and Refutations* I discuss Bacon's '*interpretatio naturae*', pointing out that it means 'the reading, or spelling out, of the book of nature', and that the term '*interpretatio*' has a legal sense, different from our modern sense: it means in Bacon 'reading' or 'expounding' the law (to the layman) *exactly as it stands*. (This interpretation of mine is fully born out by *De Augmentis*, loc. cit., and throws much light on this *whole* passage from *De Augmentis*—not only on the isolated part quoted in the note before the last.) At the same place of my *Conjectures* I also explain Bacon's idea of the purity of the intellect, and of purifying the intellect: it means purging the intellect of prejudices; that is, of theories (of *anticipationes mentis*).

Now it so happens that Dilthey (*Schriften*, vol. v, p. 318) misinterprets Bacon's '*interpretatio naturae*' which he wrongly describes as a metaphor (since he interprets it in that modern sense of 'interpretation' whose meaning is almost the same as Bacon's '*anticipatio mentis*'). Similarly Ranke (*Sämtliche Werke*, vol. 49, p. 175) misinterprets Bacon's idea of purity: assuming my conjectural interpretation and considering the context it becomes clear that in the Baconian passage discussed by Ranke, Bacon (who writes in Latin) uses '*caste*' for 'modestly' (in the intellectual sense of not rushing into anticipations or oracular pronouncements, as the context shows). Ranke, however, mistranslates '*caste*' by 'chaste' ('*keusch*'). Besides, Ranke's 'chaste and industriously' ('*keusch und fleissig*') instead of 'modestly and constantly' is not a proper translation of Bacon's '*caste et perpetuo*' (a free translation would be 'modestly and devotedly'). And there is in Ranke also a misattribution of this mistranslation which I find quite inexplicable. Ranke ascribes the passage to 'the Foreword to the *Organum*, certainly one of the most beautiful *prefaces* ever

To sum up, I have tried to show that the idea of the third world is of interest for a theory of understanding which aims at combining an intuitive understanding of reality with the objectivity of rational criticism.

written'. But what are the facts? There exists a *Praefatio* to the *Novum Organum*, but the passage quoted by Ranke is not to be found in it: it comes, rather, from the *Praefatio* of the *Instauratio Magna*, published together with the *Organum*, but separated from its *Praefatio* by more than a dozen pages (by the *Distributio Operis*, and by a short explanation which states that the first part of the *Instauratio* is missing).

The passage may be translated as follows. (My text is p. 130, '*Nos vero . . .*' of vol. 1 of *The Works of Francis Bacon*, edited by J. Spedding, R. L. Ellis, and D. D. Heath, 1889.) 'I however, dwelling modestly and constantly among the things [themselves], I never move with my intellect further away from the things than is needed in order to allow their images and their rays to focus, as they may, in the sense [of sight]'. (Bacon concludes his sentence, after a semicolon: 'so that not much is left to do for the powers of inventing and excelling'.)

Ranke's translation and comments are: ' "Lasst uns", sagt Bacon in der Vorrede zu dem Organon—gewiss einem der schönsten Prooemien, die je geschrieben worden sind—"lasst uns keusch und fleissig unter den Dingen verweilen und unsere Fassungskraft nur eben so weit über sie erheben, um ihre Bilder und Strahlen in uns aufnehmen zu können."

'Er sagte dies von der Betrachtung der *Natur*. Die Erforschung der *Geschichte* hat es freilich noch schwerer.' (And so forth: Ranke is concerned with the special difficulties of historiography—of the interpretation of *history* as opposed to the interpretation of *nature*.)

As one can see from Ranke's mistranslation of Bacon's simple Latin text, the interpretation (*hermeneutics*) of texts which, after all, is part of historiography, is indeed almost as risky as the interpretation of nature. It is a matter in which we must work with conjectures *and* refutations: that is, we must try to refute our conjectures until they fit fully into the context of the problem situation, lose arbitrary features, and achieve something like a maximum of explanatory power of what the author wanted to say.

For other examples of the conjectural method of interpretation, see especially the notes to the first volume of my *Open Society*, and the Addenda 6 to 9 of my *Conjectures and Refutations*, third edn., 1969, and fourth edn., 1972.

5. The Aim of Science

To speak of 'the aim' of scientific activity may perhaps sound a little naïve; for clearly, different scientists have different aims, and science itself (whatever that may mean) has no aims. I admit all this. And yet it seems that when we speak of science we do feel, more or less clearly, that there is something characteristic of scientific activity; and since scientific activity looks pretty much like a rational activity, and since a rational activity must have some aim, the attempt to describe the aim of science may not be entirely futile.

I suggest that it is the aim of science to find *satisfactory explanations*, of whatever strikes us as being in need of explanation. By an *explanation* (or a causal explanation) is meant a set of statements by which one describes the state of affairs to be explained (the *explicandum*) while the others, the explanatory statements, form the 'explanation' in the narrower sense of the word (the *explicans* of the *explicandum*).

We may take it, as a rule, that the *explicandum* is more or less well known to be true, or assumed to be so known. For there is little point in asking for an explanation of a state of affairs which may turn out to be entirely imaginary. (Flying saucers may represent such a case: the explanation needed may not be of flying saucers, but of reports of flying saucers; yet should flying saucers exist, then no further explanation of the *reports* would be required.) The *explicans*, on the other hand, which is the object of our search, will as a rule not be known: it will have to be discovered. Thus, scientific explanation, whenever it is a discovery, will be *the explanation of the known by the unknown*.[1]

---

[1] See the last paragraph of the text, before the final quotation, of my 'Note on

This paper is a revised version of a paper which was first published in *Ratio*, vol. i, no. 1, Dec. 1957, pp. 24–35. A brief discussion of the correction of Galileo's and Kepler's results by Newton's theory was first published in my contribution to Simon Moser (ed.), *Gesetz und Wirklichkeit*, 1949 (see especially pp. 57 f.), reprinted in Hans Albert, *Theorie und Realität*, 1964 (see especially p. 100). An English translation of this paper will be found in the Appendix to the present volume.

The *explicans*, in order to be satisfactory (satisfactoriness may be a matter of degree), must fulfil a number of conditions. First, it must logically entail the *explicandum*. Secondly, the *explicans* ought to be true, although it will not, in general, be known to be true; in any case, it must not be known to be false even after the most critical examination. If it is not known to be true (as will usually be the case) there must be *independent* evidence in its favour. In other words, it must be *independently* testable; and we shall regard it as more satisfactory the greater the severity of the independent tests it has survived.

So I have still to elucidate my use of the expression 'independent', with its opposites, '*ad hoc*', and (in extreme cases) 'circular'.

Let *a* be an *explicandum*, known to be true. Since *a* trivially follows from *a* itself, we could always offer *a* as an explanation of itself. But this would be highly unsatisfactory, even though we should know in this case that the *explicans* is true, and that the *explicandum* follows from it. *Thus we must exclude explanations of this kind because of their circularity.*

Yet the kind of circularity I have here in mind is a matter of degree. Consider the following dialogue: 'Why is the sea so rough today?'—'Because Neptune is very angry'—'By what evidence can you support your statement that Neptune is very angry?'—'Oh, don't you *see* how *very* rough the sea is? And is it not always rough when Neptune is angry?' This explanation is found unsatisfactory because (just as in the case of the fully circular explanation) the only evidence for the *explicans* is the *explicandum* itself.[2] The feeling that this kind of almost circular or *ad hoc* explanation is highly unsatisfactory, and the corresponding requirement that explanations of this kind should be avoided are, I believe, among the main motive forces of the development of science: dissatisfaction is among the first fruits of the critical or rational approach.

In order that the *explicans* should not be *ad hoc*, it must be rich in content: it must have a variety of testable consequences, and among them, especially, testable consequences which are different from the *explicandum*. It is these different testable conse-

Berkeley as a Precursor of Mach', *Brit. Journ. Philos. Sc.* **4**, 1953, p. 35. (Now in my *Conjectures and Refutations*, p. 174.)

[2] This kind of reasoning survives in Thales (Diels-Kranz[10], vol. i, p. 456, line 35); Anaximander (D.-K. A11, A28); Anaximenes (D.-K. A17, B1); Alcmaeon (D.-K. A5).

quences which I have in mind when I speak of *independent* tests, or of *independent* evidence.

Although these remarks may perhaps help to elucidate somewhat the intuitive idea of an independently testable *explicans*, they are still quite insufficient to characterize a satisfactory and independently testable explanation. For if *a* is our *explicandum*—let *a* be again 'The sea is rough today'—then we can always offer a highly unsatisfactory *explicans* which is completely *ad hoc* even though it has independently testable consequences. We can still choose these consequences as we like. We may choose, say, 'These plums are juicy' and 'All ravens are black'. Let *b* be their conjunction. Then we can take as *explicans* simply the conjunction of *a* and *b*: it will satisfy all our requirements so far stated.

Only if we require that explanations shall make use of universal statements or laws of nature (supplemented by initial conditions) can we make progress towards realizing the idea of independent, or non-*ad hoc*, explanations. For universal laws of nature *may* be statements with a rich content, so that *they may be independently tested* everywhere, and at all times. Thus if they are used as explanations, they *may* not be *ad hoc* because they *may* allow us to interpret the *explicandum* as an instance of a reproducible effect. All this is only true, however, if we confine ourselves to universal laws which are testable, that is to say, falsifiable.

The question 'What kind of explanation may be satisfactory?' thus leads to the reply: an explanation in terms of testable and falsifiable universal laws and initial conditions. And an explanation of this kind will be the more satisfactory the more highly testable these laws are and the better they have been tested. (This applies also to the initial conditions.)

In this way, the conjecture that it is the aim of science to find satisfactory explanations leads us further to the idea of improving the degree of satisfactoriness of the explanations by improving their degree of testability, that is to say, by proceeding to better testable theories; which means proceeding to theories of ever richer content, of a higher degree of universality, and of higher degree of precision.[3] This, no doubt, is fully in keeping with the actual practice of the theoretical sciences.

[3] For the theory of *testability, content,* and *simplicity,* and of degrees of *universality* and *precision,* see sections 31 to 46 of my *Logic of Scientific Discovery,* 1959 (first

We may arrive at fundamentally the same result also in another way. If it is the aim of science to explain, then it will also be its aim to explain what so far has been accepted as an *explicans*; for example, a law of nature. Thus the task of science constantly renews itself. We may go on for ever, proceeding to explanations of a higher and higher level of universality—unless, indeed, we were to arrive at an *ultimate explanation*; that is to say, at an explanation which is neither capable of any further explanation, nor in need of it.

But are there ultimate explanations? The doctrine which I have called 'essentialism' amounts to the view that science must seek ultimate explanations in terms of essences:[4] if we can explain the behaviour of a thing in terms of its essence—of its essential properties—then no further question can be raised, and none need be raised (except perhaps the theological question of the Creator of the essences). Thus Descartes believed that he had explained physics in terms of the *essence of a physical body* which, he taught, was extension; and some Newtonians, following Roger Cotes, believed that the *essence of matter* was its inertia and its power to attract other matter, and that Newton's theory could be derived from, and thus ultimately explained by, these essential properties of all matter. Newton himself was of a different opinion. It was a hypothesis concerning the ultimate or essentialist causal explanation of gravity itself which he had in mind when he wrote in the *Scholium generale* at the end of the *Principia*: 'So far I have explained the phenomena . . . by the force of gravity, but I have not yet ascertained *the cause of gravity itself* . . . and I do not arbitrarily [or *ad hoc*] invent hypotheses.'[5]

I do not believe in the essentialist doctrine of ultimate explanation. In the past, critics of this doctrine have been, as a rule, instrumentalists: they interpreted scientific theories as *nothing*

German edn., 1934; fourth German edn., 1971), where the close connection between these ideas is explained.

[4] I have discussed (and criticized) essentialism more fully in my paper 'Three Views Concerning Human Knowledge', where I also refer to my earlier discussions (in the last footnote to section ii); see *Contemporary British Philosophy*, iii, edited by H. D. Lewis, 1956, note 2 on p. 365. (This paper forms now chapter 3 of my *Conjectures and Refutations*, third edn., 1969.)

[5] See also Newton's letters to Richard Bentley of 17 Jan. and especially 25 Feb. 1693 ('1692–3'). I have quoted from this letter in section iii of my paper 'Three Views Concerning Human Knowledge' (*Conjectures and Refutations*, pp. 106 f.) where the problem is discussed a little more fully.

but instruments for prediction, without any explanatory power. I do not agree with them either. But there is a third possibility, a 'third view', as I have called it. It has been well described as a 'modified essentialism'—with emphasis upon the word 'modified'.[6]

This 'third view' which I uphold modifies essentialism in a radical manner. First of all, I reject the idea of an ultimate explanation: I maintain that every explanation may be further explained, by a theory or conjecture of a higher degree of universality. There can be no explanation which is not in need of a further explanation, for none can be a self-explanatory description of an essence (such as an essentialist definition of body, as suggested by Descartes). Secondly, I reject all *what-is questions*: questions asking what a thing is, what is its essence, or its true nature. For we must give up the view, characteristic of essentialism, that in every single thing there is an essence, an inherent nature or principle (such as the spirit of wine in wine), which necessarily causes it to be what it is, and thus to act as it does. This animistic view explains nothing; but it has led essentialists (like Newton) to shun relational properties, such as gravity, and to believe, on grounds felt to be *a priori* valid, that a satisfactory explanation must be in terms of inherent properties (as opposed to relational properties). The third and last modification of essentialism is this. We must give up the view, closely connected with animism (and characteristic of Aristotle as opposed to Plato), that it is the essential properties inherent *in each individual or singular thing* which may be appealed to as the explanation of this thing's behaviour. For this view completely fails to throw any light whatever on the question why different individual things should behave in like manner. If it is said, 'because their essences are alike', the new question arises: *why should there not be as many different essences as there are different things?*

Plato tried to solve precisely this problem by saying that like

[6] The term 'modified essentialism' was used as a description of my own 'third view' by a reviewer of my paper 'Three Views Concerning Human Knowledge' in *The Times Literary Supplement*, 55, 1956, p. 527. In order to avoid misunderstandings, I wish to say here that my acceptance of this term should not be construed as a concession to the doctrine of 'ultimate reality', and even less as a concession to the doctrine of essentialist definitions. I fully adhere to the criticism of this doctrine which I have given in my *Open Society*, vol. ii, chapter 11, section ii (especially note 42), and in other places.

individual things are the offspring, and thus copies, of the same original 'Form', which is therefore something 'outside' and 'prior' and 'superior' to the various individual things; and indeed, we have as yet no better theory of likeness. Even today, we appeal to their common origin if we wish to explain the likeness of two men, or of a bird, and a fish, or of two beds, or two motor cars, or two languages, or two legal procedures; that is to say, we explain similarity in the main genetically; and if we make a metaphysical system out of this, it is liable to become a historicist philosophy. Plato's solution was rejected by Aristotle; but since Aristotle's version of essentialism does not contain even a hint of a solution, it seems that he never quite grasped the problem.[7]

By choosing explanations in terms of universal laws of nature, we offer a solution to precisely this last (Platonic) problem. For we conceive all individual things, and all singular facts, to be subject to these laws. The laws (which in their turn *are* in need of further explanation) thus explain regularities or similarities of individual things or singular facts or events. And these laws are not inherent in the singular things. (Nor are they Platonic ideas outside the world.) Laws of nature are conceived, rather, as (conjectural) descriptions of the structural properties of nature —of our world itself.

Here then is the similarity between my own view (the 'third view') and essentialism; although I do not think that we can ever describe, by our universal laws, an *ultimate* essence of the world, I do not doubt that we may seek to probe deeper and deeper into the structure of our world or, as we might say, into properties of the world that are more and more essential, or of greater and greater depth.

Every time we proceed to explain some conjectural law or theory by a new conjectural theory of a higher degree of universality, we are discovering more about the world, trying to penetrate deeper into its secrets. And every time we succeed in falsifying a theory of this kind, we make a new important discovery. For these falsifications are most important. They teach us the unexpected; and they reassure us that, although our

---

[7] As to Plato's theory of Forms or Ideas, it is 'one of its most important functions to explain the similarity of sensible things . . .' cf. my *Open Society*, chapter 3, section v; see also notes 19 and 20, and text. The failure of Aristotle's theory to perform this function is mentioned there (in the third edn., 1957) at the end of note 54 to chapter 11.

theories are made by ourselves, although they are our own inventions, they are none the less genuine assertions about the world; for they can *clash* with something we never made.

Our 'modified essentialism' is, I believe, helpful when the question of the logical form of natural laws is raised. It suggests that our laws or our theories must be *universal*, that is to say, must make assertions about the world—about all spatio-temporal regions of the world. It suggests, moreover, that our theories make assertions about structural or relational properties of the world; and that the properties described by an explanatory theory must be, in some sense or other, deeper than those to be explained. I believe that this word 'deeper' defies any attempt at exhaustive logical analysis, but that it is nevertheless a guide to our intuitions. (This is so in mathematics: all its theorems are logically equivalent, in the presence of the axioms, and yet there is a great difference in 'depth' which is hardly susceptible of logical analysis.) The 'depth' of a scientific theory seems to be most closely related to its simplicity and so to the wealth of its content. (It is otherwise with the depth of a mathematical theorem whose content may be taken to be nil.) Two ingredients seem to be required: a rich content, and a certain coherence or compactness (or 'organicity') of the state of affairs described. It is this latter ingredient which, although it is intuitively fairly clear, is so difficult to analyse, and which the essentialists were trying to describe when they spoke of essences, in contradistinction to a mere accumulation of accidental properties. I do not think that we can do much more than refer here to an intuitive idea, nor that we need do much more. For in the case of any particular theory proposed, it is the wealth of its content, and thus its degree of testability, which decides its interest, and the results of actual tests which decide its fate. From the point of view of method, we may look upon its depth, its coherence, and even its beauty, as a mere guide or stimulus to our intuition and to our imagination.

Nevertheless, there does seem to be something like a *sufficient* condition for depth, or for degrees of depth, which can be logically analysed. I shall try to explain this with the help of an example from the history of science.

It is well known that Newton's dynamics achieved a unification of Galileo's terrestrial and Kepler's celestial physics. It is often said that Newton's dynamics can be induced from Galileo's and Kepler's laws, and it has even been asserted that it can be strictly deduced from them.[8] But this is not so; from a logical point of view, Newton's theory, strictly speaking, contradicts both Galileo's and Kepler's (although these latter theories can of course be obtained as approximations, once we have Newton's theory to work with). For this reason it is impossible to derive Newton's theory from either Galileo's or Kepler's or both, whether by deduction or induction. For neither a deductive nor an inductive inference can ever proceed from consistent premises to a conclusion that formally contradicts the premises from which we started.

I regard this as a very strong argument against induction.

I shall now briefly indicate the contradictions between Newton's theory and those of his predecessors. Galileo asserts that a thrown stone or a projectile moves in a parabola, except in the case of a free vertical fall when it moves, with constant acceleration, in a straight line. (We neglect air-resistance throughout this discussion.) From the point of view of Newton's theory, these assertions are both false, for two distinct reasons. The first is false because the path of a long-range projectile, such as an inter-continental missile (thrown in an upward or horizontal direction) will be not even approximately parabolic but elliptic. It becomes, approximately, a parabola only if the total distance of the flight of the projectile is negligible compared with the radius of the earth. This point was made by Newton himself, in his *Principia*, as well as in his popularized version, *The System of*

---

[8] What can be deduced from Kepler's laws (see Max Born, *Natural Philosophy of Cause and Chance*, 1949, pp. 129–33) is that, for all planets, the acceleration towards the sun equals at any moment k/r^2, where r is the distance at that moment between the planet and the sun, and k a constant, the same for all planets. Yet this very result formally contradicts Newton's theory (except on the assumption that the masses of the planets are all equal or, if unequal, then at any rate infinitely small as compared with the mass of the sun). This fact follows from what is here said, in the text following note 9, about Kepler's third law. But in addition, it should be remembered that neither Kepler's nor Galileo's theories contain Newton's concept of *force* which is traditionally introduced in these deductions without further ado; as if this ('occult') concept could be read off from the facts, instead of being the result of a new interpretation of the facts (that is, of the 'phenomena' described by Kepler's and Galileo's laws) in the light of a completely new theory. Only after the concept of force (and even the proportionality of gravitational and inertial mass) has been introduced is it at all possible to link the above formula for the acceleration with Newton's inverse square law of attraction (by the assumpionthat the planets' masses are negligible).

the World, where he illustrates it with the help of the figure reproduced on this page.

Newton's figure illustrates his statement that, if the velocity of the projectile increases, and with it the distance of its flight, it will 'at last, exceeding the limits of the earth, . . . pass into space without touching it'.[9]

Thus a projectile on earth moves along an ellipse rather than

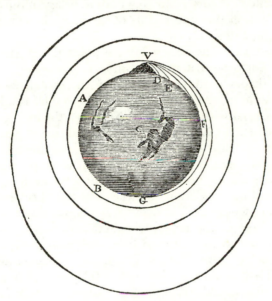

a parabola. Of course, for sufficiently short throws, a parabola will be an excellent approximation; but the parabolic track is not strictly deducible from Newton's theory unless we add to the latter a factually *false* initial condition (and one which, incidentally, is unrealizable in Newton's theory since it leads to absurd consequences) to the effect that the radius of the earth is infinite. If we do not admit this assumption, even though it is *known to be false,* then we always get an ellipse, in contradiction to Galileo's law according to which we should obtain a parabola.

A precisely analogous logical situation arises in connection with the second part of Galileo's law which asserts the existence

[9] See Newton's *Principia,* the *Scholium* at the end of section ii of Book i; p. 55 of the 1934 edn. (Motte's translation revised by Cajori). The figure, from *The System of the World,* and the quotation here given, will be found on p. 551 of this edn.

of an acceleration *constant*. From the point of view of Newton's theory, the acceleration of free-falling bodies is never constant: it always increases during the fall, owing to the fact that the body approaches nearer and nearer to the centre of attraction. This effect is very considerable if the body falls from a great height, although of course negligible if the height is negligible as compared with the radius of the earth. In this case, we can obtain Galileo's theory from Newton's if we again introduce the *false* assumption that the radius of the earth is infinite (or the height of the fall zero).

The contradictions which I have pointed out are far from negligible for long-distance missiles. To these we may apply Newton's theory (with corrections for air resistance, of course) but not Galileo's: the latter leads simply to false results, as can easily be shown with the help of Newton's theory.

With respect to Kepler's laws, the situation is similar. It is obvious that in Newton's theory Kepler's laws are only approximately valid—that is, strictly invalid—if we take into account the mutual attraction between the planets.[10] But there are more fundamental contradictions between the two theories than this somewhat obvious one. For even if, as a concession to our opponents, we neglect the mutual attraction between the planets, Kepler's third law, considered from the point of view of Newton's dynamics, cannot be more than an approximation which is applicable to a very special case: to planets whose masses are equal, or, if unequal, negligible as compared with the mass of the sun. Since it does not even approximately hold for two planets if one of them is very light while the other is very heavy, it is clear that Kepler's third law contradicts Newton's theory in precisely the same way as does Galileo's.

This can be easily shown as follows. Newton's theory yields for a two-body system—a binary star system—a law which astronomers often call 'Kepler's law' since it is closely related

---

[10] See, for example, P. Duhem, *The Aim and Structure of Physical Theory*, 1905; English translation by P. P. Wiener, 1945, Part II, chapter vi, section 4. Duhem says more explicitly what is implicit in Newton's own statement (*Principia*, Book I, proposition lxv, theorem xxv), for Newton makes it quite clear that in cases where more than two bodies interact, Kepler's first two laws will be at best only approximately valid, and even this in very special cases only, of which he analyses two in some detail. Incidentally, formula (1), below, follows immediately from Book I, proposition lix, in view of Book I, proposition xv. (See also Book III, proposition xv.)

to Kepler's third law. This so-called 'Kepler's law' says that if m_0 is the mass of one of the two bodies—say, the sun—and if m_1 is the mass of the other body—say, a planet—then, choosing appropriate units of measurement, we can derive from Newton's theory

(1) $a^3/T^2 = m_0 + m_1,$

where a is the mean distance between the two bodies, and T the time of a full revolution. Now Kepler's own third law asserts that

(2) $a^3/T^2 = constant$

that is to say, the same constant for *all* planets of the solar system. It is clear that we obtain this law from (1) only under the assumption that $m_0 + m_1 = $ constant; and since $m_0 = $ constant for our solar system if we identify m_0 with the mass of the sun, we obtain (2) from (1), provided we assume that m_1 is the same for all planets; or, if this is factually *false* (as is indeed the case, since Jupiter is several thousand times larger than the smallest planets), that the masses of the planets are *all zero as compared with that of the sun*, so that we may put $m_1 = 0$, *for all planets*. This is quite a good approximation from the point of view of Newton's theory; but at the same time, putting $m_1 = 0$ is not only strictly speaking false, but unrealizable from the point of view of Newton's theory. (A body with zero mass would no longer obey Newton's laws of motion.) Thus, even if we forget all about the mutual attraction between the planets, Kepler's third law (2) contradicts Newton's theory which yields (1).

It is important to note that from Galileo's or Kepler's theories we do not obtain even the slightest hint of how these theories would have to be adjusted—what false premises would have to be adopted, or what conditions stipulated—should we try to proceed from these theories to another and more generally valid one such as Newton's. *Only after we are in possession of Newton's theory can we find out whether, and in what sense, the older theories can be said to be approximations to it.* We may express this fact briefly by saying that, although from the point of view of Newton's theory, Galileo's and Kepler's are excellent approximations to certain special Newtonian results, Newton's theory cannot be said, from the point of view of the other two theories, to be an approximation to their results. All this shows that logic, whether deductive or inductive, cannot possibly make the step from these theories to Newton's dynamics.[11] It is only ingenuity which can make this step. Once it has been made, Galileo's and Kepler's results may be said to corroborate the new theory.

Here, however, I am not so much interested in the impossibility of induction as in *the problem of depth*. And regarding this problem, we can indeed learn something from our example. Newton's theory unifies Galileo's and Kepler's. But far from being a mere conjunction of these two theories—which play the part of *explicanda* for Newton's—*it corrects them while explaining them*. The original explanatory task was the deduction of the earlier results. Yet this task is discharged, not by deducing these earlier results but by deducing something better in their place: new results which, under the special conditions of the older results, come numerically very close to these older results, and at the same time correct them. Thus the empirical success of the old theory may be said to corroborate the new theory; and in addition, the corrections may be tested in their turn—and perhaps refuted, or else corroborated. What is brought out strongly, by the logical situation which I have sketched, is the fact that the new theory cannot possibly be *ad hoc* or circular. Far from repeating its *explicandum*, the new theory contradicts it, and corrects it. In this way, even the evidence of the *explicandum* itself becomes independent evidence for the new theory. (Incidentally, this analysis allows us to *explain the value of metrical theories*, and of measurement; and it thus helps us to avoid the mistake of accepting measurement and precision as ultimate and irreducible values.)

I suggest that whenever in the empirical sciences a new theory of a higher level of universality successfully explains some older theory *by correcting it*, then this is a sure sign that the new theory has penetrated deeper than the older ones. The demand that a new theory should contain the old one approximately, for appropriate values of the parameters of the new theory, may be called (following Bohr) the '*principle of correspondence*'.

Fulfilment of this demand is a sufficient condition of depth, as I said before. That it is not a necessary condition may be seen from the fact that Maxwell's electromagnetic wave theory did

[11] The concepts of force (cp. p. 198, note 8, above) and of action at a distance introduce further difficulties.

not correct, in this sense, Fresnel's wave theory of light. It meant an increase in depth, no doubt, but in a different sense: 'The old question of the direction of the vibrations of polarized light became pointless. The difficulties concerning the boundary conditions for the boundaries between two media were solved by the very foundations of the theory. No *ad hoc* hypotheses were needed any longer for eliminating longitudinal light waves. Light pressure, so important in the theory of radiation, and only lately determined experimentally, could be derived as one of the consequences of the theory.'[12] This brilliant passage, in which Einstein sketches some of the major achievements of Maxwell's theory and compares it with Fresnel's, may be taken as an indication that there are other sufficient conditions of depth which are not covered by my analysis.

The task of science, which, I have suggested, is to find satisfactory explanations, can hardly be understood if we are not realists. For a satisfactory explanation is one which is not *ad hoc*; and this idea—the *idea of independent evidence*—can hardly be understood without the idea of discovery, of progressing to deeper layers of explanation: without the idea that there is something for us to discover, and something to discuss critically.

And yet it seems to me that within methodology we do not have to presuppose metaphysical realism; nor can we, I think, derive much help from it, except of an intuitive kind. For once we have been told that the aim of science is to explain, and that the most satisfactory explanation will be the one that is most severely testable and most severely tested, we know all that we need to know as methodologists. That the aim is realizable we cannot assert, neither with nor without the help of metaphysical realism which can give us only some intuitive encouragement, some hope, but no assurance of any kind. And although a rational treatment of methodology may be said to depend upon an assumed, or conjectured, aim of science, it certainly does not depend upon the metaphysical and most likely false assumption

---

[12] A. Einstein, *Physikalische Zeitschrift*, **10**, 1909, pp. 817 f. The abandonment of the theory of a material ether (implicit in Maxwell's failure to construct a satisfactory material model of it) may be said to give depth, in the sense analysed above to Maxwell's theory as compared with Fresnel's; and this is, it seems to me, implicit in the quotation from Einstein's paper. Thus Maxwell's theory in Einstein's formulation is perhaps not really an example of *another* sense of 'depth'. But in Maxwell's own original form it is, I think.

that the true structural theory of the world (if any), is discoverable by man, or expressible in human language.

If the picture of the world which modern science draws comes anywhere near to the truth—in other words, if we have anything like 'scientific knowledge'—then the conditions obtaining almost everywhere in the universe make the discovery of structural laws of the kind we are seeking—and thus the attainment of 'scientific knowledge'—almost impossible. For almost all regions of the universe are filled by chaotic radiation, and almost all the rest by matter in a similar chaotic state. In spite of this, science has been miraculously successful in proceeding towards what I have suggested should be regarded as its aim. This strange fact cannot, I think, be explained without proving too much. But it can encourage us to pursue that aim, even though we may not get any further encouragement to believe that we can actually attain it; neither from metaphysical realism nor from any other source.

SELECT BIBLIOGRAPHY

An asterisk denotes an item appearing in this volume.

POPPER, KARL R., *Logik der Forschung*, 1934 (1935); enlarged edns. 1966, 1969.
—— *The Poverty of Historicism* (1944–5), 1957, 1960.
—— *Conjectures and Refutations*, 1963, 1965, 1969.
*—— *Of Clouds and Clocks*, 1965. (See ch. 6, below.)
*—— 'Naturgesetze und theoretische Systeme' in *Gesetz und Wirklichkeit*, ed. Simon Moser (1948), 1949. (Here translated as Appendix to this volume.)
—— 'Die Zielsetzung der Erfahrungswissenschaft', in *Theorie und Realität*, ed. Hans Albert, 1964, pp. 73–86.
—— 'Quantum Mechanics without "The Observer"', in *Quantum Theory and Reality*, ed. M. Bunge, 1967.
*—— 'Epistemology without a Knowing Subject', in *Logic, Methodology and Philosophy of Science*, **3**, eds. B. van Rootselaar and J. F. Staal, 1968, pp. 333–73. (See ch. 3, above.)
*—— 'On the Theory of the Objective Mind', in *Akte des 14. Internationalen Kongresses für Philosophie*, Wien, 1968, **1**, pp. 25–53. (See ch. 4, above.)

BIBLIOGRAPHICAL NOTE

The idea here discussed that theories may *correct* an 'observational' or 'phenomenal' law which they are supposed to explain (such as, for example,

Kepler's third law) was repeatedly expounded in my lectures. One of these lectures stimulated the correction of a supposed phenomenal law (see the 1941 paper referred to in my *Poverty of Historicism*, 1957, 1960, footnote on pp. 134 f.). Another of these lectures was published in Simon Moser's volume *Gesetz und Wirklichkeit* (1948), 1949. The same idea of mine was also the 'starting-point' (as he puts it on p. 92) of P. K. Feyerabend's paper 'Explanation, Reduction and Empiricism' (in Herbert Feigl and Grover Maxwell, editors, *Minnesota Studies in the Philosophy of Science*, 3, 1962) whose reference [66] is to the present paper (as first published in *Ratio*, 1, 1957). Feyerabend's acknowledgement seems to have been overlooked by the authors of various papers on related subjects.

6. Of Clouds and Clocks

AN APPROACH TO THE PROBLEM OF RATIONALITY
AND THE FREEDOM OF MAN

I

MY predecessor who in this hall gave the first Arthur Holly
Compton Memorial Lecture a year ago was more fortunate than
I. He knew Arthur Compton personally; I never met him.[1]

But I have known of Compton since my student days in the
nineteen-twenties, and especially since 1925 when the famous
experiment of Compton and Simon[2] refuted the beautiful but
short-lived quantum theory of Bohr, Kramers, and Slater.[3] This
refutation was one of the decisive events in the history of quantum theory, for from the crisis which it created there emerged
the so-called 'new quantum theory'—the theories of Born and
Heisenberg, of Schrödinger, and of Dirac.

It was the second time that Compton's experimental tests had
played a crucial role in the history of quantum theory. The first
time had been, of course, the discovery of the Compton effect,
the first independent test (as Compton himself pointed out[4]) of
Einstein's theory of light quanta or photons.

Years later, during the Second World War, I found to my
surprise and pleasure that Compton was not only a great
physicist but also a genuine and courageous philosopher; and
further, that his philosophical interests and aims coincided with

[1] When I came to Berkeley early in Feb. 1962 I was eagerly looking forward
to meeting Compton. He died before we could meet.

[2] A. H. Compton and A. W. Simon, *Phys. Rev.* **25**, 1925, pp. 309 ff. (See also W.
Bothe and H. Geiger, *Zeit. f. Phys.* **26**, 1924, pp. 44 ff., and **32**, 1925, pp. 639 ff.;
Naturwissenschaften, **13**, 1925, p. 440.)

[3] N. Bohr, H. A. Kramers, and J. C. Slater, *Phil. Mag.* **47**, 1924, pp. 785 ff., and
Zeitschr. f. Phys., **24**, 1924, pp. 69 ff. See also A. H. Compton and S. K. Allison,
X-Rays in Theory and Experiment, 1935; for example, pp. 211–27.

[4] See chapter I, section 19, of Compton and Allison (note 3).

This was the second Arthur Holly Compton Memorial Lecture, presented at
Washington University on 21 Apr. 1965.

my own on some important points. I found this when, almost by accident, I got hold of Compton's fascinating Terry Lectures which he had published in 1935 in a book entitled *The Freedom of Man*.[5]

You will have noticed that I have incorporated the title of Compton's book, *The Freedom of Man*, into my own title today. I have done so in order to stress the fact that my lecture will be closely connected with this book of Compton's. More precisely, I intend to discuss the same problems which Compton discussed in the first two chapters of this book, and again in the second chapter of another of his books, *The Human Meaning of Science*.[6]

In order to avoid misunderstandings I must stress, however, that my lecture today is not mainly about Compton's books. It is rather an attempt to look afresh at the same ancient philosophical problems with which he grappled in these two books, and an attempt to find a new solution to these ancient problems. The sketchy and very tentative solution I am going to outline here seems to me to fit in well with Compton's main aims, and I hope—indeed I believe—that he would have approved of it.

II

THE central purpose of my lecture is to try to put these ancient problems simply and forcefully before you. But first I must say something about the *clouds and clocks* which appear in the title of my lecture.

My clouds are intended to represent physical systems which, like gases, are highly irregular, disorderly, and more or less unpredictable. I shall assume that we have before us a schema or arrangement in which a very disturbed or disorderly cloud is placed on the left. On the other extreme of our arrangement, on its right, we may place a very reliable pendulum clock, a precision clock, intended to represent physical systems which are regular, orderly, and highly predictable in their behaviour.

---

[5] A. H. Compton, *The Freedom of Man*, 1935 (third edn., 1939). This book was based mainly on the Terry Foundation Lectures, delivered by Compton at Yale in 1931, and in addition on two other series of lectures given soon after the Terry Lectures.

[6] A. H. Compton, *The Human Meaning of Science*, 1940.

According to what I may call the commonsense view of things, some natural phenomena, such as the weather, or the coming and going of clouds, are hard to predict: we speak of the 'vagaries of the weather'. On the other hand, we speak of 'clockwork precision' if we wish to describe a highly regular and predictable phenomenon.

There are lots of things, natural processes and natural phenomena, which we may place between these two extremes—the clouds on the left, and the clocks on the right. The changing seasons are somewhat unreliable clocks, and may therefore be put somewhere towards the right, though not too far. I suppose we shall easily agree to put animals not too far from the clouds on the left, and plants somewhat nearer to the clocks. Among the animals, a young puppy will have to be placed further to the left than an old dog. Motor cars, too, will find their place somewhere in our arrangement, according to their reliability: a Cadillac, I suppose, is pretty far over to the right, and even more so a Rolls-Royce, which will be quite close to the best of the clocks. Perhaps furthest to the right should be placed the *solar system*.[7]

As a typical and interesting example of a cloud I shall make some use here of a cloud or cluster of small flies or gnats. Like the individual molecules in a gas, the individual gnats which together form a cluster of gnats move in an astonishingly irregular way. It is almost impossible to follow the flight of any one individual gnat, even though each of them may be quite big enough to be clearly visible.

Apart from the fact that the velocities of the gnats do not show a very wide spread, the gnats present us with an excellent picture of the irregular movement of molecules in a gas cloud, or of the minute drops of water in a storm cloud. There are, of course, differences. The cluster does not dissolve or diffuse, but it keeps together fairly well. This is surprising, considering the disorderly character of the movement of the various gnats; but it has its analogue in a sufficiently big gas cloud (such as our atmosphere, or the sun) which is kept together by gravitational forces. In the case of the gnats, their keeping together can be easily explained if we assume that, although they fly quite irregularly in all directions, those that find that they are getting

7 For the imperfections of the solar system see notes 11 and 16 below.

away from the crowd turn back towards that part which is densest.

This assumption explains how the cluster keeps together even though it has no leader, and no structure—only a random statistical distribution resulting from the fact that each gnat does exactly what he likes, in a lawless or random manner, together with the fact that he does not like to stray too far from his comrades.

I think that a philosophical gnat might claim that the gnat society is a great society or at least a good society, since it is the most egalitarian, free, and democratic society imaginable.

However, as the author of a book on *The Open Society*, I would deny that the gnat society is an open society. For I take it to be one of the characteristics of an open society that it cherishes, apart from a democratic form of government, the freedom of association, and that it protects and even encourages the formation of free sub-societies, each holding different opinions and beliefs. But every reasonable gnat would have to admit that in his society this kind of pluralism is lacking.

I do not intend, however, to discuss today any of the social or political issues connected with the problem of freedom; and I intend to use the cluster of gnats not as an example of a *social* system, but rather as my main illustration of a cloud-like *physical* system, as an example or paradigm of a highly irregular or disordered cloud.

Like many physical, biological, and social systems, the cluster of gnats may be described as a 'whole'. Our conjecture that it is kept together by a kind of attraction which its densest part exerts on individual gnats straying too far from the crowd shows that there is even a kind of action or control which this 'whole' exerts upon its elements or parts. Nevertheless, this 'whole' can be used to dispel the widespread 'holistic' belief that a 'whole' is *always* more than the mere sum of its parts. I do not deny that it may sometimes be so.[8] Yet the cluster of gnats is an example of a whole that is indeed nothing but the sum of its

[8] See section 23 of my book *The Poverty of Historicism* (1957 and later edns.), where I criticize the 'holistic' criterion of a 'whole' (or '*Gestalt*') by showing that this criterion ('a whole is more than the mere sum of its parts') is satisfied even by the favourite holistic examples of non-wholes, such as a 'mere heap' of stones. (Note that I do not deny that there exist wholes; I only object to the superficiality of most 'holistic' theories.)

parts—and in a very precise sense; for not only is it completely described by describing the movements of all the individual gnats, but the movement of the whole is, in this case, precisely the (vectorial) sum of the movements of its constituent members, divided by the number of the members.

An example (in many ways similar) of a biological system or 'whole' which exerts some control over the highly irregular movements of its parts would be a picnicking family—parents with a few children and a dog—roaming the woods for hours, but never straying far from the family car (which acts like a centre of attraction, as it were). This system may be said to be even more cloudy—that is, less regular in the movement of its parts—than our cloud of gnats.

I hope you will now have before you an idea of my two prototypes or paradigms, the clouds on the left and the clocks on the right, and of the way in which we can arrange many kinds of things, and many kinds of systems, between them. I am sure you have caught some vague, general idea of the arrangement, and you need not worry if your idea is still a bit foggy, or cloudy.

III

THE arrangement I have described is, it seems, quite acceptable to common sense; and more recently, in our own time, it has become acceptable even to physical science. It was not so, however, during the preceding 250 years: the Newtonian revolution, one of the greatest revolutions in history, led to the rejection of the commonsense arrangement which I have tried to present to you. For one of the things which almost everybody[9] thought had been established by the Newtonian revolution was the following staggering proposition:

All clouds are clocks—even the most cloudy of clouds.

This proposition, 'All clouds are clocks', may be taken as a brief formulation of the view which I shall call *'physical determinism'*.

The physical determinist who says that all clouds are clocks will also say that our commonsense arrangement, with the clouds on the left and the clocks on the right, is misleading, since

---

[9] Newton himself was not among those who drew these 'deterministic' consequences from his theory; see notes 11 and 16 below.

everything ought to be placed on the extreme right. He will say that, with all our common sense, we arranged things *not according to their nature, but merely according to our ignorance.* Our arrangement, he will say, reflects merely the fact that we know in some detail how the parts of a clock work, or how the solar system works, while we do not have any knowledge about the *detailed* interaction of the particles that form a gas cloud, or an organism. And he will assert that, once we have obtained this knowledge, we shall find that gas clouds or organisms are as clock-like as our solar system.

Newton's theory did not, of course, tell the physicists that this was so. In fact, it did not treat at all of clouds. It treated especially of planets, whose movements it explained as due to some very simple laws of nature; also of cannon balls, and of the tides. But its immense success in these fields turned the physicists' heads; and surely not without reason.

Before the time of Newton and his predecessor, Kepler, the movements of the planets had escaped many attempts to explain or even to describe them fully. Clearly, they somehow participated in the unvarying general movement of the rigid system of the fixed stars; yet they deviated from the movement of that system almost like single gnats deviating from the general movement of a cluster of gnats. Thus the planets, not unlike living things, appeared to be in a position intermediate between clouds and clocks. Yet the success of Kepler's and even more of Newton's theory showed that those thinkers had been right who had suspected that the planets were in fact perfect clocks. For their movements turned out to be precisely predictable with the help of Newton's theory; predictable in all those details which had previously baffled the astronomers by their apparent irregularity.

Newton's theory was the first really successful scientific theory in human history; and it was tremendously successful. Here was real knowledge; knowledge beyond the wildest dreams of even the boldest minds. Here was a theory which explained precisely not only the movements of *all* the stars in their course, but also, just as precisely, the movements of bodies on earth, such as falling apples, or projectiles, or pendulum clocks. And it even explained the tides.

All open-minded men—all those who were eager to learn, and who took an interest in the growth of knowledge—were converted to the new theory. Most openminded men, and especially most scientists, thought that in the end it would explain everything, including not only electricity and magnetism, but also clouds, and even living organisms. Thus physical determinism—the doctrine that all clouds are clocks—became the ruling faith among enlightened men; and everybody who did not embrace this new faith was held to be an obscurantist or a reactionary.[10]

IV

AMONG the few dissenters[11] was Charles Sanders Peirce, the great American mathematician and physicist and, I believe, one of the greatest philosophers of all time. He did not question Newton's theory; yet as early as 1892 he showed that this theory, even if true, does not give us any valid reason to believe that clouds are perfect clocks. Though in common with all other physicists of his time he believed that the world was a clock that worked according to Newtonian laws, he rejected the belief that this clock, or any other, was *perfect*, down to the smallest detail. He pointed out that at any rate we could not possibly claim to know, from experience, of anything like a perfect clock, or of anything even faintly approaching that absolute perfection which physical determinism assumed. I may perhaps quote one of Peirce's brilliant comments: '. . . one who is behind the scenes' (Peirce speaks here as an experimentalist) '. . . knows that the most refined comparisons [even] of masses [and] lengths, . . . far surpassing in precision all other [physical] measurements, . . . fall behind the accuracy of bank accounts, and that the . . . determinations of physical constants . . . are about on a par with

---

[10] The conviction that determinism forms an essential part of any rational or scientific attitude was generally accepted, even by some of the leading opponents of 'materialism' (such as Spinoza, Leibniz, Kant, and Schopenhauer). A similar dogma which formed part of the rationalist tradition was that all knowledge begins with *observation* and proceeds from there by induction. Cp. my remarks on these two dogmas of rationalism in my book *Conjectures and Refutations*, 1963, 1965, 1969, 1972, pp. 122 f.

[11] Newton himself may be counted among the few dissenters, for he regarded even the solar system as *imperfect*, and consequently as likely to perish. Because of these views he was accused of impiety, of 'casting a reflection upon the wisdom of the author of nature' (as Henry Pemberton reports in his *A View of Sir Isaac Newton's Philosophy*, 1728, p. 180).

an upholsterer's measurements of carpets and curtains . . .'.[12]
From this Peirce concluded that we were free to conjecture that
there was a certain *looseness or imperfection* in all clocks, and that
this allowed an *element of chance* to enter. Thus Peirce conjectured
that the world was not only ruled by the *strict Newtonian laws*,
but that it was also at the same time ruled by *laws of chance*, or
of randomness, or of disorder: by laws of statistical *probability*.
This made the world an interlocking system of clouds and
clocks, so that even the best clock would, *in its molecular structure*,
show some degree of cloudiness. So far as I know Peirce was the
first post-Newtonian physicist and philosopher who thus dared
to adopt the view that to some degree *all clocks are clouds*; or in
other words, that *only clouds exist*, though clouds of very different
degrees of cloudiness.

Peirce supported this view by pointing out, no doubt correctly, that all physical bodies, even the jewels in a watch, were
subject to molecular heat motion,[13] a motion similar to that of
the molecules of a gas, or of the individual gnats in a cluster of
gnats.

These views of Peirce's were received by his contemporaries
with little interest. Apparently only one philosopher noticed
them; and he attacked them.[14] Physicists seem to have ignored

[12] *Collected Papers of Charles Sanders Peirce*, **6**, 1935, 6.44, p. 35. There may of
course have been other physicists who developed similar views, but apart from
Newton and Peirce I know of only one: Professor Franz Exner of Vienna. Schrödinger, who was his pupil, wrote about Exner's views in his book *Science, Theory
and Man*, 1957, pp. 71, 133, 142 f. (This book was previously published under the
title *Science and the Human Temperament*, 1935, and Compton referred to it in *The
Freedom of Man*, p. 29.) Cp. also note 25 below.

[13] C. S. Peirce, op. cit., **6**, 6. 47, p. 37 (first published 1892). The passage,
though brief, is most interesting because it anticipates (note the remark on fluctuations in explosive mixtures) some of the discussion of macro-effects which
result from the amplification of Heisenberg indeterminacies. This discussion
begins, it appears, with a paper by Ralph Lillie, *Science*, **46**, 1927, pp. 139 ff.,
to which Compton refers in *The Freedom of Man*, p. 50. It plays a considerable part
in Compton's book, pp. 48 ff. (Note that Compton delivered the Terry Lectures in
1931.) Compton, op. cit., note 3, pp. 51 f., contains a very interesting quantitative
comparison of chance effects due to molecular heat motion (the indeterminacy
Peirce had in mind) and Heisenberg indeterminacy. The discussion was carried
on by Bohr, Pascual Jordan, Fritz Medicus, Ludwig von Bertalanffy, and many
others; more recently especially also by Walter Elsasser, *The Physical Foundations
of Biology*, 1958.

[14] I am alluding to Paul Carus, *The Monist*, **2**, 1892, pp. 560 ff., and **3**, 1892,
pp. 68 ff.; Peirce replied in *The Monist*, **3**, 1893, pp. 526 ff. (see his *Collected
Papers*, **6**, Appendix A, pp. 390 ff.).

them; and even today most physicists believe that if we had to accept the classical mechanics of Newton as true, we should be compelled to accept physical determinism, and with it the proposition that all clouds are clocks. It was only with the downfall of classical physics and with the rise of the new quantum theory that physicists were prepared to abandon physical determinism.

Now the tables were turned. Indeterminism, which up to 1927 had been equated with obscurantism, became the ruling fashion; and some great scientists, such as Max Planck, Erwin Schrödinger, and Albert Einstein, who hesitated to abandon determinism, were considered old fogies,[15] although they had been in the forefront of the development of quantum theory. I myself once heard a brilliant young physicist describe Einstein, who was then still alive and hard at work, as 'antediluvian'. The deluge that was supposed to have swept Einstein away was the new quantum theory, which had risen during the years from 1925 to 1927, and to whose advent at most seven people had made contributions comparable to those of Einstein.

V

PERHAPS I may stop here for a moment to state my own view of the situation, and of scientific fashions. I believe that Peirce

---

[15] The sudden and complete transformation of the problem-situation may be gauged by the fact that to many of us old fogies it does not really seem so very long ago that empiricist philosophers (see for example Moritz Schlick, *Allgemeine Erkenntnislehre*, second edn., 1925, p. 277) were physical determinists, while nowadays physical determinism is being dismissed by P. H. Nowell-Smith, a gifted and spirited defender of Schlick's, as an '*eighteenth-century bogey*' (*Mind*, **63**, 1954, p. 331; see also note 37 below). Time marches on and no doubt it will, in time, solve all our problems, bogies or non-bogies. Yet oddly enough we old fogies seem to remember the days of Planck, Einstein, and Schlick, and have much trouble in trying to convince our puzzled and muddled minds that these great determinist thinkers produced their bogies in the eighteenth century, together with Laplace who produced the most famous bogy of all (the 'super-human intelligence' of his *Essay* of 1819, often called 'Laplace's demon'; cp. Compton, *The Freedom of Man*, pp. 5 f., and *The Human Meaning of Science*, p. 34, and Alexander, quoted in note 35, below). Yet a still greater effort might perhaps recall, even to our failing memories, a similar eighteenth-century bogy produced by a certain Carus (not the nineteenth-century thinker P. Carus referred to in note 14 but T. L. Carus, who wrote *Lucretius de rerum naturae*, ii. 251–60, quoted by Compton in *The Freedom of Man*, p. 1).

was right in holding that all clocks are clouds, to some considerable degree—even the most precise of clocks. This, I think, is a most important inversion of the mistaken determinist view that all clouds are clocks. I further believe that Peirce was right in holding that this view was compatible with the classical physics of Newton.[16] I believe that this view is even more clearly compatible with Einstein's (special) relativity theory, and it is still more clearly compatible with the new quantum theory. In other words, I am an indeterminist—like Peirce, Compton, and most other contemporary physicists; and I believe, with most of them, that Einstein was mistaken in trying to hold fast to determinism. (I may perhaps say that I discussed this matter with him, and that I did not find him adamant.) But I also believe that those modern physicists were badly mistaken who pooh-poohed as antediluvian Einstein's criticism of the quantum theory. Nobody can fail to admire the quantum theory, and Einstein did so wholeheartedly; but his criticism of the fashionable interpretation of the theory—the Copenhagen interpretation—like the criticisms offered by de Broglie, Schrödinger, Bohm, Vigier, and more recently by Landé, have been too lightly brushed aside by most physicists.[17] There are fashions in science, and some scientists climb on the band wagon almost as readily as do some painters and musicians. But although fashions and bandwagons may attract the weak, they should be resisted rather

[16] I developed this view in 1950 in a paper 'Indeterminism in Quantum Physics and in Classical Physics', *British Journal for the Philosophy of Science*, **1**, 1950, No. 2, pp. 117–33, and No. 3, pp. 173–95. When writing this paper I knew nothing, unfortunately, of Peirce's views (see notes 12 and 13). I may perhaps mention here that I have taken the idea of opposing *clouds* and *clocks* from this earlier paper of mine. Since 1950, when my paper was published, the discussion of indeterminist elements in classical physics has gathered momentum. See Leon Brillouin, *Scientific Uncertainty and Information*, 1964 (a book with which I am by no means in full agreement), and the references to the literature there given, especially on pp. 38, 105, 127, 151 f. To these references might be added in particular Jacques Hadamard's great paper concerning geodetic lines on 'horned' surfaces of negative curvature, *Journal de mathématiques pures et appliquées*, 5th series 4, 1898, pp. 27 ff.

[17] See also my book *The Logic of Scientific Discovery*, especially the new Appendix *xi; also chapter ix of this book which contains criticism that is valid in the main, though, in view of Einstein's criticism in Appendix *xii, I had to withdraw the thought experiment (of 1934) described in section 77. This experiment can be replaced, however, by the famous thought experiment of Einstein, Podolsky, and Rosen, discussed there in Appendix *xi and *xii. See also my paper 'The Propensity Interpretation of the Calculus of Probability, and the Quantum Theory', in *Observation and Interpretation*, ed. by S. Körner, 1957, pp. 65–70, and 83–9.

than encouraged;[18] and criticism like Einstein's is always valuable: one can always learn something from it.

VI

ARTHUR HOLLY COMPTON was among the first who welcomed the new quantum theory, and Heisenberg's new physical indeterminism of 1927. Compton invited Heisenberg to Chicago for a course of lectures which Heisenberg delivered in the spring of 1929. This course was Heisenberg's first full exposition of his theory, and his lectures were published as his first book a year later by the University of Chicago Press, with a preface by Arthur Compton.[19] In this preface Compton welcomed the new theory to whose advent his experiments had contributed by refuting its immediate predecessor;[20] yet he also sounded a note of warning. Compton's warning anticipated some very similar warnings by Einstein, who always insisted that we should not consider the new quantum theory—'this chapter of the history of physics', as Compton called it generously and wisely—as being 'complete'.[21] And although this view was rejected by Bohr, we should remember the fact that the new theory failed, for example, to give even a hint of the neutron, discovered by Chadwick about a year later, which was to become the first of a long series of new elementary particles whose existence had

[18] The last sentence is meant as a criticism of some of the views contained in Thomas S. Kuhn's interesting and stimulating book *The Structure of Scientific Revolutions*, 1963.

[19] See Werner Heisenberg, *The Physical Principles of the Quantum Theory*, 1930.

[20] I am alluding to Compton's refutation of the theory of Bohr, Kramers, and Slater, see note 3 above; see also Compton's own allusion in *The Freedom of Man*, p. 7 (last sentence), and *The Human Meaning of Science*, p. 36.

[21] Cp. Compton's Preface in Heisenberg, op. cit., pp. iii ff.; also his remarks on the *incompleteness* of quantum mechanics in *The Freedom of Man*, p. 45 (with a reference to Einstein) and in *The Human Meaning of Science*, p. 42. Compton approved of the incompleteness of quantum mechanics while Einstein saw in it a weakness of the theory. Replying to Einstein, Niels Bohr asserted (like J. von Neumann before him) that the theory was *complete* (perhaps in another sense of the term). See for example A. Einstein, B. Podolsky, and N. Rosen, *Physical Review*, **42**, 1935, pp. 777–80; and Bohr's reply in **48**, 1935, pp. 696 ff.; also A. Einstein, *Dialectica*, **2**, 1948, pp. 320–4, and Bohr, pp. 312–19 of the same volume; further, the discussion between Einstein and Niels Bohr in P. A. Schilpp (ed.), *Albert Einstein: Philosopher-Scientist*, 1949, pp. 201–41, and especially 668–74, and a letter of Einstein's, published in my book, *The Logic of Scientific Discovery*, pp. 457–64; see also pp. 445–56.

not been foreseen by the new quantum theory (even though it is true that the existence of the positron could have been derived from the theory of Dirac).[22]

In the same year, 1931, in his Terry Foundation Lectures,[5] Compton became one of the first to examine the human and, more generally, the biological[23] implications of the new indeterminism in physics. And now it became clear why he had welcomed the new theory so enthusiastically: it solved for him not only problems of physics but also biological and philosophical problems, and among the latter especially problems connected with ethics.

VII

To show this, I shall now quote the striking opening passage of Compton's *The Freedom of Man*:

> The fundamental question of morality, a vital problem in religion, and a subject of active investigation in science: Is man a free agent?
>
> If . . . the atoms of our bodies follow physical laws as immutable as the motions of the planets, why try? What difference can it make how great the effort if our actions are already predetermined by mechanical laws . . . ?[24]

Compton describes here what I shall call '*the nightmare of the physical determinist*'. A deterministic physical clockwork mechanism is, above all, completely self-contained: in the perfect deterministic physical world there is simply no room for any outside intervention. Everything that happens in such a world is physically predetermined, including all our movements and therefore all our actions. Thus all our thoughts, feelings, and efforts can have no practical influence upon what happens in the physical world: they are, if not mere illusions, at best superfluous byproducts ('epiphenomena') of physical events.

In this way, the daydream of the Newtonian physicist who hoped to prove all clouds to be clocks had threatened to turn into a nightmare; and the attempt to ignore this had led to

---

[22] See the history of its discovery as told by N. R. Hanson, *The Concept of the Positron*, 1963, chapter ix.

[23] See especially the passages on 'emergent evolution' in *The Freedom of Man*, pp. 90 ff.; cp. *The Human Meaning of Science*, p. 73.

[24] Cp. *The Freedom of Man*, p. 1.

something like an intellectual split personality. Compton, I think, was grateful to the new quantum theory for rescuing him from this difficult intellectual situation. Thus he writes, in *The Freedom of Man*: 'The physicist has rarely . . . bothered himself with the fact that if . . . completely deterministic . . . laws . . . apply to man's actions, he is himself an automaton.'[25] And in *The Human Meaning of Science* he expresses his relief:

> In my own thinking on this vital subject I am thus in a much more satisfied state of mind than I could have been at any earlier stage of science. If the statements of the laws of physics were assumed correct, one would have had to suppose (as did most philosophers) that the feeling of freedom is illusory, or if [free] choice were considered effective, that the statements of the laws of physics were . . . unreliable. The dilemma has been an uncomfortable one . . .[26]

Later in the same book Compton sums up the situation crisply in the words: '. . . it is no longer justifiable to use physical law as evidence against human freedom'.[27]

These quotations from Compton show clearly that before Heisenberg he had been harassed by what I have here called the nightmare of the physical determinist, and that he had tried to escape from this nightmare by adopting something like an intellectual split personality. Or as he himself puts it: 'We [physicists] have preferred merely to pay no attention to the difficulties . . .'[28] Compton welcomed the new theory which rescued him from all this.

I believe that the only form of the problem of determinism which is worth discussing seriously is exactly that problem which worried Compton: the problem which arises from a physical theory which describes the world as a *physically complete* or a

---

[25] Cp. *The Freedom of Man*, pp. 26 f.; see also pp. 27 f. (the last paragraph beginning on p. 27). I may perhaps remind the reader that my views differ a little from the quoted passage because like Peirce I think it logically possible that the *laws* of a system be Newtonian (and so *prima facie* deterministic) and the system nevertheless indeterministic, because the system to which the laws apply may be intrinsically unprecise, in the sense, for example, that there is no point in saying that its co-ordinates, or velocities, are rational (as opposed to irrational) numbers. The following remark (see Schrödinger, op. cit., p. 143) is also very relevant: '. . . the energy-momentum theorem provides us with only *four* equations, thus leaving the elementary process to a great extent undetermined, even if it complies with them.' See also note 16.

[26] Cp. *The Human Meaning of Science*, p. ix.

[27] Ibid., p. 42.

[28] Cp. *The Freedom of Man*, p. 27.

physically closed system.[29] By a physically closed system I mean a set or system of physical entities, such as atoms or elementary particles or physical forces or fields of forces, which interact with each other—and *only* with each other—in accordance with definite laws of interaction that do not leave any room for interaction with, or interference by, anything outside that closed set or system of physical entities. It is this 'closure' of the system that creates the deterministic nightmare.[30]

VIII

I SHOULD like to digress here for a minute in order to contrast the problem of physical determinism, which I consider to be of fundamental importance, with the far from serious problem which many philosophers and psychologists, following Hume, have substituted for it.

Hume interpreted determinism (which he called 'the doctrine of necessity', or 'the doctrine of constant conjunction') as the doctrine that 'like causes always produce like effects' and that 'like effects necessarily follow from like causes'.[31] Concerning human actions and volitions he held, more particularly, that 'a spectator can commonly infer our actions from our motives and character; and even where he cannot, he concludes in

---

[29] Assume that our physical world is a *physically closed* system containing chance elements. Obviously it would not be deterministic; yet purposes, ideas, hopes, and wishes could not in such a world have any influence on physical events; assuming that they exist, they would be completely redundant: they would be what are called 'epiphenomena'. (Note that a deterministic physical system will be closed, but that a closed system may be indeterministic. Thus 'indeterminism is not enough', as will be explained in section x, below; see also note 40.)

[30] Kant suffered deeply from this nightmare and failed in his attempts to escape from it; see Compton's excellent statement on 'Kant's avenue of escape' in *The Freedom of Man*, pp. 67 f. (In line 2 on p. 68 the words '*of Pure Reason*' should be deleted.) I may perhaps mention here that I do not agree with everything Compton has to say in the field of the philosophy of science. Examples of views I do not share are: Compton's approval of Heisenberg's positivism or phenomenalism (*The Freedom of Man*, p. 31), and certain remarks (in op. cit., note 7 on p. 20) which Compton credits to Carl Eckart: although Newton himself was, it seems, not a determinist (cp. note 11), I do not think that the fairly precise idea of *physical determinism* should be discussed in terms of some vague 'law of causality'; nor do I agree that Newton was a phenomenalist in a sense similar to that in which Heisenberg may be said to have been a phenomenalist (or positivist) in the nineteen-thirties.

[31] David Hume, *A Treatise of Human Nature*, 1739 (ed. L. A. Selby-Bigge, 1888 and reprints), p. 174; see also, for example, pp. 173 and 87.

general, that he might, were he perfectly acquainted with every circumstance of our situation and temper, and the most secret springs of our . . . disposition. Now this is the very essence of necessity . . .'.[32] Hume's successors put it thus: our actions, or our volitions, or our tastes, or our preferences, are *psychologically* 'caused' by preceding experiences ('motives'), and ultimately by our heredity and environment.

But this doctrine which we may call *philosophical* or *psychological* determinism is not only a very different affair from *physical* determinism, but it is also one which a physical determinist who understands this matter at all can hardly take seriously. For the thesis of philosophical determinism, that 'Like effects have like causes' or that 'Every event has a cause', is so vague that it is perfectly compatible with physical *in*determinism.

Indeterminism—or more precisely, physical indeterminism—is merely the doctrine that *not all* events in the physical world are predetermined with absolute precision, in all their infinitesimal details. Apart from this, it is compatible with practically any degree of regularity you like, and it does not, therefore, entail the view that there are 'events without causes'; simply because the terms 'event' and 'cause' are vague enough to make the doctrine that every event has a cause compatible with physical indeterminism. While physical determinism demands complete and infinitely precise physical predetermination and the absence of *any* exception whatever, physical indeterminism asserts no more than that determinism is false, and that there are *at least some* exceptions, here or there, to precise predetermination.

Thus even the formula 'Every observable or measurable *physical* event has an observable or measurable *physical* cause' is still compatible with physical indeterminism, simply because no measurement can be infinitely precise: for the salient point about physical determinism is that, based on Newton's dynamics, it asserts the existence of a world of absolute mathematical precision. And although in so doing it goes beyond the realm of possible observation (as was seen by Peirce), it nevertheless is testable, in principle, with any desired degree of precision; and it actually withstood surprisingly precise tests.

By contrast, the formula 'Every event has a cause' says nothing about precision; and if, more especially, we look at the laws of

32 Hume, op. cit., pp. 408 f.

psychology, then there is not even a suggestion of precision. This holds for a 'behaviourist' psychology as much as for an 'introspective' or 'mentalist' one. In the case of a mentalist psychology this is obvious. But even a behaviourist may *at the very best* predict that, under given conditions, a rat will take twenty to twenty-two seconds to run a maze: he will have no idea how, by specifying more and more precise experimental conditions, he could make predictions which become more and more precise—and, *in principle, precise without limit*. This is so because behaviourist 'laws' are not, like those of Newtonian physics, differential equations, and because every attempt to introduce such differential equations would lead beyond behaviourism into physiology, and thus ultimately into physics; so it would lead us back to the problem of *physical determinism*.

As noted by Laplace, physical determinism implies that every physical event in the distant future (or in the distant past) is predictable (or retrodictable) with any desired degree of precision, provided we have sufficient knowledge about the present state of the physical world. The thesis of a philosophical (or psychological) determinism of Hume's type, on the other hand, asserts even in its strongest interpretation no more than that any *observable* difference between two events is related by some as yet perhaps unknown law to some difference—an observable difference perhaps—in the preceding state of the world; obviously a very much weaker assertion, and incidentally one which we could continue to uphold even if most of our experiments, performed under conditions which are, *in appearance*, 'entirely equal', should yield different results. This was stated very clearly by Hume himself. 'Even when these contrary experiments are entirely equal', he writes, 'we remove not the notion of causes and necessity, but . . . conclude, that the [apparent] chance . . . lies only in . . . our imperfect knowledge, not in the things themselves, which are in every case equally necessary [i.e., determined], tho' to appearance not equally constant or certain.'[33]

This is why a Humean philosophical determinism and, more

---

[33] Hume, op. cit., pp. 403 f. It is interesting to compare this with pp. 404 f. (where Hume says 'I define necessity two ways') and with his ascription to 'matter' of 'that intelligible quality, call it necessity or not' which, as he says, everybody 'must allow to belong to the will' (or 'to the actions of the mind'). In other words, Hume tries here to apply his doctrine of custom or habit, and his association psychology, to 'matter'; that is, to physics.

especially, a psychological determinism, lack the sting of physical determinism. For in Newtonian physics things really looked as if any apparent looseness in a system was in fact merely due to our ignorance, so that, should we be fully informed about the system, any appearance of looseness would disappear. Psychology, on the other hand, never had this character.

Physical determinism, we might say in retrospect, was a daydream of omniscience which seemed to become more real with every advance in physics until it became an apparently inescapable nightmare. But the corresponding daydreams of the psychologists were never more than castles in the air: they were Utopian dreams of attaining equality with physics, its mathematical methods, and its powerful applications; and perhaps even of attaining superiority, by moulding men and societies. (While these totalitarian dreams are not serious from a scientific point of view, they are very dangerous politically;[34] but since I have dealt with these dangers elsewhere I do not propose to discuss the problem here.)

IX

I HAVE called physical determinism a nightmare. It is a nightmare because it asserts that the whole world with everything in it is a huge automaton, and that we are nothing but little cogwheels, or at best sub-automata, within it.

It thus destroys, in particular, the idea of creativity. It reduces to a complete illusion the idea that in preparing this lecture I have used my brain to create *something new*. There was no more in it, according to physical determinism, than that certain parts of my body put down black marks on white paper: any physicist with sufficient detailed information could have written my lecture by the simple method of predicting the precise places on which the physical system consisting of my body (including my brain, of course, and my fingers) and my pen would put down those black marks.

[34] See especially B. F. Skinner, *Walden Two*, 1948, a charming and benevolent but utterly naïve Utopian dream of omnipotence (see especially pp. 246–50; also 214 f.). Aldous Huxley, *Brave New World*, 1932 (see also *Brave New World Revisited*, 1959), and George Orwell, *1984*, 1948, are well-known antidotes. I have criticized some of these Utopian and authoritarian ideas in *The Open Society and Its Enemies*, 1945, fourth edn., 1962, and in *The Poverty of Historicism*, e.g., p. 91. (See in both books especially my criticism of the so-called 'sociology of knowledge'.)

Or to use a more impressive example: if physical determinism is right, then a physicist who is completely deaf and who has never heard any music could write all the symphonies and concertos written by Mozart or Beethoven, by the simple method of studying the precise physical states of their bodies and predicting where they would put down black marks on their lined paper. And our deaf physicist could do even more: by studying Mozart's or Beethoven's bodies with sufficient care he could write scores which were never actually written by Mozart or Beethoven, but which they would have written had certain external circumstances of their lives been different: if they had eaten lamb, say, instead of chicken, or drunk tea instead of coffee.

All this could be done by our deaf physicist if supplied with a sufficient knowledge of purely physical conditions. There would be no need for him to know anything about the theory of music—though he might be able to predict what answers Mozart or Beethoven would have written down under examination conditions if presented with questions on the theory of counterpoint.

I believe that all this is absurd;[35] and its absurdity becomes even more obvious, I think, when we apply this method of physical prediction to a determinist.

For according to determinism, any theories—such as, say, determinism—are held because of a certain physical structure of the holder (perhaps of his brain). Accordingly we are deceiving ourselves (and are physically so determined as to deceive ourselves) whenever we believe that there are such things as arguments or reasons which make us accept determinism. Or in

---

[35] My deaf physicist is of course closely similar to Laplace's demon (see note 15); and I believe that his achievements are absurd, simply because non-physical aspects (aims, purposes, traditions, tastes, ingenuity) play a role in the development of the physical world; or in other words, I believe in *interactionism* (see notes 43 and 62). Samuel Alexander, *Space, Time and Deity*, 1920, vol. ii, p. 328, says of what he calls the 'Laplacean calculator': 'Except in the limited sense described, the hypothesis of the calculator is absurd.' Yet the 'limited sense' *includes* the prediction of *all* purely physical events, and would thus *include* the prediction of the position of all the black marks written by Mozart and Beethoven. It *excludes* only the prediction of mental experience (an exclusion that corresponds closely to my assumption of the physicist's deafness). Thus what I regard as absurd, Alexander is prepared to admit. (I may perhaps say here that I think it preferable to discuss the problem of freedom in connection with the creation of music or of new scientific theories or technical inventions, rather than with ethics, and ethical responsibility.)

other words, physical determinism is a theory which, if it is true, is not arguable, since it must explain all our reactions, including what appear to us as beliefs based on arguments, as due to *purely physical conditions*. Purely physical conditions, including our physical environment, make us say or accept whatever we say or accept; and a well-trained physicist who does not know any French, and who has never heard of determinism, would be able to predict what a French determinist would say in a French discussion on determinism; and of course also what his indeterminist opponent would say. But this means that if we believe that we have accepted a theory like determinism because we were swayed by the logical force of certain arguments, then we are deceiving ourselves, according to physical determinism; or more precisely, we are in a physical condition which determines us to deceive ourselves.

Hume saw much of this, even though it appears that he did not quite see what it meant for his own arguments; for he confined himself to comparing the determinism of *'our judgements'* with that of *'our actions'*, saying that *'we have no more liberty in the one than in the other'*.[36]

Considerations such as these may perhaps be the reason why there are so many philosophers who refuse to take the problem of physical determinism seriously and dismiss it as a 'bogy'.[37] Yet the doctrine that *man is a machine* was argued most forcefully and seriously in 1751, long before the theory of evolution became generally accepted, by de Lamettrie; and the theory of evolution gave the problem an even sharper edge, by suggesting that there may be no clear distinction between living matter and dead matter.[38] And in spite of the victory of the new quantum theory, and the conversion of so many physicists to indeterminism, de Lamettrie's doctrine that man is a machine has today perhaps more defenders than ever before among physicists, biologists, and philosophers; especially in the form of the thesis that man is a computer.[39]

[36] Humes, op. cit., p. 609 (the italics are mine).
[37] See note 15, above, and Gilbert Ryle, *The Concept of Mind*, 1949, pp. 76 ff. ('The Bogy of Mechanism').
[38] Cp. N. W. Pirie, 'The Meaninglessness of the Terms Life and Living', *Perspectives in Biochemistry*, 1937 (ed. J. Needham and D. E. Green), pp. 11 ff.
[39] See for example A. M. Turing, 'Computing Machinery and Intelligence', *Mind*, **59**, 1950, pp. 433–60. Turing asserted that men and computers are in

For if we accept a theory of evolution (such as Darwin's) then even if we remain sceptical about the theory that life emerged from inorganic matter we can hardly deny that there must have been a time when abstract and non-physical entities, such as reasons and arguments and scientific knowledge, and abstract rules, such as rules for building railways or bulldozers or sputniks or, say, rules of grammar or of counterpoint, did not exist, or at any rate had no effect upon the physical universe. It is difficult to understand how the physical universe could produce abstract entities such as rules, and then could come under the influence of these rules, so that these rules in their turn could exert very palpable effects upon the physical universe.

There is, however, at least one perhaps somewhat evasive but at any rate easy way out of this difficulty. We can simply deny that these abstract entities exist and that they can influence the physical universe. And we can assert that what do exist are our brains, and that these are machines like computers; that the allegedly abstract rules are physical entities, exactly like the concrete physical punch-cards by which we 'programme' our computers; and that the existence of anything non-physical is just 'an illusion', perhaps, and at any rate unimportant, since everything would go on as it does even if there were no such illusions.

According to this way out, we need not worry about the 'mental' status of these illusions. They may be universal properties of all things: the stone which I throw may have the illusion that it jumps, just as I have the illusion that I throw it; and my pen, or my computer, may have the illusion that it works because of its interest in the problems which it thinks that it is solving—and which I think that I am solving—while in fact there is nothing of any significance going on except purely physical interactions.

principle indistinguishable by their observable (behavioural) performance, and challenged his opponents to *specify* some observable behaviour or achievement of man which a computer would in principle be unable to achieve. But this challenge is an intellectual trap: by *specifying* a kind of behaviour we would lay down a specification for building a computer. Moreover, we use, and build, computers because they can do many things which we cannot do; just as I use a pen or pencil when I wish to tot up a sum I cannot do in my head. 'My pencil is more intelligent than I', Einstein used to say. But this does not establish that he is indistinguishable from his pencil. (Cp. the final paragraphs, p. 195, of my paper on Indeterminism, referred to in note 16 above, and chapter 12, section 5, of my book *Conjectures and Refutations*.)

You may see from all this that the problem of physical determinism which worried Compton is indeed a serious problem. It is not just a philosophical puzzle, but it affects at least physicists, biologists, behaviourists, psychologists, and computer engineers.

Admittedly, quite a few philosophers have tried to show (following Hume or Schlick) that it is merely a verbal puzzle, a puzzle about the use of the word 'freedom'. But these philosophers have hardly seen the difference between the problem of physical determinism and that of philosophical determinism; and they are either determinists like Hume, which explains why for them 'freedom' is 'just a word', or they have never had that close contact with the physical sciences or with computer engineering which would have impressed upon them that we are faced with more than a merely verbal puzzle.

X

Like Compton I am among those who take the problem of physical determinism seriously, and like Compton I do not believe that we are mere computing machines (though I readily admit that we can learn a great deal from computing machines —even about ourselves). Thus, like Compton, I am a *physical indeterminist*: physical indeterminism, I believe, is a necessary prerequisite for any solution of our problem. We have to be indeterminists; yet I shall try to show that indeterminism is not enough.

With this statement, *indeterminism is not enough*, I have arrived, not merely at a new point, but at the very heart of my problem.

The problem may be explained as follows.

If determinism is true, then the whole world is a perfectly running flawless clock, including all clouds, all organisms, all animals, and all men. If, on the other hand, Peirce's or Heisenberg's or some other form of indeterminism is true, then sheer *chance* plays a major role in our physical world. *But is chance really more satisfactory than determinism?*

The question is well known. Determinists like Schlick have put it in this way: '. . . freedom of action, responsibility, and mental sanity, cannot reach beyond the realm of causality: they stop where chance begins. . . . a higher degree of randomness . . . [simply means] a higher degree of irresponsibility.'[40]

I may perhaps put this idea of Schlick's in terms of an example I have used before: to say that the black marks made on white paper which I produced in preparation for this lecture were just the result of *chance* is hardly more satisfactory than to say that they were physically predetermined. In fact, it is even less satisfactory. For some people may perhaps be quite ready to believe that the text of my lecture can be in principle completely explained by my physical heredity, and my physical environment, including my upbringing, the books I have been reading, and the talks I have listened to; but hardly anybody will believe that what I am reading to you is the result of nothing but chance —just a random sample of English words, or perhaps of letters, put together without any purpose, deliberation, plan, or intention.

The idea that the only alternative to determinism is just sheer chance was taken over by Schlick, together with many of his views on the subject, from Hume, who asserted that 'the removal' of what he called 'physical necessity' must always result in 'the same thing with *chance*. As objects must either be conjoin'd or not, . . . 'tis impossible to admit of any medium betwixt chance and an absolute necessity'.[41]

I shall later argue against this important doctrine according to which the only alternative to determinism is sheer chance. Yet I must admit that the doctrine seems to hold good for the quantum-theoretical models which have been designed to explain, or at least to illustrate, the possibility of human freedom. This seems to be the reason why these models are so very unsatisfactory.

Compton himself designed such a model, though he did not particularly like it. It uses quantum indeterminacy, and the unpredictability of a quantum jump, as a model of a human decision of great moment. It consists of an amplifier which amplifies the effect of a single quantum jump in such a way that it may either cause an explosion or destroy the relay necessary

---

[40] See M. Schlick, *Erkenntnis*, **5**, p. 183 (extracted from the last eight lines of the first paragraph).

[41] Hume, op. cit., p. 171. See also for example p. 407: '. . . liberty . . . is the very same thing with chance.'

for bringing the explosion about. In this way one single quantum jump may be equivalent to a major decision. But in my opinion the model has no similarity to any *rational decision*. It is, rather, a model of a kind of decision-making where people who cannot make up their minds say: 'Let us toss a penny.' In fact, the whole apparatus for amplifying a quantum jump seems rather unnecessary: tossing a penny, and deciding on the result of the toss whether or not to pull a trigger, would do just as well. And there are of course computers with built-in penny-tossing devices for producing random results, where such are needed.

It may perhaps be said that some of our decisions *are* like penny-tosses: they are snap-decisions, taken without deliberation, since we often do not have enough time to deliberate. A driver or a pilot has sometimes to take a snap-decision like this; and if he is well trained, or just lucky, the result may be satisfactory; otherwise not.

I admit that the quantum-jump model may be a model for such snap-decisions; and I even admit that it is conceivable that something like the amplification of a quantum-jump may actually happen in our brains if we make a snap-decision. But are snap-decisions really so very interesting? Are they characteristic of human behaviour—of *rational* human behaviour?

I do not think so; and I do not think that we shall get much further with quantum jumps. They are just the kind of examples which seem to lend support to the thesis of Hume and Schlick that perfect chance is the only alternative to perfect determinism. What we need for understanding rational human behaviour —and indeed, animal behaviour—is something *intermediate* in character between perfect chance and perfect determinism— something intermediate between perfect clouds and perfect clocks.

Hume's and Schlick's ontological thesis that there cannot exist anything intermediate between chance and determinism seems to me not only highly dogmatic (not to say doctrinaire) but clearly absurd; and it is understandable only on the assumption that they believed in a complete determinism in which chance has no status except as a symptom of our ignorance. (But even then it seems to me absurd, for there is, clearly, something like partial knowledge, or partial ignorance.) For we know that even highly reliable clocks are not really perfect, and Schlick (if not Hume) must have known that this is largely due to factors such as friction—that is to say, to statistical or chance effects. And we also know that our clouds are not perfectly chance-like, since we can often predict the weather quite successfully, at least for short periods.

XI

THUS we shall have to return to our old arrangement with clouds on the left and clocks on the right and animals and men somewhere in between.

But even after we have done so (and there are some problems to be solved before we can say that this arrangement is in keeping with present-day physics), even then we have at best only made room for our main question.

For obviously what we want is to understand how such non-physical things as *purposes, deliberations, plans, decisions, theories, intentions,* and *values,* can play a part in bringing about physical changes in the physical world. That they do this seems to be obvious, *pace* Hume and Laplace and Schlick. It is clearly untrue that all those tremendous physical changes brought about hourly by our pens, or pencils, or bulldozers, can be explained in purely physical terms, either by a deterministic physical theory, or (by a stochastic theory) as due to chance.

Compton was well aware of this problem, as the following charming passage from his Terry Lectures shows:

It was some time ago when I wrote to the secretary of Yale University agreeing to give a lecture on November 10 at 5 p.m. He had such faith in me that it was announced publicly that I should be there, and the audience had such confidence in his word that they came to the hall at the specified time. But consider the great physical improbability that their confidence was justified. In the meanwhile my work called me to the Rocky Mountains and across the ocean to sunny Italy. A phototropic organism [such as I happen to be, would not easily] . . . tear himself away from there to go to chilly New Haven. The possibilities of my being elsewhere at this moment were infinite in number. Considered as a physical event, the probability of meeting my engagement would have been fantastically small. Why then was the audience's belief justified? . . .

They knew my purpose, and it was my purpose [which] determined that I should be there.[42]

Compton shows here very beautifully that mere physical indeterminism is not enough. We have to be indeterminists, to be sure; but we also must try to understand how men, and perhaps animals, can be 'influenced' or 'controlled' by such things as aims, or purposes, or rules, or agreements.

This then is our central problem.

XII

A CLOSER look shows, however, that there are *two* problems in this story of Compton's journey from Italy to Yale. Of these two problems I shall here call the first *Compton's problem*, and the second *Descartes's problem*.

Compton's problem has rarely been seen by philosophers, and if at all, only dimly. It may be formulated as follows:

There are such things as letters accepting a proposal to lecture, and public announcements of intentions; publicly declared aims and purposes; general moral rules. Each of these documents or pronouncements or rules has a certain content, or meaning, which remains invariant if we translate it, or reformulate it. Thus *this content or meaning is something quite abstract.* Yet it can control—perhaps by way of a short cryptic entry in an engagement calendar—the physical movements of a man in such a way as to steer him back from Italy to Connecticut. How can that be?

This is what I shall call Compton's problem. It is important to note that in this form the problem is neutral with respect to the question whether we adopt a behaviourist or a mentalist psychology: in the formulation here given, and suggested by Compton's text, the problem is put in terms of Compton's *behaviour* in returning to Yale; but it would make very little difference if we included such mental events as volition, or the feeling of having grasped, or got hold of, an idea.

Retaining Compton's own behaviourist terminology, Compton's problem may be described as the problem of the influence of the *universe of abstract meanings* upon human behaviour (and thereby upon the physical universe). Here 'universe of meanings'

---

[42] Cp. *The Freedom of Man*, pp. 53 f.

is a shorthand term comprising such diverse things as promises, aims, and various kinds of rules, such as rules of grammar, or of polite behaviour, or of logic, or of chess, or of counterpoint; also such things as scientific publications (and other publications); appeals to our sense of justice or generosity; or to our artistic appreciation; and so on, almost *ad infinitum*.

I believe that what I have here called Compton's problem is one of the most interesting problems of philosophy, even though few philosophers have seen it. In my opinion it is a real key problem, and more important than the classical body-mind problem which I am calling here 'Descartes's problem'.

In order to avoid misunderstandings I may perhaps mention that by formulating his problem in behaviouristic terms, Compton certainly had no intention of subscribing to a full-fledged behaviourism. On the contrary, he did not doubt either the existence of his own mind, or that of other minds, or of experiences such as volitions, or deliberations, or pleasure, or pain. He would therefore have insisted that there is a *second* problem to be solved.

We may identify this second problem with the classical body-mind problem, or Descartes's problem. It may be formulated as follows: how can it be that such things as states of mind—volitions, feelings, expectations—influence or control the physical movements of our limbs? And (though this is less important in our context) how can it be that the physical states of an organism may influence its mental states?[43]

Compton suggests that any *satisfactory* or *acceptable* solution of either of these two problems would have to comply with the following postulate which I shall call *Compton's postulate of freedom*: the solution must explain freedom; and it must also explain

---

[43] A critical discussion of what I call here Descartes's problem will be found in chapters 12 and 13 of my book *Conjectures and Refutations*. I may say here that, like Compton, I am almost a Cartesian, in so far as I reject the thesis of the physical completeness of all living organisms (considered as physical systems), that is to say, in so far as I conjecture that in some organisms mental states may *interact* with physical states. (I am, however, less of a Cartesian than Compton: I am even less attracted than he was by the master-switch models; cp. notes 44, 45, and 62.) Moreover, I have no sympathy with the Cartesian talk of a mental *substance* or thinking *substance*—no more than with his material *substance* or extended *substance*. I am a Cartesian only in so far as I believe in the existence of both, physical *states* and mental *states* (and, besides, in even more abstract things such as states of a discussion).

how freedom is not just chance but, rather, the result of a subtle interplay between *something almost random or haphazard*, and *something like a restrictive or selective control*—such as an aim or a standard—though certainly not a cast-iron control. For it is clear that the controls which guided Compton back from Italy allowed him plenty of freedom: freedom, say, to choose between an American and a French or Italian boat; or freedom to postpone his lecture, had some more important obligation arisen.

We may say that Compton's postulate of freedom restricts the acceptable solutions of our two problems by demanding that they should conform to *the idea of combining freedom and control*, and also to *the idea of a 'plastic control'*, as I shall call it in contradistinction to a 'cast-iron control'.

Compton's postulate is a restriction which I accept gladly and freely; and my own free and deliberate though not uncritical acceptance of this restriction may be taken as an illustration of that combination of freedom and control which is the very content of Compton's postulate of freedom.

XIII

I HAVE explained our two central *problems*—Compton's problem and Descartes's problem. In order to solve them we need, I believe, a *new theory*; in fact, a new theory of evolution, and a new model of the organism.

This need arises because the existing indeterministic theories are unsatisfactory. They are indeterministic; but we know that indeterminism is not enough, and it is not clear how they escape from Schlick's objection, or whether they conform to Compton's postulate of *freedom plus control*. Again, Compton's problem is quite beyond them: they are hardly relevant to it. And although these theories are attempts to solve Descartes's problem, the solutions they propose do not appear to be satisfactory.

The theories I am alluding to may be called 'master-switch models of control' or, more briefly, 'master-switch theories'. Their underlying idea is that our body is a kind of machine which can be regulated by a lever or switch from one or more *central control points*. Descartes even went so far as to locate the control point precisely: it is in the pineal gland, he said, that mind acts upon body. Some quantum theorists suggested (and

Compton very tentatively accepted the suggestion) that our minds work upon our bodies by influencing or selecting some quantum jumps. These are then amplified by our central nervous system which acts like an electronic amplifier: the amplified quantum jumps operate a cascade of relays or master-switches and ultimately effect muscular contractions.[44] There are, I think, some indications in Compton's books that he did not much like this particular theory or model, and that he used it for one purpose only: to show that human indeterminism (or even 'freedom') does not necessarily contradict quantum physics.[45] I think he was right in all this, including his dislike of master-switch theories.

For these master-switch theories—whether the one of Descartes, or the amplifier theories of the quantum physicists—belong to what I may perhaps call '*tiny baby theories*'. They seem to me to be almost as unattractive as tiny babies.

I am sure you all know the story of the unmarried mother who pleaded: 'But it is only a *very* tiny one.' Descartes's pleading seems to me similar: 'But it is such a tiny one: it is only an unextended mathematical point in which our mind may act upon our body.'

The quantum theorists hold a very similar tiny baby theory: 'But it is only with *one* quantum jump, and just within the Heisenberg uncertainties—and these are very tiny indeed—that a mind can act upon a physical system.' I admit that there is perhaps a slight advance here, in so far as the size of the baby is specified. But I still do not love the baby.

For however tiny the master-switch may be, the master-switch-*cum*-amplifier model strongly suggests that all our decisions are either snap-decisions (as I have called them in section x above) or else composed of snap-decisions. Now I admit that amplifier mechanisms are important characteristics of biological

---

[44] Compton discussed this theory in some detail, especially in *The Freedom of Man*, pp. 37–65. See especially the reference to Ralph Lillie, op. cit., in *The Freedom of Man*, p. 50. See also *The Human Meaning of Science*, pp. 47–54. Of considerable interest are Compton's remarks, in *The Freedom of Man*, pp. 63 f., and *The Human Meaning of Science*, p. 53, on *the character of individuality of our actions*, and his explanation of why it allows us to avoid what I may call the second horn of the dilemma (whose first horn is pure determinism), that is, the possibility that our actions are due to *pure chance*; cp. note 40.

[45] See especially *The Human Meaning of Science*, pp. viii f., and p. 54, the last statement of the section.

systems (for the energy of the reaction, released or triggered by a biological stimulus, usually exceeds greatly the energy of the triggering stimulus;[46] and I also admit, of course, that snap-decisions do occur. But they differ markedly from the kind of decision which Compton had in mind: they are almost like reflexes, and thus conform neither to the situation of Compton's problem of the influence of the universe of meanings upon our behaviour, nor to Compton's postulate of freedom (nor to the idea of a 'plastic' control). Decisions which conform to all this are as a rule reached almost imperceptibly through lengthy *deliberation*. They are reached by a kind of *maturing* process which is not well represented by the master-switch model.

By considering this process of deliberation, we may get another hint for our new theory. For deliberation always works by *trial and error* or, more precisely, by *the method of trial and of error-elimination*: by tentatively proposing various possibilities, and eliminating those which do not seem adequate. This suggests that we might use in our new theory some mechanism of trial and error-elimination.

I shall now outline how I intend to proceed.

Before formulating my evolutionary theory in general terms

I shall first show how it works in a particular case, by applying it to our first problem, that is, to Compton's problem of the *influence of meaning upon behaviour*.

After having in this way solved Compton's problem, I shall formulate the theory in a general way. Then it will be found that it also contains—within the framework of our new theory which creates a new problem-situation—a straightforward and almost trivial answer to Descartes's classical body–mind problem.

[46] This is a point of great importance, so much so that we should hardly describe any process as typically biological unless it involved the release or triggering of stored energy. But the opposite is of course not the case: many non-biological processes are of the same character; and though amplifiers and release processes did not play a great role in classical physics, they are most characteristic of quantum physics and of course of chemistry. (Radioactivity with a triggering energy equal to zero is an extreme case; another interesting case is the—in principle adiabatic—tuning-in to a certain radio frequency, followed by the extreme amplification of the signal or stimulus.) This is one of the reasons why such formulae as 'the cause equals the effect' (and, with it, the traditional criticism of Cartesian inter-actionism) have long become obsolete, in spite of the continuing validity of the conservation laws. Cp. note 43, and the *stimulating or releasing* function of language, discussed in section XIV below; see also my book, *Conjectures and Refutations*, p. 381.

XIV

LET us now approach our first problem—that is, Compton's problem of the influence of meaning upon behaviour—by way of some comments on *the evolution of languages from animal languages to human languages.*

Animal languages and human languages have many things in common, but there are also differences: as we all know, human languages do somehow transcend animal languages.

Using and extending some ideas of my late teacher Karl Bühler[47] I shall distinguish two functions which animal and human languages share, and two functions which human language alone possesses; or in other words, two lower functions, and two higher ones which evolved on the basis of the lower functions.

The two lower functions of language are these. First, language, like all other forms of behaviour, consists of *symptoms or expressions*; it is symptomatic or expressive of the state of the organism which makes the linguistic signs. Following Bühler, I call this the *symptomatic or expressive function of language.*

Secondly, for language or communication to take place, there must not only be a sign-making organism or a 'sender', but also a reacting one, a 'receiver'. The symptomatic *expression* of the first organism, the sender, releases or evokes or stimulates or triggers a reaction in the second organism, which *responds* to the sender's behaviour, thereby turning it into a *signal*. This function of language to act upon a receiver was called by Bühler the *releasing or signalling function of language.*

To take an example, a bird may be ready to fly away, and may *express* this by exhibiting certain symptoms. These may then *release or trigger* a certain response or reaction in a second bird, and as a consequence it too may get ready to fly away.

---

[47] The theory of the functions of language is due to Karl Bühler (*The Mental Development of the Child*, 1919, English translation 1930, pp. 55, 56, 57; also *Sprachtheorie*, 1934). I have added to his three functions the argumentative function (and some other functions that play no role here, such as a hortative and a persuasive function). See for example my paper 'Language and the Body–Mind Problem', in *Conjectures and Refutations*, p. 295, note 2 and text. (See also pp. 134 f.) It is not impossible that there exist in animals, especially in bees, transition stages to some descriptive languages; see K. von Frisch, *Bees: their Vision, Chemical Senses, and Language*, 1950; *The Dancing Bees*, 1955; and M. Lindauer, *Communication Among Social Bees*, 1961.

Note that the two functions, the expressive function and the release function, are *distinct*; for it is possible that instances of the first may occur without the second, though not the other way round: a bird may express by its behaviour that it is ready to fly away without thereby influencing another bird. So the first function may occur without the second; which shows that they can be disentangled in spite of the fact that, in any genuine instance of communication by language, they always occur together.

These two lower functions, the symptomatic or expressive function on the one hand, and the releasing or signalling function on the other, are common to the languages of animals *and* men; and these two lower functions are always present when any of the higher functions (which are characteristically human) are present.

For human language is very much richer. It has many functions, and dimensions, which animal languages do not have. Two of these new functions are most important for the evolution of reasoning and rationality: the *descriptive function*, and the *argumentative function*.

As an example of the descriptive function, I might now describe to you how two days ago a magnolia was flowering in my garden, and what happened when snow began to fall. I might thereby express my feelings, and also release or trigger some feeling in you: you may perhaps react by thinking of *your* magnolia trees. So the two lower functions would be present. But *in addition* to all this, I should have described to you some facts; I should have made some *descriptive statements*; and these statements of mine would be factually *true*, or factually *false*.

Whenever I speak I cannot help expressing myself; and if you listen to me you can hardly help reacting. So the lower functions are *always* present. The descriptive function *need not* be present, for I may speak to you without describing any fact. For example, in showing or expressing uneasiness—say, doubt about whether you will survive this long lecture—I need not describe anything. Yet description, including the description of conjectured states of affairs, which we formulate in the form of theories or hypotheses, is clearly an extremely important function of human language; and it is that function which distinguishes human language most clearly from the various animal languages (although there seems to be something approaching it in the language of the bees[48]). It is, of course, a function which is indispensable for science.

The last and highest of the four functions to be mentioned in this survey is the *argumentative function of language*, as it may be seen at work, in its highest form of development, in a well-disciplined *critical discussion*.

The argumentative function of language is not only the highest of the four functions I am here discussing, but it was also the latest of them to evolve. Its evolution has been closely connected with that of an argumentative, critical, and rational attitude; and since this attitude has led to the evolution of science, we may say that the argumentative function of language has created what is perhaps the most powerful tool for biological adaptation which has ever emerged in the course of organic evolution.

Like the other functions, the art of critical argument has developed by the method of trial and error-elimination, and it has had the most decisive influence on the human ability to think rationally. (Formal logic itself may be described as an 'organon of critical argument'.[49]) Like the descriptive use of language, the argumentative use has led to the evolution of ideal standards of control, or of *'regulative ideas'* (using a Kantian term): the main regulative idea of the descriptive use of language is *truth* (as distinct from *falsity*); and that of the argumentative use of language, in critical discussion, is *validity* (as distinct from *invalidity*).

Arguments, as a rule, are for or against some proposition or descriptive statement; this is why our fourth function—the argumentative function—must have emerged later than the descriptive function. Even if I argue in a committee that the University ought not to authorize a certain expenditure because we cannot afford it, or because some alternative way of using the money would be more beneficial, I am arguing not only for or against a *proposal* but also for and against some *proposition—for* the proposition, say, that the proposed use will not be beneficial, and *against* the proposition that the proposed use will be beneficial. So arguments, even arguments about proposals, as

---

[48] Cp. the books by Frisch, op. cit., and Lindauer, op. cit.

[49] See my book *Conjectures and Refutations*, chapter 1, especially the remark on p. 64 on formal logic as 'the *organon of rational criticism*'; also chapters 8 to 11, and chapter 15.

a rule bear on propositions, and very often on *descriptive* propositions.

Yet the argumentative use of language may be clearly distinguished from its descriptive use, simply because I can describe without arguing: I can describe, that is to say, without giving reasons for or against the truth of my description.

Our analysis of four functions of our language—the expressive, the signalling, the descriptive, and the argumentative functions—may be summed up by saying that, although it must be admitted that the two lower functions—the expressive and signalling functions—are *always* present whenever the higher functions are present, we must nevertheless distinguish the higher functions from the lower ones.

Yet many behaviourists and many philosophers have overlooked the higher functions, apparently because the lower ones are always present, whether or not the higher ones are.

XV

APART from the new functions of language which have evolved and emerged together with man, and with human rationality, we must consider another distinction of almost equal importance, the distinction between the evolution of *organs* and that of *tools or machines*, a distinction to be credited to one of the greatest of English philosophers, Samuel Butler, the author of *Erewhon* (1872).

Animal evolution proceeds largely, though not exclusively, by the modification of organs (or behaviour) or the emergence of new organs (or behaviour). *Human evolution* proceeds, largely, by developing new organs *outside our bodies or persons*: 'exosomatically', as biologists call it, or 'extra-personally'. These new organs are tools, or weapons, or machines, or houses.

The rudimentary beginnings of this exosomatic development can of course be found among animals. The making of lairs, or dens, or nests, is an early achievement. I may also remind you that beavers build very ingenious dams. But man, instead of growing better eyes and ears, grows spectacles, microscopes, telescopes, telephones, and hearing aids. And instead of growing swifter and swifter legs, he grows swifter and swifter motor cars.

Yet the kind of extra-personal or exosomatic evolution which interests me here is this: instead of growing better memories and brains, we grow paper, pens, pencils, typewriters, dictaphones, the printing press, and libraries.

These add to our language—and especially to its descriptive and argumentative functions—what may be described as new dimensions. The latest development (used mainly in support of our argumentative abilities) is the growth of computers.

XVI

How are the higher functions and dimensions related to the lower ones? They do not replace the lower ones, as we have seen, but they establish a kind of *plastic control* over them—a control with feed-back.

Take, for example, a discussion at a scientific conference. It may be exciting and enjoyable, and give rise to expressions and symptoms of its being so; and these expressions in their turn may release similar symptoms in other participants. Yet there is no doubt that up to a point these symptoms and releasing signals will be due to, and controlled by, the scientific *content* of the discussion; and since this will be *of a descriptive and of an argumentative nature*, the lower functions will be controlled by the higher ones. Moreover, though a good joke or a pleasant grin may let the lower functions win in the short run, what counts in the long run is a good argument—a valid argument—and what it establishes or refutes. In other words, our discussion is controlled, though plastically, by the regulative ideas of truth and of validity.

All this is strengthened by the discovery and development of the new dimensions of printing and publishing, especially when these are used for printing and publishing scientific theories and hypotheses, and papers in which these are critically discussed.

I cannot do justice to the importance of critical arguments here: it is a topic on which I have written fairly extensively,[50] and so I shall not raise it again here. I only wish to stress that critical arguments are *a means of control*: they are a means of eliminating errors, a means of selection. We *solve our problems* by

---

[50] See note 49, and my book *The Open Society and its Enemies*, especially chapter 24 and the *Addendum* to vol. ii (fourth edn., 1962); and *Conjectures and Refutations*, especially the preface and the introduction.

tentatively proposing various competing theories and hypotheses, as trial balloons, as it were; and by submitting them to critical discussion and to empirical tests, for the purpose of error-elimination.

So the evolution of the higher functions of language which I have tried to describe may be characterized as the evolution of new means for problem-solving, by new kinds of trials, and by new methods of error-elimination; that is to say, new methods for *controlling* the trials.

XVII

I CAN now give my solution to our first main problem, that is, Compton's problem of the influence of meaning upon behaviour. It is this.

The higher levels of language have evolved under the pressure of a need for the *better control* of two things: of our lower levels of language, and our adaptation to the environment, by the method of growing not only new tools, but also, for example, new scientific theories, and new standards of selection.

Now in developing its higher functions, our language has also grown abstract meanings and contents; that is to say, we have learned how to abstract from the various modes of formulating or expressing a theory, and how to pay attention to its *invariant content or meaning* (upon which its truth depends). And this holds not only for theories and other descriptive statements, but also for proposals, or aims, or whatever else may be submitted to critical discussion.

What I have called 'Compton's problem' was the problem of explaining and understanding the controlling power of meanings, such as the contents of our theories, or of purposes, or aims; purposes or aims which in some cases we may have adopted after deliberation and discussion. But this is now no longer a problem. Their power of influencing us is part and parcel of these contents and meanings; for part of the function of contents and meanings is to control.

This solution of Compton's problem conforms to Compton's restricting postulate. For the control of ourselves and of our actions by our theories and purposes is a *plastic* control. We are not *forced* to submit ourselves to the control of our theories, for we can discuss them critically, and we can reject them freely if we think that they fall short of our regulative standards. So the control is far from one-sided. Not only do our theories control us, but we can control our theories (and even our standards): there is a kind of *feed-back* here. And if we submit to our theories, then we do so freely, after deliberation; that is, after the critical discussion of alternatives, and after freely choosing between the competing theories, in the light of that critical discussion.

I submit this as my solution of Compton's problem; and before proceeding to solve Descartes's problem, I shall now briefly outline the more general theory of evolution which I have already used, implicitly, in my solution.

XVIII

I OFFER my general theory with many apologies. It has taken me a long time to think it out fully, and to make it clear to myself. Nevertheless I still feel far from satisfied with it. This is partly due to the fact that it is an *evolutionary* theory, and one which adds only a little, I fear, to existing evolutionary theories, except perhaps a new emphasis.

I blush when I have to make this confession; for when I was younger I used to say very contemptuous things about evolutionary philosophies. When twenty-two years ago Canon Charles E. Raven, in his *Science, Religion and the Future*, described the Darwinian controversy as 'a storm in a Victorian teacup', I agreed, but criticized him[51] for paying too much attention 'to the vapours still emerging from the cup', by which I meant the hot air of the evolutionary philosophies (especially those which told us that there were inexorable laws of evolution). But now I have to confess that this cup of tea has become, after all, *my* cup of tea; and with it I have to eat humble pie.

Quite apart from evolutionary *philosophies*, the trouble about evolutionary *theory* is its tautological, or almost tautological, character: the difficulty is that Darwinism and natural selection, though extremely important, explain evolution by 'the survival of the fittest' (a term due to Herbert Spencer). Yet there does not seem to be much difference, if any, between the assertion

[51] Cp. p. 106, note 1, of my book *The Poverty of Historicism*.

'those that survive are the fittest' and the tautology 'those that survive are those that survive'. For we have, I am afraid, no other criterion of fitness than actual survival, so that we conclude from the fact that some organisms have survived that they were the fittest, or those best adapted to the conditions of life.

This shows that Darwinism, with all its great virtues, is by no means a perfect theory. It is in need of a restatement which makes it less vague. The evolutionary theory which I am going to sketch here is an attempt at such a restatement.

My theory may be described as an attempt to apply to the whole of evolution what we learned when we analysed the evolution from animal language to human language. And it consists of a certain *view of evolution* as a growing hierarchical system of plastic controls, and of a certain *view of organisms* as incorporating—or in the case of man, evolving exosomatically —this growing hierarchical system of plastic controls. The Neo-Darwinist theory of evolution is assumed; but it is restated by pointing out that its 'mutations' may be interpreted as more or less accidental trial-and-error gambits, and 'natural selection' as one way of controlling them by error-elimination.

I shall now state the theory in the form of twelve short theses:

(1) All *organisms* are constantly, day and night, *engaged in problem-solving*; and so are all those evolutionary *sequences of organisms*—the *phyla* which begin with the most primitive forms and of which the now living organisms are the latest members.

(2) These problems are problems in an objective sense: they can be, hypothetically, reconstructed by hindsight, as it were. (I will say more about this later.) Objective problems in this sense need not have their conscious counterpart; and where they have their conscious counterpart, the conscious problem need not coincide with the objective problem.

(3) Problem-solving always proceeds by the method of trial and error: new reactions, new forms, new organs, new modes of behaviour, new hypotheses, are tentatively put forward and controlled by error-elimination.

(4) Error-elimination may proceed either by the complete elimination of unsuccessful forms (the killing-off of unsuccessful forms by natural selection) or by the (tentative) evolution of controls which modify or suppress unsuccessful organs, or forms of behaviour, or hypotheses.

(5) The single organism telescopes[52] into one body, as it were, the controls developed during the evolution of its *phylum*—just as it partly recapitulates, in its ontogenetic development, its phylogenetic evolution.

(6) The single organism is a kind of spearhead of the evolutionary sequence of organisms to which it belongs (its *phylum*): it is itself a tentative solution, probing into new environmental niches, choosing an environment and modifying it. It is thus related to its *phylum* almost exactly as the actions (behaviour) of the individual organism are related to this organism: the individual organism, and its behaviour, are both trials, which may be eliminated by error-elimination.

(7) Using '*P*' for problem, '*TS*' for tentative solutions, '*EE*' for error-elimination, we can describe the fundamental evolutionary sequence of events as follows:

$$P \to TS \to EE \to P.$$

But this sequence is not a cycle: the second problem is, in general, different from the first: it is the result of the new situation which has arisen, in part, because of the tentative solutions which have been tried out, and the error-elimination which controls them. In order to indicate this, the above schema should be rewritten:

$$P_1 \to TS \to EE \to P_2.$$

(8) But even in this form an important element is still missing: the multiplicity of the tentative solutions, the multiplicity of the trials. Thus our final schema becomes something like this:

$$
\begin{array}{c}
\nearrow TS_1 \searrow \\
P_1 \to TS_2 \to EE \to P_2 \\
\searrow \quad \cdot \quad \nearrow \\
\cdot \\
\cdot \\
\cdot \\
TS_n
\end{array}
$$

Background Knowledge

---

[52] The idea of 'telescoping' (though not this term which I owe to Alan Musgrave) may perhaps be found in chapter vi of Charles Darwin's *The Origin of Species*, 1859 (I am quoting from the Mentor Book edn., p. 180; italics mine): '. . . every highly developed organism has passed through many changes; and . . . each modified structure tends to be inherited, so that each modification will not . . . be quite lost. . . . *Hence the structure of each part* [of the organism] . . . *is the sum* of many

(9) In this form, our schema can be compared with that of Neo-Darwinism. According to Neo-Darwinism there is in the main *one* problem: the problem of survival. There is, as in our system, a multiplicity of tentative solutions—the variations or mutations. But there is only *one* way of error-elimination—the killing of the organism. And (partly for this reason) the fact that P_1 and P_2 will differ essentially is overlooked, or else its fundamental importance is not sufficiently clearly realized.

(10) In our system, not all problems are survival problems: there are many very specific problems and sub-problems (even though the earliest problems may have been sheer survival problems). For example an early problem P_1 may be reproduction. Its solution may lead to a new problem, P_2: the problem of getting rid of, or of spreading, the offspring—the children which threaten to suffocate not only the parent organism but each other.[53]

It is perhaps of interest to note that *the problem of avoiding suffocation by one's offspring* may be one of those problems which was solved by the evolution of *multicellular organisms*: instead of getting rid of one's offspring, one establishes a *common economy*, with various new methods of living together.

(11) The theory here proposed distinguishes between P_1 and P_2, and it shows that the problems (or the problem situations) which the organism is trying to deal with are often *new*, and arise themselves as products of the evolution. The theory thereby gives implicitly a rational account of what has usually been called by the somewhat dubious names of *'creative evolution'* or *'emergent evolution'*.[54]

(12) Our schema allows for the development of error-eliminating controls (warning organs like the eye; feed-back mechanisms); that is, controls which can eliminate errors without killing the organism; and it makes it possible, ultimately, for our hypotheses to die in our stead.

inherited changes, through which the species has passed. . . .' See also E. Baldwin in the book, *Perspectives in Biochemistry*, pp. 99 ff., and the literature there quoted.

[53] The emergence of a new problem-situation could be described as a change or a differentiation of the 'ecological niche', or the significant environment, of the organism. (It may perhaps be called a 'habitat selection'; cp. B. Lutz, *Evolution*, 2, 1948, pp. 29 ff.) The fact that *any* change in the organism *or* its habits *or* its habitat produces new problems accounts for the incredible wealth of the (always tentative) solutions.

[54] See note 23 for reference to Compton's remarks on 'emergent evolution'.

XIX

EACH organism can be regarded as a hierarchical system of *plastic controls*—as a system of clouds controlled by clouds. The controlled subsystems make trial-and-error movements which are partly suppressed and partly restrained by the controlling system.

We have already met an example of this in the relation between the lower and higher functions of language. The lower ones continue to exist and to play their part; but they are constrained and controlled by the higher ones.

Another characteristic example is this. If I am standing quietly, without making any movement, then (according to the physiologists) my muscles are constantly at work, contracting and relaxing in an almost random fashion (see TS_1 to TS_n in thesis (8) of the preceding section), but controlled, without my being aware of it, by error-elimination (EE) so that every little deviation from my posture is almost at once corrected. So I am kept standing, quietly, by more or less the same method by which an automatic pilot keeps an aircraft steadily on its course.

This example also illustrates the thesis (1) of the preceding section—that each organism is all the time engaged in problem-solving by trial and error; that it reacts to new and old problems by more or less chance-like,[55] or cloud-like, trials which are eliminated if unsuccessful. (If successful, they increase the probability of the survival of mutations which 'simulate' the solutions so reached, and tend to make the solution hereditary,[56] by incorporating it into the spatial structure or form of the new organism.)

---

[55] The method of trial and error-elimination *does not operate with completely chance-like or random trials* (as has been sometimes suggested), even though the trials may look pretty random; there must be at least an 'after-effect' (in the sense of my *The Logic of Scientific Discovery*, pp. 162 ff.). For the organism is constantly learning from its mistakes, that is, it establishes *controls* which suppress or eliminate, or at least reduce the frequency of, certain *possible* trials (which were perhaps *actual* ones in its evolutionary past).

[56] This is now sometimes called the 'Baldwin Effect'; see for example, G. G. Simpson, 'The Baldwin Effect', *Evolution*, **7**, 1953, pp. 110 ff., and C. H. Waddington, the same volume, pp. 118 ff. (see especially p. 124), and pp. 386 f. See also J. Mark Baldwin, *Development and Evolution*, 1902, pp. 174 ff. and H. S. Jennings, *The Behaviour of the Lower Organisms*, 1906, pp. 321 ff.

XX

THIS is a very brief outline of the theory. It needs, of course, much elaboration. But I wish to explain *one* point a little more fully—the use I have made (in theses (1) to (3) of section XVIII) of the terms '*problem*' and '*problem-solving*' and, more particularly, my assertion that *we can speak of problems in an objective, or non-psychological sense*.

The point is important, for evolution is clearly not a conscious process. Many biologists say that the evolution of certain organs solves certain problems; for example, that the evolution of the eye solves the problem of giving a moving animal a timely warning to change its direction before bumping into something hard. Nobody suggests that this kind of solution to this kind of problem is consciously sought. Is it not, then, just a metaphor if we speak of problem-solving?

I do not think so; rather, the situation is this: when we speak of a problem, we do so almost always from hindsight. A man who works on a problem can seldom say clearly what his problem is (unless he has found a solution); and even if he can explain his problem, he may mistake it. And this may even hold of scientists—though scientists are among those few who consciously try to be fully aware of their problems. For example, Kepler's conscious problem was to discover the harmony of the world order; but we may say that the problem he solved was the mathematical description of motion in a set of two-body planetary systems. Similarly, Schrödinger was mistaken about the problem he had solved by finding the (time-independent) Schrödinger equation: he thought his waves were charge-density waves, of a changing continuous field of electric charge. Later Max Born gave a statistical interpretation of the Schrödinger wave amplitude; an interpretation which shocked Schrödinger and which he disliked as long as he lived. He had solved a problem—but it was not the one he thought he had solved. This we know now, by hindsight.

Yet clearly it is in science that we are most conscious of the problems we try to solve. So it should not be inappropriate to use hindsight in other cases, and to say that the amoeba solves some problems (though we need not assume that it is in any sense aware of its problems): from the amoeba to Einstein is just one step.

XXI

BUT Compton tells us that the amoeba's actions are not rational,[57] while we may assume that Einstein's actions are. So there should be some difference, after all.

I admit that there is a difference: even though their methods of almost random or cloud-like trial and error movements are fundamentally not very different,[58, 55] there is a great difference in their attitudes towards error. Einstein, unlike the amoeba, consciously tried his best, whenever a new solution occurred to him, to fault it and detect an error in it: he approached his own solutions *critically*.

I believe that this consciously critical attitude towards his own ideas is the one really important difference between the method of Einstein and that of the amoeba. It made it possible for Einstein to reject, quickly, hundreds of hypotheses as inadequate before examining one or another hypothesis more carefully, if it appeared to be able to stand up to more serious criticism.

As the physicist John Archibald Wheeler said recently, 'Our whole problem is to make the mistakes as fast as possible'.[59] This problem of Wheeler's is solved by consciously adopting the critical attitude. This, I believe, is the highest form so far of the rational attitude, or of rationality.

The scientist's trials and errors consist of hypotheses. He formulates them in words, and often in writing. He can then try to find flaws in any one of these hypotheses, by criticizing it, and by testing it experimentally, helped by his fellow scientists who will be delighted if they can find a flaw in it. If the hypothesis does not stand up to these criticisms and to these tests at least as well as its competitors,[60] it will be eliminated.

It is different with primitive man, and with the amoeba. Here

[57] See *The Freedom of Man*, p. 91, and *The Human Meaning of Science*, p. 73.

[58] Cp. H. S. Jennings, op. cit., pp. 334 f., 349 f. A beautiful example of a problem-solving fish is described by K. Z. Lorenz, *King Solomon's Ring*, 1952, pp. 37 f.

[59] John A. Wheeler, *American Scientist*, **44**, 1956, p. 360.

[60] That we can only choose the 'best' of a set of competing hypotheses—the 'best' in the light of a critical discussion devoted to the search for truth—means that we choose the one which appears, in the light of the discussion, to come 'nearest to the truth'; see my *Conjectures and Refutations*, chapter 10. See also *The Freedom of Man*, pp. vii f., and especially p. 74 (on the principle of conservation of energy).

there is no critical attitude, and so it happens more often than not that natural selection eliminates a mistaken hypothesis or expectation by eliminating those organisms which hold it, or believe in it. So we can say that the critical or rational method consists in letting our hypotheses die in our stead: it is a case of exosomatic evolution.

XXII

HERE I may perhaps turn to a question which has given me much trouble although in the end I arrived at a very simple solution.

The question is: Can we show that plastic controls exist? Are there inorganic physical systems in nature which may be taken as examples or as physical models of plastic controls?

It seems that this question was implicitly answered in the negative by many physicists who, like Descartes or Compton, operate with master-switch models, and by many philosophers who, like Hume or Schlick, deny that anything intermediate between complete determinism and pure chance can exist. Admittedly, cyberneticists and computer engineers have more recently succeeded in constructing computers made of hardware but incorporating highly plastic controls; for example, computers with built-in mechanism for chance-like trials, checked or evaluated by feed-back (in the manner of an automatic pilot or a self-homing device) and eliminated if erroneous. But these systems, although incorporating what I have called plastic controls, consist essentially of complex relays of master-switches. What I was seeking, however, was a simple physical model of Peircean indeterminism; a purely physical system resembling a very cloudy cloud in heat motion, controlled by some other cloudy clouds—though by somewhat less cloudy ones.

If we return to our old arrangement of clouds and clocks, with a cloud on the left and a clock on the right, then we could say that what we are looking for is something intermediate, like an organism or like our cloud of gnats, but not alive: a pure physical system, controlled plastically and 'softly', as it were.

Let us assume that the cloud to be controlled is a gas. Then we can put on the extreme left an uncontrolled gas which will soon diffuse and so cease to constitute a physical *system*. We put on the extreme right an iron cylinder filled with gas: this is our example of a 'hard' control, a 'cast-iron' control. In between, but far to the left, are many more or less 'softly' controlled systems, such as our cluster of gnats, and huge balls of particles, such as a gas kept together by gravity, somewhat like the sun. (We do not mind if the control is far from perfect, and many particles escape.) The planets may perhaps be said to be cast-iron controlled in their movements—comparatively speaking, of course, for even the planetary system is a cloud, and so are all the milky ways, star clusters, and clusters of clusters. But are there, apart from organic systems and those huge systems of particles, examples of any 'softly' controlled small physical systems?

I think there are, and I propose to put in the middle of our diagram a child's balloon or, perhaps better, a soap bubble; and this, indeed, turns out to be a very primitive and in many respects an excellent example or model of a Peircean system *and* of a 'soft' kind of plastic control.

The soap bubble consists of two subsystems which are both clouds and which control each other: without the air, the soapy film would collapse, and we should have only a drop of soapy water. Without the soapy film, the air would be uncontrolled: it would diffuse, ceasing to exist as a system. Thus the control is mutual; it is plastic, and of a feed-back character. Yet it is possible to make a distinction between the controlled system (the air) and the controlling systems (the film): the enclosed air is not only more cloudy than the enclosing film, but it also ceases to be a physical (self-interacting) system if the film is removed. As against this, the film, after removal of the air, will form a droplet which, though of a different shape, may still be said to be a physical system.

Comparing the bubble with a 'hardware' system like a precision clock or a computer, we should of course say (in accordance with Peirce's point of view) that even these hardware systems are clouds controlled by clouds. But these 'hard' systems are built with the purpose of minimizing, so far as it is possible, the cloud-like effects of molecular heat motions and fluctuations: though they are clouds, the controlling mechanisms are designed to suppress, or compensate for, all cloud-like effects as far as possible. This holds even for computers with mechanisms simulating chance-like trial-and-error mechanisms.

Our soap bubble is different in this respect and, it seems, more similar to an organism: the molecular effects are not eliminated but contribute essentially to the working of the system which is enclosed by a skin—a permeable wall[61] that leaves the system 'open', and able to 'react' to environmental influences in a manner which is built, as it were, into its 'organization': the soap bubble, when struck by a heat ray, absorbs the heat (much like a hot-house), and so the enclosed air will expand, keeping the bubble floating.

As in all uses of similarity or analogy we should, however, look out for limitations; and here we might point out that, at least in some organisms, molecular fluctuations are apparently amplified and so used to release trial-and-error movements. At any rate, amplifiers seem to play important roles in all organisms (which in this respect resemble some computers with their master-switches and cascades of amplifiers and relays). Yet there are no amplifiers in the soap bubble.

However this may be, our bubble shows that natural physical cloud-like systems which are plastically and softly controlled by other cloud-like systems do exist. (Incidentally, the film of the bubble need not, of course, be derived from organic matter, though it will have to contain large molecules.)

XXIII

THE evolutionary theory here proposed yields an immediate solution to our second main problem—the classical Cartesian body–mind problem. It does so (without saying *what* 'mind' or 'consciousness' is) by saying something about the evolution, and thereby about the functions, of mind or consciousness.

We must assume that consciousness grows from small beginnings; perhaps its first form is a vague feeling of irritation, experienced when the organism has a problem to solve such as getting away from an irritant substance. However this may be,

---

[61] Permeable walls or membranes seem to be characteristic of all biological systems. (This may be connected with the phenomenon of biological individuation.) For the pre-history of the idea that membranes and bubbles are primitive organisms, see C. H. Kahn, *Anaximander*, 1960, pp. 111 ff.

consciousness will assume evolutionary significance—and increasing significance—when it begins to *anticipate* possible ways of reacting: possible trial-and-error movements, and their possible outcomes.

We can say now that conscious states, or sequences of conscious states, may function as systems of control, of error-elimination: the elimination, as a rule, of (incipient) behaviour, that is (incipient) movement. Consciousness, from this point of view, appears as just one of many interacting kinds of control; and if we remember the control systems incorporated for example in books—theories, systems of law, and all that constitutes the 'universe of meanings'—then consciousness can hardly be said to be the highest control system in the hierarchy. For it is to a considerable extent controlled by these exosomatic linguistic systems—even though they may be said to be *produced* by consciousness. Consciousness in turn is, we may conjecture, *produced* by physical states; yet it controls them to a considerable extent. Just as a legal or social system is produced by us, yet controls us, and is in no reasonable sense 'identical' to or 'parallel' with us, but *interacts* with us, so states of consciousness (the 'mind') control the body, and *interact* with it.

Thus there is a whole set of analogous relationships. As our exosomatic world of meanings is related to consciousness, so consciousness is related to the behaviour of the acting individual organism. And the behaviour of the individual organism is similarly related to its body, to the individual organism taken as a physiological system. The latter is similarly related to the evolutionary sequence of organisms—the *phylum* of which it forms the latest spearhead, as it were: as the individual organism is thrown up experimentally as a probe by the *phylum* and yet largely controls the fate of the *phylum*, so the behaviour of the organism is thrown up experimentally as a probe by the physiological system and yet controls, largely, the fate of this system. Our conscious states are similarly related to our behaviour. They anticipate our behaviour, working out, by trial and error, its likely consequences; thus they not only control but they try out, *deliberate*.

We now see that this theory offers us an almost trivial answer to Descartes's problem. Without saying *what 'the mind' is*, it leads immediately to the conclusion that our *mental states control* (*some of*) *our physical movements*, and that there is some give-and-take, some feed-back, and so some *interaction*, between mental activity and the other functions of the organism.[62]

The control will again be of the 'plastic' kind; in fact all of us —especially those who play a musical instrument such as the piano or the violin—know that the body does not always do what we want it to do; and that we have to learn, from our ill-success, how to modify our aims, making allowances for those limitations which beset our control: though we are free, to some considerable extent, there are always conditions—physical or otherwise—which set limits to what we can do. (Of course, before giving in, we are free to try to transcend these limits.)

Thus, like Descartes, I propose the adoption of a dualistic outlook, though I do *not* of course recommend talking of *two kinds of interacting substances*. But I think it is helpful and legitimate to distinguish *two kinds of interacting states* (or events), physio-chemical and mental ones. Moreover, I suggest that if we distinguish only these two kinds of states we still take too narrow a view of our world: at the very least we should also distinguish those artifacts which are products of organisms, and especially the products of our minds, and which can interact with our minds and thus with the state of our physical environment. Although these artifacts are often 'mere bits of matter', 'mere tools' perhaps, they are even on the animal level sometimes consummate works of art; and on the human level, the products of our minds are often very much more than 'bits of matter'—marked bits of paper, say; for these bits of paper may represent states of a discussion, states of the growth of knowledge, which may transcend (sometimes with serious consequences) the grasp of most or even all of the minds that helped to produce them. Thus we have to be not merely dualists, but pluralists; and we have to recognize that the great changes which we have brought about, often unconsciously, in our

[62] As hinted in several places, I conjecture that the acceptance of an '*interaction*' of mental and physical states offers the only satisfactory solution of Descartes's problem; see also note 43. I wish to add here that I think that we have good reason to assume that there exist mental states, or conscious states (for example in dreams) in which the consciousness of the ego (or of one's spatio-temporal position and identity) is very weak, or absent. It seems therefore reasonable to assume that full consciousness of the ego is a late development, and that it is a mistake to formulate the body-mind problem in such a way that this form of consciousness (or conscious 'will') is treated as if it were the only one.

physical universe show that abstract rules and abstract ideas, some of which are perhaps only partially grasped by human minds, may move mountains.

As an afterthought, I should like to add one last point.

It would be a mistake to think that, because of natural selection, evolution can only lead to what may be called 'utilitarian' results: to adaptations which are useful in helping us to survive.

Just as, in a system with plastic controls, the controlling and controlled subsystems interact, so our tentative solutions interact with our *problems* and also with our *aims*. This means that our aims can change and that *the choice of an aim may become a problem*; different aims may compete, and new aims may be invented and controlled by the method of trial and error-elimination.

Admittedly, if a new aim clashes with the aim of surviving, then this new aim may be eliminated by natural selection. It is well known that many mutations are lethal and thus suicidal; and there are many examples of suicidal aims. Others are perhaps neutral with respect to survival.

Many aims that at first are subsidiary to survival may later become autonomous, and even opposed to survival; for example, the ambition to excel in courage, to climb Mount Everest, to discover a new continent, or to be the first on the Moon; or the ambition to discover some new truth.

Other aims may from the very beginning be autonomous departures, independent of the aim to survive. Artistic aims are perhaps of this kind, or some religious aims, and to those who cherish them they may become much more important than survival.

All this is part of the superabundance of life—the almost excessive abundance of trials and errors upon which the method of trial and error-elimination depends.[63]

It is perhaps not uninteresting to see that artists, like scientists, actually use this trial-and-error method. A painter may put down, tentatively, a speck of colour, and step back for a

---

[63] Cp. for example my *Conjectures and Refutations*, especially p. 312.

critical assessment of its effect[64] in order to alter it if it does not solve the problem he wants to solve. And it may happen that an unexpected or accidental effect of his tentative trial—a colour speck or brush stroke—may change his problem, or create a new subproblem, or a new aim: the evolution of artistic aims and of artistic standards (which, like the rules of logic, may become exosomatic systems of control) proceeds also by the trial-and-error method.

We may perhaps here look back for a moment to the problem of physical determinism, and to our example of the deaf physicist who had never experienced music but would be able to 'compose' a Mozart opera or a Beethoven symphony, simply by studying Mozart's or Beethoven's bodies and their environments as physical systems, and predicting where their pens would put down black marks on lined paper. I presented these as unacceptable consequences of physical determinism. Mozart and Beethoven are, partly, controlled by their 'taste', their system of musical evaluation. Yet this system is not cast iron but rather plastic. It responds to new ideas, and it can be modified by new trials and errors—perhaps even by an accidental mistake, an unintended discord.[65]

In conclusion, let me sum up the situation.

We have seen that it is unsatisfactory to look upon the world as a closed physical system—whether a strictly deterministic system or a system in which whatever is not strictly determined is simply due to chance: on such a view of the world human creativeness and human freedom can only be illusions. The attempt to make use of quantum-theoretical indeterminacy is

---

[64] See, for example, Ernst H. Gombrich, *Meditations on a Hobby Horse*, 1963, especially p. 10; and the same author's *Art and Illusion*, 1960, 1962 (see the Index under 'trial and error'). Cp. also note 65.

[65] For the close similarity of scientific and artistic production see *The Freedom of Man*, Preface, pp. vii f., and the remark in *The Freedom of Man*, p. 74, referred to in note 60 above; further E. Mach, *Wärmelehre*, 1896, pp. 440 f., where he writes: 'The history of art . . . teaches us how shapes which arise accidentally may be used in works of art. Leonardo da Vinci advises the artist to look for shapes of clouds or patches on dirty or smoky walls, which might suggest to him ideas that fit in with his plans and his moods. . . . Again, a musician may sometimes get new ideas from random noises; and we may hear on occasion from a famous composer that he has been led to find valuable melodic or harmonic motifs by accidentally touching a wrong key while playing the piano.'

also unsatisfactory, because it leads to chance rather than freedom, and to snap-decisions rather than deliberate decisions.

I have therefore offered here a different view of the world—one in which the physical world is an open system. This is compatible with the view of the evolution of life as a process of trial and error-elimination; and it allows us to understand rationally, though far from fully, the emergence of biological novelty and the growth of human knowledge and human freedom.

I have tried to outline an evolutionary theory which takes account of all this and which offers solutions to Compton's and Descartes's problems. It is, I am afraid, a theory which manages to be too humdrum *and* too speculative at the same time; and even though I think that testable consequences can be derived from it, I am far from suggesting that my proposed solution is what philosophers have been looking for. But I feel that Compton might have said that it presents, in spite of its faults, a possible answer to his problem—and one which might lead to further advance.

7. Evolution and the Tree of Knowledge

I WAS much gratified by the invitation to deliver the Herbert Spencer Lecture, and not only because of the honour of being called upon to pay homage to a thinker of great courage and originality. What pleased me especially was the suggestion, made by the Board of Management of this lectureship, that I might decide to choose for my lecture some such subject as 'The Method of the Biological Sciences'. This suggestion gives me the opportunity to develop here a number of ideas which, though I find them exciting and worthy of discussion, I might never have presented in public had I not received this encouragement.

All the ideas which I intend to put before you bear on problems of method in biology. Yet I shall not confine myself to this field. My plan for the three parts of this lecture is to begin with some remarks on the general theory of knowledge; next to turn to certain problems of method bearing on the theory of evolution; and finally to trespass upon, or rather dabble in, certain parts of the theory of evolution itself. To be quite specific, I shall put before you, in the third part of my lecture, a conjecture of mine which is intended to solve, within the framework of a Darwinian or Neo-Darwinian theory of natural selection, some of the classical difficulties under which this theory has laboured hitherto.

I call these difficulties 'classical', because they were discovered early, and succinctly analysed, both by Herbert Spencer, shortly after he accepted Darwin's theory of natural selection, and by Samuel Butler, shortly after he rejected it. Indeed, Darwin himself, as Spencer pointed out, had already been much concerned with the difficulties to which I am alluding.[1]

---

[1] See especially Spencer's paper 'The Factors of Organic Evolution', first

Based on the Herbert Spencer Lecture, delivered in Oxford on 30 Oct. 1961. The more significant additions, including whole new footnotes, have been indicated by square brackets, and the Appendix has been added in 1971.

My programme for this lecture extends, therefore, from the general theory of knowledge through the methods of biology to the theory of evolution itself. This programme, I am afraid, is a little ambitious for one lecture; and if in addition it were part of my programme to *convince* you, my position would indeed be desperate. It is therefore fortunate that I have no intention of convincing anybody of the truth of any of my theses, and least of all of the truth of my new Neo-Darwinian conjecture which I shall propose to you at the end of my lecture. For although I hope that this conjecture may perhaps help us to get a little nearer to the truth, I do not dare even to hope that it is true; indeed, I fear that it contains very little truth. It certainly contains neither the final truth, nor the whole truth of the matter. Thus I do not wish to convince you, simply because I am not convinced myself. Yet I do hope, and I shall try my best, to rekindle your interest in these problems. I admit that they have at times become somewhat stale, and I have even somewhere expressed my agreement with Professor Raven's remark that the evolutionary controversy was 'a storm in a Victorian teacup'. Yet although this description may be quite fair if we think of the storm raised by Darwin's assertion of our kinship with the apes, there were other, and to my mind more exciting, theoretical problems raised by the Darwinian controversy.

1. *Some Remarks on Problems and the Growth of Knowledge*

I now turn to the first part of my lecture: to the general theory of knowledge.

The reason why I feel I have to start with some comments on the theory of knowledge is that I disagree over it with almost everybody, except perhaps Charles Darwin and Albert Einstein. (Einstein, incidentally, explained his view of these

published in his *Essays* (for example in vol. i of the 'Library Edition' of 1891, pp. 389 ff.). It is interesting to note that among the many important ideas in this paper there are formulations of an approach that is now called the 'organismic approach to biology' and widely believed to be an innovation; see for example p. 410, where Spencer speaks of changes in certain organs and says that 'all the other . . . organs become implicated in the change. The functions performed by them have to constitute *a moving equilibrium*'. (Italics mine.) In modern terms, Spencer here describes the organism as 'an open system in fluent equilibrium' (or 'in an approximately steady state').

matters in his Herbert Spencer Lecture of 1933.)[2] The main point at issue is the relation between observation and theory. I believe that theory—at least some rudimentary theory or expectation—always comes first; that it always precedes observation; and that the fundamental role of observations and experimental tests is to show that some of our theories are false, and so to stimulate us to produce better ones.

Accordingly I assert that we do not start from observations but always from *problems*—either from practical problems or from *a theory which has run into difficulties*. Once we are faced with a problem, we may begin to work on it. We may do so by attempts of two kinds: we may proceed by first attempting to guess or to conjecture a solution to our problem; and we may then attempt to criticize our usually somewhat feeble guess. Sometimes a guess or a conjecture may withstand our criticism and our experimental tests for some time. But as a rule, we soon find that our conjectures can be refuted, or that they do not solve our problem, or that they solve it only in part; and we find that even the best solutions—those able to resist the most severe criticism of the most brilliant and ingenious minds —soon give rise to new difficulties, to new problems. Thus we may say that *the growth of knowledge proceeds from old problems to new problems, by means of conjectures and refutations.*

Some of you, I suppose, will agree that we usually start from problems; but you may still think that our problems must have been the result of observation and experiment, since all of you are familiar with the idea that there can be nothing in our intellect which has not entered it through our senses.

But it is just this venerable idea which I am combating.[3] I assert that every animal is born with expectations or anticipations, which could be framed as hypotheses; a kind of hypothetical knowledge. And I assert that we have, in this sense, some degree of inborn knowledge from which we may begin, even though it may be quite unreliable. This inborn

---

[2] Albert Einstein, *On the Methods of Theoretical Physics*, 1933. (Also in his *The World As I See It.*) [Sir Peter Medawar has pointed out to me that I ought to have mentioned here, besides Darwin and Einstein, Claude Bernard, *An Introduction to the Study of Experimental Medicine* (1865), 1927.]

[3] [I have since tried to trace this doctrine to Parmenides who formulated it in order to combat it. See p. 165 of the second edition (1965) of my *Conjectures and Refutations.*]

knowledge, these inborn expectations, will, if disappointed, create *our first problems*; and the ensuing growth of our knowledge may therefore be described as consisting throughout of corrections and modifications of previous knowledge.

Thus I am turning the tables on those who think that observation must precede expectations and problems; and I even assert that for *logical reasons*, observation cannot be prior to all problems, although obviously it will often be prior to some problems—for example to those problems which arise from an observation that disappoints some expectation or refutes some theory. The fact that observation cannot precede all problems may be illustrated by a simple experiment which I wish to carry out, by your leave, with yourselves as experimental subjects.[4] My experiment consists of asking you to *observe*, here and now. I hope you are all co-operating, and observing! However, I fear that at least some of you, instead of observing, will feel a strong urge to ask: 'WHAT do you want me to observe?'

If this is your response, then my experiment was successful. For what I am trying to illustrate is that, in order to observe, we must have in mind a definite question which we might be able to decide by observation. Darwin knew this when he wrote: 'How odd it is that anyone should not see that all observation must be for or against some view . . .'[5] [Neither 'observe!' (without indication of *what*) nor 'observe this spider!' is a clear imperative. But 'observe *whether* this spider climbs up, or down, as I expect it will!' would be clear enough.]

I cannot, of course, hope to convince you of the truth of my thesis that observation comes after expectation or hypothesis. But I do hope that I have been able to show you that there may exist an alternative to the venerable doctrine that knowledge, and especially scientific knowledge, always start from observation.[6]

---

[4] [I have repeated here an account of an experiment which I have also described on p. 46 of the second edition (1965) of my *Conjectures and Refutations*.]

[5] Francis Darwin (ed.), *More Letters of Charles Darwin*, vol. i, 1903, p. 195. See also J. O. Wisdom, *Foundations of Inference in Natural Science*, 1952, p. 50, and Nora Barlow, *The Autobiography of Charles Darwin*, 1958, p. 161. Darwin's passage ends with the words (which I admit slightly weaken it as a support of my thesis) 'if it is to be of any service!'.

[6] The still more venerable doctrine that all knowledge starts from perception or sensation, which is here, of course, also rejected, is at the root of the fact that 'problems of perception' are still widely considered to form a respectable part of philosophy, or more precisely of the theory of knowledge.

Now let us look a little more closely at this method of conjecture and refutation which, according to my thesis, is the method by which our knowledge grows.

We start, I say, with a problem, a difficulty. It may be practical or theoretical. Whatever it may be when we first encounter the problem we cannot, obviously, know much about it. At best, we have only a vague idea what our problem really consists of. How, then, can we produce an adequate solution? Obviously, we cannot. We must first get better acquainted with the problem. But how?

My answer is very simple: by producing an inadequate solution, and by *criticizing* it. Only in this way can we come to understand the problem. For to understand a problem means to understand its difficulties; and to understand its difficulties means to understand why it is not easily soluble—why the more obvious solutions do not work. We must therefore produce these more obvious solutions; and we must criticize them, in order to find out *why* they do not work. In this way, we become acquainted with the problem, and may proceed from bad solutions to better ones—provided always that we have the creative ability to produce new guesses, and more new guesses.

This, I think, is what is meant by 'working on a problem'. And if we have worked on a problem long enough, and intensively enough, we begin to know it, to understand it, in the sense that we know what kind of guess or conjecture or hypothesis will not do at all, because it simply misses the point of the problem, and what kind of requirements would have to be met by any serious attempt to solve it. In other words, we begin to see the ramifications of the problem, its sub-problems, and its connection with other problems. (It is only at this stage that a new conjectured solution should be submitted to the criticism of others, and perhaps even published.)

If we now consider this analysis, we find that it fits in with our formula, which stated that the progress of knowledge is from old problems to new problems, by means of conjectures and of critical attempts to refute them. For even the process of becoming better and better acquainted with a problem proceeds in accordance with this formula.

At the next step our tentative solution is discussed, and criticized; everybody tries to find a flaw in it and to refute it, and whatever the result of these attempts may be, we shall certainly learn from them. If the criticism of our friends, or of our opponents, is successful, we shall have learned much about our problem: we shall know more about its inherent difficulties than we did before. And if even our most acute critics do not succeed, if our hypothesis is able to resist their criticism, then again, we shall have learned much: both about the problem and about our hypothesis, its adequacy, and its ramifications. And as long as our hypothesis survives, or at least as long as it does better, in the face of criticism, than its competitors, it may, temporarily and tentatively, be accepted as part of current scientific teaching.

All this may be expressed by saying that the growth of our knowledge is the result of a process closely resembling what Darwin called 'natural selection'; that is, *the natural selection of hypotheses*: our knowledge consists, at every moment, of those hypotheses which have shown their (comparative) fitness by surviving so far in their struggle for existence; a competitive struggle which eliminates those hypotheses which are unfit.[7]

This interpretation may be applied to animal knowledge, pre-scientific knowledge, and to scientific knowledge. What is peculiar to scientific knowledge is this: that the struggle for existence is made harder by the conscious and systematic criticism of our theories. Thus, while animal knowledge and pre-scientific knowledge grow mainly through the elimination of those holding the unfit hypotheses, scientific criticism often makes our theories perish in our stead, eliminating our mistaken beliefs before such beliefs lead to our own elimination.

This statement of the situation is meant to describe how knowledge really grows. It is not meant metaphorically, though of course it makes use of metaphors. The theory of knowledge which I wish to propose is a largely Darwinian theory of the growth of knowledge. From the amoeba to Einstein, the growth of knowledge is always the same: we try to solve our problems, and to obtain, by a process of elimination, something approaching adequacy in our tentative solutions.

---

[7] See my *Logic of Scientific Discovery*, especially pp. 108 and 131, and also my *Poverty of Historicism*, p. 133.

And yet, something new has emerged on the human level. In order that this may be seen at a glance, I shall contrast the evolutionary tree with what may be called the growing tree of knowledge.

The evolutionary tree grows up from a common stem into more and more branches. It is like a family tree: the common stem is formed by our common unicellular ancestors, the ancestors of all organisms. The branches represent later developments, many of which have, to use Spencer's terminology, 'differentiated' into highly specialized forms each of which is so 'integrated' that it can solve its particular difficulties, its problems of survival.

The evolutionary tree of our tools and instruments looks very similar. It started presumably with a stone and a stick; yet under the influence of more and more specialized problems it has branched into a vast number of highly specialized forms.

But if we now compare these growing evolutionary trees with the *structure of our growing knowledge*, then we find that the growing tree of human knowledge has an utterly different structure. Admittedly, the growth of applied knowledge is very similar to the growth of tools and other instruments: there are always more and more different and specialized applications. But pure knowledge (or 'fundamental research' as it is sometimes called) grows in a very different way. It grows almost in the opposite direction to this increasing specialization and differentiation. As Herbert Spencer noticed, it is largely dominated by a tendency towards increasing integration towards unified theories.[8] This tendency became very obvious when Newton combined the terrestrial mechanics of Galileo with Kepler's theory of celestial movements; and it has persisted ever since.

When we spoke of the tree of evolution we assumed, of course, that the direction of time points upwards—the way the tree grows. Assuming the same upward direction of time, we should have to represent the tree of knowledge as springing from countless roots which grow up into the air rather than

[8] [Spencer also writes, criticizing Comte (*Essays*, 1891, vol. ii, p. 24): 'The progress of science is duplex. It is at once from the special to the general and from the general to the special. It is analytical and synthetical at the same time.' As examples of this principle, Spencer mentions ten discoveries in physics, including the theories of Galileo and Newton (ibid., pp. 25 ff.).]

down, and which ultimately, high up, tend to unite into one common stem. In other words, the evolutionary structure of the growth of pure knowledge is almost the opposite of that of the evolutionary tree of living organisms, or of human implements, or of applied knowledge.

This integrative growth of the tree of pure knowledge has now to be explained. It is the result of our peculiar aim in our pursuit of pure knowledge—the aim of satisfying our curiosity by explaining things. And it is, moreover, the result of the existence of a human language which enables us not only to describe states of affairs, but also to argue about the truth of our descriptions; that is to say, to criticize them.

In seeking pure knowledge our aim is, quite simply, to understand, to answer how-questions and why-questions. These are questions which are answered by giving an explanation. Thus all problems of pure knowledge are *problems of explanation*.

These problems may well originate in practical problems. Thus the practical problem, 'What can be done to combat poverty?', has led to the purely theoretical problem, 'Why are people poor?', and from there to the theory of wages and prices, and so on; in other words, to pure economic theory, which of course constantly creates its own new problems. In this development the problems dealt with—and especially the unsolved problems—multiply, and they become differentiated, as they always do when our knowledge grows. Yet *the explanatory theory itself* has shown that integrative growth first described by Spencer.

To take an analogous example from biology, we have the most urgent practical problem of combating epidemics such as smallpox. Yet from the praxis of immunization we move to the theory of immunology and from here to the theory of antibody formation—a field of pure biology famous for the depth of its problems, and for the power of its problems to multiply.

Problems of explanation are solved by proposing explanatory theories; and an explanatory theory can be criticized by showing that it is either inconsistent in itself or incompatible with the facts or incompatible with some other knowledge. Yet this criticism assumes that what we wish to find are *true* theories— theories which agree with the facts. It is, I believe, this idea of *truth as correspondence with the facts* which makes rational criticism possible. Together with the fact that our curiosity, our passion to explain by means of unified theories, is universal and unlimited, our aim of getting nearer to the truth explains the integrative growth of the tree of knowledge.

In pointing out the difference between the evolutionary tree of instruments and that of pure knowledge I hope to offer, incidentally, something like a refutation of the now so fashionable view that human knowledge can only be understood as an instrument in our struggle for survival. The point made may serve as a warning against too narrow an interpretation of what I have said about the method of conjecture and refutation, and the survival of the fittest hypothesis. Yet it in no way conflicts with that I have said. For I did not state that the fittest hypothesis is always the one which helps our own survival. I said, rather, that the fittest hypothesis is the one which best solves the *problem* it was designed to solve, and which resists criticism better than competing hypotheses. If our problem is a purely theoretical one—one of finding a purely theoretical explanation —then the criticism will be regulated by the idea of truth, or of getting nearer to the truth, rather than by the idea of helping us to survive.

Speaking here of truth, I wish to make clear that our aim is to find true theories or at least theories which are nearer to the truth than the theories which are known to us at present. Nevertheless this does not mean that we can know for certain of any of our explanatory theories that they are true. We may be able to criticize an explanatory theory, and to establish its falsity. But a good explanatory theory is always a bold anticipation of things to come. It ought to be testable, and criticizable, but it will not be capable of being shown to be true; and if we take the word 'probable' in any of the many senses which satisfy the calculus of probabilities, then it can never be shown to be 'probable' (that is to say, more probable than its negation).

This fact is far from surprising. For although we have acquired the art of rational criticism, and the regulative idea that a true explanation is one which corresponds to the facts, nothing else has changed; the fundamental procedure of the growth of knowledge remains that of conjecture and refutation, of the elimination of unfit explanations; and since the elimination of a finite number of such explanations cannot reduce the infinity of the surviving possible explanations, Einstein may err, precisely as the amoeba may err.

Thus we cannot attribute truth, or probability, to our theories. The use of such standards as truth, and approximation to the truth, plays a role only within our criticism. We may reject a theory as untrue; and we may reject a theory as being less close an approximation to truth than one of its predecessors, or competitors.

I may perhaps put together what I have been saying in the form of two brief theses.

(i) We are fallible, and prone to error; but we can learn from our mistakes.

(ii) We cannot justify our theories, but we can rationally criticize them, and tentatively adopt those which seem best to withstand our criticism, and which have the greatest explanatory power.

This concludes the first part of my lecture.

2. *Remarks on Methods in Biology, and Especially in the Theory of Evolution*

In the second part of my lecture—which I have had to cut severely to make room for the third part—I propose to discuss briefly a number of problems concerning the methods of biology.

I shall start with two general theses. My first thesis is this.

(1) If anyone should think of scientific method as a way which leads to success in science, he will be disappointed. There is no royal road to success.

My second thesis is this.

(2) Should anybody think of scientific method, or of *The Scientific Method*, as a way of justifying scientific results, he will also be disappointed. A scientific result cannot be justified. It can only be criticized, and tested. And no more can be said in its favour than that it seems, after all this criticism and testing, better, more interesting, more powerful, more promising, and a better approximation to truth, than its competitors.

In spite of these two intentionally discouraging theses something more positive may be said. There is something like a secret of success, and I shall give it away. It is this.

In any stage of your researches be as clear as you can about your problem, and watch the way it changes and becomes more definite. Be as clear as you can about the various theories you hold, and be aware that we all hold theories unconsciously, or take them for granted, although most of them are almost certain to be false. Try again and again to formulate the theories which you are holding and to criticize them. And try to construct alternative theories—alternatives even to those theories which appear to you inescapable; for only in this way will you understand the theories you hold. Whenever a theory appears to you as the only possible one, take this as a sign that you have neither understood the theory nor the problem which it was intended to solve. And look upon your experiments always as tests of a theory—as attempts to find faults in it, and to overthrow it. If an experiment or observation seems to support a theory, remember that what it really does is to weaken some alternative theory—perhaps one which you have not thought of before. And let it be your ambition to refute and replace your own theories: this is better than defending them, and leaving it to others to refute them. But remember also that a good defence of a theory against criticism is a necessary part of any fruitful discussion since only by defending it can we find out its strength, and the strength of the criticism directed against it. There is no point in discussing or criticizing a theory unless we try all the time to put it in its strongest form, and to argue against it only in that form.

The process of discovery or of learning about the world which I have described here may be said to be *evocative* rather than *instructive*, to use a distinction explained and used in Sir Peter Medawar's Reith Lectures.[9] We learn about our environment not through being instructed by it, but through being challenged by it: our responses (and among them our expectations, or anticipations or conjectures) are evoked by it, and we learn through the elimination of our unsuccessful responses—that is, *we learn from our mistakes*. An evocative method of this kind, however, can *imitate or simulate* instruction: its result may look as if we had obtained our theories by starting from observation and proceeding by induction. This idea of an evocative process of evolution *simulating* an instructive process

[9] [Peter B. Medawar, *The Future of Man*, Methuen, 1961.]

is characteristic of Darwinism, and plays an important part in what follows here.

Darwin's discovery of the theory of natural selection has often been compared to Newton's discovery of the theory of gravitation. This is a mistake. Newton formulated a set of universal laws intended to describe the interaction, and consequent behaviour, of the physical universe. Darwin's theory of evolution proposed no such universal laws. There are no Darwinian laws of evolution. In fact, it was Herbert Spencer who tried to formulate universal laws of evolution—the laws of 'differentiation' and 'integration'. As I have tried to indicate these are not without interest and may be quite true. But they are vague, and in comparison with Newton's laws they are almost devoid of empirical content. (Darwin himself found Spencer's laws to be of little interest.)

Nevertheless, Darwin's revolutionary influence upon our picture of the world around us was at least as great, though not as deep, as Newton's. For Darwin's theory of natural selection showed that it is *in principle possible to reduce teleology to causation by explaining, in purely physical terms, the existence of design and purpose in the world.*

What Darwin showed us was that the mechanism of natural selection can, in principle, simulate the actions of the Creator, and His purpose and design, and that it can also simulate rational human action directed towards a purpose or aim.

If this is correct, then we could say from the point of view of *biological method*: Darwin showed that we are all completely free to use teleological explanation in biology—even those of us who happen to believe that all explanation ought to be causal. For what he showed was, precisely, that *in principle* any particular teleological explanation may, one day, be reduced to, or further explained by, a causal explanation.

Although this was a great achievement, we have to add that the phrase *in principle* is a very important restriction. Neither Darwin nor any Darwinian has so far given an actual causal explanation of the adaptive evolution of any single organism or any single organ. All that has been shown—and this is very much—is that such explanations might exist (that is to say, they are not logically impossible).

I hardly need to say that my way of looking at Darwinism will be highly objectionable to many biologists who believe that teleological explanations in biology are just as bad, or almost as bad, as theological explanations. Their influence was strong enough to make a man like Sir Charles Sherrington plead, in a highly apologetic mood, that 'we do not obtain due profit from the study of any particular type-reflex unless we can discuss its immediate purpose as an adapted act'.[10]

One of the more obvious points of Darwinism—but one which is important for the third part of my lecture—is that only an organism which exhibits in its behaviour a strong tendency or disposition or propensity to struggle for its survival will in fact be likely to survive. Thus such a disposition will tend to become part of the genetic structure of all organisms; it will show itself in their behaviour and in much, if not in all, of their organization. This certainly means not merely simulating but explaining, if only in principle, teleology by natural selection.

Similarly one can say that Lamarckism, and especially the doctrine that organs evolve *under the influence of their use* and degenerate under the influence of their disuse, has been in a certain sense *explained* in terms of natural selection by J. M. Baldwin (a Princeton philosopher) [by Waddington and Simpson] and by Erwin Schrödinger.[11] Their method of explanation is further developed and, it seems to me, considerably extended in the hypothesis which I am going to present in the third part of my lecture, and for this reason I shall not analyse it here. But I wish to make clear that what Baldwin [Waddington, Simpson], and Schrödinger have shown is how Lamarckian evolution by instruction may be *simulated* by Darwinian evolution by natural selection.

This is a type of explanation which also exists in physics. A simple example would be the hypothesis first proposed by

---

[10] I quote from Sir Charles Sherrington, *The Integrative Action of the Nervous System*, 1906, 1947, p. 238.

[11] See J. M. Baldwin, *Development and Evolution*, 1902, and Erwin Schrödinger, *Mind and Matter*, 1958, especially the chapter 'Feigned Lamarckism', pp. 26 ff. [Originally, I also referred here to Sir Julian Huxley's *Evolution—The Modern Synthesis*, 1942. Sir Peter Medawar has drawn my attention to the fact that the reference is dubious in this context, and he has drawn my attention to Waddington's paper; see above, p. 245, note 56.]

Kant and later by Laplace which attempts to explain the fact that all the planets of our planetary system move in more or less similar planes, which are not far apart, in the same direction round the sun. This 'Nebular Hypothesis' (as Spencer usually called it) assumes as a typical initial situation a rotating nebula, out of which the planets are formed by some process of condensation (or, according to Spencer, of differentiation and integration). In this way the theory explains, or simulates, what may first appear to be a consciously designed arrangement. [It might be mentioned here that Kant's and Laplace's nebular hypothesis might be augmented, or possibly even replaced, by a hypothesis of the 'survival' type. According to this hypothesis, a system of planets moving in widely divergent planes, or moving partly in unlike directions, would be less stable, by some orders of magnitude, than a system like ours; so that there is only a small probability of encountering a system of the less stable type.] Another example from physics would be the following: Newton's theory of gravity operates with attractive forces acting at a distance. [G. L. Le Sage published in 1782 a theory which explains this Newtonian action at a distance by simulating it. In this theory there are no attractive forces, but merely bodies *pushing* other bodies.[12]] Einstein's gravitational theory may be said to show how an explanatory system in which there are neither pushes nor attractive forces may simulate a Newtonian system. Now it is important that the simulated explanation—that is, Newton's theory—may be described as an *approximation* to Einstein's theory and to the truth. The theory of natural selection proceeds in a similar way. In any particular case it starts from a simplified model-situation—a situation consisting of certain species in certain environmental conditions—and it tries to show why, in this situation, certain mutations would have survival value. Thus even if Lamarckism is false, as it seem to be, it should be respected by Darwinists as a first approximation to Darwinism.[13]

The real difficulty of Darwinism is the well-known problem

[12] [G. L. Le Sage (translated by Abbot: 'The Newtonian Lucretius'), *Annual Report of the Smithsonian Institution*, 1898, pp. 139–60.]

[13] [In the original lecture, two passages from this paragraph stood at a different place (approximately one page later on).]

of explaining evolutions which are *apparently goal-directed* such as that of our eyes, by an incredibly large number of very small steps; for according to Darwinism, each of these steps is the result of a purely accidental mutation. That all these independent accidental mutations should have had survival value is difficult to explain. [This is especially the case for the Lorenzian inherited behaviour.] The 'Baldwin effect'—that is, the theory of a purely Darwinian development that simulates Lamarckism—seems to me an important step towards an explanation of such developments.

I believe that the first person to see the difficulty clearly was Samuel Butler, who summed it up in the question: 'Luck or Cunning?', meaning here 'Accident or Design?'. Bergson's system of Creative Evolution may similarly be regarded as a comment on this difficulty: his *élan vital* is just a name which he gave to whatever may cause or control those *apparently goal-directed* changes. Any animistic or vitalistic explanation of this type is of course *ad hoc*, and quite unsatisfactory. Yet it may be possible to reduce it to something better—as Darwin did when he showed that teleological explanations may be simulated—and thereby to show that it was an approximation to the truth—or at least to a more tenable theory. (I attempt to produce such a theory in the third part of this lecture.)

A word may be added here on the logical form of a theory of natural selection. This is a very interesting subject, and I should have liked to expound it here at length. However, I can only briefly mention a point or two.

The theory of natural selection is a *historical* one: it constructs a *situation* and shows that, given that situation, these things whose existence we wish to explain are indeed likely to happen.

To put it more precisely, Darwin's theory is a *generalized* historical explanation. This means that the situation is supposed to be *typical* rather than *unique*. Thus it may be possible to construct at times a simplified *model* of the situation.

I may perhaps say here very briefly that what I regard as Darwin's central idea—his attempt to explain genetic changes which led to better adaptation in the sense of *better chances for the individual animal or plant to survive*—has recently suffered an eclipse. This is due very largely to the fashionable pursuit of mathematical exactness, and to the attempt to define survival value statistically, in terms of actual survival (of a gene, or some other genetic unit, in a population).

But survival, or success in the sense of an increase in numbers, may be due to either of two distinguishable circumstances. A species may succeed or prosper because it has managed, say, to improve its speed, or its teeth, or its skill, or its intelligence; or it may succeed or prosper merely because it has managed to increase its fecundity. It is clear that a sufficient increase in fecundity depending fundamentally on genetical factors, or a shortening of the period of immaturity, may have the same survival value as, or even a greater survival value than, say, an increase in skill or in intelligence.

From this point of view it may be a little hard to understand why natural selection should have produced anything beyond a general increase in rates of reproduction, and the elimination of all but the most fertile breeds.[14] [There may be many different factors involved in the processes which determine the rates of reproduction and of mortality, for instance the ecological conditions of the species, its interplay with other species, and the balance of the two (or more) populations.] But be this as it may, it should be possible, I think, to overcome the considerable difficulties which stand in the way of measuring the *success in the adaptation of the individual organisms* of a species perhaps by subtracting its fecundity value (its birth-rate) from its over-all population increase (its survival rate). In other words, I propose to call species *A better adapted* than species *B* (in a Lamarckian and a Darwinian sense), if, for example, their populations increase equally even though *A* has a lower birth-rate than *B*. In a case like this we could say that the *individual members* of species *A* are, on the average, fitter to survive than those of species *B*, or that they are better adapted to their environment than those of *B*.

Without some distinction such as this (and the distinction could be given an elaborate statistical basis) we are liable to

[14] This is only one of the countless difficulties of Darwin's theory to which some Neo-Darwinists seem to be almost blind. Particularly difficult to understand from this point of view is the transition from uni-cellular to multi-cellular organisms, which have new and peculiar difficulties in reproducing and, especially, in surviving after reproduction, and which introduce into life something new, namely death; for all multicellular individuals die.

lose sight of the original problems of Lamarck and Darwin, and especially of the explanatory power of Darwin's theory— its power to explain adaptation and purpose-like developments by natural selection which *simulates* evolution of a Lamarckian character.

To conclude this second part of my lecture I may remind you that, as already indicated, I do not believe in induction. Hume has shown, I think conclusively, that induction is invalid; but he still believed that though invalid, and not rationally justifiable, it is universally practised by animals and men. I do not think that this is true. The truth is, I think, that we proceed by a method of *selecting* anticipations or expectations or theories—by the method of trial and error-elimination, which has often been taken for induction because *it simulates induction.* I believe that the venerable myth of induction has led to much dogmatism in biological thinking. It has also led to the de-nunciation of what are often called 'armchair scientists'—that is to say, theoreticians. But there is nothing wrong with armchairs. They have faithfully supported Kepler, Newton, Maxwell, and Einstein; Bohr, Pauli, de Broglie, Heisenberg, and Dirac; and Schrödinger, in both his physical and his biological speculations.

I speak with feeling since I am not even an armchair biologist but something worse—a mere armchair philosopher.

But so, after all, was Herbert Spencer, whose name, as I freely admit, I am here exploiting shamelessly as a cover for my own misdeeds in the field of biological speculation.

3. *A Conjecture: 'Genetic Dualism'*

I now come to the third and main part of my lecture—the presentation of a conjecture or hypothesis which, if it withstands criticism, may perhaps strengthen the theory of natural selection, even though it keeps strictly within the logical boundaries of an orthodox Neo-Darwinian (or, if you prefer, 'New Synthesis') framework.

My conjecture is, of course, a generalized historical hypo-thesis: it consists in the construction of a typical situation in which natural selection might produce the results which we hope to explain with its help.

The problem to be solved by it is the old problem of ortho-genesis versus accidental and independent mutation—Samuel Butler's problem of *luck or cunning*. It arises from the difficulty of understanding how a complicated organ, such as the eye, can ever result from the purely accidental co-operation of inde-pendent mutations.

Briefly, my solution of the problem consists in the hypothesis that in many if not all of those organisms whose evolution gives rise to our problem—they may include perhaps some very low organisms—we may distinguish more or less sharply [at least] *two distinct parts*: roughly speaking a *behaviour-controlling part* like the central nervous system of the higher animals, and an *executive part* like the sense organs and the limbs, together with their sustaining structures.

This, in brief, is the situation which my conjecture assumes. It will be combined with the orthodox Neo-Darwinian assump-tion that mutational changes in one of these two parts will, as a rule, though perhaps not always, be independent of muta-tional changes in the other part.

This situational hypothesis postulates a *dualism* that strongly resembles a mind-body dualism. Yet it is compatible with the most radical forms of mechanistic materialism as well as with the most radical forms of animism. For all that is demanded by my dualistic hypothesis—which I may perhaps describe as '*genetic dualism*'—can be formulated as follows:

In the cases which we wish to explain, certain inherited dispositions or propensities like those of self-preservation, seeking food, avoiding dangers, acquiring skills by imitation, and so on, may be regarded as subject to mutations that do not as a rule induce any significant change in any of the organs of the body, including the sense organs, except those organs (if any) which are the genetic carriers of the dispositions or propensities referred to.

Before explaining the consequences of this hypothesis, let me point out at once that the hypothesis of genetic dualism may be false. It would be false if the genes (or whatever may take the place of these inheritance-controlling units) which control, for example, the embryonic development of the human eye, were always the same genes as those which control our innate visual curiosity—our disposition or propensity to make use of our eyes as much as possible in all kinds of situations where there is sufficient light for us to see anything at all. Or to put it a little differently: if our innate tendency to *use* our eyes, or our ears, hands, legs, and so on, is always transmitted by heredity in precisely the same way as our *having* eyes, ears, hands, legs, and so on, then my dualistic hypothesis would be false. It would also be false if it were altogether a mistake to distinguish sharply between *possessing* an organ and *using* an organ—if, for example, possession and use were merely two different abstractions from what is biologically or genetically one and the same reality. I shall refer to the assumption that this is so as *genetic monism*, or as the *monistic hypothesis*.

I believe that it is the tacit acceptance of something like this genetic monism which is responsible for the fact that my dualistic hypothesis has not (at least not to my knowledge) been fully developed and discussed so far. The acceptance of a monistic hypothesis was perhaps favoured by the fact that the main problem of the theory of evolution was to explain the origin of species—that is to say, the origin of differentiation in the organs of animals and plants, rather than the origin of specific types of behaviour or propensities to behave.

However this may be, I shall now discuss the working of my dualistic hypothesis with the help of a *mechanical model*. More precisely, I shall substitute a servo-mechanism—a machine— for the developing organism. But before doing so, I wish to make quite clear that my conjecture is not identical with this model, and that those who accept my conjecture are in no way committed to the view that organisms are machines. Furthermore, my model does not contain mechanical ana- logues for all the relevant elements of the theory. For example, it contains no mechanism for bringing about mutations or other genetic changes, the reason being that this is not my problem.

I take as my model an aeroplane—for example a fighter plane—steered by an automatic pilot. The aeroplane, we assume, is built for certain definite purposes, and the automatic pilot is furnished with a number of inbuilt reactions, which amount to 'instructions' to attack a weaker enemy, to support a friend in attack and defence, to flee from a stronger enemy, and so on. The mechanical parts of the automatic pilot upon which these 'instructions' depend constitute the physical basis of what I shall call the *aim-structure* of my model.

In addition, there is built into the automatic pilot the physical basis of what I shall call its *skill-structure*. This consists of such things as stabilization mechanisms; mechanisms for interpreting detectors, in order to identify and distinguish between enemies and friends; steering controls; aiming controls; and so on. It is not assumed that the aim-structure and the skill-structure are clearly distinguished. Together they constitute what I propose to call the *central propensity structure* of the automatic pilot, or, if you like, its 'mind'. The physical system—the switches, wires, valves, batteries, and so on, including those embodying the 'instructions' for the automatic pilot—may be described as the physical basis of its central propensity structure, or of its 'mind'. I shall in what follows simply call this *physical system* the 'automatic pilot'.

It is known that it is also possible to build into such a servomechanism certain propensities to 'learn'—for example to improve some of its skills—by trial and error. But we may neglect this point to start with. Instead, we assume initially that the aim-structure and the skill-structure are rigid, and exactly adjusted to the executive organs of the plane, such as its engine power.

Let us now assume that our fighter plane is reproducible—it does not matter whether self-reproducing, or reproduced by a factory copying its various physical parts—though subject to accidental mutations, and let us group the possible mutations into four classes.

(1) Mutations affecting the automatic pilot.

(2) Mutations affecting an organ—say the rudder or the engine—which is controlled by the automatic pilot.

(3) Mutations affecting a self-regulating organ not under the control of the automatic pilot—say, an independent thermostat regulating the temperature of the engines.

(4) Mutations affecting two or more organs at once.

Now it seems clear that in a complicated organism like this, almost all accidental mutations will be disadvantageous, and most will even be lethal. They will thus be eliminated, we may assume, by natural selection. This will hold with special force for accidental mutations affecting more than one organ—say the automatic pilot *and* another organ. Such mutations are bound to be unfavourable; the probability that they might both be favourable, or even complementary, must be almost zero.

This is one of the biggest differences between my dualistic hypothesis and the monistic hypothesis. According to the monistic hypothesis, a favourable mutation of an organ, say an increase in the power of one of the engines, will always be *used* favourably, and that is all there is to it. Any favourable mutation is improbable, but its probability need not be vanishingly small. But according to the dualistic hypothesis, a favourable change of an organ would, in many cases, be only *potentially* favourable. To make any difference, the improvement would have to be *used*; and this new use might depend on a *complementary* accidental change in the central propensity structure. But the probability of two such accidental changes which would be at the same time both independent and complementary must indeed be vanishing.

It may therefore seem at first sight that a dualistic model can only increase the difficulties of a purely selectionist theory, and this may be another reason why most Darwinians seem to have tacitly adopted a monistic hypothesis.

Now to take an example. Let us say a mutation gives all the engines greater power so that the plane may fly faster. This must be considered favourable both for attacking an enemy and for fleeing; and we can assume that its aim-structure will induce the automatic pilot to make full use of the increased power and speed. But its skill-structure will be adjusted to the old engine-power and top speed. Or in other words, the detailed reactions of the skill-performing mechanism will be adjusted to the old engines and the old speed; and since we have assumed that the pilot cannot 'learn' in the sense of improving its skill, the speed will be too fast for it, and according to my dualistic hypothesis, the plane will crash. Genetic monism, on the other hand, would assume that, with the increased engine power, the increased skill comes of itself, because it is only another aspect of the same thing—according to the assumption that we must not, for genetic purposes, distinguish between an organ and its use.

You will remember our four possibilities of mutational change:

(1) Change of the structure of the automatic pilot.
(2) Change of an organ directly controlled by the pilot.
(3) Change of a self-controlling system.
(4) Change of more than one organ at a time.

Case (4)—that is, a change in more than one organ—may, as we have seen, be neglected by both the dualistic and the monistic hypothesis, because favourable changes of this kind are too improbable.

Case (3)—that is, a change of a self-controlling organ—may be dealt with here by remarking that a self-controlling organ is either a small dualistic sub-system to which our dualistic hypothesis has to be applied again, or else one for which the monistic hypothesis holds, and which develops in accordance with the usual theory.

Case (2)—that is, change of an organ directly controlled by the pilot—is likely to be unfavourable, as our example of increased engine power and speed shows, even if the mutation as such would be favourable from the point of view of a monistic hypothesis.

Thus we are left with case (1), that of mutational changes in the inherited central propensity structure. My thesis is that favourable changes in this structure create no special difficulty. For example a favourable mutation in the aim-structure may induce the plane to flee from the enemy in a greater number of cases than previously; or perhaps the opposite propensity may turn out to be favourable (that is, the propensity to attack the enemy in a greater number of cases). We do not know which will be more favourable but, according to our assumption, natural selection will find out.

Similarly with skills. We know that a human pilot may improve his skill without changing the structure of his plane. This shows that favourable mutations in the automatic pilot's skill-structure are possible, without complementary changes in the rest of the structure. Of course, favourable mutations are always improbable. But we do know that a human pilot may, without changing his plane, adopt new aims, and develop new skills, without crashing; and some of these new aims and new skills may be favourable from the point of view of, say, self-preservation; therefore, corresponding new aims and skills of the automatic pilot may survive.

We are thus led to the following first result: if we start from a dualistic organism in which a controlling central propensity structure and a controlled executive structure are in exact balance, then mutations of the central propensity structure seem to be a little less likely to be lethal than mutations of the controlled executive organs (even potentially favourable ones).

Our second and main result is this. Once a new aim or tendency or disposition, or a new skill, or a new way of behaving, has evolved in the central propensity structure, this fact will influence the effects of natural selection in such a way that previously unfavourable (though potentially favourable) mutations become actually favourable if they support the newly established tendency. *But this means that the evolution of the executive organs will become directed by that tendency or aim, and thus 'goal-directed'.*

We may illustrate this by considering two kinds of favourable mutation of the central propensity structure: those in which what might be called all-round aims or skills are *improved*, and those in which aims or skills are *specialized*.

Examples of the first kind are mutations that introduce aims which are only indirectly favourable, such as a mutation which introduces an aim, or a tendency, or a wish, to improve some skill of the organism. Now once a mutation like this is established, another mutation, which makes the skill-structure more flexible, may become more favourable; and by such mutations of the skill-structure, the organism might acquire the propensity to 'learn', in the sense of improving its skill, by trial and error.

Moreover, once we have obtained a more flexible central propensity structure, otherwise lethal mutations of the executive organs, such as greater speed, may become extremely favourable, even if they were previously unfavourable.

The point here is that the mutations of the central structure will be *leading*. That is to say, only those mutations of the executive organs will be preserved which fit into the general tendencies previously established by the changes of the central structure.

A similar thing may be said about the second kind of change; that is, about *specializing* changes of the central structure. Changes in the environment may favour the narrowing of the aim-structure. For example, if only *one* kind of food is easily available—perhaps a kind originally not much favoured— change of taste (that is, a change of the aim-structure) may be highly favourable. This change of aim may lead to a specialization of the whole organism, such as of its skills in getting food, and of the shape of its organs. To take an example, this theory would suggest that the specialized beak and tongue of the woodpecker developed, by selection, *after* it began to change its tastes and its feeding habits, rather than the other way round. Indeed, we may say that had the woodpecker developed its beak and tongue before changing its taste and skill, the change would have been lethal: it would not have known what to do with its new organs.

Or take a classical Lamarckian example—the giraffe: its propensities or feeding habits must have changed *before* its neck, according to my theory; otherwise a longer neck would not have been of any survival value.

I must now stop expounding my theory and say a few words about its explanatory power.

To put it briefly, my dualistic hypothesis allows us, in principle, to accept not only simulated Lamarckism, but also a simulated vitalism and animism; and it thus 'explains' these theories as first approximations. It thereby allows us, in principle, to explain the evolution of complex organs such as the eye by many steps leading in a definite direction. The direction may indeed, as the vitalists asserted, be determined by a mind-like tendency—by the aim-structure or skill-structure of the organism which may develop a tendency, or a wish, to use the eye, and a skill in interpreting the stimuli received from it.

At the same time, there is no reason to think that the monistic hypothesis will always be false. It may be that, in the course of evolution, different kinds of organisms develop which are to a greater or lesser extent either monistic or dualistic in their genetic mechanism. In this way we might perhaps explain at least some of the outbreaks of apparently goal-directed evolutionary changes—while other changes which are less goal-directed may be explained by assuming that we are faced with the development of genetically monistic structures.

This is perhaps the place to confess that I was led to my conjecture of genetic dualism through being puzzled by a case that constitutes a prima facie refutation of my conjecture—and by trying to make clear to myself why this case was so puzzling. It was the case of the four-winged mutation (*tetraptera*) of *drosophila*, the famous two-winged fruit fly. What puzzled me about it was this: why did the four-winged mutation not crash? How could it have the skill to use its four wings? Perhaps this case does actually refute my conjecture. But it seems more likely that it does not. (Perhaps the wing-structure of the insect is largely self-regulating, or a monistic part of an essentially dualistic animal; or perhaps the mutation is an atavism—as indeed it is supposed to be—and the skill-structure, though not the aim-structure, pertaining to the use of four wings has survived atavistically the older and probably gradual change from four wings to two.) Apart from worrying about this case, I was mainly led on by considerations of the evolution of man, of human language, and of the tree of human knowledge.

To conclude with just one strong point in favour of genetic dualism: students of animal behaviour have shown the existence of complex inborn behaviour—behaviour which involves a fairly skilful, highly specialized, and highly co-ordinated use of many organs. It seems to me difficult if not impossible to believe that this behaviour is merely another aspect of the anatomical structure of the many organs which participate in it.

In spite of this and other arguments against the monistic hypothesis I do not think that my own dualistic hypothesis can be very easily tested. Yet I do not think that it is untestable. However, before possible tests can be seriously discussed, the hypothesis will have to be critically examined from the point of view of whether it is consistent; whether, if true, it would solve the problems it sets out to solve, and whether it can be improved, by simplifying it, and by sharpening it. At the moment I offer it as no more than a possible line of thought.

ADDENDUM

The Hopeful Behavioural Monster

THE above lecture was delivered ten years ago, in 1961. Some of its ideas—the spearhead theory of behavioural mutations— were further developed in 'Of Clouds and Clocks'. But although intensely interested in evolutionary theory, I am no expert in any of its fields; and an expert discouraged me from publishing the Spencer Lecture.

However, through all those years it appeared to me that the *distinction of the genetic bases for* (1) *aims or preferences*, (2) *skills, and* (3) *anatomical executive tools* seems to be an important contribution to a theory of evolution of the Darwinian type. What I called 'genetic dualism' (and should have called 'genetic pluralism') seemed to me to offer an explanation of genetic trends or 'orthogenesis'.

It appeared to me an improvement on the theory which Richard B. Goldschmidt proposed in the form of his famous 'hopeful monsters'; and I think it useful to compare the two theories.

Goldschmidt (1878–1958) published in 1940 a book, *The Material Basis of Evolution*,[1] in which he pointed out that Darwin's many small variations lead to many great difficulties. First, there is the tendency to return to an average population, even if mutations have occurred. Secondly, there is the great difficulty, experienced in all selection experiments, of achieving changes beyond certain definite limits: the attempt to go further leads almost invariably to sterility and extinction.

Both arguments make difficulties for the Darwinian theory of an evolution from very few original living forms—perhaps even only one. Yet it is precisely this theory which we wish to explain, a phenomenon for whose reality there is a great amount of empirical evidence.

The orthodox explanation is that immense periods of time allow small variations to accumulate, and that geographical separation especially often prevents the re-establishment of an

---

[1] Richard B. Goldschmidt, *The Material Basis of Evolution*, Yale University Press, New Haven, 1940.

average population. Goldschmidt found these ideas to be insufficient; and without breaking with the idea of natural selection, he broke with the idea that every evolutionary change has to be explicable in terms of a very great number of very small variations. He assumed that from time to time big mutations occur, which are usually lethal and eliminated, but some of which survive; thus he explained both the genuine differences *and* the obvious character of cousinship between the various forms of life. The big mutations he described as *'hopeful monsters'*. The theory has its attractive side: monsters do occur from time to time. But there are great difficulties. Usually such mutations would be lethal (an organism is too finely balanced to stand up to sudden accidental great changes), and where they are not lethal, the likelihood of a reversal to the original form is very great.

I have always been very interested in Goldschmidt's theories,[2] and I drew Goldschmidt's 'hopeful monsters' to the attention of I. Lakatos, who referred to them in his 'Proofs and Refutations'.[3]

But it was only a few days ago, when reading a new critical book *Darwin Retried* by Norman Macbeth,[4] that it struck me that it might be time to revive Goldschmidt's 'hopeful monsters' in a new form.

Goldschmidt himself thought mainly, if perhaps not exclusively, of anatomical monsters—organisms with non-negligible or even drastic differences of a structural kind from their parents. I suggest that we start with behavioural or *ethological monsters*: organisms whose differences from their parents consist primarily in their deviating *behaviour*.

Of course, this behaviour has its genetical basis. But the genetic basis appears to allow a certain range to the behavioural response, depending perhaps on no more than the momentary physiological state in which the organism reacts to its environmental stimulus, or perhaps on an unusual combination of stimuli, or perhaps on a genetic variant in the disposition to behave. In all these cases, new and monstrous behaviour can and does appear without any observable anatomical

[2] See Richard B. Goldschmidt, op. cit., and also his 'Some Aspects of Evolution', *Science*, **78**, 1933, pp. 539–47.

[3] I. Lakatos, 'Proofs and Refutations', *B.J.P.S.* **14**, 1963, p. 24.

[4] Norman Macbeth, *Darwin Retried*, Gambit Incorporated, Boston, 1971; see especially chapter 17.

novelty. The novelty may have its material basis in some change restricted to a special part of the nervous system, but this change can be the result of a wound or some other accident, and does not need to be genetically determined. On the other hand, it may well be due to a genuine genetic mutation in that part of the genetic system especially responsible for behaviour; a mutation which is not necessarily linked with a gross change in the anatomy. Ultimately the novelty of the behaviour may be due to a real novelty in the environmental circumstances—in the ecology of the organism.

In each of these cases, the behavioural monster may radically deviate in its behaviour from its parents. But there is no immediate reason why the deviation should be lethal. Admittedly, the monstrous behaviour may upset the balance of the organism, but it need not do so; or it may upset it in a way which is not necessarily lethal for the organism (as when a fly, moving over my writing paper, gets its legs soaked in ink and has some trouble in cleaning them).

Novelty of behaviour, and monstrosity (in Goldschmidt's sense) of behaviour are thus much less likely to be lethal than anatomical monstrosity. On the other hand, through natural selection monstrous behaviour may have the greatest impact upon the elimination of the anatomical variations.

To take the famous example of the eye, the novel *behaviour* which makes use of light-sensitive spots (already existent) may greatly increase their selective value, which previously perhaps was negligible. In this way, *interest* in seeing may be successfully fixed genetically and may become the leading element in the orthogenetic evolution of the eye; even the smallest improvements in its anatomy may be selectively valuable if the aim-structure and the skill-structure of the organism make sufficient use of it.

I thus submit a variation of Darwinism in which behavioural monsters play a decisive part. Behavioural novelty leads, if successful, to the selection of those ecological niches which in their turn operate selectively—operate, that is, to make use of these behavioural novelties and thus exert a selection pressure in a partly predetermined direction: in the direction determined by some genetically possible undetermined *aim*, for example a taste for a new kind of food, or an enjoyment of utilizing light-sensitive regions of the skin. Thus we may get orthogenesis which, after all, was Goldschmidt's main problem.

Even such properties of organisms as youthful playfulness may have turned out useful in a changing world in which behavioural monstrosity—that is, variability plus possible orthogenesis—can help survival.

In this way the (often) leading role played by changes (genetic changes, or even genetically undetermined ones) of the aim-structure, and in the second line by changes in the skill-structure, over genetically based changes of anatomical structure, might be explained. The anatomical structure can change only slowly, in the main. But its changes will for this very reason remain insignificant if they are not guided by those in aim-structure and skill-structure. Thus the evolution of a genetic apparatus establishing a primacy of aim-structure and skill-structure over anatomical structure might, in principle, be explained on Darwinian lines.

It will be seen that this Darwinian theory of hopeful behavioural monsters 'simulates' not only Lamarckism, but Bergsonian vitalism also.

8. A Realist View of Logic, Physics, and History

MAN, some modern philosophers tell us, is alienated from his world: he is a stranger and afraid in a world he never made. Perhaps he is; yet so are animals, and even plants. They too were born, long ago, into a physico-chemical world, a world they never made. But although they did not make their world, these living things changed it beyond all recognition and, indeed, remade the small corner of the universe into which they were born. Perhaps the greatest of these changes was made by the plants. They radically transformed the chemical composition of the earth's whole atmosphere. Next in magnitude are perhaps the achievements of some marine animals which built coral reefs and islands and mountain ranges of limestone. Last came man, who for a long time did not change his environment in any remarkable way, apart from contributing, by deforestation, to the spread of the desert. Of course, he did build a few pyramids; but only during the last century or so did he begin to compete with the reef-building corals. Still more recently he began to undo the work of the plants by slightly, though significantly, raising the carbon dioxide content of the atmosphere.

Thus we have not made our world. So far we have not even changed it much, compared with the changes achieved by marine animals and plants. Yet we have created a new kind of product or artifact which promises in time to work changes in our corner of the world as great as those worked by our predecessors, the oxygen-producing plants, or the island-building corals. These new products, which are decidedly of our own making, are our myths, our ideas, and especially our scientific theories: theories about the world we live in.

Based on the Opening Address to the First International Colloquium held at the University of Denver, 16–20 May 1966. First published in W. Yougrau and A. D. Breck (eds.), *Physics, Logic and History*, Plenum Press, 1970, pp. 1–30.

I suggest that we may look upon these myths, these ideas and theories, as some of the most characteristic products of human activity. Like tools, they are organs evolving outside our skins. They are exosomatic artifacts. Thus we may count among these characteristic products especially what is called 'human knowledge'; where we take the word 'knowledge' in the objective or impersonal sense, in which it may be said to be contained in a book; or stored in a library; or taught in a university.

When referring to human knowledge, I shall usually have this objective sense of the word 'knowledge' in mind. This allows us to think of knowledge produced by men as analogous to the honey produced by bees: the honey is made by bees, stored by bees, and consumed by bees; and the individual bee which consumes honey will not, in general, consume only the bit it has produced itself: honey is also consumed by the drones which have not produced any at all (not to mention that stored treasure of honey which the bees may lose to bears or beekeepers). It is also interesting to note that, in order to keep up its powers to produce more honey, each working bee has to consume honey, some of it usually produced by other bees.

All this holds, by and large, with slight differences, for oxygen-producing plants and for theory-producing men: we, too, are not only producers but consumers of theories; and we have to consume other people's theories, and sometimes perhaps our own, if we are to go on producing.

'To consume' means here, first of all, 'to digest', as in the case of the bees. But it means more: our consumption of theories, whether those produced by other people or by ourselves, also means criticizing them, changing them, and often even demolishing them, in order to replace them by better ones.

All these are operations which are necessary for the *growth of our knowledge*; and I again mean here, of course, knowledge in the objective sense.

I suggest that it looks at present as if it is this growth of human knowledge, the growth of our theories, which turns our *human history* into a chapter so radically new in the history of the universe, and also in the history of life on earth.

All three of these histories—the history of the universe, the history of life on earth, and the history of man and of the growth of his knowledge—are, of course, themselves chapters of our knowledge. Consequently, the last of these chapters—that is, the history of knowledge—will consist of knowledge about knowledge. It will have to contain, at least implicitly, theories about theories, and especially theories about the way in which theories grow.

I shall, therefore, before going any further into my topic, present a general tetradic schema which I have found more and more useful as a description of the growth of theories. It is as follows:

$$P_1 \to TT \to EE \to P_2.$$

Here 'P' stands for 'problem'; 'TT' stands for 'tentative theory'; and 'EE' stands for '(attempted) error-elimination', especially by way of critical discussion. My tetradic schema is an attempt to show that the result of criticism, or of error-elimination, applied to a tentative theory, is as a rule the emergence of a new problem; or, indeed, of several new problems. Problems, after they have been solved and their solutions properly examined, tend to beget problem-children: new problems, often of greater depth and ever greater fertility than the old ones. This can be seen especially in the physical sciences; and I suggest that we can best gauge the progress made in any science by the distance in depth and expectedness between P_1 and P_2: the best tentative theories (and all theories are tentative) are those which give rise to the deepest and most unexpected problems.

My tetradic schema can be elaborated in various ways; for example, by writing it as follows:

$$P_1 \begin{cases} \nearrow TT_a \to EE_a \to P_{2a} \\ \to TT_b \to EE_b \to P_{2b} \\ \searrow TT_n \to EE_n \to P_{2n}. \end{cases}$$

In this form the schema would indicate that, if we can, we should propose many theories as attempts to solve some given problem, and that we should critically examine each of our tentative solutions. We then find that each gives rise to new problems; and we may follow up those which promise the most novel and most interesting new problem: if the new problem,

P_{2b}, say, turns out to be merely the old P_1 in disguise, then we say that our theory only manages to *shift the problem* a little; and in some cases we may take this as a decisive objection to the tentative theory, TT_b.

This shows that error-elimination is only *part* of our critical discussion: our critical discussion of the competing tentative theories may compare them, and assess them, from many different points of view. The decisive point is, *of course*, always: how well does our theory solve its problems; that is, P_1?

At any rate, one of the things we wish to achieve is to learn something new. According to our schema, progressiveness is one of the things we demand of a good tentative theory: and it is brought out by the critical discussion of it: the theory is progressive if our discussion shows that *it has really made a difference to the problem we wanted to solve*; that is, if the newly emerging problems are different from the old ones.

If the newly emerging problems are different then we can hope to learn a great many new things when we proceed to solve them in turn.

Thus my tetradic schema can be used to describe the emergence of new problems and, consequently, the emergence of new solutions—that is, new theories; and I even want to present it as an attempt to make sense of the admittedly vague idea of emergence—as an attempt to speak of emergence in a rational manner. I should like to mention that it can be applied not only to the emergence of new scientific problems and, consequently, new scientific theories, but to the emergence of new forms of behaviour, and even new forms of living organisms.

Let me give you an example. P_1 may be, say, a certain problem concerning the survival of a species, such as the problem of reproduction, of producing offspring. According to Darwin, this survival problem has found a good solution if the species survives; any other tentative solution will be eliminated by the disappearance of both the solution and the species.

According to my schema, the attempted error-elimination—that is, the struggle for survival—will bring out the inherent weakness of each of the proposed solutions in the form of a *new problem*. For example, the new problem may be that the parent organisms and their offspring are threatening to suffocate one another. This new problem may, in turn, be solved; for example, the organisms may develop a method of scattering or disseminating their offspring; or else the new problem may be solved by the establishment of a common economy, comprising several organisms. Perhaps the transition from unicellular to multicellular organisms proceeded in this way.

However this may be, my schema shows that there may be more than Darwin's alternative, '*survive or perish*', inherent in the process of error-elimination: error-elimination may bring out new emerging problems, specifically related to the old problem *and* to the tentative solution.

In what follows I shall use my schema, sometimes only implicitly; and I shall refer to emergence, assuming that my schema makes this idea sufficiently respectable within what I hope will be a rational discussion. I propose to deal with some aspects of the growth of knowledge under four headings:

1. Realism and Pluralism: Reduction versus Emergence.
2. Pluralism and Emergence in History.
3. Realism and Subjectivism in Physics.
4. Realism in Logic.

1. *Realism and Pluralism: Reduction versus Emergence*

Man produces not only scientific theories but many other ideas—for example, religious or poetical myths or, say, plots for stories.

What is the characteristic difference between a scientific theory and a work of fiction? It is not, I hold, that the theory is possibly true while the descriptions in the story are not true, although truth and falsity have something to do with it. The difference is, I suggest, that the theory and the story are embedded in different critical traditions. They are meant to be judged by quite different traditional standards (even though these standards may have something in common).

What characterizes the theory is that it is offered as a solution to a scientific problem; that is, either a problem that has arisen before, in the critical discussion of earlier tentative theories, or (perhaps) a problem discovered by the author of the theory now offered, but discovered within the realm of the problems and solutions belonging to the scientific tradition.

However, I am not leaving it at that. For the scientific tradition in its turn is, or was until recently, characterized by what may be called *scientific realism*. That is to say, it was inspired by the ideal of finding *true solutions* to its problems: solutions which corresponded to the facts.

This regulative ideal of finding theories which correspond to the facts is what makes the scientific tradition a realist tradition: it distinguishes between the world of our theories and the world of facts to which these theories belong.

Moreover, the natural sciences with their critical methods of problem solving, and some of the social sciences too, especially history and economics, have represented for quite a long time our best efforts in problem solving and fact finding (by fact finding I mean, of course, the discovery of statements or theories which correspond to facts). Thus these sciences contain, by and large, the best statements and theories from the point of view of truth; that is, those giving the best description of the world of facts, or of what one calls 'reality'.

Now let us look at certain relations that hold between some of these sciences.

Take physics and chemistry for example; sciences which make assertions about all physical things and physical states, including living organisms.

Physics and chemistry are not very different, and there seems to be no great difference in the kind of things to which they apply, except that chemistry, as it is usually understood, becomes inapplicable at very high temperatures and also, perhaps, at very low ones. It therefore would not be very surprising if the hopes, held for a long time, that chemistry can be reduced to physics, were to come true, as indeed they seem to be doing.

Here we have a real paradigm case of a *'reduction'*; by a *reduction* I mean, of course, that all the findings of chemistry can be fully explained by (that is to say, deduced from) the principles of physics.

Although such a reduction would not be very surprising, it would be a very great scientific success. It would not only be an exercise in unification, but a real advance in understanding the world.

Let us assume that this reduction has been carried out

completely. This might give us some hope that we may also reduce one day all the biological sciences to physics.

Now this would be a spectacular success, far greater than the reduction of chemistry to physics. Why? Because the kind of things to which physics and chemistry apply are really very similar from the start. Only think how difficult it would be to say whether the atomic theory is a physical or a chemical theory. In fact, for a long time it was both; and it is this common bond which provides the link which may lead, or perhaps has led, to their unification.

With living organisms the situation is different. They are, no doubt, subject to all kinds of physical and biological laws. Yet there appears to be some prima facie difference between living organisms and non-living things. Admittedly, we learn from science that there are transitory or intermediate stages, and also intermediate systems; and this gives us hope that a reduction might be achieved one day. Moreover, it seems not at all improbable that recent tentative theories about the origin of life on earth might be successfully put to the test, and that we might be able to create primitive living organisms artificially.

But even this would not necessarily mean a complete reduction. This is shown by the fact that chemists were able to create all sorts of chemicals, inorganic and organic, before understanding even their chemical composition, to say nothing about their physical structure. Thus even the control of chemical processes by purely physical means is not as such equivalent to a reduction of chemistry to physics. Reduction means much more. It means *theoretical* understanding: the *theoretical* penetration of the new field by the old field.

Thus we might find a recipe for creating some primitive forms of life from non-living matter without understanding, theoretically, what we were doing. Admittedly, this would be a tremendous encouragement to all those who seek for a reduction, and rightly so. But the way to a reduction might still be long; and we could not know whether it was not even impassable: there may be no theoretical reduction of biology to physics, just as there seems to be neither a theoretical reduction of mechanics to electrodynamics, nor a theoretical reduction the other way round.

If the situation is such that, on the one hand, living

organisms may originate by a natural process from non-living systems, and that, on the other hand, there is no complete theoretical understanding of life possible in physical terms, then we might speak of life as an *emergent* property of physical bodies, or of matter.

Now I want to make it quite clear that as a rationalist I wish and hope to understand the world and that I wish and hope for a reduction. At the same time, I think it quite likely that there may be no reduction possible; it is conceivable that life is an *emergent* property of physical bodies.

My point here is that those believers in reduction who, for some philosophical or other reason, adopt *a priori* the dogmatic position that reduction must be possible, in a way destroy their triumph should reduction ever be achieved. For what will then be achieved ought to have been achieved all the time; so their triumph will be only the uninteresting one of having been proved right by events.

Only those who assert that the question cannot be settled *a priori* can claim that any successful reduction would be a tremendous discovery.

I have dwelt on this point so long because it has some bearing on the position of the next rung of the ladder—the emergence of consciousness.

There are philosophers, called 'radical behaviourists' or 'physicalists', who think that they have *a priori* reasons, such as *Ockham's razor*, for asserting that our introspection of mental states or events, and our reports about mental states or events, are simply introspections and reports about ourselves *qua* physical systems: they are reports about physical states of these systems.

Two philosophers expected here this morning have defended such a view with brilliant arguments. They are Herbert Feigl and Willard Van Orman Quine. I should like to make a few critical remarks about their views.

Quine says, with a reference to Carnap and Feigl, that if theoretical progress can be 'achieved by . . . positing distinctive mental states . . . behind physical behaviour, surely as much . . . could be achieved by positing . . . certain correlative physiological states and events instead. . . . Lack of a detailed physiological explanation of the states is scarcely an objection to acknowledging them as states of human bodies. . . . The bodily states exist anyway; why add the others?'[1]

Let me point out that Quine speaks here as a realist: 'The bodily states exist anyway', he says. Nevertheless, from the point of view I am adopting here, he is not what I should call a 'scientific realist': he does not wait to see whether science will achieve a reduction here, as perhaps it may one day; instead he applies Ockham's razor,[2] pointing out that mental *entities* are not necessary for the theory.

But who knows what Ockham or anybody else might mean here by necessity? If mental entities or, better, mental states should exist—and I myself do not doubt that they do exist—then positing mental states is necessary for any true explanation of them; and should they one day be reduced to physical states, then this will be a tremendous success. But there will be no success at all if we reject their existence by merely noting that we can explain things without them, by the simple method of confining ourselves to physical things and their behaviour.

To sum up my argument in brief: philosophical speculations of a materialistic or physicalistic character are very interesting, and may even be able to point the way to a successful scientific reduction. But they should be frankly tentative theories (as I think Feigl's theories are). Some physicalists do not, however, consider their theories as tentative, but as proposals to express everything in a physicalistic language; and they think these proposals have much in their favour because they are undoubtedly *convenient*: inconvenient problems such as the body-mind problem do indeed, most conveniently, disappear. So these physicalists think that there can be no doubt that these problems should be eliminated as pseudo-problems.

To this I would reply that by the same method we could have eliminated *a priori* all chemical states and problems connected with them: we could have said that they were obviously physical, and that there was no need to specify them in detail: that all we needed to do was to postulate the existence of some physical state correlative to each chemical state.

I think it is clear that the general adoption of such a proposal would have led to the attitude of not looking for the detailed

[1] W. V. Quine, *Word and Object*, 1960, p. 264.
[2] W. V. Quine, *From a Logical Point of View*, second rev. edn., 1961, p. 2.

reduction of chemistry to physics. No doubt, it would have dissolved the analogue of the body-mind problem—the problem of the relation of physics to chemistry; but the solution would have been linguistic; and as a consequence we should not have learned anything about the real world.

All this leads me to assert that realism should be at least tentatively pluralistic, and that realists should subscribe to the following pluralistic postulate:

We must beware of solving, or dissolving, factual problems linguistically; that is, by the all too simple method of refusing to talk about them. On the contrary, we must be pluralists, at least to start with: we should first emphasize the difficulties, even if they look insoluble, as the body-mind problem may look to some.

If we can then reduce or eliminate some entities by way of scientific reduction, let us do so by all means, and be proud of the gain in understanding.

So I would say: let us work out in every case the arguments for emergence in detail, *at any rate before attempting reduction.*

To sum up and sharpen the considerations advanced in this section:

The reduction of chemistry to physics, apparently now well on the way, may be described as a paradigm case of a genuine scientific reduction which satisfies all the requirements of a good scientific explanation.

'Good' or 'scientific' reduction is a process in which we learn much that is of great importance: we learn to understand and to explain the theories about the field to be reduced (in this case chemistry) and we learn a great deal about the power of the reducing theories (in this case physics).

It is conceivable, although not yet certain, that the reduction of chemistry to physics will be completely successful. It is also conceivable, though less likely, that we may one day have *good reductions* of biology, including physiology, to physics, and of psychology to physiology, and thus to physics.

I call *bad reduction* or *ad hoc* reduction the method of reduction by merely linguistic devices; for example, the method of physicalism which suggests that we postulate *ad hoc* the existence of physiological states to explain behaviour which we previously explained by postulating (though not by postulating *ad hoc*) mental states. Or in other words, by the linguistic device of saying that I report on a *physiological* state of mine when I report that I now feel that I understand the Schrödinger equation.

This second kind of reduction or the use of Ockham's razor is bad, because it prevents us from seeing the problem. In the picturesque as well as hard-hitting terminology of Imre Lakatos, it is a disastrous case of a *'degenerating problem shift'*; and it may prevent either a good reduction, or the study of emergence, or both.

In order to avoid this disastrous method we must in each case try to learn as much as possible about the field which we hope to reduce. It may be that the field resists reduction; and in some cases, we may even possess arguments to show why the field cannot be reduced. In this case we may have an example of genuine emergence.

I may perhaps end my comments on the degenerating problem shift of behaviourism (especially linguistic behaviourism) with the following remark.

Behaviourists and materialists are anti-idealists: and they are, rightly, opponents of Berkeley's *'esse = percipi'* or

$$to\ be\ =\ to\ be\ observable.$$

According to them, 'to be' is 'to be material', 'to behave as a body in space and time'. Nevertheless, it may be said that they do adhere, unconsciously, to Berkeley's equation, although they put it in a slightly different verbal form:

$$to\ be\ =\ to\ be\ observed$$

or perhaps

$$to\ be\ =\ to\ be\ perceived.$$

For they say that only those things exist which can be observed. They do not realize that *all observation involves interpretation in the light of theories,* and that what they call 'observable' is what is observable in the light of pretty old-fashioned and primitive theories. Though I am all for common sense, I am also for enlarging the realm of common sense by learning from science. At any rate, *it is not science but dubious philosophy (or outdated science) which leads to idealism, phenomenalism, and positivism; or to materialism and behaviourism,* or to any other form of anti-pluralism.

2. *Pluralism and Emergence in History*

I shall not speak about the history of the universe, but only say a few words about the history of life on earth.

It seems that a very promising start has recently been made towards reconstructing the conditions under which life *emerged* on earth; and I think we may, perhaps, expect some major success soon. But while sanguine about emergence, even experimental emergence, I feel very sceptically inclined about reduction. This is due to certain thoughts of mine about the evolution of life.

It seems to me that evolutionary processes or major evolutionary changes are as unpredictable as historical processes or major historical changes. I hold this view because I am strongly inclined towards an indeterminist view of the world, somewhat more radical than Heisenberg's: my indeterminism includes the thesis that even classical physics is indeterministic, and is thus more like that of Charles Sanders Peirce, or that of Alfred Landé. And I think that evolution proceeds largely probabilistically, under constantly changing conditions or problem situations, and that every tentative solution, whether more successful or less successful or even completely unsuccessful, creates a new problem situation. This seems to me to prevent a complete reduction as well as a complete understanding of the processes of life, although it does not prevent constant and far-reaching progress towards such understanding. (This argument should not be taken to be like Bohr's application of his idea of complementarity to living organisms—an argument which seems to me very weak indeed.)

But I want to speak in this section mainly about human history, about the story of mankind. This, as I have indicated, is very largely the history of our knowledge—of our theories about the world—and, of course, of the repercussions of these products, which are of our own making, upon ourselves and our further productions.

It is obvious that one can adopt a physicalist or materialist attitude towards these theoretical products of ours; and it might be suspected that my emphasis upon the objective sense of knowledge—my emphasis upon theories as contained in books collected in libraries and as taught in universities—indicates that I sympathize with the physicalist or materialist interpretation of theories; I mean an interpretation which sees language as consisting of physical objects—noises, or printed letters—and which sees ourselves as conditioned, or dispositioned, to react to these noises or letters with certain characteristic kinds of physical behaviour.

But nothing is further from my intention than to encourage *ad hoc* reductions of this kind. Admittedly, if forced to choose between any subjectivist or personalist view of human knowledge and the materialist or physicalist view I have just tried to sketch, I should choose the latter; but this is emphatically *not* the alternative.

The history of ideas teaches us very clearly that ideas emerge in logical or, if the term is preferred, in dialectical contexts.[3] My various schemata such as

$$P_1 \to TT \to EE \to P_2$$

may indeed be looked upon as improvements and rationalizations of the Hegelian dialectical schema: they are rationalizations because they operate entirely within the classical logical organon of rational criticism, which is based upon the so-called law of contradiction; that is to say, upon the demand that contradictions, whenever we discover them, must be eliminated. Critical error-elimination on the scientific level proceeds by way of a conscious search for contradictions.

Thus history, and especially the history of ideas, teaches us that if we want to understand history, we must understand ideas and their objective logical (or dialectical) relationships.

I do not believe that anybody who has ever seriously gone into any chapter of the history of ideas will think that a reduction of these ideas could ever be successful. But I take it as my task here not so much to argue against the possibility of any reduction, as to argue for the recognition of emergent entities, and for the need to recognize and describe these emergent *entia* before one can seriously think about their possible elimination by way of reduction.

One of my main arguments for the emergent character of

---

[3] K. R. Popper, 'What is Dialectic?' in *Conjectures and Refutations*, 1963.

theories I have given elsewhere.[4] My argument depends upon the conjecture that there is such a thing as a genuine growth of scientific knowledge; or in practical terms, that tomorrow, or a year hence, we may propose and test important theories of which nobody has seriously thought so far. If there is growth of knowledge in this sense, then it cannot be predictable by scientific means. For he who could so predict today by scientific means our discoveries of tomorrow could make them today; which would mean that there would be an end to the growth of knowledge.

On the other hand, unpredictability in principle has always been considered as the salient point of emergence; and it seems to me that my argument shows at any rate that the growth of knowledge must be unpredictable in principle.

But there are other arguments for the emergent character of theories, or of knowledge in the objective sense. I shall only mention an argument or two against the very popular and very naïve view that theories can be reduced to the mental states of those who produce them, or of those who understand them. (Whether or not these mental states themselves may then perhaps be reduced to physical states in turn will not be further discussed.)

The idea that a theory in its objective or logical sense may be reduced to the mental states of those who hold the theory takes, as a rule, the form that the theory just *is* a thought. But this is a trivial mistake: it is the failure to distinguish between two senses of the word 'thought'. In its subjective sense, the word 'thought' describes a mental experience or a mental process. But two mental experiences or processes, though they may stand in causal relations to each other, cannot stand in logical relations to each other.

Thus, if I say that certain ideas of the Buddha agree with certain ideas of Schopenhauer, or that they contradict certain ideas of Nietzsche, then I am not speaking about the mental thought-processes of these people or about their interrelations. If I say, however, that Nietzsche was influenced by certain ideas of Schopenhauer, then I do mean that certain thought-processes of Nietzsche's were causally influenced by his reading of Schopenhauer. So we have actually these two different

[4] K. R. Popper, *The Poverty of Historicism*, 1957, Preface.

worlds, the world of *thought-processes*, and the world of the *products* of thought-processes. While the former may stand in *causal* relationships, the latter stand in *logical* relationships.

The fact that certain theories are incompatible is a logical fact, and holds quite independently of whether or not anybody has noticed or understood this incompatibility. These purely objective logical relationships are characteristic of the entities which I have called theories, or knowledge, in the objective sense.

This may also be seen from the fact that the person who produces a theory may very often not understand it. Thus it might be argued without paradox that Erwin Schrödinger did not fully understand the Schrödinger equation, at any rate not until Max Born gave his statistical interpretation of it; or that Kepler's area law was not properly understood by Kepler, who seems to have disliked it.

In fact, understanding a theory is something like an infinite task, so that we may well say that a theory is never fully understood, even though some people may understand some theories extremely well. Understanding a theory has, indeed, much in common with understanding a human personality. We may know or understand a man's system of dispositions pretty well; that is to say, we may be able to predict how he would act in a number of different situations. But since there are infinitely many possible situations, of infinite variety, a full understanding of a man's dispositions does not seem to be possible. Theories are similar: a full understanding of a theory would mean understanding all its logical consequences. But these are infinite in a non-trivial sense: there are infinitely many situations of infinite variety to which the theory might be applicable; that is to say, upon which some of its logical consequences may bear; and many of these situations have never been thought of; their possibility may not yet have been discovered. But this means that nobody, neither its creator nor anybody who has tried to grasp it, can have a full understanding of all the possibilities inherent in a theory; which shows again that the theory, in its logical sense, is something objective and something objectively existing—an object that we can study, something that we try to grasp. It is no more paradoxical to say that theories or ideas are our products and yet not fully understood by us than to say that our children are our products and yet not fully understood by us, or that honey is a product of the bee, yet not fully understood by any bee.

Thus, the study of the history of our theories or ideas—and a good case could be made for the view that all human history is largely a history of our theories or ideas—should make us all pluralists. For what exist, for the historian, are people in physical, social, mental, and ideological problem situations; people producing ideas by which they try to solve these problems, ideas which they try to grasp, to criticize, to develop.

The student of the history of ideas will find that ideas have a kind of life (this is a metaphor, of course); that they can be misunderstood, rejected, and forgotten; that they can reassert themselves, and come to life again. Without metaphor, however, we can say that they are not identical with any man's thought, or belief; that they can exist even if universally misunderstood, and rejected.

All this may be reminiscent of Plato and Hegel. But there are great differences here. Plato's 'ideas' were eternal, unchanging conceptions or notions; Hegel's were dialectically self-changing conceptions or notions. The ideas which I find most important are not conceptions or notions at all. They correspond not to words but to statements or propositions.

In opposition to Plato and Hegel I consider *tentative theories* about the world—that is, hypotheses together with their logical consequences—as the most important citizens of the world of ideas; and I do not think (as Plato did) that their strangely non-temporal character makes them eternal and thereby *more real* than things that are generated and are subject to change, and to decay. On the contrary, a thing that can change and perish should for this very reason be accepted as prima facie real; and even an illusion is, *qua* illusion, a real illusion.

This is important in connection with the problem of time, and of change.

A historian cannot, I think, accept the doctrine that time and change are illusions; a doctrine upheld by some great physicists and philosophers such as Parmenides, Weyl, and Schrödinger. Nothing is more real than an event, an occurrence; and every event involves some change.

That the pluralistic universe in which the historian lives, with its individual men living individual lives, trying to solve their problems, producing children, and ideas about them, hoping and fearing and deceiving themselves and others, but always theorizing, and often seeking not only happiness but also truth—that this pluralistic universe should be successfully 'reduced' to one or another kind of monism—this seems to me not only unlikely, but impossible. But this is not my point here. My point is that only after recognizing the plurality of what there is in this world can we seriously begin to apply Ockham's razor. To invert a beautiful formulation of Quine's,[5] only if Plato's beard is sufficiently tough, and tangled by many entities, can it be worth our while to use Ockham's razor. That the razor's edge will be dulled in being used for this tough job is only to be expected. The job will no doubt be painful. But it is all in a day's work.

3. *Realism and Subjectivism in Physics*

There are two important fields in modern physics in which physicists have allowed subjectivism not only to enter, but to play an essential role: Boltzmann's theory of the subjectivity of the direction of time, and Heisenberg's interpretation of the indeterminacy formulae as determining a lower limit to the effect of the observer's interference with the observed object.

There was also another intrusion of the subject, or of the observer, when Einstein brought in the observer in a number of imaginary thought experiments intended to elucidate relativity; but this is a field from which the observer was exorcized, slowly but steadily, by Einstein himself.

I shall not discuss this point further, nor shall I discuss the subjective theory of time which, in trying to tell us that time and change are human illusions, forgets that they are very real illusions which have in no way been reduced to anything else (and which, I conjecture, are not amenable to reduction). I shall not discuss all this because I have done so only recently. I merely want to say a few words about the Heisenberg formulae and their interpretation.

These formulae are usually derived in a fairly complicated

5 W. V. Quine, *From a Logical Point of View*, second rev. edn., 1961, p. 2.

manner; there is, for example, an interesting derivation by Weyl[6] and another rather complicated one by Born.[7]

Yet in fact the Heisenberg formula for energy depends neither on wave mechanics nor on Heisenberg's matrix mechanics; nor do we need the commutation relations (which according to Hill[8] are insufficient for the derivation of the formulae). It simply does not depend on the revolutionary new quantum mechanics of 1925–6, but follows directly from Planck's old quantum postulate of 1900:

$$(1) \qquad\qquad E = h\nu.$$

From this we get immediately

$$(2) \qquad\qquad \Delta E = h\,\Delta\nu.$$

By using the principle of harmonic resolving power,

$$(3) \qquad\qquad \Delta\nu \approx 1/\Delta t,$$

we obtain from (2) and (3)

$$(4) \qquad\qquad \Delta E \approx h/\Delta t,$$

which leads at once to

$$(5) \qquad\qquad \Delta E \Delta t \approx h;$$

that is to say, a form of Heisenberg's so-called *indeterminacy formulae*.

In precisely the same way we obtain the Heisenberg formula for position and momentum from Duane's principle (whose analogy to Planck's principle has recently been stressed by Alfred Landé). It may be written

$$(6) \qquad\qquad \Delta p_i \approx h/\Delta q_i.$$

According to Landé this may be interpreted as follows: a body (such as a grid or a crystal) endowed with the space-periodicity Δq_i is entitled to change its momentum p_i in multiples of $\Delta p_i \sim h/\Delta q_i$.

From (6) we obtain at once

$$(7) \qquad\qquad \Delta p_i \approx h/\Delta q_i.$$

which is another form of Heisenberg's indeterminacy formulae.

Considering that Planck's theory is a statistical theory, the

---

[6] H. Weyl, *The Theory of Groups and Quantum Mechanics*, 1931, pp. 72 and 393.

[7] M. Born, *The Natural Philosophy of Cause and Chance*, 1949, pp. 189–91.

[8] E. L. Hill, in *Mind, Matter, and Method, Essays in Philosophy and Science in Honor of Herbert Feigl* (eds. P. Feyerabend and G. Maxwell), 1966, p. 442.

Heisenberg formulae can be most naturally interpreted as statistical *scatter relations*, as I proposed more than thirty years ago.[9, 10] That is, they say nothing about the possible precision of measurements, nor anything about limits to our knowledge. But if they are scatter relations, they tell us something about the limits to the homogeneity of quantum-physical states, and therefore, though indirectly, about predictability.

For example, the formula $\Delta p_i \Delta q_i \approx h$ (which can be obtained from Duane's principle just as $\Delta E \Delta t \approx h$ can be obtained from Planck's principle) tells us, simply, that if we determine the coordinate x of a system (say, an electron) then, upon repetition of the experiment, the momentum will scatter.

Now, how can such an assertion be tested? By making a long series of experiments with a fixed shutter opening Δx and by measuring, in every single case, the momentum p_x. If these momenta scatter as predicted, then the formula has survived the test. But this shows that in order to test the scatter relations, we have actually measured, in every case, p_x with a precision far greater than Δp_x; for otherwise we could not speak of Δp_x as the scatter of p_x.

Experiments of the kind described are carried out every day in all physical laboratories. But they refute Heisenberg's indeterminacy interpretation, since measurements (though not the predictions based upon them) are more precise than this interpretation permits.

Heisenberg himself noted that such measurements are possible, but he said that it was 'a matter of personal belief' or 'personal taste' whether or not we attach any meaning to them; and ever since this remark they have been universally disregarded as meaningless. But they are not meaningless, for they have a definite function: they are tests of the very formulae in question; that is, of the indeterminacy formulae *qua* scatter relations.

There is, therefore, no reason whatever to accept either Heisenberg's or Bohr's subjectivist interpretation of quantum mechanics. Quantum mechanics is a statistical theory because

[9] K. R. Popper, *The Logic of Scientific Discovery*, 1959, 1968, 1972 (first German edn. 1934).

[10] K. R. Popper, 'Quantum Mechanics without "The Observer"', in *Quantum Mechanics and Reality* (ed. M. Bunge), 1967.

the problems it tries to solve—spectral intensities, for example —are statistical problems. There is, therefore, no need here for any philosophical defence of its non-causal character.

The irreducibility of statistical theories to deterministic theories (rather than the incompatibility of these two kinds of theories) should, however, be established. Arguments to this effect have been offered by Landé, and very different ones by myself.

To sum up, there is no reason whatsoever to doubt the realistic and objectivistic character of all physics. The role played by the observing subject in modern physics is in no way different from the role he played in Newton's dynamics or in Maxwell's theory of the electric field: the observer is, essentially, the man who tests the theory. For this, he needs a lot of other theories, competing theories and auxiliary theories. All this shows that we are not so much observers as thinkers.

4. *Realism in Logic*

I am opposed to looking upon logic as a kind of game. I know about so-called alternative systems of logic and I have actually invented one myself, but alternative systems of logic can be discussed from very different points of view. One might think that it is a matter of choice or convention which logic one adopts. I disagree with this view.

My theory is briefly this. I look upon logic as the theory of deduction or of derivability, or whatever one chooses to call it. Derivability or deduction involves, essentially, *the transmission of truth and the retransmission of falsity*: in a valid inference truth is transmitted from the premisses to the conclusion. This can be used especially in so-called 'proofs'. But falsity is also retransmitted from the conclusion to (at least) one of the premisses, and this is used in disproofs or refutations, and especially in *critical discussions*.

We have premisses and a conclusion; and if we show that the conclusion is false, and assume that the inference is valid, we know that at least one of our premisses must be false. This is how logic is constantly used in critical discussion, for in a critical discussion we attempt to show that something is not in order with some assertion. We attempt to show it; and we may not succeed: criticism may be validly answered by counter-criticism.

What I should wish to assert is (1) that criticism is a most important methodological device; and (2) that if you answer criticism by saying, 'I do not like your logic: your logic may be all right for you, but I prefer a different logic, and according to my logic this criticism is not valid', then you may undermine the method of critical discussion.

Now I should distinguish between two main uses of logic, namely (1) its use in the demonstrative sciences—that is to say, the mathematical sciences—and (2) its use in the empirical sciences.

In the demonstrative sciences logic is used in the main for proofs—for the transmission of truth—while in the empirical sciences it is almost exclusively used critically—for the re-transmission of falsity. Of course, applied mathematics comes in too, in which we implicitly make use of the proofs of pure mathematics, but the role of mathematics in the empirical sciences is somewhat dubious in several respects. (There exists a wonderful article by Schwartz to this effect.[11])

Thus in the empirical sciences logic is mainly used for criticism; that is, for refutation. (Remember my schema $P_1 \rightarrow TT \rightarrow EE \rightarrow P_2$.)

Now, what I wish to assert is this. If we want to use logic in a critical context, then we should use a very strong logic, the strongest logic, so to speak, which is at our disposal; for we want our criticism to be *severe*. In order that the criticism should be severe we must use the full apparatus; we must use all the guns we have. Every shot is important. It doesn't matter if we are over-critical: if we are, we shall be answered by counter-criticism.

Thus we should (in the empirical sciences) use the full or classical or two-valued logic. If we do not use it but retreat into the use of some weaker logic—say, the intuitionist logic, or some three-valued logic (as Reichenbach suggested in connection with quantum theory)—then, I assert, we are not critical enough; it is a sign that something is rotten in the state

---

[11] J. Schwartz, 'The Pernicious Influence of Mathematics on Science', in *Logic, Methodology and Philosophy of Science* (eds. E. Nagel, P. Suppes, and A. Tarski), 1962, pp. 356–60.

of Denmark (which in this case is the quantum theory in its Copenhagen interpretation, as I indicated earlier).

Now let us look, by contrast, at proofs. Every mathematician knows that considerable interest lies in proving a theorem with the help of a *minimum apparatus*. A proof which uses stronger means than necessary is mathematically unsatisfactory, and it is always interesting to find the weakest assumptions or minimum means which have to be used in a proof. In other words, we want the proof not only to be sufficient—that is to say valid—but we want it if possible to be necessary, in the sense that a minimum of assumptions have been used in the proof. This, I admit, is a somewhat sophisticated view. In unsophisticated mathematics we are happy and grateful if we can prove anything, but in more sophisticated mathematics we really want to know what is *necessary* for proving a theorem.

So if one can prove mathematical theorems with methods weaker than the full battery of classical logic, then this is extremely interesting from a mathematical point of view. Thus in proof theory we are interested in weakening if possible our classical logic, and we can, for example, introduce intuitionist logic or some other weaker logic such as positive logic, and investigate how far we can get without using the whole battery.

I think, incidentally, that the term 'intuitionist logic' is a misnomer. It is just a name for a very interesting and somewhat weakened form of classical logic invented by Brouwer and formalized by Heyting. I certainly do not want to say anything in favour of the philosophical theory called intuitionism though I should like to say something in favour of the Brouwer-Heyting logic. But I trust it will not be supposed that I am in any sense defending the authority of intuition in philosophy or logic or anywhere else. Leaving aside for the moment Brouwerian logic, one might say that intuitionism is the doctrine that intuitions are not only important but generally *reliable*. As against this I think that intuitions are very important but that as a rule they do not stand up to criticism. So I am not an intuitionist. However, Brouwerian or so-called 'intuitionist logic' is, from the standpoint of the present discussion, important because it is just a part, a genuine part, and thus a weakened form, of classical logic; that is to say, every inference which is valid from the point of view of intuitionist logic is also valid from the point of view of classical logic, while the opposite is not the case: we have inferences which may be validly drawn in classical logic but which are not valid in intuitionist logic. Thus if I can prove a theorem (so far proved only by classical means) with intuitionist logic, I have made a real mathematical discovery; for mathematical discoveries do not consist only in finding new proofs of new theorems, but they consist also in finding new proofs of old theorems; and a new proof of a theorem will be especially interesting if it uses weaker means than the old proof. A proof using stronger means one can always have for the asking, *a fortiori*; yet finding a weaker proof is a real mathematical achievement.

So intuitionistic logic is a very interesting approach to mathematics because it tries to prove as many mathematical theorems as possible with reduced logical means.

Intuitionistic logic has a further advantage: one can show that in it the so-called 'law of excluded middle' is not demonstrable (although it is a well-formed formula of the system). One can also show that if in any system whatsoever some well-formed formula is not demonstrable, then the system must be consistent. Generally speaking, the weaker the logical means we use, the less is the danger of inconsistency— the danger that a contradiction is derivable. So intuitionist logic can also be looked upon as an attempt to make more certain that our arguments are consistent and that we do not get into hidden inconsistencies or paradoxes or antinomies. How safe such a weakened logic is, as such, is a question into which I do not want to enter now; but obviously it is at least a little safer than the full classical logic. I do not suppose it is always safe, but that is not my point. My point is this. If you wish to prove, or to establish something, you should use weak means. But for disestablishing it—that is to say, for criticizing it—we may use strong means. Of course someone might say, 'Look here, I can refute you even with weak means; I do not even need to use the whole of intuitionist logic.' Still, that is not very important. The main thing is that for the rationalist *any* criticism is welcome—though he may reply to it by criticizing the criticism.

Now this rationalist view is a realist view of logic. First, because it looks upon logic partly in connection with the methodology of the natural sciences which, I have tried to argue, is a realistic affair. Secondly, and this is a very special point, because it looks upon logical inference as truth transmitting or falsity re-transmitting; that is to say, it is concerned with the idea of truth.

I would assert that not the least important of the achievements of Alfred Tarski is that by introducing two ideas into logic, he has actually made logic very much a realistic affair. The first is Tarski's idea (partly anticipated by Bolzano) that logical consequence is truth transmission. The second, I would say, is the rehabilitation of the correspondence theory of truth, the rehabilitation of the idea that truth is simply correspondence with the facts.

I think I may differ here a little from Quine, because I think that this idea of Tarski's ought to be interpreted as destructive of relativism, and because I think that Tarski's claim that his theory of truth is an 'absolutistic' theory of truth is correct. In order to explain this point, I will recount a very old story with a slightly new point to it. The old story is the story of the three main theories of truth. The new point is the elimination of the word 'truth' from the story, and with it, of the appearance that we are dealing here with words, or verbal definitions. However, for this elimination some preparatory discussion is needed.

Of the three main theories of truth, the oldest was the correspondence theory, the theory that truth is correspondence with the facts, or to put it more precisely, that a statement is true if (and only if) it corresponds to the facts, or if it adequately describes the facts. This is the theory which I think Tarski has rehabilitated. The second theory is the so-called coherence theory: a statement is regarded as true if (and only if) it coheres with the rest of our knowledge. The third theory is that truth is pragmatic utility or pragmatic usefulness.

Now, the coherence theory has all sorts of versions of which I shall mention just two. According to the first, truth is coherence with our beliefs, or more precisely, a given statement is true if it coheres with the rest of our beliefs. This I find a bit disconcerting because I do not want to put beliefs into logic, for well-known reasons. (If Peter believes p, and if p and q are interdeducible, we might say that Peter is logically bound to believe *q*. Yet he may not know that *p* and *q* are interdeducible, and he may in fact disbelieve *q*.)

According to the second version of the coherence theory a certain given statement, of which we do not know whether it is true or not, is to be accepted as true if (and only if) it coheres with the statements we have previously accepted. This version has the effect of making our knowledge utterly conservative: 'entrenched' knowledge can hardly be overthrown.

The theory of pragmatic utility is especially concerned with the problem of theories in the natural sciences such as physics. It says that we should accept a physical theory as true if it turns out in tests, and other applications, to be pragmatically useful, or successful.

I propose now to use something like a trick. My trick consists in this. I shall very soon, until very near the end of this paper, stop referring to *truth*. I shall not any longer ask, 'What is truth?' There are several reasons. My main reason is that I believe that 'What is?' or 'What are?' questions or, in other words, all verbal or definitional questions, should be eliminated. 'What is?' or 'What are?' questions I regard as pseudo-questions; they do not all seem to be so pseudo, but I do think they all are pseudo-questions. Questions such as, 'What is life?' or 'What is matter?' or 'What is mind?' or 'What is logic?' I think should not be asked. They are typically unfruitful questions.

So I think we should also discard the question, 'What is truth?'

My first reason (just mentioned) for discarding the question 'What is truth?' one may call 'anti-essentialism'. My second reason is even more important. It is that we should altogether avoid, like the plague, discussing the meaning of words. Discussing the meaning of words is a favourite game of philosophy, past and present: philosophers seem to be addicted to the idea that words and their meaning are important, and are the special concern of philosophy.

I will for your convenience present again here—on the next page—a table which I have used before. (See p. 124 above.)

On the left we have *words or concepts and their meanings*, and on the right we have *statements or propositions or theories and their truth*.

Now I have been taught by the experience of a lifetime in this field that one should always try to get away from the left side of the table and to keep to the right side. One should always keep to assertions, to theories, and the question of their truth. One should never get involved in verbal questions or questions of meaning, and never get interested in words. If challenged by the question of whether a word one uses really means this or perhaps that, then one should say: 'I don't know, and I am not interested in meanings; and if you wish, I will gladly accept *your* terminology.' This never does any

---

IDEAS
that is

DESIGNATIONS *or* TERMS   STATEMENTS *or* PROPOSITIONS
or CONCEPTS   *or* THEORIES

may be formulated in

WORDS   ASSERTIONS

which may be

MEANINGFUL   TRUE

and their

MEANING   TRUTH

may be reduced, by way of

DEFINITIONS   DERIVATIONS

to that of

UNDEFINED CONCEPTS   PRIMITIVE PROPOSITIONS

The attempt to establish (rather than reduce) by these means their

MEANING   TRUTH

leads to an infinite regress

---

harm. One should never quarrel about words, and never get involved in questions of terminology. One should always keep away from discussing concepts. What we are really interested in, our real problems, are factual problems, or in other words, problems of theories and their truth. We are interested in theories and how they stand up to critical discussion; and our critical discussion is controlled by our interest in truth.

Having said this, I intend now to stop using the word 'truth'. Our problem is no longer: Is truth correspondence? Is truth coherence? Is truth usefulness? This being so, how can we formulate our real problem?

Our problem can be sharply formulated only by pointing out that the opponents of the correspondence theories all made an *assertion*. They all asserted that there cannot be such a thing as the correspondence between a statement and a fact. This is their central assertion. They say that this concept is meaningless (or that it is undefinable, which, incidentally, in my opinion does not matter, since definitions do not matter). In other words, the whole problem arises because of doubts, or scepticism, concerning correspondence: whether there is such a thing as a correspondence between a statement and a fact. It is quite clear that these doubts are serious (especially in view of the paradox of the liar).

It is also quite clear that, but for these doubts, the upholders of the coherence theory and of the theory of pragmatic usefulness would really have nothing to argue against. Nobody denies that pragmatic usefulness and such matters as predictive power are important. But should there exist something like the *correspondence of a theory to the facts*, then this would obviously be more important than mere self-consistency, and certainly also much more important than coherence with any earlier 'knowledge' (or 'belief'); for if a theory corresponds to the facts but does not cohere with some earlier knowledge, then this earlier knowledge should be discarded.

Similarly, if there exists something like the correspondence of theory to the facts, then it is clear that a theory which corresponds to the facts will be as a rule very useful; more useful, *qua* theory, than a theory which does not correspond to the facts. (On the other hand, it may be very useful for a criminal before a court of justice to cling to a theory which does not correspond to the facts; but as it is not *this* kind of usefulness which the pragmatists have in mind, their views raise a question which is very awkward for them: I mean the question, 'Useful for whom?'.)

Although I am an opponent of pragmatism as a philosophy of science, I gladly admit that pragmatism has emphasized something very important: the question whether a theory has some application, whether it has, for example, predictive power. *Praxis*, as I have put it somewhere, is invaluable for the theoretician as a spur and at the same time as a bridle: it is a spur because it suggests new problems to us, and it is a bridle because it may bring us down to earth and to reality if we get lost in over-abstract theoretical flights of our imagination. All this is to be admitted. And yet, it is clear that the pragmatist position will be superseded by a realist position if we can meaningfully say that a statement, or a theory, may or may not correspond to the facts.

Thus the correspondence theory does not deny the importance of the coherence and pragmatist theories, though it does imply that they are not good enough. On the other hand, the coherence and pragmatist theories assert the impossibility or meaninglessness of the correspondence theory.

So without ever mentioning the word 'truth' or asking, 'What does truth mean?' we can see that the central problem of this whole discussion is not the verbal problem of defining 'truth' but the following substantial problem: can there be such a thing as a statement or a theory which corresponds to the facts, or which does not correspond to the facts?

Behind the doubts concerning the possibility of speaking about correspondence, there are various strong arguments.

First of all, there are paradoxes or antinomies which arise out of this correspondence idea. Secondly, there are the countless unsuccessful attempts to say more precisely what the correspondence between a statement and a fact consists of. There is the attempt of Schlick, who said that correspondence is to be explained by a one-one relationship between the linguistic statement and the fact; that is, by uniqueness. A statement, he said, is 'true', or corresponds to the facts, if it stands to the facts of the world in a one-one relationship or in a unique relationship: non-correspondence or 'falsity' is the same as ambiguity. Of course, this is an unacceptable view, for many vague and ambiguous statements (such as 'there are a few people somewhere in America') may correspond to the facts; and vice versa, every general proposition or theory which corresponds to the facts corresponds to many facts, so that there is not a one-one relationship.

Moreover, a statement which does not correspond to the facts may be quite unambiguous. A murderer may say unambiguously, 'I have not killed him.' There is no ambiguity in this assertion; but it does not correspond to the facts. Clearly, Schlick's attempt to explain correspondence misfires. Another even worse attempt is Wittgenstein's.[12] Wittgenstein suggested

[12] L. Wittgenstein, *Tractatus Logico-Philosophicus*, 1922.

that a proposition is a picture of reality and that correspondence is a relationship very much like the one that holds between the groove on a gramophone record and the sounds which it denotes: a kind of projective relationship between facts and statements. The untenability of this view can easily be shown. One is reminded of the famous story of Livingstone being introduced by an interpreter to a Negro king whom he asked, 'How are you?'. The Negro king answered with one word, and the interpreter began to talk and talk and talk and talk, for ten minutes, translating the word to Livingstone in the form of a long story of the king's sorrows. Then Livingstone asked whether the king was in need of medical assistance, and then the king began to talk and talk and talk and talk and talk. And the interpreter translated it with one word: 'No.'

No doubt this story is invented. But it is well invented; and it illustrates the weakness of the projection theory of language, especially as a theory of the correspondence between a statement and a fact.

But this is not all. The matter is even more serious; namely, Wittgenstein, after having formulated this theory, said that it is impossible to discuss the relationship of language to reality, or to discuss language at all. (Because language cannot be discussed by language.) This is a field in which words fail us. 'It shows itself' is his favourite expression to indicate the failure of words. Any attempt to go deeper into the relationship between language and reality or to discuss language more deeply or statements more deeply is, accordingly, bound to be meaningless. And although he says in the Preface of his book, 'the *truth* of the thoughts that are here set forth seems to me unassailable and definitive', he ends up by saying, 'Anybody who understands me eventually recognizes them [the propositions of the *Tractatus*] as nonsensical.' (Because talk about language is meaningless.) No doubt this refers, apart from other things, especially to his theory of projection. His remark that his readers will see that what he says is meaningless thus confirms what the opponents of the correspondence theory have always said of the correspondence theory, namely that it is meaningless to speak about the correspondence between a statement and a fact.

So we are back at the real issue. It is this: is there or is there not a tenable correspondence theory? Can we or can we not speak meaningfully of the correspondence between a statement and a fact?

Now my assertion is that Tarski has rehabilitated the correspondence theory. This, I think, is a great achievement, and it is a great philosophical achievement. I say this because it has been denied by many philosophers (for example, by Max Black) that there is something philosophically important in Tarski's achievement.

The key to the rehabilitation of the correspondence theory is a very simple and obvious observation made by Tarski. That is, if I want to speak about correspondence between a statement *S* and a fact *F*, then I have to do so in a language in which I can speak about both: statements such as *S*, and facts such as *F*. This seems to be frightfully trivial; but it is nevertheless decisive. It means that the language in which we speak in explaining correspondence must possess the means needed to *refer* to statements, and to *describe* facts. If I have a language which has both these means at its disposal, so that it can refer to statements *and* describe facts, then in this language —the *meta*language—I can speak about correspondence between statements and facts without any difficulty, as we shall see.

A metalanguage is a language in which we talk about some other language. For example, a grammar of the German language, written in English, uses English as a metalanguage in order to talk about German. The language about which we talk in the *metalanguage* (in this case English) is usually called the *'object language'* (in this case German). The characteristic thing about a metalanguage is that it contains (metalinguistic) *names* of words and of statements of the object language, and also (metalinguistic) *predicates*, such as 'noun (of the object language)' or 'verb (of the object language)' or 'statement (of the object language)'. If a metalanguage is to suffice for our purpose it must also, as Tarski points out, contain the usual means necessary to speak about at least all those *facts* about which the object language can speak.

All this is the case if we use English as our metalanguage in order to speak about German (as the object language under investigation).

For example, we shall be able to say in the English meta-language such things as:

The German words '*Das Gras ist grün*' form a statement of the German language.

On the other hand, we shall be able to describe in our (English) metalanguage the fact which the German statement '*Das Gras ist grün*' describes. We can describe this fact in English simply by saying that grass is green.

We can now make a statement in the metalanguage about the *correspondence of a statement of the object language to the facts* as follows. We can make the assertion: *The German statement '*Das Gras ist grün*' corresponds to the facts if, and only if, grass is green.* (Or: '. . . *only if it is a fact that grass is* green.')

This is very trivial. It is, however, important to realize the following: in our assertion, the words '*Das Gras ist grün*', put within *quotes*, function as a metalinguistic (that is, an *English*) name of a *German* statement; on the other hand, the English words 'grass is green' occur in our assertion above *without* any quotation marks: they do not function as a name of a statement, but simply as the description of a *fact* (or alleged fact).

This makes it possible for our assertion to express a relation-ship between a (German) *statement*, and a *fact*. (The *fact* is neither German nor English, although it is, of course, described or spoken about in our metalanguage, which is English: the fact is non-linguistic, it is a fact of the real world, although we need of course a language if we wish to talk about it.) And what our metalinguistic assertion asserts is that a certain (German) statement *corresponds to a certain fact* (a non-linguistic fact, a fact of the real world) under conditions which are precisely stated.

We can, of course, replace the German object language by any other—even by English. Thus we can make the metalin-guistic assertion:

*The English statement '*Grass is green*' corresponds to the facts if, and only if, grass is green.*

This looks even more trivial. But it can hardly be denied; nor can it be denied that it expresses the conditions under which a statement corresponds to the facts.

Generally speaking, let '*S*' be a (metalinguistic) *name* of a statement of the object language, and let '*f*' be the *abbreviation* of an expression of the metalanguage that describes the (supposed) fact *F* which *S* describes. Then we can make the following metalinguistic assertion:

A statement *S* of the object language corresponds to the facts if, and only if, *f*. (Or: . . . if it is a fact that *f*.)

Note that while '*S*' is here a metalinguistic name of a statement, '*f*' is not a name, but an abbreviation of an expression of the metalanguage describing a certain fact (the fact which we can name '*F*').

We can now say that what Tarski did was to discover that in order to speak about the correspondence between a statement *S* and a fact *F*, we need a language (a metalanguage) in which we can *speak about* the statement *S* *and state* the fact *F*. (The former we speak about by using the *name* '*S*', the latter by using a metalinguistic expression '*f*' which *states or describes F*.)

The importance of this discovery is that it dispels all doubt about the meaningfulness of talking about the correspondence of a statement to some fact or facts.

Once this is done, we can, of course, replace the words 'corresponds to the facts' by the words 'is true'.

Tarski, apart from this, introduced a method of giving a *definition* of truth (in the sense of the correspondence theory) for any consistent *formalized system*. But this is not, I think, his main achievement. His main achievement is the rehabilitation of talk about correspondence (and truth). Incidentally, he showed under what circumstances such talk may lead to paradoxes, and how we can avoid these paradoxes; *and he also showed how in ordinary talk about truth we can, and do, avoid paradoxes.*

Once we have settled that we can use 'truth' in the sense of the correspondence of statements to facts, there is really nothing of importance to be added about the word 'truth'. There is no doubt that correspondence to the facts is what we usually call 'truth'; that in ordinary language it is correspondence that we call 'truth', rather than coherence or pragmatic usefulness. A judge who admonishes a witness to speak the truth and nothing but the truth does not admonish the witness to speak what he thinks is useful either for himself or for anybody else. The judge admonishes a witness to speak the truth and nothing but the truth, but he does not say, 'All we require of you is that you do not get involved in contradictions', which he would say were he a believer in the coherence theory. But this is not what he demands of the witness.

In other words, the ordinary sense of 'truth' as it is used in courts of law is, no doubt, correspondence. But my main point is that this may be regarded as an afterthought, and as an unimportant afterthought. For if anybody should want to say, 'No, in ordinary language, "truth" is used in a different sense', I should not quarrel with him. I should suggest that we forget all about terminology: I should be prepared to use the terminology of my opponent, pointing out, however, that we have *at least* these three meanings at our disposal: this is the only thing about which I should be prepared to quarrel; but I should refuse to quarrel about words.

I should point out, though, that the correspondence theory of truth is a realistic theory; that is to say, it makes the distinction, which is a realistic distinction, between a theory and the facts which the theory describes; and it makes it possible to say that a theory is true, or false, or that it corresponds to the facts, thus relating the theory to the facts. It allows us to speak of a reality different from the theory. This is the main thing; it is the main point for the realist. The realist wants to have both a theory and the reality or the facts (don't call it 'reality' if you don't like it, just call it 'the facts') which are different from his theory *about* these facts, and which he can somehow or other compare with the facts, in order to find out whether or not it corresponds to them. Of course, the comparison is always extremely difficult.

One last word about Tarski's theory. Its whole purpose is often misinterpreted: it is wrongly assumed that it is intended to yield a *criterion of truth*. For coherence was so intended, and likewise pragmatic usefulness; they strengthened the traditional view that any serious theory of truth should present us with *a method of deciding* whether or not a given statement is true.

Tarski has proved many things from his definition of truth. Among other things, he has proved that in a sufficiently powerful language (and in every language in which we can formulate mathematical or physical theories) there can be no criterion of truth; that is, no criterion of correspondence: the question of whether a proposition is true is not in general decidable for the languages for which we may form the concept of truth. Thus the concept of truth plays mainly the role of a regulative idea. It helps us in our search for truth that we know there is something like truth or correspondence. It does not give us a means of finding truth, or of being sure that we have found it even if we have found it. So there is no criterion of truth, and we must not ask for a criterion of truth. We must be content with the fact that the idea of truth as correspondence to the facts has been rehabilitated. This has been done by Tarski; and I think that he has thereby rendered an immense service to the realistic outlook.

Although we have no criterion of truth, and no means of being even quite sure of the falsity of a theory, it is easier to find out that a theory is false than to find out that it is true (as I have explained in detail elsewhere). We have even good reasons to think that most of our theories—even our best theories—are, strictly speaking, false; for they oversimplify or idealize the facts. Yet a false conjecture may be nearer or less near to the truth. Thus we arrive at the idea of nearness to the truth, or of a better or less good approximation to the truth; that is, at the idea of *'verisimilitude'*. I have tried to show that this idea can be rehabilitated in a way similar to Tarski's rehabilitation of the idea of truth as correspondence to the facts.[13]

In order to do so I have used mainly the two Tarskian ideas mentioned here. One is the idea of truth. The other is the idea of logical consequence; or more precisely, of the set of logical consequences of a conjecture, or the content of a conjecture.

By incorporating into logic the idea of verisimilitude or approximation to truth, we make logic even more 'realistic'. For it can now be used to speak about the way in which one theory corresponds better than another to the facts—the facts of the real world.

To sum up. As a realist I look upon logic as the *organon of criticism* (rather than of proof) in our search for true and highly informative theories—or at least for new theories that contain more information, and correspond better to the facts, than our older theories. And I look upon criticism, in its turn, as our main instrument in promoting the growth of our knowledge about the world of facts.

[13] K. R. Popper, *Conjectures and Refutations*, 1963, 1972, Chapter 10 and Addenda.

9. Philosophical Comments on Tarski's Theory of Truth

OUR main concern in science and in philosophy is, or ought to be, the search for truth, by way of bold conjectures and the criticial search for what is false in our various competing theories.[1]

This was my view thirty-seven years ago in July 1934 when I first met Alfred Tarski at a conference in Prague organized by the Vienna Circle. I must stress, however, that in those days, before I had learned from Tarski about his theory of truth, my intellectual conscience was far from clear about the assumption that our main concern was the search for truth. I had written in my book, *Logik der Forschung* (1934), whose page proofs I had with me in Prague and showed to Tarski (but I doubt whether he was interested): 'the striving for knowledge and the search for truth are . . . the strongest motives of scientific discovery'.[2] Yet I was uneasy about the notion of truth; and there is a whole section in that book in which I tried to defend the notion of truth as commonsensical and harmless by saying

---

[1] This formulation of our main concern in science is somewhat improved, for the natural sciences, in the last section of this paper. A word may be said here about terminology.

I find uninteresting (because mainly verbal) the problem of whether we should speak of 'sentences', 'statements', or 'propositions'; the main critics of Tarski's terminology of 'sentences' assert that sentences are uninterpreted strings of words following certain rules of grammar and can therefore be neither true nor false. They overlook the fact that Tarski speaks explicitly of *'meaningful sentences'* and only of *interpreted languages*. In order to show my contempt of this kind of verbal criticism I have simply adopted the terminology of my opponents, and I speak throughout my paper of 'statements' rather than of 'sentences'. Thus I use 'statement' as synonym for an interpreted, meaningful sentence or proposition.

[2] K. R. Popper, *The Logic of Scientific Discovery*, section 85, p. 278.

Based on a talk given at a Symposium in Honour of Alfred Tarski on the occasion of his 70th Birthday, held at the University of California 23–30 June 1971.

that, if we want, we can avoid its use in the methodology of science by speaking of deducibility and similar logical relations instead.[3]

The reason for my uneasiness concerning the notion of truth was, of course, that this notion had been for some time attacked by some philosophers, and with good arguments. It was not so much the antinomy of the liar which frightened me, but the difficulty of explaining the correspondence theory: what could the correspondence of a statement to the facts be? In addition, there was a view which, though I decidedly never held it, I felt unable to combat effectively. The view I am alluding to is that if we wish to speak about truth, we should be able to give a criterion of truth. I *did* hold that it was nevertheless legitimate to speak of truth. But I was unable to defend my view that the absence of a criterion of truth could not be used as an argument against the logical legitimacy of the notion of truth.

I am glad that I never gave written expression to this particular uneasiness, which was utterly unjustified, as everybody here today will be aware.[4] As we now know, truth is by no means the only notion whose importance and legitimacy is unimpaired by the fact that there exists no general criterion of its applicability in specific cases. A famous example of a similar kind is the notion of deducibility: we know that for many theories the decision problem for theoremhood is insoluble; and unless we confine ourselves to a decidable theory, a theory for which the decision problem can be positively solved, there exists no criterion or general procedure permitting us to decide in each particular case whether or not an alleged theorem of the theory is a *valid theorem*; that is, whether or not it is deducible with the logical means provided by the theory. (This is the sense in which I use the terms 'valid theorem', 'valid derivation', etc.)

Thus we do not have a general criterion of validity or theoremhood for undecidable theories. Nevertheless the notion of validity or theoremhood is perfectly clear, even for un-decidable theories: an alleged theorem is actually valid if and only if there exists a valid derivation of it, whether or not the

---

[3] Op. cit., section 84.

[4] See especially note 1 on p. 254 of A. Tarski, *Logic, Semantics, Metamathematics*, Clarendon Press, Oxford, 1956.

derivation has been or will be discovered by us. The absence of a criterion in no way contributes to the vagueness of the term 'valid theorem'. Rather, it is in this case a direct consequence of our inability to check through the infinity of all valid derivations, in order to find whether or not any of them ends with the alleged theorem. We may be lucky and discover a proof or a disproof of the alleged theorem; but if we are not so lucky, then, unless the theory permits of a decision procedure, we have no means of finding out whether the formula in question is a theorem or not.

Today, all this is almost too trivial to be mentioned. Yet there are still plenty of philosophers who believe that any notion, for example the notion of truth, is logically legitimate only if a criterion exists which enables us to decide whether or not an object falls under that notion. Thus there is an article[5] in volume 3 of the *Encyclopedia of Philosophy* of 1967 in which my view that there is no general criterion of truth for scientific theories is summed up in a brisk but quite misleading sentence attributing to me the opinion that 'Truth itself is just an illusion.' In volume 2 of the same *Encyclopedia* we are told that it is implicit in the later writings of Wittgenstein 'that a concept is vacuous if there is no criterion for its application'.[6]

The term 'positivism' has many meanings, but this (Wittgensteinian) thesis that 'a concept is vacuous if there is no criterion for its application' seems to me to express the very heart of positivistic tendencies. (The idea is very close to Hume.) If this interpretation of positivism is accepted, then positivism is refuted by the modern development of logic, and especially by Tarski's theory of truth, which contains the *theorem*: for sufficiently rich languages, there can be no general criterion of truth.

This theorem is, of course, of the greatest interest if we remember the classical conflict between the Stoics (and later the Cartesians) on the one side, and the Sceptics on the other. Here we have one of the rare examples where a classical philosophical conflict may be said to have been settled by a theorem belonging to logic or to metalogic. But one cannot

---

[5] *The Encyclopedia of Philosophy*, ed. Paul Edwards, Macmillan, 1967, vol. 3, p. 37.
[6] Op. cit., vol. 2, p. 260. See my *Open Society*, ii, 4th edn., Addendum 1, sect. 3.

say that the example is widely known or appreciated among philosophers.

Yet it is not my intention here to enter into a polemic with those philosophers who deny that Tarski's theory of truth has a philosophical significance. Instead I wish to recall my intense joy and relief when I learned in 1935 that the following were consequences of Tarski's theory of truth:

(1) that this concept was definable in logical terms which nobody had questioned before, *and therefore logically legitimate*;

(2) that it was applicable to every unambiguously formulated (closed) statement (of any non-universalistic language), provided it was not applicable to its negation, *and therefore obviously not vacuous*, in spite of the fact

(3) that it was not linked to any general criterion, although every sentence derivable from a true sentence or from a true theory was, demonstrably, true;

(4) that the class of true sentences was a deductive system, and

(5) that it was an undecidable deductive system provided the language under consideration was rich enough. (In connection with this result, Tarski referred to Gödel.)

As mentioned before, I first met Tarski in July 1934 in Prague. It was early in 1935 that I met him again in Vienna, in Karl Menger's Colloquium, of which Tarski and Gödel were members, and in which I also met such great men as Skolem and Abraham Wald. It was in those days that I asked Tarski to explain to me his theory of truth, and he did so in a lecture of perhaps twenty minutes on a bench (an unforgotten bench) in the *Volksgarten* in Vienna. He also allowed me to see the sequence of proof sheets of the German translation of his great paper on the concept of truth, which were then just being sent to him from the editor of *Studia Philosophica*. No words can describe how much I learned from all this, and no words can express my gratitude for it. Although Tarski was only a little older than I, and although we were, in those days, on terms of considerable intimacy, I looked upon him as the one man whom I could truly regard as my teacher in philosophy. I have never learned so much from anybody else.

Nevertheless, there are peripheral points on which I may perhaps disagree with him. I was always a commonsense philosopher, and a commonsense realist.[7] My attitude was that it was commonsensical to hold that common sense was often wrong—perhaps more often than right; but that it was plain that in philosophy we had to start from common sense, if only to find out, by criticism, where it was wrong. I was interested in the real world, in the cosmos, and I was thoroughly opposed to every idealism, positivism, or even neutralism in philosophy. If there was not a real world, as rich as and even much richer than the world we know so superficially from our daily life, and if the study of this world was not the main task of philosophy, then I would not be interested in philosophy. I never found out precisely what Tarski's attitude to realism was. He seemed to be impressed by Kotarbinski's 'reism', but also by Vienna positivism; and he stressed the neutrality of his concept of truth.

As I was a critical commonsense realist and conscious of the fact that I therefore held a 'metaphysical' theory,[8] I was greatly interested in what appeared to me a realist aspect of Tarski's theory of truth, an aspect whose mere existence, I suspect, he may deny.[9]

Tarski's theory, as you all know, and as he stressed first, is a *rehabilitation* and an elaboration of the classical theory that truth is correspondence to the facts; and this seems to *me* to support metaphysical realism. Tarski's theory is, at the same time, also a rehabilitation and elaboration of some of the classical *criticism* of this correspondence theory, for it points out

[7] I am a realist in two senses of the word. Firstly, I believe in the reality of the physical world. Secondly, I believe that the world of theoretical entities is real, as I have explained in my papers 'Epistemology Without a Knowing Subject', 'On the Theory of the Objective Mind', and 'A Realist View of Logic, Physics, and History' (now chapters 3, 4, and 8 of the present volume). In these, I maintain my opposition to essentialism—the reality of *concepts*—but assert the reality of *problems*, *theories*, *mistakes*, etc.

(As to the first sense I may even describe myself as a materialist in so far as I believe in the reality of matter, although I am emphatically *not* a materialist in the sense in which 'materialism' is the view that (extended) matter is something ultimate or irreducible, or that it alone is real. On the contrary, I believe that there may be a true theory of matter which explains the extension of matter by intensities such as forces, as was first suggested by Leibniz, Boscovic, and Kant.)

[8] Cp. my *Logic of Scientific Discovery*, p. 252, text to note *1.

[9] Cp. A. Tarski, 'The Semantic Conception of Truth and the Foundations of Semantics', *Philosophy and Phenomenological Research*, 4, 1944, pp. 341–76; see especially section 19.

the degree to which those who suspected the correspondence theory of being paradoxical were right. This latter part is, essentially, solved by Tarski's doctrine that the semantics (L_1) of an object language (L_0)—that is, the metalanguage that contains the concept 'true in L_0' as a definable concept—must be *essentially richer* (of a higher order) than the object language (L_0).

The object language L_0 may contain, as we know, its own syntax and, more especially, descriptive names of all its own expressions. But L_0 cannot, without risk of antinomy, contain specifically semantic terms like *denotation, satisfaction,* or *truth*; that is, notions which relate the *names of the expressions* of L_0 to the *facts or objects* to which these expressions refer.

All this gave me material for thoughts that developed for many years. I will briefly communicate a few of these thoughts.

II

I F, as Tarski's theory suggests, truth is correspondence to the facts, then let us for a moment abandon the word 'truth' altogether and instead only talk of 'the correspondence of statements to the facts they describe'.

It was, I think, the apparent impossibility of discovering or explaining this correspondence which made all pre-Tarskian correspondence theories of truth so suspect; suspect even to people like myself who valued the correspondence theory simply because of its commonsense and realist character.[10]

Now let us be bold, and take it seriously that there are statements that correspond to the facts. Any theory dealing with this situation must be able to speak (1) of the statements of some language, which we call the language under investigation or the object language,[11] and (2) of facts and purported facts.

(1) In order to speak of statements, we must have at our disposal *names* of statements, for example *quotation names* or

---

[10] For details, see *C. & R.*, p. 223.

[11] It appears that the term 'object language' was originally introduced to mean 'language that speaks about (physical) objects'. I use it in the sense of 'language that is the object of investigation'; it is investigated by a theory formulated in a metalanguage. (This, of course, gives rise to the idea of an infinite hierarchy of metalanguages.)

descriptive names of statements. This means that any correspondence theory must be formulated in a metalanguage; that is, a language in which one can discuss, or speak about, the expressions of some object language under investigation.

(2) In order to speak about any relation between the statements and the facts, we must have at our disposal descriptions of facts; that is to say, we must be able to describe, in our metalanguage, all those facts which we can describe in the object language. Thus the metalanguage must possess translations of the statements of the object language, or it must contain the object language as *part of itself* (a method that avoids the unpleasant problem of the existence of faithful translations).

So we find that any theory that deals with the correspondence between statements and facts, and therefore with some relation between statements and facts, must be formulated in a metalanguage which apart from the usual logical words, has at its disposal three types of expressions:

(1) Names of statements; that is, of the linguistic expressions of some object language; they are part of the 'morphology' or 'syntax' of that object language.

(2) Statements describing the facts (including the non-facts) under discussion in that object language; that is, translations of the object language into the metalanguage. (In order to avoid the pitfalls of translation, the object language may be made part of the metalanguage, as already hinted.)

(3) In addition to these two fundamental types of expression, there is a third type: terms denoting predicates of, and relations between, these two fundamental kinds of expression, for example such predicates as 'X corresponds to the facts' or such relations as 'X corresponds to the facts if and only if y'. (This last kind of term is semantical and of a higher order than the object language to which it refers.)

These are the three almost obvious minimum requirements for any language in which we can formulate a correspondence theory.

A language which satisfies these three minimum requirements Tarski called a 'semantical metalanguage'.

I see the greatness and boldness of Tarski's achievement in the fact that he discovered these minimum requirements, and also that he found out that the predicates or relations mentioned under (3), which relate expressions to the world of facts, went essentially beyond the means at our disposal in the object language.[12]

It is clear that once we have the three categories of expressions at our disposal, we can in the semantical metalanguage make such assertions as

P corresponds to the facts if and only if *p*,

whereby we assume that the upper case italics such as '*P*' are variables standing for the metalinguistic *names* of those objectlinguistic fact-describing statements whose metalinguistic *translations* are represented by the corresponding lower case italics such as '*p*'.

In teaching Tarski's theory of truth I found that it made matters easier for me, and for at least some of my students, if I spoke in this way about *correspondence to the facts* rather than about *truth*. Incidentally, I also found that it made matters easier to use among our examples *false* statements of the object language.

Let us take German as our object language and English as our metalanguage, and let us remember that the English translation of the German sentence '*Der Mond besteht aus grünem Käse*' is 'The moon is made of green cheese'. Taking these false statements, we can of course construct the true semantical assertion:

'The German statement "*Der Mond besteht aus grünem Käse*" corresponds to the facts if and only if the moon consists of green cheese.'

The use of false statements of the object language is, however, a very minor point. On the other hand, speaking of correspondence to the facts (instead of truth) seems to be a real help to some students. It allows them to see more clearly that, and

[12] A philosophically only slightly less important result about the terms mentioned under (3) is that, *qua* terms of the metalanguage, they have the same morphological character as the terms mentioned under (1): that is to say, they belong to the morphology developed *in* the metalanguage (even though not to that part of it which contains the morphology or syntax *of* the object language and can be developed in the object language itself).

why, the statement which is taking the place of the lower case italicized variable '*p*' is, and why it *must* be, a metalinguistic statement of some *fact* (or some purported fact); that is to say, the metalinguistic description of some state of affairs also described in the object language.

III

THERE is a claim of Tarski's, in the second paragraph of his famous paper on truth,[13] that in defining truth he does not need to employ any concepts which are semantical (that is, which relate linguistic expressions to the things expressed). But since he defines 'truth' with the help of the concept of satisfaction, and the latter concept is clearly semantical (it is so listed by Tarski himself in the first paragraph of his paper xv, p. 401 of *Logic, Semantics, Metamathematics*), even a careful reader may be excused if he is at first a little puzzled. The solution of the puzzle may be put as follows. Every sufficiently rich language speaking about some subject matter may (according to results found independently by Tarski and Gödel) contain its own 'morphology' or 'syntax', while (as Tarski has shown) no consistent language may contain the means of defining its own semantics. What Tarski needs for his definition is, as we have seen, a semantical metalanguage which is of a higher order than the object language whose semantics it contains. But those terms which are semantical terms with respect to the *object* language may within the metalanguage as such have the same status as its other morphological or syntactical terms. Thus the semantics of an object language L_n may be part of the syntax of the higher order metalanguage (L_{n+1}, say): no terms of a non-morphological or non-syntactical character need to enter L_{n+1}. This amounts to a reduction of the semantics of L_n to the syntax of L_{n+1}.

This point is of general philosophical interest, not only because semantical terms were regarded with suspicion, but also because a reduction of terms of a suspect character to terms of an accepted kind is something that merits our attention. At any rate, Tarski's achievement in reducing terms which

---

[13] Cp. p. 152 of Woodger's English translation, *Logic, Semantics, Metamathematics*, Clarendon Press, Oxford, 1956.

belong to the semantics of L_n to the non-semantical terms of L_{n+1} removes all grounds for suspicion.

I admit that this reduction is important because it is a rare event in philosophy that we are able to introduce an entirely new (and suspect) category of terms on the basis of (unsuspect) established categories; it is a rehabilitation, an act of saving the honour of a suspect term.

On the other hand, I regard definitions, and questions of reducibility, as philosophically not particularly important. If we cannot define a term, nothing prevents us from using it as an undefined term: the use of some undefined terms is not only legitimate but unavoidable, for every defined term must, in the last resort, be defined with the help of some undefined terms.[14] In my opinion, *it is not his successful description of a method for defining 'true'* which makes Tarski's work philosophically so important, but his *rehabilitation of the correspondence theory of truth,* and the proof that there is no further difficulty lurking here once we have understood the essential need for a semantical metalanguage which is richer than the object language *and* its syntax. It is clear enough that if we like we may start with primitive semantical terms (as was done by R. M. Martin)[15] instead of with their careful avoidance. We would achieve essentially the same semantic theory of truth or correspondence to the facts. But without Tarski's theory, which provides a semantical metalanguage free from any specifically semantical terms, the philosophers' suspicion of semantical terms may not have been overcome.

IV

As mentioned before, I am a realist. I admit that an idealism such as Kant's can be defended to the extent that it says that *all our theories are man-made,* and that we try to impose them upon the world of nature. But I am a realist in holding that the question whether our man-made theories are true or not depends upon the real facts; real facts which are, with very few exceptions, emphatically not man-made. Our man-made

[14] Thus Tarski has stressed that the concept of truth may be introduced by way of axioms, rather than by way of a definition.

[15] Cp. R. M. Martin, *Truth and Denotation, A Study in Semantical Theory,* Routledge and Kegan Paul, London, 1958.

theories may clash with these real *facts*, and so, in our search for truth, we may have to adjust our theories or to give them up.

Tarski's theory allows us to *define truth* as correspondence to the facts; but we can use it also to *define reality* as that to which true statements correspond. For example, we may distinguish *real facts*, that is (alleged) facts that are real, from (*alleged*) *facts that are not real* (that is, from non-facts). Or to put it more explicitly, we can say that an alleged fact, such as the moon's consisting of green cheese, is a real fact if and only if the statement which describes it—in this case the statement 'The moon is made of green cheese'—is *true*; otherwise the alleged fact is not a real fact (or, if you prefer to say so, it is not a fact at all).

And just as Tarski allows us to replace the term 'truth' by 'the set of true statements (or sentences)', so we can replace the term 'reality' by 'the set of real facts'.

Thus I suggest that if we can define the concept of truth, we can also define the concept of reality. (Of course, problems of order arise, analogous to the problems of the order of languages in Tarski's work; see especially his Postscript, pp. 268–77, of *Logic, Semantics, Metamathematics*.) This is not intended to suggest that the term 'truth' is in some sense or other more basic than the term 'reality': I am anxious to reject any such suggestion, because of its idealistic flavour.[16] I simply mean that if it is possible to define 'truth' as 'correspondence to the facts' or, what amounts to the same, as 'correspondence to reality', then it is equally possible to define 'reality' as 'correspondence to the truth'. And since I am a realist, I like to be able to reassure myself that the concept of reality is not 'vacuous', or suspect for any other reason; no more than is the concept of truth.

V

AMONG those older theories of Tarski's which are accessible to an unsophisticated philosopher such as myself, there is his Calculus of Systems. I was in Paris in 1935 when, if I remember rightly, Tarski completed his paper on the Calculus of Systems.[17] I have taken the greatest interest in it.

[16] See K. R. Popper, *Conjectures and Refutations*, note 33 on p. 116, with an acknowledgement to Alexandre Koyré.

[17] See A. Tarski, op. cit., pp. 342–83.

I have tried to combine some of the more obvious results of Tarski's paper on Truth with his paper on the Calculus of Systems. We at once get the following most trivial theorems in which it is assumed that the languages spoken of are not universalistic.

Theorem. The set T of true statements of any language is a deductive system in the sense of Tarski's Calculus of Systems. It is complete.[18]

As a deductive system, T is a consequence class; that is, it is identical with the class $Cn(T)$ of its own logical consequences $(T = Cn(T))$. It is a complete system in the sense that if a statement not belonging to T is added to T, the resulting class is inconsistent.

Theorem. The set of true statements of any sufficiently rich language is a non-axiomatizable deductive system in the sense of Tarski's Calculus of Systems.

These two theorems are quite trivial, and in what follows it will be assumed that the languages in question are sufficiently rich to satisfy the second of these theorems.

I now introduce a new concept, the notion of the *truth content* of a statement *a*.

Definition. The set of all true statements following from any given statement *a* is called the *truth content of a*. It is a deductive system.

Theorem. The truth content of any true statement *a* is an axiomatizable system $A_T = A$; the truth content of any false statement *a* is the deductive system $A_T \subset A$, where A_T is non-axiomatizable, provided the object language in question is rich enough.

This definition, and this theorem, may be generalized: Tarski's calculus of deductive systems may be regarded as a generalization of the calculus of statements, since to every statement (or class of logically equivalent statements), *a*, there corresponds a (finitely) *axiomatizable* system, *A*, such that

$$A = Cn(A) = Cn(\{a\});$$

and *vice versa*: to every *axiomatizable* deductive system, *A*, there corresponds a statement (or a class of logically equivalent state-

---

[18] I follow in the main Tarski's symbolism (especially in using upper case italics to denote deductive systems) except for writing 'T' for the class of true statements where Tarski writes 'Tr'.

ments), *a*. But since there are also deductive systems or consequence classes which are not axiomatizable, so that there is no statement or finite class of statements whose consequence class they are, the transition from statements to consequence classes or deductive systems, or from the calculus of statements to the Calculus of Systems, may be described as a generalization.

Thus we have, more generally, for every consequence class or deductive system A a system A_T, the truth content of A which is identical with A if and only if A consists only of true statements, and which is in any case a subsystem of A: obviously, it is the product class or meet of the sets A and T.

The question may be asked whether we have corresponding to the *truth content A_T* of *a* or of A also something to be called the *falsity content A_F* of *a* or of A. An obvious suggestion that presents itself is to define the class of all the false statements which belong to the deductive system A as the falsity content of A. Yet this suggestion is not quite satisfactory if we use (as I suggest) the term '*content*' as a third synonym of 'deductive system' or 'consequence class'; for this class, supposed to consist only of false statements, is not a deductive system: every deductive system A contains true statements—in fact, an infinity of them—and so the class consisting only of the false statements belonging to A cannot be a content.

In order to introduce the idea of the falsity content A_F of a statement *a* or a consequence class A, one may fall back on the idea of the *relative content* of A, given B, which may be introduced as a generalization of a Tarskian deductive system or (*absolute*) *content*, $A = Cn(A)$. I shall explain this idea, and in view of some possible intuitive criticism, I shall also introduce the idea of a *content measure*. In the end, I shall introduce, with the help of the idea of the measures of truth content and of falsity content, the idea of approximation to truth or verisimilitude.

VI

TARSKI speaks of greater and smaller deductive systems or consequence classes. Indeed, the set of deductive systems (of some given language) is partially ordered by the inclusion relation, which coincides with the deducibility relation. The following remark made by Tarski in his paper on the Calculus of Systems may be used as a clue to the relativization of a consequence class or content or deductive system: '. . . among deductive systems a smallest exists, i.e. a system which is a sub-system of all other deductive systems. It is the system $Cn(\mathrm{o})$, the set of consequences of the empty set. This system, which here for brevity will be denoted by 'L', can be interpreted as the set of all logically valid sentences (or, more generally, as the set of all those sentences which from the start we recognize as true when undertaking the construction of the deductive theory that is the object of our . . . investigation).'[19]

This suggests that we may use a system other than the zero system L 'as the set of all those sentences which *from the start we recognize as true* when undertaking the construction . . .'. Let us denote, as before, the deductive system in whose content we are interested by the variable 'A' and 'the set of all those sentences which from the start we recognize as true' by the variable 'B'. Then we can write

$$Cn(A, B)$$

as the relativization of Tarski's $Cn(A)$, which becomes a special case when $B = L = Cn(\mathrm{o})$:

$$Cn(A) = Cn(A, L).$$

We can write 'A, B' as an abbreviation for '$Cn(A, B)$' just as Tarski writes 'A' for '$Cn(A)$'. The quoted passage from Tarski then suggests the following:

Definition: $A, B = Cn(A, B) = Cn(A + B) - Cn(B).$

This obviously leads to the following:

Theorem. $A = Cn(A) = A, L = Cn(A, L) = Cn(A + L) - Cn(L).$

Confining ourselves to the relative way of writing we then have for the truth content

$$A_T = A_T, L = Cn((A \cdot T) + L) - Cn(L)$$

and for the falsity content

$$A_F = A, A_T = Cn(A + A_T) - Cn(A_T) = Cn(A) - Cn(A_T)$$

---

[19] A. Tarski, *Logic, Semantics, Metamathematics*, Clarendon Press, Oxford, 1956, p. 343.

which turns the falsity content A_F into a relative content whose extension coincides (as originally suggested) with the class of all false statements of A.

VII

AGAINST the proposed definition of the falsity content A_F as the relative content A, A_T the following objection may be raised. This definition is intuitively backed by a quotation from Tarski in which Tarski takes L to be the smallest or the zero deductive system. But in our definition

$$A = A, L = Cn(A+L) - Cn(L),$$

we are taking the word zero too literally: we now see that L should be taken as a set of *measure zero* rather than as a set which, in view of our expression '$-Cn(L)$', is literally empty or else no longer present, according to our definition, since it was subtracted (so that only the non-logical statements of A are left, which was not intended).

Whether we take this objection seriously or not, it disappears in any case if we decide to operate with a *measure of content*, $ct(A)$, or $ct(A, B)$, instead of the content or consequence class $Cn(A)$ or $Cn(A, B)$ itself.

In 1934, Tarski had drawn the attention of the conference in Prague to an axiomatization of the calculus of the relative probability of a deductive system A, given a deductive system B, due to Stephan Mazurkiewicz,[20] which was based on Tarski's Calculus of Systems. Such an axiomatization can be regarded as introducing a measure function of the deductive systems or contents $A, B, C,...$, even though this particular function, the probability function, $p(A, B)$

---

[20] Tarski referred to S. Mazurkiewicz, 'Über die Grundlagen der Wahrscheinlichkeitsrechnung I', *Monatshefte f. Math. & Phys.*, **41**, 1934, pp. 343–52. It emerges from footnote 2 on p. 344 of this paper that Tarksi's Calculus of Systems was known to Polish mathematicians as early as 1930. The system of Mazurkiewicz has a certain finitistic character, in contrast to my own system (see *L. Sc. D.*, pp. 326–58), which can be interpreted in various ways, for example as a calculus of the probabilities of deductive systems.

I may perhaps mention that in the present volume I am using as symbols for measure functions, such as probability, content, and verisimilitude, lower case italics: for instance $p(A)$, $ct(A)$, $vs(A)$; while in the Addenda to *Conjectures and Refutations*, where I first dealt with the latter two measure functions, I wrote *Ct* and *Vs*.

increases with decreasing relative content. This suggests the introduction of a content measure by a definition such as

Definition: $ct(A, B) = 1 - p(A, B)$

which increases and decreases with increasing and decreasing relative content. (Other definitions are of course possible but this seems the simplest and the most obvious one.) We obtain at once

$$ct(L) = 0$$
$$ct(A_T) = 1 - p(A.T, L) = 1 - p(A.T)$$
$$ct(A_F) = 1 - p(A, A_T)$$

corresponding to our previous results.

This suggests that we can introduce the idea of the *truthlikeness or verisimilitude* of a statement *a* in such a way that it increases with its truth content and decreases with its falsity content. This can be done in several ways.[21]

The most obvious way is to take $ct(A_T) - ct(A_F)$ as a measure of the verisimilitude of *A*. However, for reasons which I will not discuss here, it seems to me slightly preferable to define verisimilitude $vs(A)$ by this difference multiplied by some normalizing factor, preferably the following:

$$1/(p(A_T, L) + p(A, A_T)) = 1/(2 - ct(A_T) - ct(A_F)).$$

In this way we obtain the following:

Definition: $vs(A) = (ct(A_T) - ct(A_F))/(2 - ct(A_T) - ct(A_F))$,

which of course can also be written in the *p*-notation:

$$vs(A) = (p(A, A_T) - p(A_T, L))/(p(A, A_T) + p(A_T, L)).$$

This leads to

$$-1 \leqslant vs(A) \leqslant +1,$$

and especially to

$$vs(L) = 0,$$

that is to say, verisimilitude measures not that kind of approximation to truth which may be achieved by saying nothing (this is measured by lack of content, or probability), but the approach to 'the whole truth' through a greater and greater truth content. Verisimilitude in this sense is, I suggest, a more adequate aim of science—especially of the natural sciences—than truth, for two reasons. First, because we do not think that *L* represents the aim of science, even though $L = L_T$. Secondly, because we may

---

[21] Cp. K. R. Popper, *Conjectures and Refutations*, Addendum 3, pp. 391–7.

prefer theories which we think are false to others, even to true ones such as *L*, if we think that their truth content sufficiently exceeds their falsity content.

I have in these last sections merely sketched a programme of combining Tarski's theory of truth with his Calculus of Systems so as to obtain a concept of *verisimilitude* which allows us to speak, without fear of talking nonsense, of *theories which are better or worse approximations to truth*. I do not, of course, suggest that there can be a criterion for the applicability of this notion, any more than there is one for the notion of truth. But some of us (for example Einstein himself) sometimes wish to say such things as that we have reason to conjecture that Einstein's theory of gravity is *not true*, but that it is a *better approximation to truth* than Newton's. To be able to say such things with a good conscience seems to me a major desideratum of the methodology of the natural sciences.

ADDENDUM

A Note on Tarski's Definition of Truth

IN his famous paper on the Concept of Truth,[1] Tarski describes a method of defining the idea of truth, or more precisely, the idea of '*x* is a true statement (of the language *L*)'. The method

[1] Cp. A. Tarski, 'Der Wahrheitsbegriff in den formalisierten Sprachen' (*Studia Philosophica*, vol. i, 1935, pp. 261 ff.). ['The Concept of Truth in Formalized Languages', in A. Tarski, *Logic, Semantics, Metamathematics*, 1956, paper VIII, pp. 152 to 278.] I understand that Tarski prefers to translate '*Aussage*' and '*Aussagefunktion*' by 'sentence' and 'sentence-function' (while I am using here 'statement' and 'statement-function') and that these terms are used in Professor J. H. Woodger's translation of Tarski's logical papers, soon to be published by the Clarendon Press, Oxford. [The book was published in 1956. There were a few other differences between my translation and Woodger's.]

First published in *Mind*, **64**, N.S., 1955. Apart from the remarks in square brackets and some new *italics* and a few slight stylistic corrections, I have made only the following changes: I now replace, following Woodger's translation of 1956, 'fulfil' and 'fulfilment', etc., by 'satisfy' and 'satisfaction'; as a consequence I have, in Definition 22b, changed my former 'satisfies' twice into 'complies with'. I changed the last words of the text of the Note from 'an infinite sequence' to 'infinite sequences' and I inserted page number and other references to Woodger's translation. [All additions are in square brackets.] Otherwise I have left the Addendum as it was first published.

is first applied to the language of the class calculus, but it is a method which can be applied very generally to many different (formalized) languages, including languages which would allow the formalization of some empirical theories. What characterizes his method is that the definition of 'true statement' is based upon a definition of the *relation of satisfaction*, or more precisely, of the phrase 'the infinite sequence *f* satisfies the statement-function *X*'.[2] *This relation of satisfaction is of interest on its own account*, quite apart from the fact that it is crucial for the definition of truth (and that the step from the definition of satisfaction to that of truth presents hardly any problem). The present note is concerned with the problem of employing, in the definition of satisfaction, *finite instead of infinite sequences*. This, I believe, is a desideratum from the point of view of an application of the theory to the empirical sciences, and also from a didactic point of view.

Tarski himself briefly discusses two methods[3] which employ finite sequences of varying length instead of infinite sequences. But he points out that these alternative methods have certain disadvantages. The first of them, he indicates, leads to 'considerable [or 'rather serious'] complications' (*ziemlich bedeutenden Komplikationen*) in the definition of satisfaction (Definition 22), while the second has the disadvantage of 'a certain artificiality' (*eine gewisse Künstlichkeit*), in so far as it leads to a definition of truth (Definition 23 [p. 195]) with the help of the concept of an 'empty sequence' or a 'sequence of zero length'.[4] What I wish to point out in this note is that a comparatively slight variation of Tarski's procedure allows us to operate with finite sequences

---

[2] Cp. op. cit., pp. 311 [193], 313 [195]. Note that the class of statement-functions [or sentential functions] includes that of statements, i.e. of *closed* statement-functions.

[3] The first alternative method is sketched in Tarski's note 40 on pp. 309 f. [p. 191, note 1]. (It is not explicitly stated that this method may be used for the purpose of avoiding infinite sequences, but it is clear that it can be so used.) The second method is described in note 43, pp. 313 f. [p. 195, note 1]. The method suggested in this note of Tarski's, which is technically different from the one used by Tarski in his text, is used by Carnap in his *Introduction to Semantics* (1942), pp. 47 f. [more precisely, pp. 45–8]. Although Carnap refers to Tarski, he overlooks Tarski's anticipation of this particular method. (There is even a third method, indicated by Tarski in note 87 on p. 368 [p. 245, note 2]. This device is very simple, but undoubtedly highly artificial, in Tarski's sense of artificiality; moreover, this method only relates to the definition of truth itself, not to that of fulfilment [satisfaction], which has an interest of its own.)

[4] This artificial concept is also used by Carnap.

without getting involved in the complications or artificialities (e.g. empty sequences) Tarski had in mind. The method allows us to preserve the very natural procedure of the condition (δ) of Tarski's Definition 22 [p. 193] (and thus to avoid the detour of introducing relations—or attributes—of a degree equal to the number of the *free* variables of the statement-function under consideration). My variant of Tarski's method is a slight one; but in view of the fact that Tarski refers to other variants which have considerable disadvantages, but not to this one, it may be worth while to describe what is perhaps a small improvement.[5]

In order to do so, it is useful to mention, informally, first the idea of a *place number n* (or the *n*th place) of a finite sequence of things, and secondly, the idea of the *length* of a finite sequence *f*, i.e. the number of places of *f* (in symbols, $Np(f)$) which is identical with its greatest place number, and of the comparison of different finite sequences with respect to their length. We mention, thirdly, that a thing may occupy a certain place—the *n*th, say—in the sequence, and may, therefore, be described as [the *n*th individual or] the *n*th thing or the *n*th member of the sequence in question. It should be noted that one and the same thing may occur in different places of a sequence, and also in different sequences.[6]

---

[5] The main difference between my method and those suggested by Tarski (mentioned in note 3 above) consists in this. Tarski suggests that we correlate with a given function (either infinite sequences or) finite sequences of a definite length (dependent on the function) while I use finite sequences which are 'of sufficient length' (Definition 22a), i.e. not too short for the function in question. Accordingly, my finite sequences can be of *any length* (beyond a certain minimum which depends on the function). But the admission of finite sequences of any length (provided it is sufficient) does not involve any vagueness, since we easily obtain a *theorem* (cp. Tarski's Lemma A, p. 317 [198]) according to which, if *f* fulfils *x*, then every extension *g* of *f* also fulfils *x* (where *g* is an extension of *f* if and only if, for every f_i there exists a g_i such that $g_i = f_i$). Thus the theorem informs us that we only need to consider the *shortest* finite sequences of those which are adequate to the function under consideration (to be sure, to the total compound function under consideration, as opposed to its components).

[6] The 'things' [as I call them here; I might have called them, like Tarski, 'individuals' but for the fact that I wanted to avoid mentioning the perhaps slightly confusing complication that Tarski's 'individuals' happen to be the individual *classes* of the calculus of classes] considered by Tarski in this section of his work are *classes*; in view of the development of Tarski's §§ 4 and 5, I shall speak here of 'sequences of things' instead of sequences of classes, assuming that a relation $f_i \subset f_k$ is defined for all things f_i and f_k.

Like Tarski, I use 'f_1', 'f_2', ... 'f_i', 'f_k', ... 'f_n', as names of the things which occupy the first, second, ith, kth ... nth place of the sequence f. I use the same notation as Tarski does, except that I use [for typographical reasons] '$P_k y$' as the name of the universalization [or universal quantification] of the expression y with respect to the variable v_k.[7] It is assumed that to Tarski's definition (11)[8] is added a definition of 'v_k occurs in the statement-function x'—an assumption which in no way goes beyond Tarski's methods, and which in fact is implicit in Tarski's own treatment.

We can now proceed to replace Tarski's Definition 22 [p. 193]. We shall replace it by two definitions, the preliminary Definition 22a, and the Definition 22b which corresponds to Tarski's own definition.

Definition 22a

A finite sequence of things f is *adequate to* the statement-function x (or of *sufficient length with respect to x*) if and only if

for every natural number n,

if v_n occurs in x, then the number of places of f is at least equal to n (i.e. $Np(f) \geqslant n$).

Definition 22b[9]

The sequence f *satisfies* the statement-function x if and only if

f is a finite sequence of things, and x is a statement-function, and

    (1) f is adequate to x,
    (2) x complies with one of the following four conditions:

---

[7] Cp. Tarski's Definition 6 on p. 292 [176].

[8] Op. cit., p. 294 [178]. Tarski defines explicitly only the phrase 'The variable v_k occurs *freely* in the statement function x' [or 'v_k is a *free* variable of the sentential function x'].

[9] This is exactly like Tarski's Definition 22 [p. 193], except that (1) is added to Tarski's condition (in order to replace his infinite sequences by finite ones), and that our (δ) (*b*) contains a minor adjustment, in so far as it refers to the length of f (and of g). [There is a drawback in translating '*erfüllen*' by 'to satisfy'; it is this: in the definition of 'f satisfies x', use is made of the intuitive idea 'x complies with (i.e. satisfies) such-and-such *conditions*'. But the two 'satisfies' are quite distinct technically, even though intuitively they very nearly coincide. In the German text, no terminological distinction is made on p. 311, but on p. 312, footnote, corresponding to footnote 1 on p. 193 of the English edition, a distinction occurs between '*erfüllt*' and '*befriedigt*'. There is of course no circularity in Definition 22.]

(α) There exist natural numbers i and k such that $x = \iota_{i,k}$ and $f_i \subset f_k$.

(β) There exists a statement-function y such that $x = \bar{y}$, and f does not satisfy y.

(γ) There exist two statement-functions y and z such that $x = y+z$ and f satisfies either y or z or both.

(δ) There exists a natural number k and a statement-function y such that

(a) $x = P_k y$,

(b) every finite sequence g whose length is equal to f satisfies y, provided g complies with the following condition: for every natural number n, if n is a place number of f and $n \neq k$, then $g_n = f_n$.

Tarski's Definition 23 [p. 193] can now be replaced by one of the following two equivalent[10] definitions.

Definition 23+

x is a *true statement* (i.e. $x \in Wr$) if and only if (a) x is a statement ($x \in As$) and (b) every finite sequence of things which is adequate to x satisfies x.

Definition 23++

x is a *true statement* (i.e. $x \in Wr$) if and only if (a) x is a statement ($x \in As$) and (b) there exists at least one finite sequence of things which satisfies x.

It may be noted that the formulation of 23++ does not need to refer to the adequacy of the sequence. It may be further noted that in 23+ (which corresponds exactly to Tarski's definition), but not in 23++, the condition (a) may be replaced by 'x is a statement-function', thus achieving a certain generalization by comprising statement-functions with free variables, for example, the function $\iota_{i,i}$; i.e. the universally valid (*allgemeingültige* ['correct in every individual domain']) statement-functions.[11]

In an analogous way, 23++, if extended to functions, leads to the notion of a satisfiable (*erfüllbare*) statement-function.

---

[10] The equivalence emerges from Tarski's consideration; cp. op. cit., p. 313, lines 13 to 16 [p. 194, lines 12 to 15].

[11] Cp. op. cit., p. 320 [201], Definition 27 and *seq.*

I will conclude by saying that, in its application to an empirical theory (at least partially formalized), and especially to non-quantified statement-functions of such a theory, the definition of *fulfilment* [*or satisfaction*], i.e. Definition 22b, seems to be perfectly 'natural' from an intuitive point of view, mainly owing to the avoidance of infinite sequences.[12]

[12] We may use it, for example, to define an instantiation of a law (not written as a universalization, i.e. written without universal prefix) as a finite sequence of things which satisfies it; or, in my opinion more important, to define a *refuting instance* of any statement-function (open or closed) as a finite [and adequate] sequence of things which do *not* satisfy it.

The Bucket and the Searchlight: Two Theories of Knowledge

THE purpose of this paper is to criticize a widely held view about the aims and methods of the natural sciences, and to put forward an alternative view.

I

I SHALL start with a brief exposition of the view I propose to examine, which I will call *'the bucket theory of science'* (or *'the bucket theory of the mind'*). The starting point of this theory is the persuasive doctrine that before we can know or say anything about the world, we must first have had perceptions—sense experiences. It is supposed to follow from this doctrine that our knowledge, our experience, consists either of accumulated perceptions (naïve empiricism) or else of assimilated, sorted, and classified perceptions (a view held by Bacon and, in a more radical form, by Kant).

The Greek atomists had a somewhat primitive notion of this process. They assumed that atoms break loose from the objects we perceive, and penetrate our sense organs, where they become perceptions; and out of these, in the course of time, our knowledge of the external world fits itself together [like a self-assembling jigsaw puzzle]. According to this view, then, our mind resembles a container—a kind of bucket—in which perceptions and knowledge accumulate. (Bacon speaks of perceptions as 'grapes, ripe and in

---

A lecture delivered (in German) at the European Forum of the Austrian College, Alpbach, Tyrol, in August 1948, and first published, in German, under the title *'Naturgesetze und theoretische Systeme'* in *Gesetz und Wirklichkeit*, edited by Simon Moser, 1949. Not previously published in English. [Textual additions made in this translation are put into square brackets, or indicated in the footnotes.]

The paper anticipates many of the ideas developed more fully in this volume and in *Conjectures and Refutations*, and in addition it contains some ideas which I have not published elsewhere. Most of the ideas, and the expressions: 'the bucket theory of the mind' and 'the searchlight theory of science [and of the mind]' go back to my New Zealand days and are first mentioned in my *Open Society*. I read a paper under the title 'The Bucket Theory of the Mind' in the Staff Club of the London School of Economics in 1946. This Appendix is especially closely related to Chapters 2 and 5 of the present volume.

season' which have to be gathered, patiently and industriously, and from which, if pressed, the pure wine of knowledge will flow.)

Strict empiricists advise us to interfere as little as possible with this process of accumulating knowledge. True knowledge is pure knowledge, uncontaminated by those prejudices which we are only too prone to add to, and mix with, our perceptions; these alone constitute experience pure and simple. The result of these additions, of our disturbing and interfering with the process of accumulating knowledge, is error. Kant opposes this theory: he denies that perceptions are ever pure, and asserts that our experience is the result of a process of assimilation and transformation—the combined product of sense perceptions and of certain ingredients added by our minds. The perceptions are the raw material, as it were, which flows from outside into the bucket, where it undergoes some (automatic) processing—something akin to digestion, or perhaps to systematic classification—in order to be turned in the end into something not so very different from Bacon's 'pure wine of experience'; let us say, perhaps, into fermented wine.

I do not think that either of these views suggests anything like an adequate picture of what I believe to be the actual process of acquiring experience, or the actual method used in research or discovery. Admittedly, Kant's view might be so interpreted that it comes much nearer to my own view than does pure empiricism. I grant, of course, that science is impossible without experience (but the notion of 'experience' has to be carefully considered). Though I grant this, I nevertheless hold that perceptions do not constitute anything like the raw material, as they do according to the 'bucket theory', out of which we construct either 'experience' or 'science'.

II

In science it is *observation* rather than perception which plays the decisive part. But observation is a process in which we play an intensely *active* part. An observation is a perception, but one which is planned and prepared. We do not 'have' an observation [as we may 'have' a sense experience] but we 'make' an observation. [A navigator even 'works' an observation.] An observation is always preceded by a particular interest, a question, or a problem—in short, by something theoretical.[1] After all, we can put every question

---

[1] By the word 'theoretical' I do not mean here the opposite of 'practical' (since our interest might very well be a practical one); it should rather be understood in the sense of 'speculative' [as with a speculative interest in a pre-existing problem] in contrast to 'perceptive'; or 'rational' as opposed to 'sensual'.

in the form of a hypothesis or conjecture to which we add: 'Is this so? Yes or no?' Thus we can assert that every observation is preceded by a problem, a hypothesis (or whatever we may call it); at any rate by something that interests us, by something theoretical or speculative. This is why observations are always selective, and why they presuppose something like a principle of selection.

Before elaborating these points any further I shall try to introduce, as a digression, a few remarks of a biological nature. Although these are not meant to constitute a basis or even an argument for the main thesis which I intend to propose later, they may perhaps be helpful in getting over, or in circumventing, certain objections to it, and in this way facilitate later its understanding.

III

WE know that all living things, even the most primitive, react to certain stimuli. These reactions are specific; that is to say, for each organism (and for each type of organism) the number of possible reactions is limited. We can say that every organism possesses a certain innate set of possible reactions, or a certain disposition to react in this or that way. This set of dispositions may change with the advancing age of the organism (partly perhaps under the influence of sense impressions or perceptions) or it may remain constant; however this may be, at any instant in the life of the organism it is, we may assume, invested with such a set of possibilities and dispositions to react, and this set constitutes what may be called its [momentary] inner state.

Upon this inner state of the organism will depend how it will react to its external environment. This is why physically identical stimuli may at different times produce different reactions, whilst physically different stimuli may result in identical reactions.[2]

Now we shall say that an organism '*learns from experience*' only if its dispositions to react change in the course of time, and if we have reason to assume that these changes do not depend merely on innate [developmental] changes in the state of the organism but also on the changing state of its external environment. (This is a necessary condition, though not a sufficient one, for saying that the organism learns from experience.) In other words, we shall regard the process by which the organism learns as a certain kind of change, or modification, in its dispositions to react, and not, as would the

---

[2] Compare F. A. von Hayek, 'Scientism and the Study of Society', *Economica*, N.S. 9, 10, and 11 (1942, 1943, and 1944); [now also in his *The Counter-Revolution of Science*, 1952].

bucket theory, as an (ordered or classified or associated) accumulation of memory traces, left over by perceptions that are past.

These modifications in the organism's disposition to react, which go to make up the processes of learning, are closely connected with the important notion of an '*expectation*', and also with that of a '*disappointed expectation*'. We may characterize an expectation as a *disposition to react, or as a preparation for a reaction*, which is adapted to [or which anticipates] a state of the environment yet to come about. This characterization seems to be more adequate than one that describes an expectation in terms of states of consciousness; for we become conscious of many of our expectations only when they are disappointed, owing to their being unfulfilled. An example would be the encountering of an unexpected step in one's path: it is the unexpectedness of the step which may make us conscious of the fact that we expected to encounter an even surface. Such disappointments force us to *correct* our system of expectations. The process of learning consists largely in such corrections; that is, in the elimination of certain [disappointed] expectations.

IV

LET us now return to the problem of observation. An observation always presupposes the existence of some system of expectations. These expectations can be formulated in the form of queries; and the observation will be used to obtain either a confirming or a correcting answer to expectations thus formulated.

My thesis that the question, or the hypothesis, must precede the observation may at first have seemed paradoxical; but we can see now that it is not at all paradoxical to assume that expectations— that is, dispositions to react—must precede every observation and, indeed, every perception: for certain dispositions or propensities to react are innate in all organisms whereas perceptions and observations clearly are not innate. And although perceptions and, even more, observations, play an important part in the process of *modifying* our dispositions or propensities to react, some such dispositions or propensities must, of course, be present first, or they could not be modified.

These biological reflections are by no means to be understood as implying my acceptance of a behaviourist position. I do not deny that perceptions, observations, and other states of consciousness occur, but I assign to them a role very different from the one they are supposed to play according to the bucket theory. Nor are these biological reflections to be regarded as forming in any sense an assumption on which my arguments will be based. But I hope that they will help towards a better understanding of these arguments. The same may be said of the following reflections, which are closely connected with these biological ones.

At every instant of our pre-scientific or scientific development we are living in the centre of what I usually call a *'horizon of expectations'*. By this I mean the sum total of our expectations, whether these are subconscious or conscious, or perhaps even explicitly stated in some language. Animals and babies have also their various and different horizons of expectations though no doubt on a lower level of consciousness than, say, a scientist whose horizon of expectations consists to a considerable extent of linguistically formulated theories or hypotheses.

The various horizons of expectations differ, of course, not only in their being more or less conscious, but also in their content. Yet in all these cases the horizon of expectations plays the part of a frame of reference: only their setting in this frame confers meaning or significance on our experiences, actions, and observations.

Observations, more especially, have a very peculiar function within this frame. They can, under certain circumstances, destroy even the frame itself, if they clash with certain of the expectations. In such a case they can have an effect upon our horizon of expectations like a bombshell. This bombshell may force us to reconstruct, or rebuild, our whole horizon of expectations; that is to say, we may have to correct our expectations and fit them together again into something like a consistent whole. We can say that in this way our horizon of expectations is raised to and reconstructed on a higher level, and that we reach in this way a new stage in the evolution of our experience; a stage in which those expectations which have not been hit by the bomb are somehow incorporated into the horizon, while those parts of the horizon which have suffered damage are repaired and rebuilt. This has to be done in such a manner that the damaging observations are no longer felt as disruptive, but are integrated with the rest of our expectations. If we succeed in this rebuilding, then we shall have created what is usually known as an *explanation* of those observed events [which created the disruption, the problem].

As to the question of the temporal relation between observation on the one hand and the horizon of expectations or theories on the other, we may well admit that a new explanation, or a new hypothesis, is generally preceded in time by *those* observations which destroyed the previous horizon of expectations and thus were the stimulus to our attempting a new explanation. Yet this must not be understood as saying that observations generally precede expectations or hypotheses. On the contrary, each observation is preceded by expectations or hypotheses; by those expectations, more especially, which make up the horizon of expectations that lends those observations their significance; only in this way do they attain the status of real observations.

The question, 'What comes first, the hypothesis (H) or the observation (O)?' reminds one, of course, of that other famous question: 'What came first, the hen (H) or the egg (O)?' Both questions are soluble. The bucket theory asserts that [just as a primitive form of an egg (O), a unicellular organism, precedes the hen (H)] observation (O) always precedes every hypothesis (H); for the bucket theory regards the latter as arising from observations by generalization, or association, or classification. By contrast, we can now say that the hypothesis (or expectation, or theory, or whatever we may call it) precedes the observation, even though an observation that refutes a certain hypothesis may stimulate a new (and therefore a temporally later) hypothesis.

All this applies, more especially, to the formation of scientific hypotheses. For we learn only from our hypotheses what kind of observations we ought to make: whereto we ought to direct our attention; wherein to take an interest. Thus it is the hypothesis which becomes our guide, and which leads us to new observational results.

This is the view which I have called the *'searchlight theory'* (in contradistinction to the *'bucket theory'*). [According to the searchlight theory, observations are secondary to hypotheses.] Observations play, however, an important role as *tests* which a hypothesis must undergo in the course of our [critical] examination of it. If the hypothesis does not pass the examination, if it is falsified by our observations, then we have to look around for a new hypothesis. In this case the new hypothesis will come after those observations which led to the falsification or rejection of the old hypothesis. Yet what made the observations interesting and relevant and what altogether gave rise to our undertaking them in the first instance, was the earlier, the old [and now rejected] hypothesis.

In this way science appears clearly as a straightforward continuation of the pre-scientific repair work on our horizons of expectations. Science never starts from scratch; it can never be described as free from assumptions; for at every instant it presupposes a horizon of expectations—yesterday's horizon of expectations, as it were. Today's science is built upon yesterday's science [and so it is the result of yesterday's searchlight]; and yesterday's science, in turn, is based on the science of the day before. And the oldest scientific theories are built on pre-scientific myths, and these, in their turn, on still older expectations. Ontogenetically (that is, with respect to the development of the individual organism) we thus regress to the state of the expectations of a newborn child; phylogenetically (with respect to the evolution of the race, the phylum) we get to the state of expectations of unicellular organisms. (There is no danger here of a vicious infinite regress—if for no other reason than that every organism is born with *some* horizon of expectations.) There is, as it were, only one step from the amoeba to Einstein.

Now if this is the way science evolves, what can be said to be the characteristic step which marks the transition from pre-science to science?

V

THE first beginnings of the evolution of something like a scientific method may be found, approximately at the turn of the sixth and fifth centuries B.C., in ancient Greece. What happened there? What is new in this evolution? How do the new ideas compare with the traditional myths, which came from the East and which, I think, provided many of the decisive suggestions for the new ideas?

Among the Babylonians and the Greeks and also among the Maoris in New Zealand—indeed, it would seem, among all peoples who invent cosmological myths—tales are told which deal with the beginning of things, and which try to understand or explain the structure of the Universe in terms of the story of its origin. These stories become traditional and are preserved in special schools. The tradition is often in the keeping of some separate or chosen class, the priests or medicine men, who guard it jealously. The stories change only little by little—mainly through inaccuracies in handing them on, through misunderstandings, and sometimes through the accretion of new myths, invented by prophets or poets.

Now what is new in Greek philosophy, what is newly added to all this, seems to me to consist not so much in the replacement of the myths by something more 'scientific', as in a *new attitude towards the myths*. That their character then begins to change seems to me to be merely a consequence of this new attitude.

The new attitude I have in mind is *the critical attitude. In the place of a dogmatic handing on of the doctrine* [in which the whole interest lies in the preservation of the authentic tradition] *we find a critical discussion of the doctrine.* Some people begin to ask questions about it; they doubt the trustworthiness of the doctrine: its *truth*.

Doubt and criticism certainly existed before this stage. What is new, however, is that doubt and criticism now become, in their turn, part of the tradition of the school. A tradition of a higher order replaces the traditional preservation of the dogma: in the place of traditional theory—in place of the myth—we find the tradition of criticizing theories (which at first themselves are hardly more than myths). It is only in the course of this critical discussion that observation is called in as a witness.

It can hardly be a mere accident that Anaximander, the disciple of Thales, developed a theory which explicitly and consciously diverges from that of his master, and that Anaximenes, the disciple of Anaximander, diverges just as consciously from his master's doctrine. The only explanation seems to be that the founder of the school himself challenged his disciples to criticize his theory, and that they turned this new critical attitude of their master's into a new tradition.

It is interesting that this happened only once, so far as I know. The earlier Pythagorean school was almost certainly a school of the old kind: its tradition does not embrace the critical attitude but is confined to the task of preserving the doctrine of the master. It was undoubtedly only the influence of the critical school of the Ionians which later loosened the rigidity of the Pythagorean school tradition and so paved the way leading to the philosophical and scientific method of criticism.

The critical attitude of ancient Greek philosophy can hardly be better exemplified than by the famous lines of Xenophanes:

> Yet if cattle or horses or lions had hands and could draw
> And could sculpture like men, then the horses would draw
>   their gods
> Like horses; and cattle like cattle; and each would then shape
> Bodies of gods in the likeness, each kind, of its own.

This is not only a critical challenge—it is a statement made in the full consciousness and mastery of a critical methodology.

Thus it seems to me that it is the tradition of criticism which constitutes what is new in science, and what is characteristic of science. On the other hand it seems to me that the task which science sets itself [that is, the explanation of the world] and the main ideas which it uses, are taken over without any break from prescientific mythmaking.

VI

WHAT is the task of science? With this question I have ended my preliminary examination of biological and historical trends, and I now come to the logical analysis of science itself.

The task of science is partly theoretical—*explanation*—and partly practical—*prediction and technical application*. I shall try to show that these two aims are, in a way, two different aspects of one and the same activity.

I will first examine the idea of an explanation.

One often hears it said that an explanation is the reduction of the unknown to the known; but we are rarely told how this is to be done. At any rate, this notion of explanation is not one that was ever used in the actual practice of explanation in science. If we look at the history of science in order to see what kinds of explanation were used and accepted as satisfactory at one time or another, then we find a very different notion of explanation in practical use.

I gave a short sketch of this history (I do not mean the history of the concept of explanation but the history of the practice of explanation) to the philosophical seminar this morning.[3] Unfortunately, time prevents me from dealing with this question here again at length. Yet I should mention here one general result. In the course of the historical development of science many different methods and kinds of explanation have been regarded as acceptable; but they all have one aspect in common: the various methods of explanation all consist of a *logical deduction*; a deduction whose conclusion is the *explicandum*—a statement of the thing to be explained—and whose premises consist of the *explicans* [a statement of the explaining laws and conditions]. The main changes that have occurred in the course of the history of science consist in the silent abandonment of certain implicit demands regarding the character of the *explicans* (that it can be intuitively grasped, that it is to be self-evident, etc.); demands which turn out not to be reconcilable with certain other demands whose crucial significance becomes more and more obvious as time goes on; in particular the demand for the independent testability of the *explicans* [which forms the premises and thus the very heart of the explanation].

[3] (Added in the translation.) Part of the fuller story will be found (though somewhat condensed and with reduced emphasis upon what has been in actual practice accepted as an explanation) in my Venice lecture: 'Philosophy and Physics: Theories of the Structure of Matter', now contained in my book *Philosophy and Physics* (1972). Other parts are to be found in the first half of my *Conjectures and Refutations*, especially chapters 6, 3, and 4. (This last chapter will be found to overlap with, and expand, some parts of the present lecture.)

Thus an explanation is always the deduction of the *explicandum* from certain premisses, to be called the *explicans*.

Here is a somewhat gruesome example, just for the purpose of illustration.[4]

A dead rat has been discovered and we wish to know what has happened to it. The *explicandum* may be stated thus: 'This rat here has died recently.' This *explicandum* is definitely known to us—the fact lies before us in stark reality. If we want to explain it, we must try out some conjectural or hypothetical explanations (as the authors of detective stories do); that is to say, explanations which introduce something *unknown*, or at any rate much less known, to us. Such a hypothesis may be, for instance, that the rat died of a large dose of rat poison. This is useful as a hypothesis in so far as, firstly, it helps us to formulate an *explicans* from which the *explicandum* can be deduced; secondly, it suggests to us a number of independent tests— tests of the *explicans* which are quite independent of whether the *explicandum* is true or not.

Now the *explicans*—which is our hypothesis—does not only consist of the sentence 'This rat has eaten some bait containing a large dose of rat poison', for from this statement alone one cannot validly deduce the *explicandum*. Rather, we shall have to use, as *explicans*, two different kinds of premisses—*universal laws* and *initial conditions*. In our case the universal law might be put like this: 'If a rat eats at least eight grains of rat poison it will die within five minutes.' The (singular) initial condition (which is a singular statement) might be: 'This rat ate at least eighteen grains of rat poison, more than five minutes ago.' From these two premisses together we may now indeed deduce that this rat recently has died [that is, our *explicandum*].

Now all this may seem somewhat obvious. But consider one of my theses—the thesis, namely, that what I have called the *'initial conditions'* [the conditions pertaining to the individual case] never suffice by themselves as an explanation, and that we always need a general law as well. Now this thesis is by no means obvious; on the contrary, its truth is often not admitted. I even suspect that most of you would be inclined to accept a remark like 'this rat has eaten rat poison' as quite sufficient to explain its death, even if no explicit statement of the universal law regarding the effects of rat poison is added. But suppose for a moment that we were living in a world in which anybody (and also any rat) who eats a lot of that chemical called 'rat poison' will feel especially well and happy for a week to come and more lively than ever before. If a universal law like this were valid, could the statement 'This rat has eaten rat

4 I have made the example slightly less gruesome in the translation.

poison' still be acceptable as an explanation of death? Obviously not.

Thus we have reached the important result, often overlooked, that any explanation that utilizes the singular initial conditions alone would be incomplete, and that *at least one universal law* is needed besides, even though this law is, in some cases, so well known that it is omitted as if it were redundant.

To sum up this point. We have found that an explanation is a deduction of the following kind:

U	(Universal Law)	} Premisses
I	(Specific Initial Conditions)	} (constituting the *Explicans*)
$\overline{E}$	(*Explicandum*)	Conclusion

VII

BUT are all explanations of this structure *satisfactory*? Is, for instance, our example (which explains the death of the rat by reference to rat poison) a satisfactory explanation? We do not know: the tests may show that whatever the rat may have died of, it was not rat poison.

If some friend should be sceptical of our explanation and ask, 'How do you know that this rat ate poison?', it will obviously not be sufficient to answer, 'How can you doubt it, seeing that it is dead?'. Indeed, any reason which we may state in support of any hypothesis must be other than, and independent of, the *explicandum*. If we can only adduce the *explicandum* itself as evidence, we feel that our explanation is circular, and therefore quite *unsatisfactory*. If, on the other hand, we are able to reply, 'Analyse the contents of its stomach, and you will find a lot of poison', and if this prediction (which is new—that is, not entailed by the *explicandum* alone) proves true, we shall at least consider our explanation a fairly good hypothesis.

But I have to add something. For our sceptical friend may also question the truth of the universal law. He may say, for instance, 'Granted, this rat has eaten a certain chemical; but why should it have died of it?'. Again, we must not answer: 'But don't you see it is dead? That just shows you how dangerous it is to eat this chemical.' For this again would make our explanation circular and unsatisfactory. In order to make it satisfactory we should have to submit the universal law to test cases which are independent of our *explicandum*.

With this, my analysis of the formal schema of explanation may be regarded as concluded, but I shall add some further remarks and analyses to the general schema I have outlined.

First, an observation about the ideas of cause and effect. The state of affairs described by the singular *initial conditions* can be called the '*cause*', and the one described by the *explicandum* the '*effect*'. I feel, however, that these terms, encumbered as they are with associations from their history, are better avoided. If we still want to use them, we should always remember that they acquire a meaning only relative to a theory or a universal law. It is the theory or the law which constitutes the *logical link* between cause and effect, and the statement '*A* is the cause of *B*' should be analysed thus: 'There is a theory *T* which can be, and has been, independently tested, and from which, in conjunction with an independently tested description *A*, of a specific situation, we can logically deduce a description, *B*, of another specific situation.' (That the existence of such a *logical* link between 'cause' and 'effect' is presupposed in the very use of these terms has been overlooked by many philosophers, including Hume.)[5]

VIII

THE task of science is not confined to searching for purely theoretical explanations; it also has its practical sides: prediction-making as well as technical applications. Both of these can be analysed by means of the same logical schema which we introduced to analyse explanation.

(1) *The derivation of predictions.* Whereas in the search for an explanation the *explicandum* is given—or known—and a suitable *explicans* has to be found, the derivation of predictions proceeds in the opposite direction. Here the theory is given, or assumed to be known (perhaps from textbooks), and so are the specific initial conditions (they are known, or assumed to be known, by observation). What remain to be found are the logical consequences: certain logical conclusions which are not yet known to us from observation. These are the *predictions*. In this case, the prediction *P* takes the place of the *explicandum E* in our logical schema.

(2) *Technical application.* Consider the task of building a bridge which has to comply with certain practical requirements, laid down in a list of specifications. What we are given are the specifications, *S*, which describe a certain required state of affairs—the bridge to be built. (*S* are the customer's specifications, which are given prior to,

---

[5] (Added in translation.) I made these comments on the notions 'cause' and 'effect' first in section 12 of my *Logik der Forschung* (*The Logic of Scientific Discovery*). See also my *Poverty of Historicism*, pp. 122 f.; my *Open Society and Its Enemies*, especially note 9 to chapter 25; and 'What can Logic do for Philosophy?', *Aristotelian Society, Supplementary Volume*, **22**, 1948, pp. 145 ff.

and are distinct from, the architect's specifications.) We are given, further, the relevant physical theories (including certain rules of thumb). What are to be found are certain initial conditions which may be realized technically and which are of such a nature that the specifications may be deduced from them, together with the theory. So in this case, *S* takes the place of *E* in our logical schema.[6]

This makes it clear how, from a logical point of view, both the derivation of predictions and the technical application of scientific theories may be regarded as mere inversions of the basic schema of scientific explanation.

The use of our schema, however, is still not exhausted: it may also serve to analyse the *procedure of testing our explicans*. The testing procedure consists in the derivation from the *explicans* of a prediction, *P*, and in comparing it with an actual, observable, situation. If a prediction does not agree with the observed situation, then the *explicans* is shown to be false; it is falsified. In this case we still do not know whether it is the universal *theory* which is false, or whether the *initial conditions* describe a situation which does not correspond with the real situation—so that the initial conditions are false. [Of course, it may well be that the theory *and* the initial conditions are false.]

The falsification of the prediction shows that the *explicans* is false, yet the reverse of this does not hold: it is incorrect and grossly misleading to think that we can interpret the 'verification' of the prediction as 'verifying' the *explicans* or even a part of it. For a true prediction may easily have been validly deduced from an *explicans* that is false. It is even quite misleading to regard *every* 'verification' of a prediction as something like a practical *corroboration* of the *explicans*: it would be more correct to say that only such 'verifications' of predictions which are 'unexpected' [without the theory under examination] may be regarded as corroborations of the *explicans*, and so of the theory. This means that a prediction can be used to corroborate a theory only if its comparison with observations might be regarded as a serious attempt at testing the *explicans*—a serious

---

[6] (Added in the translation.) This analysis must not be interpreted as implying that the technologist or the engineer is concerned only with '*applying*' theories which are supplied by the pure scientist. On the contrary, the technologist and the engineer are constantly faced with *problems to be solved*. These problems are of various degrees of abstraction, but are usually, at least in part, of a theoretical character; and in trying to solve them, the technologist or engineer uses, like everybody else, the method of conjecture, or trial, and testing, or refutation, or error elimination. This is well explained on p. 43 of J. T. Davies, *The Scientific Approach*, 1965, a book in which many good applications and illustrations of the searchlight theory of science can be found.

attempt at refuting it. A ['risky'] prediction of this kind may be called 'relevant to a test of the theory'.[7] After all, it is fairly obvious that the passing of an examination can give an idea of the qualities of the student only if the examination which he passes is sufficiently severe, and that an examination can be designed which even the weakest student will pass easily.[8]

In addition to all this, our logical scheme permits us, finally, to analyse the difference between the tasks of a *theoretical* and of a *historical* explanation.

The theoretician is interested in finding, and testing, universal laws. In the course of testing them he uses other laws, of the most diverse kinds (many of them quite unconsciously) as well as diverse specific initial conditions.

The historian on the other hand, is interested in finding descriptions of states of affairs in certain finite, specific spatio-temporal regions— that is to say, what I have called specific initial conditions—and in testing or checking their adequacy or accuracy. In this kind of testing he uses, in addition to other specific initial conditions, universal laws of all kinds—usually rather obvious ones—which belong to his horizon of expectations, though, as a rule, he is not conscious that he uses them. In this he resembles the theoretician. [Their difference, however, is very marked: it lies in the difference between their various interests, or problems: in the difference of what each regards as problematic.]

In a logical schema [similar to our previous ones] the procedure of the theoretician may be represented in the following manner:

$$\begin{array}{cccc} U_0 & U_0 & U_0 & \cdots \\ U_1 & U_2 & U_3 & \cdots \\ \underline{I_1} & \underline{I_2} & \underline{I_3} & \cdots \\ P_1 & P_2 & P_3 & \cdots \end{array}$$

[7] A relevant prediction corresponds, in a certain sense, to an acid test, or to an '*experimentum crucis*'; for in order that a prediction P may be relevant to a test of a theory T, it must be possible to state a prediction P' which does not contradict the initial condition and the remainder of our horizon of expectations for the time being, other than T (assumptions, theories, etc.), and which, combined with the initial conditions and the remainder of the horizon of expectations, contradicts P. This is what is meant if we say that $P(= E)$ ought to be (without T) 'unexpected'.

[8] Experienced examiners will feel that the word 'easily' is somewhat unrealistic. As the President of a Governmental Board of Examiners in Vienna sometimes said musingly: 'If a student, in answering the examination question "How much is 5 plus 7?" puts down "eighteen", then we give him a pass. But if he answers "green", then I sometimes think afterwards that we really ought to have ploughed him.'

U_0 is here the universal law, the universal hypothesis, which is under examination. It is kept constant throughout the tests, and used, together with various other laws U_1, U_2, ... and various other initial conditions I_1, I_2, ... in order to derive various predictions P_1, P_2, ... which may then be compared with observable actual facts.

The procedure of the historian may be represented by the following schema:

$$
\begin{array}{cccc}
U_1 & U_2 & U_3 & \ldots \\
I_1 & I_2 & I_3 & \ldots \\
\underline{I_0} & \underline{I_0} & \underline{I_0} & \ldots \\
P_1 & P_2 & P_3 & \ldots
\end{array}
$$

Here, I_0 is the historical hypothesis, the historical description, which is to be examined or tested. It is kept constant throughout the tests; and it is combined with various (mostly obvious) laws, U_1, U_2, ... and with corresponding initial conditions, I_1, I_2, ... for deriving various predictions, P_1, P_2, etc.

Both our schemata are, of course, highly idealized and over-simplified.

IX

EARLIER I have tried to show that an explanation will be *satisfactory* only if its universal laws, its theory, can be tested independently of the *explicandum*. But this means that any satisfactory explanatory theory must always assert *more* than what was already contained in the *explicanda* which originally led us to put it forward. In other words, satisfactory theories must, as a matter of principle, transcend the empirical instances which gave rise to them; otherwise they would, as we have seen, merely lead to explanations which are circular.

Here we have a methodological principle which stands in direct contradiction to all positivistic and naïvely empiricist [or inductivist] tendencies. It is a principle which demands that we should dare to put forward bold hypotheses that open up, if possible, new domains of observations, rather than those careful generalizations from 'given' observations which have remained [ever since Bacon] the idols of all naïve empiricists.

Our view that it is the task of science to put forward explanations, or (what leads essentially to the same logical situation)[9] to create the theoretical foundations for predictions and other applications—this view has led us to the methodological demand that our theories should be testable. Yet there are *degrees of testability*. Some theories are *better* testable than others. If we strengthen our methodological demand and aim at *better and better testable* theories, then we arrive at a methodological principle—or a statement of the task of science —whose [unconscious] adoption in the past would rationally explain a great number of events in the history of science: it would explain them as steps towards carrying out the task of science. (At the same time it gives us a statement of the task of science, telling us what should in science be regarded as *progress*; for in contrast to most other human activities—art and music in particular—there really is, in science, such a thing as progress.)

An analysis and comparison of the degrees of testability of different theories shows that the testability of a theory grows with its *degree of universality* as well as with its *degree of definiteness, or precision.*

The situation is fairly simple. Along with the degree of universality of a theory goes an increase in the range of those events about which the theory can make predictions and thereby also the domain of possible falsifications. But a theory which is more easily falsified is at the same time one that is better testable.

We find a similar situation if we consider the degree of definiteness or precision. A precise statement can be more easily refuted than a vague one, and it can therefore be better tested. This consideration also allows us to explain the demand that qualitative statements should if possible be replaced by quantitative ones by our principle of increasing the degree of testability of our theories. (In this way we can also explain the part played by *measurement* in the testing of theories; it is a device which becomes increasingly important in the course of scientific progress, but which should not be used [as it often is] as a characterizing feature of science, or the formation of theories, in general. For we must not overlook the fact that measuring procedures began to be used only at a fairly late stage in the development of some of the sciences, and that they are even now not used

---

[9] (Added in the translation.) I have in later years (from 1950 on) made a sharper distinction between the theoretical or explanatory and the practical or 'instrumental' tasks of science, and I have stressed the logical priority of the theoretical task over the instrumental task. I have tried to stress, more especially, that predictions have not only an instrumental aspect, but also, and mainly, a theoretical one, as they play a decisive role in testing a theory (as shown earlier in the present lecture). See my *Conjectures and Refutations*, especially chapter 3.

in all of them; and we must also not overlook the fact that all
measurement is dependent on theoretical assumptions.)

x

A GOOD example from the history of science that may be used to
illustrate my analysis is the transition from the theories of Kepler
and Galileo to the theory of Newton.

That this transition has nothing whatever to do with induction,
and that Newton's theory cannot be regarded as anything like a
generalization of those two earlier theories may be seen from the
undeniable [and important] fact that Newton's theory *contradicts*
them. *Thus Kepler's laws cannot be deduced from Newton's* [although it
has been often asserted that they can be so deduced, and even that
Newton's can be deduced from Kepler's]: Kepler's laws can be obtained from Newton's only *approximately*, by making the [false] assumption that the masses of the various planets are negligible compared
with the mass of the sun. Similarly, Galileo's law of free falling
bodies cannot be deduced from Newton's theory: on the contrary,
it contradicts it. Only by making the [false] assumption that the
total length of all falls is negligible compared with the length of the
radius of the earth can we obtain Galileo's law *approximately* from
Newton's theory.

This shows, of course, that Newton's theory cannot be a
generalization obtained by induction [or deduction] but that it is a
new hypothesis which can irradiate the way to the falsification of the
old theories: it can irradiate, and point the way to those domains
in which, according to the new theory, the old theories fail to yield
good approximations. (In Kepler's case this is the domain of the
theory of perturbations, and in Galileo's case it is the theory of
variable accelerations, since according to Newton gravitational
accelerations vary inversely with the square of the distance.)

Had Newton's theory achieved no more than the union of Kepler's
laws with Galileo's, it would have been only a *circular explanation
of these laws* and therefore unsatisfactory as an explanation. Yet its
power of illumination and its power of convincing people consisted
just in its power to throw light on the way to independent tests,
leading us to [successful] predictions which were incompatible with
the two older theories. It was the way to new empirical discoveries.

Newton's theory is an example of an attempt to explain certain
older theories of a lower degree of universality, which not only leads
to a kind of unification of these older theories but at the same time
to their falsification (and so to their correction by restricting or

determining the domain within which they are, in good approximation, valid).[10] A case which occurs perhaps more often is this: an old theory is first falsified; and the new theory arises later, as an attempt to explain the partial success of the old theory as well as its failure.

XI

IN connection with my analysis of the notion (or rather the practice) of explanation a further point seems significant. From Descartes [and perhaps even from Copernicus] to Maxwell, most physicists tried to explain all newly discovered relations by means of *mechanical models*; that is to say, they tried to reduce them to laws of push or pressure with which we are acquainted from handling everyday physical things—things belonging to the realm of 'physical bodies of medium size'. Descartes made this into a kind of programme for all the sciences; he even demanded that we should restrict ourselves to models that work merely by push or pressure. This programme suffered its first defeat with the success of Newton's theory; but this defeat (which was a serious affliction to Newton and his generation) was soon forgotten, and gravitational attraction was admitted into the programme on equal terms with push and pressure. Maxwell, too, first tried to develop his theory of the

    [10] (Added in the translation.) The incompatibility of Newton's theory with that of Kepler was stressed by Pierre Duhem, who wrote of Newton's '*principles of universal gravity*' that it is '*very far from being derivable by generalization and induction from the observational laws of Kepler*' in that it '*formally contradicts these laws. If Newton's theory is correct, Kepler's laws are necessarily false.*' (The quotation is from p. 193 of P. P. Wiener's translation of Duhem's *The Aim and Structure of Physical Theory*, 1954. The term '*observational*' applied here to the '*laws of Kepler*' should be taken with a good grain of salt: Kepler's laws were wild conjectures, just as much as Newton's were: they cannot be induced from Tycho's observations—no more than Newton's can from Kepler's laws.) Duhem's analysis is based on the fact that our solar system contains *many* heavy planets for whose mutual attraction allowance has to be made in accordance with Newton's theory of perturbation. We can, however, go beyond Duhem: even if we take Kepler's laws as holding for a set of *two-body systems*, each of them containing a central body of the mass of the sun and *one* planet (of varying mass and distance in the various different systems belonging to the set), even then Kepler's third laws fails if Newton's laws are true, as I have shown briefly in *Conjectures and Refutations*, note 28 to chapter 1 (p. 62) and in some detail in my paper 'The Aim of Science', (1957), now Chapter 5 of the present volume, also in *Theorie und Realität*, edited by Hans Albert, 1964, chapter 1, pp. 73 ff., especially pp. 82 f. In this paper I say a little more about explanations which *correct their (apparently 'known' or 'given') explicanda while explaining them approximately*. This is a view which I have developed fairly fully in my lectures since 1940 (first in a course of lectures given to the Christchurch branch of the Royal Society of New Zealand; cp. the footnote on pp. 134 f. of my *Poverty of Historicism*).

electromagnetic field in the form of a mechanical model of the ether; but in the end he gave up the attempt. With this, the mechanical model lost most of its significance: only the equations which originally were meant to describe the mechanical model of the ether remained. [They were interpreted as describing certain non-mechanical properties of the ether.]

With this transition from a mechanical to an *abstract theory* a stage is reached in the evolution of science at which in practice no more is demanded of explanatory theories than that they can be tested independently; we are ready to work with theories which can be intuitively represented by diagrams such as pictures [or by 'picturable' or 'visualizable' mechanical models], if they are obtainable: this yields 'concrete' theories; or else, if these are not obtainable, we are ready to work with 'abstract' mathematical theories [which, however, may be quite 'understandable' in a sense I have analysed elsewhere].[11]

Our general analysis of the notion of explanation is of course unaffected by the failures of any particular picture or model. It applies to all kinds of abstract theories in the same manner as it applies to mechanical and other models. In fact, models are, from our point of view, nothing but attempts to explain new laws in terms of old laws which have already been tested [together with assumptions about typical initial conditions, or the occurrence of a typical structure—that is to say, the model in a narrower sense]. Models often play important parts in the extension and elaboration of theories; but it is necessary to distinguish a new model in a setting of old theoretical assumptions from a new theory—that is, from a new system of theoretical assumptions.

XII

I HOPE that some of my formulations which at the beginning of this lecture may have seemed to you far-fetched or even paradoxical will now appear less so.

There is no road, royal or otherwise, which leads of necessity from a 'given' set of specific facts to any universal law. What we call 'laws' are hypotheses or conjectures which always form a part of some larger system of theories [in fact, of a whole horizon of expectations] and which, therefore, can never be tested in isolation. The progress of science consists in trials, in the elimination of errors, and in further trials guided by the experience acquired in the course

---

[11] (Added in the translation.) A fuller analysis of 'understanding' is given in Chapter 4 of the present volume.

of previous trials and errors. No particular theory may ever be regarded as absolutely certain: every theory may become problematical, no matter how well corroborated it may seem now. No scientific theory is sacrosanct or beyond criticism. This fact has often been forgotten, particularly during the last century, when we were impressed by the often repeated and truly magnificent corroborations of certain mechanical theories, which eventually came to be regarded as indubitably true. The stormy development of physics since the turn of the century has taught us better; and we have now come to see that it is the task of the scientist to subject his theory to ever new tests, and that no theory must be pronounced final. Testing proceeds by taking the theory to be tested and combining it with all possible kinds of initial conditions as well as with other theories, and then comparing the resulting predictions with reality. If this leads to disappointed expectations, to refutations, then we have to rebuild our theory.

The disappointment of some of the expectations with which we once eagerly approached reality plays a most significant part in this procedure. It may be compared with the experience of a blind man who touches, or runs into, an obstacle, and so becomes aware of its existence. *It is through the falsification of our suppositions that we actually get in touch with 'reality'.* It is the discovery and elimination of our errors which alone constitute that 'positive' experience which we gain from reality.

It is of course always possible to save a falsified theory by means of supplementary hypotheses [like those of epicycles]. But this is not the way of progress in the sciences. The proper reaction to falsification is to search for new theories which seem likely to offer us a better grasp of the facts. Science is not interested in having the last word if this means shutting off our minds from falsifying experiences, but rather in learning from our experience; that is, in learning from our mistakes.

There is a way of formulating scientific theories which points with particular clarity to the possibility of their falsification: we can formulate them in the form of prohibitions [or *negative existential statements*] such as, for example, 'There does not exist a closed physical system, such that energy changes in one part of it without compensating changes occurring in another part' (first law of thermodynamics). Or, 'There does not exist a machine which is 100 per cent efficient'(second law). It can be shown that universal statements and negative existential statements are logically equivalent. This makes it possible to formulate all universal laws in the manner indicated; that is to say, as prohibitions. However, these are prohibitions intended only for the technicians and not for the scientist. They tell the former how to proceed if he does not want to squander his energies. But to the scientist they are a challenge to test and to falsify; they stimulate him to try to discover those states of affairs whose existence they prohibit, or deny.

Thus we have reached a point from which we can see science as a magnificent adventure of the human spirit. It is the invention of ever new theories, and the indefatigable examination of their power to throw light on experience. The principles of scientific progress are very simple. They demand that we give up the ancient idea that we may attain certainty [or even a high degree of 'probability' in the sense of the probability calculus] with the propositions and theories of science (an idea which derives from the association of science with magic and of the scientist with the magician): the aim of the scientist is not to discover absolute certainty, but to discover better and better theories [or to invent more and more powerful searchlights] capable of being put to more and more severe tests [and thereby leading us to, and illuminating for us, ever new experiences]. But this means that these theories must be falsifiable: it is through their falsification that science progresses.

Index of Names

Compiled by J. F. G. Shearmur

Words formed from proper names have, in general, been listed under the name of the person concerned. References of particular importance are in *italic*.

n = footnote; ns = footnotes

Index of Subjects

Compiled by J. F. G. SHEARMUR

Entries of particular importance have been *italicized*; where entries are subdivided, subheadings are arranged in order of the keyword in the subheading; a dash indicates the repetition of the previous subheading, a second dash of the previous sub subheading.

n = footnote; ns = footnotes; t = term explained

theory of knowledge, see *knowledge* (*theory of & biology*); of language, 70, 84, 160n, *235-40*; laws of, 241, 267; logical character of theory of, 69-70, 241-2, 267, 269-70, 272, 296; problems of method in theory of, 265-72; of mind or consciousness, 250-1, 252n, 345; problems of organism in, see *problems* (*evolutionary*); & self-transcendence, 147-50; tree of, 262-3; unpredictability of, 296

exactness, precision, 58, 133n, 202, 218n, 220-2, 270-1, 356-7

excluded middle, 128, 133, 307

executive organs, 273-84, see also *evolution*

existential statements, 12n, 13-14, 360

expectations, 3-4, 9, 21, 23-4, *25-6*, 62-3, 66, 69, 71, 146, 259, 266, 344-6, 360, see also *knowledge* (*subjective*); horizon of, 25, *345*t-*346*, 354&n, 359, see also *background knowledge*; inborn, see *inborn*; unconscious, 24-5, 344

experience, 4, 7, *12*, 36, 61, 64, 104, 148, 342-3, 345, 360; & decoding, *36-7*, *63-4*, 65, 73, 88

experiments: crucial, 14-15, 354n; as tests, 266

explanation, 28, 91, 122-3, *191-204*, 263-5, 267-8, 294, 345, *349-56*, see also *causality, reduction, simulation*; ad hoc or circular, 192-3, 202, 270, 294, 351, 355, 357; & deduction, 349-51; & correction of explicandum, see *explicandum*; historical, see *historical*; history of, 349, 358-9; & initial conditions, 91, 193, *350-5*; of the known by the unknown, 191, 349-50; & models, 269-70, 358-9; & prediction, 195, 349, 352-4&n, 356; schematic representation of, 351, 354-5; of success in search for knowledge, 23, 28, 98, 204; ultimate, 123, 194-5, 360, see also *essentialism*; & universal laws, 193, 196-7, 350-1, 354-5

explanatory power, 53, 143

explicandum, 191-3, 349-52, 355, see also *explanation*; correction of when explained, 16, *197-202, 204-5, 357-8&n*

explicans, 191-4, 349-50, 352-3, see also *explanation*

expression, 107, 120-1, 146-7, 149, 158, 160n, 167, 183, 235, 239; as function of language, see *language* (*functions of, expressive*)

expressionism, 146-7, see also ⎡*world 2* (*world 3 taken by some as expression of*)

eye, 72, 146, 154n, 273-4; evolution of, 244, 246, 270, 273, 279, 283-4

facts, 46, 103, 290, 315, 317, 324-5, 329; correspondence to, see *correspondence*; hard, 104

fallibility, 41, 64, 121, 134, 265, see also *knowledge* (*conjectural*)

falsification, see *refutation*

falsity, 13-14; 158, 237, 312; content, *48-52&n*, 53, 57-9, *81, 331-5*; & nearness to truth, 55-6, 318, see also *verisimilitude*; retransmission of, 31, 304-5, 308; in 'world 3', 156

feedback, 112-13, 117, 119, 122, 125, 147, 161, 239, 241, 244, 248-9, 252

first world, see *world 1*

force or attraction (Newtonian), 174, 198n, 202n, 269, 358

formalism, 133&n, 134, 137

Forms (Plato), 106, 123-5, 153-4, 156, 196&n

foundations (basis) of knowledge, 33-4, 37, 42, 63, see also *starting-point*

freedom, 125-6, **Ch. 6**, 209, 217-18, 223n, 227, 231-3&n, 254-5, see also *control* (*plastic*); Compton's postulate of, 231-2, 234, 240; & determinism, 218-19, 222-3&n, 224, 226, 233n, 254; & indeterminism, 219n, 226-30, 232, 233n, 254-5

future & past, 2, 27, 69, 90, 96, see also *induction* (*problem of, traditional*)

Galileo's theory: & Newton's theory, 16, 191n, *197-8&n*, 199-202, 262&n, 357-8; of the tides, *170-6&ns*, 189n

Geisteswissenschaften (humanities), 158, 162, *183-6*, see also *understanding*

genetic: code, 73, 84, 149-50; dualism (pluralism), 145, 149-50, 243, 251, 253-4, *272-84*; monism, 273-4, 276-7, 279-80

genetically *a priori*, 92, see also *inborn*

geometry, 92, 129, 131, 173, 174n, 175n

Gestalten, 62, 209n

gnats, *208-10*, 248-9

goal-directed changes as evolutionary problem, 269–70, 279–80, see also *genetic dualism*

God, 22, 41; 'dice-playing' (Einstein), 183–4; (or Christianity) & theory of knowledge, 64, 68, 77, 127, 130, 194; & world 3, 124–5, 154n

gods: & planets, 173; & pluralism, 153–4; Xenophanes on, 348

'goodness' of theories, see *preference*

gravity, 9, 52–3, 57, 101, 184, *269*

guesses: knowledge as, see *knowledge (conjectural)*

habit, 148–9, see also *custom*

harmony of the world, 179n, 246

heat, molecular motion, 213&n, 249, see also *indeterminism (Peircean)*

hen & egg, 346

hermeneutics, 162&n, 183–6, *187n*, 189&n 190n, see also *understanding*

heuristics, 24, 114, 133, see also *problem solving*

historical: explanation, 179, 186–90&ns, 354–5, see also *situational analysis*; evolution & —, 269–70, 272; understanding, 163, 167, 170–81, 186–90&ns, see also *understanding*

historicism, 196

history, 67, 167–8, *185–90&ns*, 286–7, 296–301; of science, 6, 58, 170–80&ns, 185, 349, 356, see also *Galileo's theory* etc.

holism, 209&n, 210

hope, 98–9; hopeful monsters, 281–4

humanities, 158, 162, 183–6, see also *understanding*

'Hume's problem', see *induction (problem of, logical, Hume's)*

hypotheses: die in our stead, see *elimination*; all knowledge as consisting of, see *knowledge (conjectural)*; Newton on, 194

idealism, 36n, *38–44*, 64–5, 68&n, 86–7, 99n, 105, 295, 323, 328

Ideas (Plato), 106, 123–6, 153–4, 156, 158, 196n, 300

illusions (appearance), reality of, 37, 39n, 300

immediacy, see *directness*

immunization (Albert), 30, 38n, 39, 360

impressions, 62–3, 68, 88, 93, 100, see also *perception*

imprinting (Lorenz), 96

inborn (innate, psychologically *a priori* etc.), see also *aims*; behaviour, 270, 280; beliefs, 27; dispositions, 63, 66, 71, 121, 273, 343–4; expectations, 5n, 24, 258–9; instincts, 24–5; knowledge, 61, 71&n, 92, 258–9; structure, 72, see also *genetic dualism*

indeterminacy, Heisenberg's formula, 213n, 233, 301–4, see also *quantum theory*

indeterminism (physical), *212–17&ns*, 218n, 219n, 226–9, 232–3, 248, 254–5, 296; is not enough, 219n, *226*, 230, 232, 254, see also *control (plastic)*; & freedom, 219n, 226–30, 232, 233n, 254–5; in a Newtonian world, 212–15&ns, 218n, 296; Peircean, 212–15&ns, 248–9, 296; & quantum theory, 214–15, 227–8, 233, 254–5

induction, **Ch. 1**, 58, 85–103, 145–6, 198, 202, 272, 359, see also *bucket theory*; & corroboration, 84; & demarcation, 1n, 12, 29–30; & correction of *explicandum* in explanation, 197–202, 357, 358n; & infinite regress, 86, 91; invalidity of (or inductive principles), 11, 28, 86, 94–5, 272; (alleged) justification of (or inductive principles), 4, 27–9, 90, 93–4, 97–9; principles or rules of, 4n, 5, 8–9, 11, 27–9, 86, 91–2, 98; probabilistic theories of, 4, 17–18&n, 19, 28, 89&n, 90, 101–3, 264–5; problems of, **Ch. 1**; commonsense —, 3, 27; logical —: Hume's —— & Hume's solution, *3–5*&ns, 6–9, 11–12, 22–3, 85–97, 100, 272; reformulations of —— , 7–8, 9–13; —— & universal scientific theories, 5, 7–9, 93; pragmatic —, 21–3, 28–9; psychological —: Hume's —— & Hume's solution, 3–4, 6, 11–12, 86, 90, 94–7, 100, 272; reformulation of——, 23–7; traditional —, 2, 12, 22, 27–9, 90; criticism of —— , 2, 28–9, 90, 97–9; *author's solutions of the various* —, 1&n, 2–3, *6–13*, 13–20, *21–2*, 23–5, *26–9*, 90–1, 93–7; by repetition, 3–4, 6–7, 23, 27, 94, *98*, 100; simulated, 98, 272; unreliability of so-called, 97–9

inductive inferences, 2, 28, 89–90, 94, 96, 198

scientism, 185&n, 186
searchlight, **Appendix**, 341n, 346, 353n, 357, 361
second world, see *world 2*
selection, 97, 144, 149, 239, 272, see also *learning, natural selection*
self, 73, 104, 149; consciousness of, 35–6&n, *74*, 252n; criticism, 147; expression, 119, 147–8, see also *language (functions of, expressive)*; transcendence, 121, 146–9
semantical: metalanguage, see *metalanguage*; paradoxes, see *paradoxes*; terms, 60, 324–5, 327–8
sense: data, 62–5, 77, 104, 145–6; experience, 63, 93, 104, 128, 341, see also *bucket theory*; intuition (Kant), 130–1; organs, 72, 88, 145–6, 341
senses, 3, 61, 72, 87–8, 127, 258
sentences (Tarski), 44&n, 45n, 319n, 322, 335n
sequences, finite & infinite, 336–40&ns
signalling function of language, see *language (functions of, signalling)*
similarity, 24, 196&n, see also *universals*
simplicity, 16, 143, 193n, 197
simulation, 149, 245, 250, 266–70, 272, 279, 284
situation (Collingwood), 187–9, see also *problem situation*
situational analysis or logic, 70, 109, 167, *178–9t&ns*, 182–3, 186–90, see also *problem situation, understanding*
skill-structure, 275–81, 283–4
sociology of knowledge, 114, 222n
solar (planetary) system, 249; imperfect (Newton), 212n
sources of knowledge, 60, 77&n, 130–2, 134, 136, see also *bucket theory*
space: intuition of, 129–30&n, 131, 136; Kantian theory of, 110, 129–30&n, 131; Newtonian, 184n
spearhead theory of behavioural mutations, 243, 251, 278–9, 281, 283–4, see also *genetic dualism*
specialization, 182&n, 185
Spirit, Absolute or Objective (Hegel), 106, 125–6; see also *world 3 & Hegel*
starting-point, 35–6, 72–3, 103–5, 154, 341, see also *foundations, problems*; common sense & criticism as, 33–5, 60, 69, 72, 99, 104, 323

state: of a discussion, 107, 231n, 252, see also *world 3*; mental, 106–8, 147, 154, 157n, 158, 231&n, 251–2&n, 292–3, 298, see also *world 2*; physical, 154, 231n, 251–2&n, 293, 298, see also *world 1*
statement-functions, 335–40&ns
statements: calculus of & Calculus of Systems, 330–1; existential, 12n, 13–14, 360; & facts, see *correspondence*
statistical theory: & determinism, 304; quantum theory as, 303–4
stimulus & reaction, 234&n, 343–4
Stoicism, 124, 153, *157&n, 158*, 321
structures, biological, 112–14, see also *world 3 (biological analogues)*
subjective: approach to knowledge, see *bucket theory, world 2 (world 3 taken by some as expression of)*; knowledge, see *knowledge (subjective), world 2*
subjectivism, 38n, 44, 76, 85, 93, 104, 138, *140–2*, 297, *301–4*, see also *bucket theory*
substance, 231n, 252
success in search for knowledge: explanation of would prove too much, 23, 98, 204; improbable if our theories are correct, 11, 23, 28–9, 204
sufficient reason, 3, 25, 30&n, 75–6&n, 77, 100; & law of excluded middle, 127–8&n; for preference, see *preference*
'sun will rise and set once in 24 hours', 3, 10, 20, 26, 28, 97–8
supplementary hypotheses, 360, see also *immunization*
survival, 4, 19, 69–70, 241–2, 244, 253, 262, 268, 270–1&n, 288–9; mutations, & genetic monism & dualism, 275–84
symmetry & laws of nature, 184n
syntax or morphology of language, 324–5, 326n, 327–8
syntheticity, 83–4, 85–6, 91–2, 130
systems, see also *clocks, clouds*; biological or organic, 149–50, 210, 250n; calculus of (Tarski), see *Tarski's*; open, 250, 255; physical, 207, 249, 275; physically closed, 217–19&n, 225, 231n, 254, see also *determinism (physical)*

tabula rasa, 61t, 66&n, 71, 73, see also *bucket theory*